CONTINUUM

Problems
in French Literature
from the Late Renaissance
to the Early Enlightenment

CONTINUUM

Problems
in French Literature
from the Late Renaissance
to the Early Enlightenment

CONTINUUM

Problems
in French Literature
from the Late Renaissance
to the Early Enlightenment

Volume 1

RETHINKING CLASSICISM

Overviews

AMS PRESS
NEW YORK

CONTINUUM

ISSN   0899-4307

Continuum: Problems in French Literature from the Late Renaissance to the Early Enlightenment is published with support from the Center for Advanced Studies, the College of Arts and Sciences, and the Department of French of the University of Virginia.

International Standard Book Number
Series: 0-404-63750-7
Vol. 1:   0-404-63751-5

All manuscripts submitted to *Continuum* should be prepared in accordance with *The MLA Style Manual* (1985): double-spaced, with parenthetical documentation, explanatory or elaborative endnotes, and a list of works cited. Submission of two copies will speed refereeing; OCR-readable type (i.e., letter-quality Prestige Elite or Courier 10) will facilitate eventual production.

Address editorial correspondence, submissions, and review books to David Lee Rubin, *Continuum*, French Department, 302 Cabell Hall, University of Virginia, Charlottesville, Virginia, 22903. To subscribe, write to AMS Press, 56 East 13th Street, New York, N. Y. 10003.

Contents

A Letter from the Editor   vii

Rethinking Classicism—Overviews

DOMNA C. STANTON
Classicism (Re)constructed:
    Notes on the Mythology of Literary History   1

RALPH ALBANESE
Le Discours scolaire au XIXeme siècle: le cas Molière   31

JULES BRODY
What *Was* French Classicism?   51

ROBERT J. NELSON
French Classicism: Dimensions of Application   79

ALAIN NIDERST
Les Classicismes: les mots et les choses   105

HERBERT C. DE LEY
Monchrestien's *Aman* and Racine's *Esther*:
    Toward a Game Theory of French Classicism   119

BARBARA WOSHINSKY
Classical Uncertainties   133

ERIKA HARTH
Classical Discourse: Gender and Objectivity   151

NICHOLAS CRONK
The Singular Voice:
    Monologism and French Classical Discourse   175

G. J. MALLINSON
Fiction, Morality and the Reader: Reflections on
    the Classical Formula *Plaire et Instruire*   203

Comment on Recent Books

MARCEL GUTWIRTH
The Labyrinth of the Comic, by Richard Keller Simon   231

MICHAEL S. KOPPISCH
The French Essay, by Theodore P. Fraser   237

DORANNE FENOALTEA
Poems in their Place, edited by Neil Fraistat   243

MARGARET M. MCGOWAN
The Dancing Body in Renaissance Choreography,
     by Mark Franko   249

FLOYD GRAY
A travers le seizième siècle, by Henri Weber   259

ALISON WEBER
Culture of the Baroque, by José Antonio Maravell   263

MARIE-ODILE SWEETSER
Corneille, Tasso, and Modern Poetics,
     by A. Donald Sellstrom   269

PHILIP A. WADSWORTH
La Fontaine, by Marie-Odile Sweetser   277

ROGER DUCHENE
Appelle-moi Pierrot: Wit and Irony in the Letters of
     Mme de Sévigné, by Jo Ann Marie Recker   281

JEAN DUBU
Racine, le jansénisme, et la modernité, by M.-F. Bruneau;
Dramatic Narrative: Racine's récits, by Nina C. Ekstein;
Re-lectures raciniennes, edited by Richard L. Barnett   283

EDWARD C. KNOX
La Bruyère. Amateur de caractères, by Floyd Gray   293

Index   297

A Letter from the Editor

i

Continuum will explore, and promote exploration of, theoretical, historical, and interpretive issues in the study of early modern French literature (and, whenever possible, allied disciplines). Responsible risk-taking will be fostered by ample deadlines after the announcement of topics, and by the opportunity to develop new insights and arguments, as well as ideas and methods, more fully than is usual in scholarly periodicals.

The inaugural number, "Rethinking Classicism—Overviews," illustrates more eloquently than a programmatic statement both our intentions and our approach. Now almost complete, the second number, on textual aspects of "Rethinking Classicism," will confirm first impressions, with essays by Mitchell Greenberg (on *L'Astrée*), C. J. Gossip (on the first "classical" tragedy), Susan Read Baker (on Corneille's personation and impersonation), John D. Lyons (on the discourse of Corneille's *Discours*), Richard Goodkin (on Racine and the excluded third [person]), and Louis Marin (on Port Royal versus the theater). In addition, there will be review-articles by Gérard Defaux, François Rigolot, Donald Stone, Ronald Tobin, Richard Danner, James Gaines and others.

Ideally, our readers will be our writers and *vice versa.* We therefore welcome *your* participation—be it in the form of publishable dialogue with the essayists or reviewers, or recommendation of themes and prospective authors (or proposal of articles) for future numbers. As for the latter, we announce a volume on literature and the other arts, with a May 15, 1989, deadline for proposals and a May 15, 1990, deadline for submissions. A detailed prospectus is available from the editor.

ii

The idea of *Continuum* arose in conversations between Hugh Davidson, Mary McKinley and the editor as early as the summer of 1981. At that time, however, and for several years following, there appeared to be no way of producing the publication attractively *and* economically. As a result, the project lay dormant until 1986. Then, through a chance meeting with Daniel Russell, co-founder of *Emblematica*, the editor learned of electronic publishing and the interest shown by AMS Press in new scholarly annuals. After further discussions with Hugh Davidson, Mary McKinley, Aram Vartanian, Roland Simon, Scott Bryson, and Richard T. Arndt,* as well as Suzanne Guerlac and Alexandra Dennis (who suggested a name well-suited to the project's intentions), an advisory board was appointed, and a prospectus drawn up for submission to Gabriel Hornstein, president of AMS. There ensued brief negotiations which led to improvements in the proposal, a generous contract, and unstinting moral support from New York.

Critically important financial aid was made available first by W. Dexter Whitehead, Dean of the Graduate School of Arts and Sciences and Director of the Center for Advanced Studies at the University of Virginia, then—upon the recommendation of Robert T. Denommé, chairman of the French Department—by Hugh M. Kelly, Dean of the Faculty of Arts and Sciences.

Raymond C. La Charité shared a research report which simplified our choice of hard- and soft-ware, demonstration and purchase of which were arranged by Anne Lind of Omni-Comp, Charlottesville. Throughout the production of Volume 1, we benefitted from the knowledge, the skills and the patience, of Mrs. Lind; Gail Moore, Director, Cabell Hall Word Processing Center; three members of the Academic Computing Center: Alan Batson, Director; Alice Howard, Manager of User Services, and Mike Beach, Programmer-Analyst; and, of course, the contributors.

To all, our deepest thanks.

iii

One member of the founding group did not share in the pleasures (and trials) of preparing *Continuum* 1, for which he was to have written an essay on classicism as a phenomenon implicating all the arts. I refer, of course, to Robert Nicolich, who died November 19, 1986. To his memory we affectionately dedicate this inaugural volume.

D. L. R.

Charlottesville, Virginia
December 19, 1988

*John D. Lyons joined us as associate editor in the autumn of 1987. His influence will be evident beginning with the third volume, manuscripts for which are now under consideration.

Rethinking Classicism—Overviews

Classicism (Re)constructed: Notes on the Mythology of Literary History

Domna C. Stanton
University of Michigan

"The genesis and development of *classicisme* and *classique* as literary-historical terms have not been fully studied," Jules Brody wrote two decades ago, in an anthology of texts from the 1750s to the 1960s that documented the ways in which a "critical notion has grown,... been variously interpreted and applied," in fact, become petrified (v, viii). Citing the clichés still identified with classicism—reason, clarity, order, rules, imitation of the ancients, artificiality, grandiosity, impersonality, abstraction—Brody rightly insisted this was "a timely moment to re-examine the question"(viii). But this call to re-examine classicism, more radically, to expose its construction as an ontology, has essentially been ignored. On the contrary, although *la nouvelle critique* has displayed a "fascination" with classicism (Doubrovsky, *YFS*, 19), it has markedly reified the notions of *l'âge classique*, classical discourse, and classical episteme. The moment that Brody referred to is, then, even more timely today, but largely because of the perspectives provided by critical theory over the past twenty years, a period of crisis in Western discourses that has produced what Lyotard calls the "delegitimization of master narratives." The sceptical impulse governing this crisis has put into question "what we know," demystified the doxal and canonical by analyzing the historical processes of their authority, the functions and interests that their production and reproduction or their re-vision served—in short, by probing the connections between *savoir* and *pouvoir*. In this light, the questions to be addressed to classicism are no longer, "Qu'est-ce qu'un classique?", the title of an 1850 essay by Sainte-Beuve, or "Qu'est ce que le classicisme?", the title of Peyre's 1933 study, which aim for "more accurate" definitions; but rather, "comment et pourquoi le classicisme?", on the understanding that the term is "under erasure," and that the sign does not (necessarily) have a referent.

Now as Brody recognized, any attempt to re-examine classicism, to "make it strange" in order to re-construct its emergence is particularly difficult, and meets with special resistance. For more than any other -ism, classicism has been upheld as the essence of French literature, and identified with the nation's cultural patrimony, indeed with what is quintessentially French. A sacrosanct notion, classicism may be viewed as a myth, not only as a discourse whose semes give symbolic expression to a vision of human nature and society, but as a construction of the real that has been imposed and accepted as true through various ideological and institutional processes, and internalized in the behavior, even the self-definition of human subjects, a phenomenon that Bourdieu calls the *habitus*. More specifically, however, classicism has functioned as a myth in the Barthesian sense of a discourse that hides its arbitrariness and its historicity under the mask or alibi of Nature, the universal and essential. Following Barthes's scheme, the signifier of the myth—the work of a set of writers, arbitrarily selected from the large pool of seventeenth-century and sometimes eighteenth-century authors—is denied its "richness of meaning" (*Mythologies*, 202), the complexity, plurality and contradictions of significance, and absorbed, reified and transfixed to illustrate the concept of classicism. The refusal to acknowledge the myth as the product of a specific discursive locus, historical situation and ideology, says Barthes, makes the concept all the more powerfully convincing as truth.

That classicism, like all myths, dies hard, is not the only reason for the difficulty that the reconstruction of its ontology entails. For unlike Barthes's synchronic analysis of contemporary mass culture, a study of the myth of classicism should examine its semes and their rewriting, their shifts in value in different socio-historical situations over two and a half centuries. Such a study would entail an archeology or genealogy of classicism, to use Foucault's preferred terms. It would focus on the functions of classicism as the projection of the values of a group or class—the writer, the teacher/scholar, the bourgeoisie—and its complex imbrication in the discourses of various institutions—etatic and nationalistic, pedagogical and literary, philosophical and religious. Of necessity, however, my study of classicism will be partial. By this, I do not simply recognize the incompleteness and fragmentariness of all historical reconstructions. I mean that my study of key moments in the making and perpetuation of this myth by specific groups and individuals from the eighteenth century to today is partial by its subjectivity; it is the product of my discursive situation, which affords the possibility of what Barthes terms the ironic distance of demystification. By that token, what follows is also a story, a narrative that may have some validity, but makes no "classical" claim to truth.

I

Like all stories, the narrative of French classicism does not begin in the beginning, but in retrospect. The labelling of certain French writers as classical, it has rightly been said, did not occur in the seventeenth century, but in an eighteenth century at once nostalgic, critical and progressive. No seventeenth-century writer could regard him/herself as classical, when that adjective, used only in the phrase "autheur classique," according to the *Dictionnaire de l'Académie Française* (1694), meant "un autheur ancien fort approuvé, et qui fait authorité dans la matière qu'il traitte," such as "Aristote, Platon, Tite-Live etc." And yet, the attribution of the term, with its semes of canonicity, authority and exemplarity[1], to authors of modern France, rather than of ancient Greece and Rome, did not miraculously originate with Voltaire's *Le Siècle de Louis XIV* (1751), as literary historians have often claimed. More collectively, it was the *Querelle des anciens et des modernes* that writers were trying to resolve in the 1740s when they hailed certain "modern" seventeenth-century authors, but dubbed them "classical." Paradoxically, however, the chief modernist argument for historical and cultural progress, and thus for the reign of Louis XIV as its highest point, generated the somewhat inconsistent vision of a rarefied circle and a fragile moment, outside of which and after which there could only be imperfection and corruption. As Monsieur de la Chapelle declared to the Académie Française in 1699:

> On dirait qu'il y a une sorte de fatalité ou, pour parler mieux, un ordre saint de la Providence qui fixe dans tous les arts, chez tous les peuples du monde, un point d'excellence qui ne s'avance ni ne s'étend jamais. Ce même ordre immuable détermine un

> nombre certain d'hommes illustres, qui naissent, fleurissent, se trouvent ensemble dans un court espace de temps, où ils sont séparés du reste des hommes communs que les autres temps produisent, et comme enfermés dans un cercle, hors duquel il n'y a rien qui ne tienne ou de l'imperfection de ce qui commence, ou de la corruption de ce qui vieillit.[2]

This mythic vision, which was both self-serving to its authors and serviceable to a monarchy by divine right, would grow to encompass the entire century in the writings of Des Fontaines, Prévost and the Marquis d'Argens before Voltaire coined the phrase, *le siècle de Louis XIV*. Reproducing in that work the myth and mysteries of cyclical periodization, with the notable addition of a long and laborious phase of maturation,[3] Voltaire gave expression to one of the most enduring conceptions of literary historiography:

> Le siècle de Louis XIV a donc en tout la destinée des siècles de Léon X, d'Auguste, d'Alexandre. Les terres qui firent naître dans ces temps illustres tant de fruits du génie avaient été longtemps préparées auparavant. On a cherché en vain dans les causes morales et dans les causes physiques la raison de cette tardive fécondité, suivie d'une longue stérilité. La véritable raison est que, chez les peuples qui cultivent les beaux-arts, il faut beaucoup d'années pour épurer la langue et le goût. Quand les premiers pas sont faits, alors les génies se développent... [Mais] les vérités morales une fois annoncées avec éloquence ... tout cela devient lieu commun. On est réduit à imiter, ou à s'égarer...le génie n'a qu'un siècle, après quoi il faut qu'il dégénère (II, 57-59).[4]

Writing after this fall into decadence, Voltaire projected his nostalgic vision of the genius-filled *siècle de Louis XIV* as the model and inspiration for humanity itself; his work, he said, comprised "l'histoire de l'esprit humain puisée dans le siècle le plus glorieux à l'esprit humain."[5] But this essentializing view represented a critical response to the perceived deficiencies of the present. "Je me console avec le siècle de Louis XIV," he wrote, "de toutes les sottises du siècle présent" (*Correspondance*, 577-78). More personally, as Becq has emphasized, it was the problematic status of the eighteenth-century *homme de lettres*, who witnessed the decline of the patronage system and ambivalently confronted his emerging autonomy, that underlay Voltaire's cult for a king who supported artists and gave them power (480ff). Molière and Boileau, Corneille and Racine, Bossuet and Bourdaloue, Lulli and Quinault "enseignèrent à la nation à penser, à sentir, et à s'exprimer," declared Voltaire, "tous ces grands hommes furent connus et protégés de Louis XIV...." (II, 54-55). As with Des Fontaines, Prévost and D'Argens, Voltaire's seventeenth century was a fantasy

of the writer's power in a society that supported artistic merit as
crucial to the nation's eminence, in contrast to his contemporaries'
need to establish their own "republic of letters" for mutual assistance
and praise.[6] Notwithstanding Voltaire's implicit criticism of the
reign of Louis XV, his vision of *le siècle de Louis XIV* did not
challenge the monarchy. Since his work contained a paean to
France as "de toutes les nations celle qui a produit le plus de ces
ouvrages," and its language as "la langue d'Europe" (II, 59),[7]
Voltaire, the royal historiographer as of 1745, sustained the
aspirations of the post- regency monarchy to power and to cultural
hegemony over Europe.

   Now Voltaire did not actually label the moderns canonized in *Le
Siècle de Louis XIV* as "auteurs classiques." Nor does his
description of what he calls "l'école de ces génies" (II, 56) contain a
taxonomy of common traits. However, his strong preference for the
second half of the century over the first, which would become a
literary historical topos, is based on the idea of a necessary evolution
toward a purified and fixed linguistic idiom; "la langue," he writes
of Vaugelas, "commençait à s'épurer et à prendre une forme
constante" (II, 46). More concerned with poetics than thematics,
Voltaire extols Racine for being "toujours élégant, toujours correct,
toujours vrai," and criticizes La Fontaine as "bien moins châtié dans
son style, bien moins correct dans son langage" (II, 53, 55).

   These ideals of elegance and conformity to linguistic norms
recur in Du Marsais' *Encyclopédie* article, *Classique*, which sealed
the identification of modern French writers as classical. Signaling a
new usage of the term, related to the Latin *auctores classici* or "les
auteurs du premier ordre... tels que Cicéron, Virgile, Horace, etc.,"
Du Marsais writes:

> On peut dans ce dernier sens donner le nom d'auteurs classiques
> français aux bons auteurs du siècle de Louis XIV et de celui-ci;
> mais on doit plus particulièrement appliquer le nom de classiques
> aux auteurs qui ont écrit tout à la fois élégamment et
> correctement, tels que Despréaux, Racine, etc." (Brody, 7).

If Du Marsais creates a hierarchy between superior classical authors,
who are elegant and correct, and the merely "good," he also enlarges
the boundaries of "the classical" era to include the present, thus
undermining the Voltairian nostalgia for the past. In the same spirit,
the "Discours préliminaire" to the *Encyclopédie* affirms the
superiority of the moderns over the ancients, adding to Voltaire's list
of classical authors Montesquieu and Voltaire himself. While
acknowledging the general inferiority of contemporary literary
works to those of "le siècle de Louis XIV," D'Alembert's

Discours" hails the philosophical spirit of his time and looks forward to "un nouveau siècle de lumière" (161), the end result of the subversion of the old order of knowledge, which the Encyclopedic enterprise symbolized. That subversion, which was predicated on a new, arbitrary and ideological classification of phenomena, such as the "classical," would culminate in a political and cultural revolution that redefined modern classical authors as ancient, emblems of an oppressive *ancien régime*.

II

When Hugo declared in 1856, "Je fis souffler un vent révolutionnaire/ Je mis un bonnet rouge au vieux dictionnaire," and proclaimed himself the Danton and Robespierre of semantics and poetics (vv. 65-66, 141), he was, of course, mythifying romanticism as the triumph of the *roturiers* over classical masters and discourses. More accurately, however, the Revolution of 1789 insured the accession of the bourgeoisie to power. And the proverbial battle of romanticism against classicism involved the struggle of bourgeois writers for discursive authority at a moment when the classical artists, canonized by Voltaire's generation, reigned supreme. The idealization of a republican Greece and Rome during the revolutionary period, which Marx would interpret as the need to reconnect with the past during historical crises, the cult of "neoclassicism" during the Napoleonic Empire, and the associations with le siècle de Louis XIV promoted during the Restauration all played a part in the enthronement of what would be called "classicism" ca. 1825.[8] Already in de Staël's *Corinne* (1807), then, the conventional and superficial comte d'Erfeuil extols Bossuet, La Bruyère, Montesquieu and Buffon as "[de] véritables autorités classiques; ...[ils] ne peuvent être surpassés; surtout les deux premiers, qui appartiennent à ce siècle de Louis XIV, qu'on ne saurait trop louer, et dont il faut imiter autant qu'on le peut, les parfaits modèles"(176). Equally fixated on the classics and hostile to the romantics, according to Stendhal's *Racine et Shakespeare* (126-27), Chateaubriand expressed his preference for "le siècle de Louis XIV" over his own, because of its "healthy" religious and monarchic doctrines, and for "geniuses" like Bossuet, Fénelon, Pascal and the writers of Port-Royal, who produced "les meilleurs livres classiques"; indeed, "nous ne faisons que les répéter" (2: 163-168). It was, of course, this scene of repetition that the romantics wanted to shatter.

Of necessity, perhaps, the romantics (af)firmed their identity by hyperbolizing their difference from classical writers. As de Staël's *De l'Allemagne* and Stendhal's *Racine et Shakespeare* suggest, the primary goal of the romantics was to wrest the notion of modernity away from Voltaire's seventeenth-century writers. Returning to pre-Voltairian notions, de Staël's "De la poésie classique et de la poésie romantique" limits the classical to pagan antiquity in order to show that "la littérature des Anciens est chez les modernes une littérature transplantée" (1: 213). There can be no French classics, then, only the adaptation of ancient masterpieces to French taste through an imposition of arduous rules that do not derive from "nature" or historical memory, and that can never produce great art: "la simplicité de l'art, chez les modernes, tournerait facilement à la froideur et à l'abstraction, tandis que celle des Anciens était pleine de vie" (1: 213). More reductively, de Staël elaborates a set of binary oppositions that associates the classical with simplicity, clarity and purity, and a focus on action or the external world of events, and the modern or romantic with emotional complexity, individuality and interiority, an emphasis on "cette réflexion inquiète qui nous dévore" (212). In idealizing romantic modernity, de Staël thus identifies French writers deemed modern classics with coldness and abstraction, slavish imitation of the ancients, conformity to rules, and the outdated ideals of simplicity, clarity, purity—semes that are still today's clichés.

As this new quarrel between ancients and moderns intensified in the 1820's, Stendhal's *Racine et Shakespeare* extended the terms of de Staël's argument to the theater where the battle, according to Gautier's *Histoire du romantisme,* would finally be won. In his set of responses to Auger's attack on romanticism at the Académie Française, Stendhal de-historicizes and universalizes the romantic by equating it with the modern in all epochs, specifically with novelty, risk-taking and courage, and thus with pleasure for the spectator/reader; classical, by opposition, is equated with prudence and imitation, the retrograde and outmoded, and thus with *ennui*. Accordingly, Sophocles and Euripedes, Racine and Molière were "eminently romantic" in their own time, but the belief that their imitation is pleasurable to modern spectators, Stendhal declares, "c'est du classicisme"(71); it is absurd to try "de reproduire les caractères et les formes qui plaisaient vers 1670" (196). Notwithstanding Racine's genius for his time, the work of this "dieu des classiques"—a term Stendhal links with the Academicians' "ridiculous" attempts to dictate their "literary code"(136) to the public—has an *"extrême dignité... qui nous glace aujourd'hui"*

(70). The "air de grandeur" that Voltaire had exalted in *le siècle de Louis XIV* had become glacial dignity for Stendhal and de Staël, and his ideal of elegant and correct discourse emblematized "le mot noble" that Hugo's "vocable ignoble" (v.143) had purportedly decimated.

To be sure, the radical break with the past that the romantics proclaimed was their own fantasy of power. For while they denounced the classical as imitative, they hailed the imitation of Shakespeare, Walter Scott, or *la littérature du Nord*, now coded as openness to new, foreign sources of inspiration (*De l'Allemagne*, 1: 213). At the same time, de Staël and Stendhal validated the romantic by appealing to a nationalist ideology, just as Voltaire did his moderns. Insisting that each nation should have its own literature, modeled on its own character, Stendhal paradoxically argued that by imitating Shakespeare, France could create "une tragédie vraiment nationale" that would surpass England's (165). And because romantic literature has its roots "dans notre propre sol," said de Staël, "elle est la seule qui puisse croître et se vivifier de nouveau; elle exprime notre religion; elle rappelle notre histoire" (*De l'Allemagne*, 1: 214). In the spirit of the times, she also claimed that whereas a classicizing French poetry can only be appreciated by "les esprits cultivés," a nationalist, romantic poetry would finally become familiar "aux gens du peuple et aux bourgeois même des villes" (214). In perpetuating the notion of a literature for the people, however, the moderns did not differ from the ancients; in fact, that myth contained a hidden complicity between the romantics and the defenders of classicism who dominated the educational institutions of nineteenth-century bourgeois France.

III

Although the Conventions of 1790-1795 aspired to create an egalitarian system of primary education for the people, the chief pedagogical achievement of the revolution was a system of secondary education for *les notables* modeled on the jesuitical colleges of the *ancien régime*.[9] The often-noted supremacy of the nineteenth-century lycées over both elementary and higher education, which would become nation-wide only in the last two decades of the century, devolved from the concerted effort to provide the bourgeoisie the legitimate culture that the noble alone once possessed. In fact, a lycée education for a select minority[10] constituted the requisite badge of distinction for entering the professional cadres of society. And yet, the "need" for this distinction does not veil the arbitrariness of what is defined as legitimate culture nor, as Bourdieu has emphasized, its fundamental goal of reproducing the dominant order. Indeed, since the dawn of the nineteenth century, according to Althusser, the "system of scolarity" has become the primary ideological state apparatus (18-21).

Nowhere is this more evident than in literature, which became an autonomous field and was institutionalized in the schools in the period 1800-1850. To be sure, the relation between literature and teaching is tautological, as Barthes has observed: "la littérature...c'est ce qui s'enseigne, un point c'est tout. C'est un objet d'enseignement."[11]. And this tautology is especially notable in the literary manual: authors appear therein because they are literary, and they are literary because they appear in manuals (Mouralis, 32). More problematic, however, was the literary status of nineteenth-century authors: for if they gained legitimacy with the autonomization of literature, they were also excluded from the lycée curriculum, a factor that may partly account for the fervor of the romantic battle against the classics.

The teaching of literature as rhetoric in the lycées was, of course, dominated by the classics of Greece and Rome.[12] Not surprisingly, then, the progressive gesture of including modern French writers, which was officially sanctioned by the *Loi Fontaines* in 1803, was limited to seventeenth-century "classics," with a couple of eighteenth-century additions, as Chervel's study of the French texts taught in the lycées from 1800-1900 reveals. In *Rhétorique/Première*, for instance, which represents a more complete list of the same authors taught in the earlier grades, the pantheon comprised in the order of their appearance: Bossuet, Fléchier, Boileau, La Bruyère, Fénelon, Massillon, Montesquieu, Buffon, Molière, Racine, Voltaire, Pascal, Corneille, La Fontaine. Only in the last two decades are sixteenth-century writers introduced through the reductive, but ideologically significant *morceaux choisis*; and in 1895, Montaigne, Rousseau, and Diderot are added, as well as Lamartine, Hugo and unnamed nineteenth-century historians (185ff).

The purpose of reading these classics was didactic in the narrowest and broadest senses. Racine, for instance, was extolled and reduced to a model of diction and style, as the title of Fontanier's 1818 work confirms: *Etudes de la langue française sur Racine, ou Commentaire général et comparatif sur la diction et le style de ce grand classique...pour servir de cours pratique de langue française et suppléer à l'insuffisance des grammaires.* More broadly, however, because the new secular educational system was constantly criticized by the church, which had lost its pedagogical function, studies of the modern classics had to fulfill a moral mission as "une discipline qui s'ajoute aux exemples du foyer domestique, à la religion, aux lois de la patrie," insisted Nisard, the director of the Ecole Normale Supérieure (1: vii).[13] Indeed, the prominence of Bossuet and Fénelon, Fléchier and Massillon among the authors taught exposes the use of literature to instill virtue in future leaders.[14] This moralistic aim permeates Cousin's *Du vrai, du beau et du bien*, a series of lectures first delivered in 1815-1821, and revised in 1853 after his demise as a "liberal" minister of education. The theory of *spiritualisme*, which he propounds in opposition to nineteenth-century materialism and atheism, and which upholds the "moderate freedoms" of a constitutional monarchy over the "dictatorship" of democracy (ix), finds in a religious and absolutist seventeenth century the ideal association of the good and the beautiful. The author of numerous works of erudition on seventeenth century letters and society, Cousin strives to rehabilitate and honor what he terms *une école* "fort légèrement traitée" (208) that comprises Corneille, Racine, Molière, La Fontaine, Boileau, and of course, Bossuet. In the process, the faults highlighted by de Staël, Stendhal and Hugo become supreme virtues once more: simplicity, austerity, nobility of language, even elitism (218). Unlike the romantics, however, Cousin goes on to underscore the superior reason, *bon sens* and genius for composition of a school of writers who championed the spirit over the senses. And he presents this vision of classicism, which would become a cliché, as the model his students should imitate. "Revenez," Cousin exhorts, "revenez aux maîtres de notre grande école nationale du XVIIe siècle" (220).

In a similar vein, Nisard's *Histoire de la littérature française* (1844), the product of ten years of teaching at the Ecole Normale Supérieure, extols the great national authors as "des maîtres aimés et obéis"(1: vii). Writing on the eve, and then in the aftermath of the revolution of 1848[15], Nisard presents these authors as the incarnation of *l'esprit français* in an expressed nationalistic effort to return to the immutable truth that the "errors" of the recent past have clouded with doubt (1: 8-11). The triumph of Christian discipline, "algebraic clarity" and reason (1: 32), and of the collective good over individual freedom and desire, *l'esprit français* was most fully realized by "l'époque glorieuse qu'on appelle le siècle de Louis XIV" (2: 347), and to which Nisard devotes more than half of his four-volume work.[16] Using the tautological alibi that the writers he privileges are those who have justly survived (1: 34), Nisard hails Descartes as the first author who conveys "une image parfaite de l'esprit français" (2: 84); and in the doxally superior second half of the century, which he sharply differentiates from the first, he singles out Pascal, La Fontaine, Bossuet, Fénelon, but above all, Boileau as its personification. More than in any earlier critic, Nisard's Boileau embodies the spirit of discipline and of conformity to rules for the greater good. Comparing him to Richelieu, the Académie Française and Louis XIV, Nisard proudly observes that "le législateur du Parnasse" tolerated no infractions to his "arrêts de justice" (2: 297, 394). Even today, he maintains, "nous nous dirigeons par ses règles" (2: 313); "Boileau est dans nos veines. On n'est pas libre en France de ne pas lire Boileau" (2: 240-41). Like Boileau himself, *l'esprit français* of seventeenth-century writers constituted for Nisard, "une des forces morales dans notre pays" (4: 371).

The restrictiveness of a conception of classicism, such as Nisard's, was to be the focus of Sainte-Beuve's 1850 article, "Qu'est-ce qu'un classique?" Writing this "causerie" as the prolific critic of *Le Constitutionnel*, who had become disenchanted with romanticism in the late 1830's, but had not yet become a professor at the Ecole Normale Supérieure, Sainte-Beuve could see classicism as the defensive reaction and construction of "quelques esprits résistants" to the romantic onslaught (10). It was they and the venerable academicians in their 1835 dictionary, he argued, who perpetuated the view of classical authors as models of purity, sobriety, correctness and elegance, conformity to rules, moderation and reason. Observing that writers who exemplified those principles would be merely mediocre, Sainte-Beuve insisted it was time "de renoncer à ces définitions restrictives et craintives" (11), "de maintenir l'idée et le culte, tout en l'élargissant" (18). So saying, he showed that every nation has its classics—Italy its Dante, England its Shakespeare—and thus, somewhat tautologically, that "classical" implies "quelque chose...qui fait ensemble et tradition, qui se compose, se transmet et qui dure" (9). More specifically, Sainte-Beuve elaborated a synthetic definition comprising the humanistic essentialism of a Voltaire, the moralism of a Cousin, the spirit of commonality of a Nisard, but also and more paradoxically, the contemporary particularity that Stendhal associated with the romantic. "Un vrai classique," Sainte-Beuve declared:

> c'est un auteur qui a enrichi l'esprit humain...qui lui a fait faire
> un pas de plus, qui a découvert quelque vérité morale non
> équivoque, ou ressaisi quelque passion éternelle dans ce coeur

> où tout semblait connu et exploré;...qui a parlé à tous dans un
> style à lui et qui se trouve aussi celui de tout le monde, dans un
> style nouveau sans néologisme, nouveau et antique, aisément
> contemporain de tous les âges. Un tel classique a pu être un
> moment révolutionnaire, il a pu le paraître du moins, mais il ne
> l'est pas;...il n'a renversé ce qui le gênait que pour rétablir bien
> vite l'équilibre au profit de l'ordre et du beau (11).

The meaning of this equilibrium between "l'ordre" and "le beau" becomes apparent in Sainte-Beuve's inaugural lecture "De la tradition en littérature" at the Ecole Normale Supérieure in 1858. Speaking now as a professor who must not deviate from "[les] lieux consacrés"(43), he defines as classical "les littératures à l'état de santé et de fleur heureuse, les littératures en plein accord et en harmonie avec leur époque, avec leur cadre social, avec les principes et les pouvoirs dirigeants de la société," in contrast to romantic literatures, which are in conflict with the dominant order, "inquiètes, chercheuses, excentriques...errantes" (39-40). If he emphasizes here, as in much of his work, the sociological relation between author and public, Sainte-Beuve's devaluation of literatures of opposition contains its own conservative agenda. Praising "la noble et forte harmonie du grand siècle" (Allem, ed., 251), which produced the only classical literature in France, Sainte-Beuve constructed a myth of serenity, which would become a cliché: "La littérature classique... ne gémit pas...ne s'ennuie pas...Le classique ...aime sa patrie, son temps, ne voit rien de plus désirable, ni de plus beau...L'activité dans l'apaisement serait sa devise" (*Qu'est-ce qu'un classique?*, 40-41). Among his many articles on seventeenth-century authors, filled with anecdotal biographies and literary judgments both favorable and critical,[17] none more clearly illustrates his theory of the classic's harmony with his time than those on Boileau. "La littérature et la poétique de Boileau," he writes, "sont merveilleusement d'accord avec la religion, la philosophie, l'économie politique, la stratégie et tous les arts du temps" (Allem, ed., 225). While the deficiencies of the poet are noted, Boileau the critic emerges once again as the calm, just and powerful oracle for writers like Molière, Racine, La Fontaine, who would have yielded to their weaknesses without his restraints (244-45, 251). No less mythic than Nisard's view, then, Sainte-Beuve's representation of Boileau—"un des hommes qui m'ont le plus occupé depuis que je fais de la critique," he admits (233)—may be a projection of the power that the nineteenth-century critic and pro-fessor wished to possess. Indeed, Nisard seemed to confuse desire with reality, when he stated: "Nous vivons à une époque et sous une forme de gouvernement où la réputation dans les lettres, comme la réputation au barreau chez les Romains, est une sorte de candidature universelle à tous les emplois de l'Etat" (1: 10). In an effort to ensure that their *savoir* was the avenue to *pouvoir*, literary scholars now began to appropriate the positivistic methods of the natural and social sciences.

IV

When Taine excoriated Cousin in 1857 as "un fils du XVIIe égaré dans un autre siècle" (*Les Philosophes français*, 192), he challenged both his "cult" for the classics and his method. A second-rate Bossuet declaiming on morality and virtue, and a bibliomane possessed by an antiquated fervor for erudition, Cousin was no historian, said Taine: he did not seek "le trait dominant" of the times, "[et] pourquoi de ce trait naissent les autres...le système des facultés et des passions qui s'y est formé et qui l'a rempli," and which could be understood "comme un corps organisé après avoir noté la structure et mécanisme de toutes ses parties" (110). So saying, Taine was already propounding his influential theory that an individual, a body of literature or a historical period could be analyzed by the same method used in physical mechanics. This obsession with incorporating the prestigious methods of the new sciences, which underlies the work of both Taine and Lanson, the most powerful figures in literary studies in the period 1860-1930, was partly a response to the crisis in academic institutions and discourses after 1850. The uprisings of 1848, which led to an expanded, but more tightly controlled educational system, under the *Loi Falloux;* and the growing sense in the 1860s that French education was inferior to that of other countries and needed to be overhauled reached crisis levels in 1870 with Germany's military victory, and resulted in significant reforms, especially at the university level. What were previously institutions for training lycée teachers would now become rigorous research centers on the German model, insisted Taine, a member of the 1877 commission founded to create a modern, nation-wide university system. For the literary faculties, as Taine and later Lanson realized, the choice was either to achieve scientific rigor and thus legitimacy or else fall into oblivion along with the now discredited field of rhetoric.

Although the ensuing professorial quarrel between moderns and ancients hinged on methodological issues, Taine attacked Cousin's deification of the seventeenth century like a latter-day romantic. He declared Boileau illegible, Corneille and Racine devoid of Shakespeare's vitality and, more globally, the classics' "style régulier" and "lieux communs" the source of a "mortel ennui" (*Les Philosophes français*, 104). Two decades later, in *Les Origines de la France contemporaine* (1876-1893), Taine's deterministic theory of "la race, le milieu, le moment" produced a rigid vision of a seventeenth- and eighteenth-century *esprit classique* that was the antithesis of the romantic spontaneity, originality, energy, and excess he championed. Under an absolutist monarchy and a functionless aristocracy devoted to a leisurely life of salon conversation, argued Taine, language was purified, clarified and classified, but it lost its poetic potential, "toutes les métaphores risquées et piquantes, presque toutes ces façons de parler inventées et primesautières qui...font jaillir dans l'imagination la forme colorée, exacte et complète des choses, mais dont la trop vive secousse choquerait les bienséances de la conversation polie" (1: 294). Like classical grammar (38), language thus became the exclusive instrument of "la raison raisonnante," which cannot embrace "la plénitude et la complexité des choses réelles" (300), not the vitality of the past or the profound particularity of an individual, much less of any class outside of *les honnêtes gens*.[18] With this "raison raisonnante" as its chief faculty, *l'esprit classique* was the "mold," "the fixed form" of every sentence, discourse, and mind before the Revolution (1: 289): "Suivre en toute recherche... la méthode des mathématiciens; extraire, circonscrire, isoler quelques notions très simples et très générales; puis abandonnant l'expérience, les comparer, les combiner, et du composé artificiel ainsi obtenu, déduire par le pur raisonnement toutes les conséquences qu'il enferme: tel est le procédé naturel de l'esprit classique" (46), he claimed, but it could be argued, of *l'esprit tainien* as well.

Taine's vision of classicism was a powerful force in literary studies, well beyond his death in 1893, as Bray's *La Formation de la doctrine classique en France* (1927) confirms. Although a model of Lansonian erudition and citation, Bray's study of prefaces, pamphlets and treatises on poetics from 1600 to 1660 is dominated by the notions of "le culte des règles," the excessive rule of reason, the loss of imagination, the denegation of the individual.[19] Thus the poet, prisoner of an immutable code (106), can only pretend to be free, "libre de bien faire, comme l'est un enfant bien élevé, à qui la pensée de faire le mal ne peut venir" (113). And since reason is "le plus profond et le plus solide des fondements de l'esthétique classique" (114), it does not represent an individual achievement, but "une sorte d'entité métaphysique, supérieure aux raisons individuelles qui n'en sont que des reflets, permanente et universelle, intangible et incorruptible" (126). In this vein, the ideal of good taste "n'est là encore qu'une forme de la raison" (137), which marks yet again the triumph of prosaism (121), the demise of poetry and beauty.

The synthesis of Taine and Lanson, which Bray's work represents, seems to contradict Lanson's strenuous efforts to establish *l'histoire littéraire*—the method that would dominate literary studies until the 1950s—in opposition to the deterministic model of the natural sciences. And yet, Lanson's *Histoire de la littérature française* (1895), which was to sell 350,000 copies before 1920, begins with a Tainian chapter on "le caractère de la race," just as his primary focus on a writer's sources and influences may be regarded as a re-writing of *le milieu* and *le moment*. At bottom, however, Lanson strove to incorporate the new positivistic methods of history, which had openly rejected its ties to literature ca. 1870. "On ne saurait trop applaudir," he wrote in 1901, "...à cet effort pour créer la science littéraire, non point à l'instar des sciences de la nature mais par une spécialisation de la méthode historique" (quoted in Compagnon, 56).[20] Disseminated by the *Revue d'Histoire Littéraire* from 1894 on, and legitimized by the Sorbonne chair Lanson held after 1904, literary history was meant to forge the passage from the ancient to the modern republic of letters, and at the same time, to form "la conscience intellectuelle, morale et civique" of his contemporaries (Compagnon, 84). "La religion est évanouie, la science est lointaine," Lanson stated in 1895, in a re-writing of Nisard, "par la littérature seule leur arrivent les sollicitations qui les arrachent à l'égoïsme étroit ou au métier abrutissant" (*Histoire*, viii).

Lanson's "progressive" method marked a return to the original text, now buttressed by an exhaustive collection of bibliographical, biographical, and contextual data, a dream of plenitude that would earn him the label, "le roi du fichier."[21] Moreover, like the method of l'explication de texte, which Lanson and Brunot established in the lycées to replace the antiquated stress on rote memory,[22] the university discipline of *l'histoire littéraire* featured "la description des individualités" (*Histoire*, vii), especially the originality of genius, which Taine had left wholly unexplained, insisted Lanson after Sainte-Beuve.[23] Not surprisingly, then, Lanson's representation of "la littérature classique" in his broad "tableau de la vie littéraire de la nation" from the tenth to the nineteenth centuries contained strong echoes of Sainte-Beuve. Following an organic model of evolution, however, Lanson's classico-centrist survey of the century began with "les préparateurs" (Malherbe, Balzac, Chapelain, Descartes), and "the first generation of classics"(Corneille, Pascal); focused on "les grands noms" (Boileau, Molière, Racine, La Fontaine, Bossuet, and Bourdaloue, as well as La Rochefoucauld, Retz and Sévigné); and closed with "the end of the classical age" (La Bruyère, Fénelon and the quarrel of the ancients and moderns). But Lanson included writers deemed second and third-rate, like the "burlesque" and the "précieux," since their lack of original genius paradoxically made them more emblematic of *l'esprit classique* and *français*: thus a Voiture sonnet "ramasse et suppose toute la civilisation de la première moitié du XVIIe siècle, monarchie absolue, société polie, domination intellectuelle de l'Italie et de l'Espagne, et la brutalité récente enchaînée dans un cérémonial minutieux" (quoted in Compagnon, 156). By contrast, the genius of a Corneille or a Molière remained an inexplicable residue, "cet effroyable inconnu" that no study of sources and influences could fathom, in fact, an irreducible and tautological originality (Compagnon, 190). It was thus not by deduction, but through a pre-formed induction that Lanson traced the perfection of "les grands artistes classiques" to a combination of "[la] souveraineté de la raison et [le] respect de l'antiquité" (*Histoire*, 390). Indeed, classical reason did not degenerate into sterile eighteenth-century cartesianism, he argued against Taine,[24] because it was contained by a preoccupation with form derived from the ancients, but wholly modernized; as a result, art was strengthened by the creation of a "rigorous classical doctrine" (413). Although the preeminence of reason did impoverish language, lyricism and the sense of history, classicism achieved its own realism and naturalism, Lanson maintained, the personification of which was Boileau, once again. While he underscored the defects of the poet, like Sainte-Beuve, and even his absolutism, like Taine, Lanson primarily chastised Boileau's inability to do literary history: "Aussi ne s'est-il pas soucié de ce qu'on appelle l'histoire littéraire, l'étude du développement des littératures et des genres, l'examen des conditions et des milieux, qui dans une certaine mesure déterminent la direction du génie littéraire..." (487). Projecting his own values onto Boileau, Lanson exposed the myth of literary history's transcendant impartiality.

Lanson's reluctant admission that his method could not explain the difference of "genial texts" was to disappear from the work of his disciples. Mornet, the most faithful of them all, and the inheritor of Lanson's Sorbonne chair, valorized classical reason without emphasizing the problematic individuality of esthetic form in his

Histoire de la clarté classique (1929). Even more classico-centrist than Lanson, Mornet dismisses the middle ages and the sixteenth century to focus on the clarity, order, logic and penchant for general truth of *l'esprit classique*, which he claims gave French thought and style its most original and fecund qualities, its permanence and universality. Thus, although he views classical clarity as the deliberate and arduous achievement of two generations of seventeenth-century writers, wrought in denial of the violence and disorder of their lives, Mornet still defines it as "une des formes essentielles de notre pensée" (357). Exposing both the class bias and function of this myth, he admits to being "attaché au goût de la clarté par des habitudes profondes,... surtout [des] habitudes professionnelles" (354), even as he recognizes that some adaptation to "real life" must occur "dans le milieu scolaire [où]... le goût et les habitudes d'une clarté scrupuleuse et savante se sont le plus...despotiquement installés" (356). Nevertheless, judging by his definition of literary history—the discovery of a general truth, clearly presented and supported by a precise and ordered set of reasons—the method Mornet advocates and incarnates remains the emblem of classical clarity.

By 1940, however, when Mornet published his *Histoire de la littérature classique, 1660-1700, ses caractères véritables, ses aspects méconnus*, things had become less clear. In opposition to Bray, Mornet insists that the idea of a coherent classical doctrine was created by literary historians, just as the emphasis on imitation of the ancients was devised by romantics; that the so-called *irréguliers* (e.g. Théophile and Saint-Amant) upheld the same, often contradictory principles as *les réguliers*; that classical comedy and tragedy in no way exemplify the notions of reason, simplicity, and the cult of nature; indeed, that the writers rightly enthroned as classical were but a small minority who did not represent "l'esprit du siècle," since they privileged pleasure over rules, and feeling or the ineffable *je ne sais quoi* over reason (8-12, 14-22, 103-11, 371-72). So saying, Mornet was not simply re-writing Sainte-Beuve; his more complex oppositional vision of "notre époque classique" had been influenced by other sources, as his praise for the work of Lancaster and Brown suggests (2, 4)—by foreign scholars who had a different investment in, and perception of, French classicism.

V

If the idea of classicism from Voltaire to Mornet is inextricably linked to the nationalist ideology of *l'esprit français*, then it stands to reason that scholars from other countries could more easily put the myth, or at least some of its aspects, into question. In the period 1940-1960, a number of these professors tried to cast a fresh, unprejudiced look at French classicism, like so many ingenuous observers in Voltairian tales.[25]   First among these, however, was Peyre, who left France to become the father of French studies in America; *Le Classicisme français* (1942), he said, was "le résultat de notre expérience de Français qui a vécu a l'étranger et a exposé hors de France, à des publics ... ni alourdis de préjugés favorables ni refroidis par un enseignement scolaire jadis impatiemment subi, l'histoire de notre littérature" (12).[26]   From this perspective, Peyre maintained that the traditional meanings of *auteurs classiques*—the ones taught in schools; the best writers; or those of classical antiquity and their later imitators—should not designate a small group of authors in the period 1660-1685, who were, for example, far less obsessed with the past than the romantics. Systematically challenging the clichés of French classicism, Peyre argued that its proverbial rationalism actually represented intellectuality, "[le] besoin de comprendre" (68); that its penchant for analyzing general human traits was not indicative of coldness, impersonality, or anti-individualism; that it did not ignore the external world, but privileged a more profound interior truth; that it did not involve submission to a code of rules, since its supreme dictum was pleasure; and that its *moralistes* were not moralistic or didactic, but psychologically perspicacious.   However, as he examined the construction of the myth by enlightenment and romantic authors, and especially by professors in the period 1830-1850, Peyre upheld the work of Racine and Molière, La Fontaine and Bossuet as "une réussite unique" (16), combining Sainte-Beuve with the later Mornet to revitalize, but nonetheless perpetuate "[un] classicisme essentiel" (235), and beyond, "[le] classicisme profond de la littérature et de l'art français" (237).

Not surprisingly, then, in his 1947 attack on the legend of French classicism, written in Italian, Benedetto singled Peyre out for attack as the perpetrator of an "absurd myth" of miraculous artistic perfection (Brody, 145). Elaborated by French critics as a wish fulfillment fantasy, the idea(l) of French classicism had not changed, he explained, because of a nationalistic drive to rival the glory of Greece. "We are asked to believe," Benedetto wrote indignantly,

that France, working from the very depths of her *moi*, realized,
at that point in time, the same ideal of eternal and universal
beauty that the ancients had realized in their masterpieces—an
ideal to which perhaps all peoples aspire, but which lies within
the reach of that people alone which carries it *ab origine* in its
blood and which has naturalized it to its genius (Brody, 134).

Accordingly, the foreign critic who would challenge this "myth" and
show that the qualities of the classics are not privileged French
property is constantly dismissed as incapable of real understanding.
Nevertheless, Benedetto (re)constructs a classicism of clarity, order
and discipline, after Mornet; of reason combined with concern for
poetic form, inspired by antiquity, after Lanson; of psychological
acuity coupled with grandiosity and solemnity, and of truth with
beauty; but he claims these represent the humanistic values of all
modern European literature since the Renaissance, and that includes
Italy, of course.   Moreover, Benedetto undermines the myth of a
serene, unified French classical school, highlighting both the
unbridgeable differences between a Molière and a Racine, and the
"real" drama of writers' lives, which is reflected in their work. And
yet, Benedetto ultimately rediscovers in what he terms a "style Louis
XIV," dominated by the ideal of *Honnêteté*, a French propensity for
literature that subordinates the self to society, reason and
universals, that combines measure with pleasure, and substance
with elegance (147) to produce a significant "equilibrium" (144-47).
So doing, Benedetto revealed that the foreigner, working within a
specific discursive and professional context, was not really writing
from elsewhere; his difference, it turns out, was largely more of the
same.
     The value and the limitations of such oppositional criticism may
also be gauged by Borgerhoff's *The Freedom of French Classicism*
(1950). For while this Princeton professor challenges Bray's rules
and restrictions by emphasizing the independence of writers from
Corneille to Fénelon, and their conviction that rigid formal standards
destroy literature (235-36), he aims to demythologize and
complexify classicism, not to eliminate the concept.   Thus he
maintains that the myth of rationalism was created by romantics
opposed to eighteenth-century logicalism; that the ideals of
simplicity and naturalness were a means of combatting scholasticism
and pedantry; and he reaffirms, after Mornet, the preeminence of
pleasure, but especially, of feeling and intuition, the mysterious and
the inexplicable, in effect, the Pascalian order of the heart (235-44).
Rejecting the cliché of equilibrium in favor of tension and
contradiction, Borgerhoff upholds what he calls the paradox, the

oxymoron of classicism: "it found an anchor in the certainty of the indefinable and the rationally incomprehensible, and in so doing it enabled itself to express the infinite complexity of man's nature as few other literatures have done" (245). Through this paradox, however, Borgerhoff paradoxically revalidates the notion of a unified century (253ff), and even of an ideal, essential classicism.

More radically, or so it seems at the outset, Moore's *French Classical Literature* (1961) calls for "the end of ...the scandal of a literature...proclaimed as the finest product of a nation's culture," but thought to be "artificial, affected, unexciting, and old-fashioned," formal and rigid, imitative and rule-bound (9-10). Because French critics and professors have insisted on unquestioning admiration, there has been little inquiry and research, says Moore, citing as exceptions the work of Mornet and Adam in France, Lancaster in his native England, Brody in America. However, his ideal "unbiased and critical reader," who would restore works to "their original context," intention and meaning, "freed from accretions of interpretations" (18- 20), reproduces what have become topoi among foreign scholars—the preeminence of pleasure over rules, and of unrest over serenity. Praising the work of historians, Moore stresses the social, political and scientific ferment of the century, and thus the achievement of classical order and unity as a needed response to forces of violence, disorder, anarchy. In this revisionist mode, Moore limits classicism to "a common spirit" (19) in the 1660's and 1670's that represents a very small part of the production of a small number of writers, but he admits to having "no startling new interpretation to offer" (18). Although he began by entertaining the possibility of doing "without the term" (12), he is finally "content to go on thinking of the leading French writers of this period as 'classical'" (18), infusing "a new content into an old word" (13) that conveys their vital innovations, but avoids the dangers of anachronism (20).

Caught between a dissatisfaction with the old myth of classicism and an inability to formulate a radically new concept or then to dispense completely with the notion, Moore's work suggests an impasse that is confirmed in Brody's *French Classicism, A Critical Miscellany* (1966), with which I began. For while the foreign scholars who dominate the last part of his volume—and these include Peyre, Benedetto, Borgerhoff and Moore as well as Edelman and Brody himself—were distanced enough to challenge the clichés of French literary historians, and to vivify and complexify classicism, they also reproduced some old and some new myths, and revealed a deep-seated investment in perpetuating the idea(l). So too, then, Brody's introduction exposes the role of teacher-scholars who "followed the fruitless tactic of trying to make over into literary virtues those very attributes which in the romantic view were identified as vices" (vi). By contrast, he emphasizes the "rebellious innovation" of authors who wrote in "open defiance of traditional orthodoxies" (vi), and the modernism of the forms they used, which had no firm ancient antecedents. And yet, Brody insists, "it is an empirical fact" that Sévigné and Racine, La Rochefoucauld and Pascal "do have something in common," urging that it be identified before the emerging concept of the baroque[27] once again robs classical literature of its "profundity and imaginative power"; but the identification of that "something," he conceded, was not "even remotely in view" (viii). However, while Brody dramatized this classical impasse, the debate over *la nouvelle critique* had already exploded across the ocean. That quarrel would focus on the modernity of the classics, which Brody extolled, but most especially, on the modernity of their interpretation, which Moore considered dangerous.

VI

When Raymond Picard published his blistering *Nouvelle critique ou nouvelle imposture* (1965) in response to Barthes's *Sur Racine* (1963), he catalyzed the latest "querelle des anciens et des modernes," which represented yet again a struggle for *pouvoir* as (and over) *savoir*. To be sure, Barthes had used Racine's proverbial "transparence classique" (10) ironically and provocatively to justify the application of all new methodologies to this *œuvre*, in his own case, "une sorte d'anthropologie racinienne, à la fois structurale et [psycho]analytique" (9). More aggressively, in "Histoire ou littérature," the closing section of his text, Barthes had attacked Picard's study of Racine as the emblem of "la critique universitaire," fixated in "le cadre désuet" of the institution, and Lansonian notions of erudition and authorial genius (153, 158). Chastising the university's belief in objective criticism, Barthes argued that critics must recognize their "impuissance à dire vrai sur Racine," their investment in a particular methodology, and thus the subjectivity of their reading, which in effect "fait partie de la littérature" (166).[28] That Picard, the specialist, mustered chapter and verse to brand Barthes's interpretation of Racine absurdly unknowing and unfounded set the stage for his demonstration that the author of *Sur Racine*, like "his friends," was dogmatic and impressionistic, prone to global statements and the naive biographism of psychoanalytic criticism. In this way,"the new critic" emerged as an ancient, a synthesis of Brunetière and Faguet, whose methods Lanson had criticized at the turn of the century. Picard cast himself as the defender of science, even more, of Racinian ambiguity and of "purely" literary studies, over and against the neologistic, jargonistic Barthes and his "school" for whom the explanation of literature was always elsewhere—in marxism, existentialism, structuralism, or psychoanalysis. Scandalized that Barthes had transformed Racine into a sex-obsessed D.H. Lawrence, Picard declared, in a revelation of his own ideological preconceptions:

> Il y a une vérité de Racine, sur laquelle tout le monde peut arriver à se mettre d'accord. En s'appuyant en particulier sur les certitudes du langage, sur les implications de la cohérence psychologique, sur les impératifs de la structure du genre, le chercheur patient et modeste parvient à dégager des évidences qui déterminent en quelque sorte des zones d'objectivité (69).

As a non-specialist, Barthes displayed enormous arrogance, but more serious by far, his text was monstrously dangerous— "tératologique" (88)—since its denial that Racine's *œuvre* represented "[une] activité volontaire et lucide" (138), warned Picard, heralded the destruction of literature.

That Picard labeled *la nouvelle critique* a "mythology," not an intellectual methodology (135), found an ironic echo in Barthes's *Critique et vérité*(1966). He compared the violence of the university critic's response to "quelque rite d'exclusion mené dans une communauté archaïque contre un sujet dangereux" (10), one who challenges doxal language, and thus the power of those who police it. In turn, Barthes interpreted the idea of Racinian and French clarity, in Picard or Nisard, as a political concept that mythified a specific historical idiom into a universal (28-30). And, with an irony that could not have escaped Picard, Barthes used the clichés of classicism—clarity, rational objectivity, verisimilitude and taste—to label Picardians representatives of *l'ancienne critique*, committed to the "classical" ideal of the full, conscious, objective writing subject. In advocating a modern, pluralistic criticism of works deemed "eternal" (51), however, Barthes ironically reconfirmed the clichés of classicism. So too, then, when he saw in La Rochefoucauld's maxims both a modern impulse toward a discontinuous, disorderly "spectacle du sens" (79), and a classical tendency to close, eternalize and essentialize meaning, he was partly reiterating the classical topoi that had marked (and marred) his *Degré zéro de l'écriture* (1952). In that early work on the evolution of the concept of literature, Barthes had rigidified the differences between the classical and the modern, like a latter-day de Staël, reproducing the topos of a clear, unproblematic, abstract, algebraic language that lacked freshness and invention, denseness and *volupté* (35-38). Extending the era of *l'écriture classique* from 1650 to 1850, in contrast to recent tendencies to narrow it, Barthes defined it as a class literature that witnessed the triumph of the bourgeoisie and its ideology. Within this conventional marxist scheme, classicism provided the necessary base against which the radical modernity of the post-1850 period could be upheld, and beyond, the ideal of an uncontaminated "adamic language" could be imagined (64-65). As Barthes observed in *Mythologies*, the modern critic can either demythify doxal concepts or create his own poetic myths. No different than scholars from afar, Barthes did both.

Like the early Barthes, marxist historians and critics used the clichés of classicism to expose the oppressiveness of monarchic absolutism as the triumph of the state, class inequality and bourgeois capitalism. While their studies of tensions and contradictions problematized and enlivened the frozen image of *le siècle de Louis XIV,* they also harked back to Taine's determinism, with a different etiology and teleology. Thus by using the method/ideology of dialectical materialism, and of Lukacs in particular, Goldmann's *Le Dieu Caché* (1959), which Barthes praised in *Sur Racine,* discerned a pattern of alternation between true tragedies and "intra-worldly" dramas in Racine's œuvre that paralleled the ideological struggles at Port Royal. Notwithstanding this socio-critical complexification of "transparent" or "eternal literature," Goldmann's proclaimed "scientific objectivity" tended to essentialize Racine's and Pascal's "vision du monde," and to sustain the Lukacsian notion of classicism as an unproblematic bourgeois unity, marked by a Sainte-Beuvian harmony between man and the world (51-52). Indeed, for all of its extraordinary impact in recent years, Bakhtin's *Rabelais and his World* (translated in 1968) contains a no less dogmatic representation of the seventeenth century: the demise of the pre-capitalist carnaval of spontaneous folk culture with the enthronement of the "new order of the absolute monarchy" (101), and an official classical culture of univocal meaning, rationalism and seriousness. In that process, Bakhtin's utopian carnival and the contestation of its grotesque realism were degraded and relegated to low literary genres; bourgeois individualism closed off, privatized the body; and personal invective replaced challenges to ultimate authority.[29]

It was such marxist dogma that Foucault challenged in his *Histoire de la sexualité* (1976) when he countered the hypothesis that sexuality had been repressed in *l'âge classique* to provide energetic workers for the needs of bourgeois capitalism and the state. And yet, Foucault's iconoclastic argument that church and state incited the confession of sexuality at the dawn of *l'âge classique* to control and define sexual human subjects concluded that both the *scientia sexualis* and the repressive theory itself were "originairement, historiquement bourgeoise[s]" (168), emblems of its triumph over the nobiliary "symbolique du sang" (195). More reductive by far, Foucault's *Histoire de la folie à l'âge classique* (1972) interpreted the internment of various categories of people into asylums as the product of a complicity between the absolute monarchy, the bourgeoisie and the counter-reformation church to eliminate those who did not sustain or enhance the political, moral, and above all, economic order (61-64). In contrast to the pre-classical and even "baroque" experience of cosmic, tragic madness, *la folie à l'âge classique* became part of reason itself, evoked only to be excluded and overcome by the cartesian subject. But as Derrida would argue in "Cogito et l'histoire de la folie," madness in Descartes remained an originating "flaw" that undermined rationality, and necessitated God's presence to ensure the truth of "clear and distinct ideas." So saying, Derrida was responding to an attack, in which Foucault had branded him the ultimate representative of a classical system, grounded in a metaphysics of the text as origin (*Folie*, 602). That "classical" was the ultimate insult to level at a post-structuralist critic suggests the ideological function of its reification as an immutable system of thought, what Foucault called an episteme in *Les Mots et les choses*. Although he emphasized that it still dominated aspects of modernity, Foucault's "classical episteme" in this 1966 structuralist study typically collapsed the seventeenth with a far more often cited eighteenth century into a closed system demarcated by moments of "rupture." Predictably, this episteme comprised an algebraic "science universelle de la mesure et de l'ordre" (70), featuring studies of classification and of genesis, the binarization of the sign, and the representational concept that idea and sign are "parfaitement transparents l'un à l'autre" (79); thus classical meaning, claimed Foucault, "ne [pouvait] faire problème" (80). Commenting on the elusiveness and indeterminacy of Foucault's claims, Descombes concluded that "his histories [were] novels" (116-17). More accurately, perhaps, Foucault's histories, like all constructions of the classical, are ideological mythologies. In that, there is no difference between *l'ancienne* and *la nouvelle critique*.

* * *

In my (re)construction, the myth of classicism from the first to the latest *querelle des anciens et des modernes* seems to have what Barthes called in his *Mythologies* a nauseating monotony. Set in place by reactive romantics, and in turn, by reactive academics, the clichés shift in value over time, alternating from the positive to the negative; they may be more reductive or more complex, but they have a fundamental similarity. Indeed, just as the academics of the period 1830-1850 hark back to Voltaire, and Taine to the romantics, all later representations of classicism from Lanson to Foucault seem to echo Sainte-Beuve or Taine, or both of them, in the case of Lanson and Barthes. Dogmatic and subjective, like all criticism, Picard notwithstanding, the definition of the classical has constituted a way of using a mythical *savoir* to gain *pouvoir* for one's own discourse and methodology, in opposition to a perceived enemy whose threat could be reduced by labeling it antiquated; thus today's moderns became tomorrow's ancients. In this light, Foucault's insistence that oppositional discourse is not necessarily liberating (*Histoire de la sexualité*, 108ff), and Picard's observation that it does not *ipso facto* create a *nouvelle critique* (9) are valid, but only partially, in my view. For oppositional or even reactive discourse does challenge and displace some aspects of the doxal, even though it also reconfirms and further reifies others. The insight that underlies the partial challenge seems to produce blindness about the sameness of the rest; or then, the capacity to challenge a part may be predicated on keeping (most of) the whole in place. This is to suggest that no privileged position exists from which one can speak differently, not even for the foreign scholars of the 1940s-1960s who perceived the nationalism that governed the classical myths of their French colleagues. Like the enlightenment or the romantic writer, the academic was bound by the parameters of a discursive and institutional formation, within which classicism was both so ingrained and so functional as a synonym or an antonym to the values of the self that it could not be, and never has been, eliminated.

To be sure, this is still a partial answer to the questions with which I began: "comment et pourquoi le classicisme?" More broadly, the perpetuation of classicism as a utopian or dystopian myth, a *faculté maîtresse* or an episteme, a transcendent universal or an indefinable, but real, "something" exposes the ancient and abiding imperative to classify discourse, to give it an arbitrary order. "Rien n'est plus essentiel à une société que le classement de ses langages," Barthes observes in *Critique et vérité* (45); but if he claims that "changer ce classement...c'est faire une révolution," how much more revolutionary would the elimination of classifications, like classicism, be. That such dis-ordering is difficult to conceive may reveal the fear that underlies the classificatory drive, as Foucault observes in *L'Ordre du discours*:

> Il y a sans doute dans notre société, et j'imagine dans toutes les autres, mais selon un profil et des scansions différentes, une profonde logophobie, une sorte de crainte sourde...contre cette masse de choses dites, contre le surgissement de tous ces énoncés, contre tout ce qu'il peut y avoir de violent, de discontinu, de batailleur, de désordre aussi et de périlleux, contre ce grand bourdonnement incessant et désordonné du discours (52-3).

That fear cannot be eliminated, but it can be held up to view with irony, if not nausea. Since there is no miraculous exit from the bonds of our discursive prisonhouse, the only choice, I believe, is to say with Sartre, "Eh bien, continuons."

Notes

[1]Cf the definition of *classique* in Richelet's dictionary (1680): "auteur qui est dans le rang des plus considérables et qui mérite d'être pris pour modèle."

[2]Quoted in Apostolidès, 45. However, Apostolidès exaggerates the widespread acceptance of this view by what he calls anachronistically "l'intellectuel d'Etat."

[3]According to Mouralis, Voltaire may have derived the notion of progressive maturation from Boileau's *Art poétique* (22).

[4]For another version of this myth, which stresses the characteristics of the decadent phase, see Marmontel, quoted in Brody, 10.

[5]Quoted in Lanson, *Histoire de la littérature française*, 704.

[6]As Darnton points out, this need eventually led to the mythification of the independent man of letters as a heroic warrior, and in Voltaire and D'Alembert, as the progressive force of history (207-09).

[7]See also Voltaire's remarks on the superiority of French music (2: 55).

[8]According to the Robert, *classicisme* enters the language in 1825; but the term does not appear in the 1835 edition of the *Dictionnaire de l'Académie Française*.

[9]The Revolution did make French the language of all the people—rather than of the monarchy, nobility and bourgeoisie—by waging open war, a kind of "linguistic terrorism" (Balibar, 97), on the idioms that half of the population spoke exclusively to ensure the uniformity essential to the ideology of nationality, and the efficient workings of bourgeois capitalism.

[10]Free admission to the lycées was not instituted until 1927-1937 (see Balibar, 147).

[11]Barthes, "Réflexions sur un manuel," in Doubrovsky, *L'Enseignement de la littérature*, 170.

[12]The association between teaching and the classics goes back to the Latin, as Du Marsais had observed in his *Encyclopédie* article, *Classique*: "ce mot ne se dit

que des auteurs que l'on explique dans les collèges; les mots et les façons de parler de ces auteurs servent de modèle aux jeunes gens" (Brody, 6).

[13]The Ecole Normale Supérieure had been founded in 1795 for the purpose of training lycée teachers, which confirms yet again the dominance of the secondary schools over all other parts of the educational system in the nineteenth century.

[14]On the religious function that the teaching of literature assumed, see also Charles, 268.

[15]Nisard's work first appeared in 1844; he began to write the last volume in 1848 and finished it in 1854, according to its preface.

[16]Nisard's work begins with a volume on the middle ages and the sixteenth century combined; the last volume is largely devoted to the eighteenth century, and closes with a chapter on Chateaubriand.

[17]For instance, Sainte-Beuve objects to the consecration of Racine as a model for imitation, not only because this limits his qualities to grammar and diction, but because his primary talents are poetic, rather than dramaturgical, and thus, of little use to "le drame nouveau" (*Œuvres*, 758). So saying, Sainte-Beuve implicitly criticizes the academic view of Racine, and sides with the romantics.

[18]However, Taine's own characterizations of the peasant, the worker or the provincial bourgeois are far from positive; see *Les Origines*, 2: 15-16. Moroever, he opposes the democratic ideal and the "irruptions" of a brutal populace (2: 315).

[19]Bray also opposes classical elitism in the name of a popular literature (126, 128, 133, 136).

[20]I am indebted to Compagnon for his insightful remarks on Lanson in *La Troisième République des lettres*.

[21]The term was coined by Lucien Febvre, according to Compagnon (163), who also emphasizes the continuity between philology and Lanson's literary history. On the primary importance of reading the original text, see for example, Lanson's *Histoire de la littérature française*, vi- vii.

[22]On the influence of the emerging field of pedagogy, see Compagnon, 85ff.

[23]See Sainte-Beuve, "Taine," *Nouveaux Lundis,* May 30, 1864, and for Lanson's criticism of Taine, Compagnon, 178ff. Despite his influence on Lanson, Sainte-Beuve was also to be criticized in *Hommes et livres* as a biographical critic and literary painter, rather than a historian.

[24]Lanson would come to favor the "enlightened" eighteenth century over the "undemocratic" seventeenth century, in the aftermath of a debate about the relative merits of Bossuet and Voltaire, and would hold the chair of literary history for the eighteenth century at the Sorbonne from 1923 until his retirement in 1928. See Compagnon, 108, 145ff.

[25]See, for example, Auerbach, whose *Mimesis* was published in Germany in 1945, and who adopted the stance of "the impartial observer, that is, anyone who has not grown up with these masterpieces from childhood and early school days" (342). Nevertheless, his method of "Historism," which is inspired by Taine with greater emphasis on sociology (344-45, 391-92), serves to iterate the notion that the monarchic, aristocratic seventeenth century and its classical rules produced literary texts that were not realistic, concrete or historical (345-47).

[26]However, Peyre had strong reservations about the degree to which the foreigner could grasp French classicism: "...l'étranger, faute de se défier des mots et des classifications chargés de tromperie, a souvent abordé le classicisme français avec des préventions, des antipathies, ou même des sympathies mal éclairées, qui ont ajouté aux incompréhensions mutuelles entres les littératures et les peuples" (205). This view, couched in much stronger terms, appeared in Peyre's *Qu'est-ce que le classicisme?*, published in France a decade earlier: "Aucun autre peuple moderne n'ayant ...créé une littérature classique exactement comparable à la nôtre, l'étranger a abordé notre classicisme avec des préventions, des antipathies, ou même des sympathies mal éclairées, qui l'ont toujours empêché de le comprendre pleinement" (Paris: Droz, 1933, 171-72).

[27]E.g., Rousset, who elaborated a series of binary oppositions in which the baroque is associated with metamorphosis, mobility and vacillation, restlessness

and anxiety, a focus on events, the present, and multiple points of view, while the classical, is associated with immobility, stability, serenity, a fixed center, a single point of view, lack of events, absence of time, and a stress on the past; see 159-64.

[28]Barthes's insistance that the critic's production constitutes *écriture* has been seminal, and controversial in its promotion of the commentator to equal rank with "the author," but in many ways, it harks back to Sainte-Beuve, perhaps the last critic to regard criticism as literature. As my reconstruction suggests, criticism and the conception of classicism after 1850 became the property of the professorial class and of academic institutions. To be sure, scholars of French classicism have often incorporated in their work remarks by Gide and Valéry (see, e.g.,Brody, 65-76; Peyre, *passim*), but Barthes's theories of the critic-as-writer and his own practice, whose "poetic charm" even Picard could not deny (76), represent an effort to reclaim critical discourse from the university, to reconnect it with the *avant garde* and, as his *Mythologies* indicate, with popular culture as well.

[29]On Bakhtin's view of the seventeenth century, see also Stanton, 128-31.

Works Cited

Althusser, Louis. "Idéologie et appareils idéologiques d'état." *La Pensée* 151 (June, 1970), 3-38.

Apostolidès, Jean Marie. *Le Roi Machine.* Paris: Minuit, 1981.

Auerbach, Erich. *Mimesis.* New York: Doubleday Anchor, 1957.

Bakhtin, Michael. *Rabelais and his World.* Trans. Helene Iswolsky. Bloomington: Indiana University Press, 1984.

Balibar, Renée and Dominique Laporte. *Le Francais National: Politique et pratiques de la langue nationale sous la révolution française.* Paris: Hachette, 1974.

Barthes, Roland. *Critique et vérité.* Paris: Seuil, 1966.

—. "La Rochefoucauld: Réflexions ou Sentences et maximes." *Le Degré Zéro de l'écriture suivi de Nouveaux Essais critiques.* Paris: Points, 1972, 69-98.

—. *Le Degré Zéro de l'écriture suivi de Nouveaux Essais critiques.* Paris: Points, 1972.

—. *Mythologies.* Paris: Points, 1957.

—. *Sur Racine.* Paris: Seuil, 1963.

Becq, Annie. *Genèse de l'esthétique moderne: De la raison classique à l'imagination créatrice.* Paris: Jean Touzot, 1984.

Borgerhoff, E.B.O. *The Freedom of French Classicism.* Princeton: Princeton University Press, 1950.

Bourdieu, Pierre. *La Reproduction.* Paris:Minuit, 1970.

Bray, René. *La Formation de la doctrine classique en France.* Paris: Hachette, 1927.

Brody, Jules, ed. *French Classicism: A Critical Miscellany.* Englewood Cliffs, NJ: Prentice Hall, 1966.

Charles, Michel. *L'Arbre et la source.* Paris: Seuil,1985.

Chateaubriand. *Le Génie du Christianisme.* 2 vols. Paris: Garnier, 1930.

Chervel, André. *Les Auteurs français, latins et grecs au programme de l'enseignement secondaire de 1800 jusqu'à nos jours.* Paris: Publications de la Sorbonne, 1986.

Compagnon, Antoine. *La Troisième République des lettres.* Paris: Seuil, 1983.

Cousin, Victor. *Du vrai, du beau et du bien.* Paris: Didier, 1856.

D'Alembert. "Discours Préliminaire." *Encyclopédie, ou dictionnaire raisonné des sciences, des arts et des métiers.* 2 vols. Paris: Garnier Flammarion, 1986.

Darnton, Robert. *The Great Cat Massacre and Other Episodes in French Cultural History.* New York: Basic Books, 1984.

Derrida, Jacques. "Cogito et l'histoire de la folie." *L'Ecriture et la différence.* Paris: Seuil,1967, 51-97.

Descombes, Vincent. *Le Même et l'autre.* Paris: Minuit, 1979.

De Staël. *Corinne ou l'Italie.* Paris: Folio, 1985.

—. *De l'Allemagne.* 2 vols. Paris: Garnier Flammarion, 1968.

Doubrovsky, Serge, ed. *L'Enseignement de la littérature.* Paris: Plon, 1971.

—. "New Critics and Old Myths." *Yale French Studies* 38 (1967), 18-26.

Fontanier, Pierre. *Etudes de la langue française sur Racine, ou Commentaire général et comparatif sur la diction et le style de ce grand classique...pour servir de cours pratique de langue française, et suppléer à l'insuffisance des grammaires.* Paris: Chez Belin-Le- Prieur, 1818.

Foucault, Michel. *Histoire de la folie à l'âge classique.* Paris: Gallimard, 1972.

—. *Histoire de la sexualité.* vol 1: *La Volonté de savoir.* Paris: Gallimard, 1976.

—. *Les Mots et les choses.* Paris: Gallimard, 1966.

—. *L'Ordre du discours.* Paris: Gallimard, 1971.

Gautier, Théophile. *Histoire du romantisme.* Paris: Charpentier, 1877.

Goldmann, Lucien. *Le Dieu caché.* Paris: Gallimard, 1959.

Hugo, Victor. "Réponse à un acte d'accusation. *Œuvres poétiques de Victor Hugo.* Ed. Pierre Albony. Vol. 2. Paris: Gallimard (Bibliothèque de la Pléiade), 494-500.

Lanson, Gustave. *Histoire de la littérature française.* Paris: Hachette, 1895.

—. *Hommes et livres.* Paris: Le Cène, Oudin et Cie., 1895.

Lyotard, Jean-François. *La Condition Post-Moderne.* Paris: Minuit, 1979.

Moore, Will G. *French Classical Literature.* Oxford: Oxford University Press, 1961.

Mornet, Daniel. *Histoire de la clarté classique.* Paris: Payot, 1929.

—. *Histoire de la littérature classique. 1660-1700, ses caractères véritables, ses aspects méconnus.* Paris: Armand Colin,1947.

Mouralis, Bernard. *Les Contre-Littératures.* Paris: Presses Universitaires de France, 1975.

Nisard, Désiré. *Histoire de la littérature française.* 4 vols. Paris: Firmin Didot, 1879.

Peyre, Henri. *Le Classicisme français.* New York: Editions de la Maison Française, 1942.

Picard, Raymond. *Nouvelle Critique ou nouvelle imposture.* Paris: Jean-Jacques Pauvert, 1965.

Rousset, Jean. *La Littérature de l'âge baroque en France: Circé et le paon.* Paris: José Corti, 1953.

Sainte-Beuve. *Les Grands Ecrivains classiques (XVIIe Siècle: Les Poètes).* Ed. Maurice Allem. Paris: Garnier, 1927.

—. *Œuvres.* Vol. 1 *(Premiers Lundis: Début des Portraits Littéraires).* Ed. Maxime Leroy. Paris: Gallimard (Bibliothèque de la Pléiade), 1956.

—. *Qu'est-ce qu'un classique? suivi de deux autres traités.* Heidelberg: Editiones Heidelbergenses, 1946.

—. "Taine." *Nouveaux Lundis.* Vol. 8. Paris: Calmann Lévy, 1885, 66-88.

Stanton, Domna C. "On la *contestation* and le *carnaval*: A Paradoxical Preface," *PFSCL* 30 (1987), 123-41.

Stendhal. *Racine et Shakespeare.* Paris: Garnier Flammarion, 1970.

Taine, Hippolyte. *Les Philosophes français du XIXe siècle.* Paris: Hachette, 1857.

—. *Les Origines de la France contemporaine. l'Ancien Régime.* 2 vols. Paris: Hachette, 1904.

Voltaire. *Correspondance.* Ed. Théodore Besterman. Vol 1. Paris: Gallimard (Bibliothèque de la Pléiade), 1963.

—. *Le Siècle de Louis XIV.* 2 vols. Paris: Garnier Flammarion, 1966.

Le Discours scolaire au XIXème siècle: le cas Molière

Ralph Albanese, Jr.
University of Nebraska—Lincoln

"La littérature, c'est ce qui s'enseigne, un point, c'est tout." R. BARTHES, "Réflexions sur un manuel" (170).

Parmi les multiples traits de modernité propres au dix-neuvième siècle, la mise en place de l'institution littéraire joue un rôle prépondérant. L'organisation de l'Ecole et les progrès continus de la scolarisation constituent en effet une seconde révolution française, moins tempétueuse peut-être mais plus significative que la première. Héritée de Rousseau, la nouvelle perception de l'écrivain en tant que modèle pédagogique, ainsi que l'entrée de la littérature dans une zone de justification scolaire, font partie intégrante d'une culture française "post-révolutionnaire."[1] L'évolution de l'enseignement littéraire au XIXème siècle, notamment au niveau du cycle secondaire, comporte de nombreuses mutations sur le plan des Instructions officielles, des programmes, des exercices et des manuels scolaires. La constitution des auteurs français en "classiques," c'est-à-dire, leur inscription dans le cursus scolaire, leur création en tant qu'objets de lecture, mérite certes une étude attentive. Nous nous proposons ici de nous en tenir à une analyse de l'image scolaire de Molière au XIXème siècle; il va de soi que cette image s'insère dans un culte du canon classique où Boileau, La Fontaine et Bossuet ont une place privilégiée. D'autre part, nous espérons mettre en lumière, par l'exemple du poète comique, la genèse du mythe scolaire du classicisme.

Le statut de Molière dans les programmes de l'enseignement secondaire est étroitement lié à l'évolution des institutions scolaires au XIXème siècle. Quoique sa place soit plus ou moins inexistante au début du siècle—l'auteur de *Tartuffe* ne fut guère prisé par Napoléon, qui lui préférait la mâle vigueur de Corneille, ni par la Restauration, qui redoutait son esprit critique et sa modération—sa popularité va en progressant pour atteindre son apogée dans les années 1880-1914. Rendre compte de cette longue période d'émergence de Molière depuis la Révolution jusqu'en 1880, c'est d'abord mettre en évidence les finalités de l'enseignement rhétorique. Marquée par la cohabitation des auteurs latins, grecs et français, les auteurs anciens jouissant d'une prépondérance réelle, cette pédagogie traditionnelle visait à développer l'aptitude discursive de l'élève, à lui faire apprendre les règles sous-jacentes à l'art du bien dire et du bien écrire. D'où la part considérable accordée aux orateurs sacrés tels que Bossuet et Massillon, ou bien à l'oeuvre de Corneille, dont l'évidente dimension rhétorique offrait une mine de citations. Cela dit, la sélection des auteurs était moins importante qu'elle ne le serait vers la fin du siècle, car tout auteur— "ancien" ou "moderne"—se révélait source de discours. On ne s'étonne donc guère que l'enseignement rhétorique ait fait de l'utilisation du "morceau choisi" une démarche pédagogique principale. Le découpage systématique des oeuvres, leur fragmentation en morceaux d'éloquence sans cesse réitérés servait à faciliter la récitation: l'élève devait se pénétrer du modèle afin de produire un discours "spontané."

Dans le cas de Molière, on a affaire à un traitement "par touches," de nombreux manuels présentant des scènes choisies de *Dom Juan* ou de *L'Avare*, par exemple, où l'insubordination filiale d'un Dom Juan ou d'un Cléante était fort bien mise en cause.[2] Au même titre que les narrations, les maximes à développer, souvent à partir d'un lieu commun de morale ou de critique, le Discours des Morts représentait un exercice scolaire en vigueur jusqu'à la fin du siècle. C'est ainsi qu'en 1853, par exemple, un sujet de discours français exige que l'élève compose un dialogue à partir d'une rencontre imaginaire entre Molière et Aristophane (Valton 35). De telles rencontres font la matière d'autres sujets analogues, où l'auteur du *Misanthrope* s'entretiendrait, tour à tour, avec Plaute [1897], Boileau [1897] et Rousseau [1900] (Perez 396; Delmont 451; Caruel 669); ce dernier exercice avait pour thème un sujet à valeur archétypale au XIXème siècle, à savoir: "Molière (dans son portrait d'Alceste) a-t-il rendu la vertu ridicule?" Or le Discours des Morts connaît de multiples variations jusqu'au début du XXème siècle, et certains sujets exigent, de même, la rédaction d'une composition adoptant la forme d'un dialogue. Tantôt l'exercice prolonge l'existence scénique des héros de comédie: "Henriette, mère de famille, élèverait ses propres filles" (*Revue universitaire*, 1908); "M. Jourdain et Chrysale, tous deux irrités contre leur femme ..." (*ibid.*, 1894); "Alceste et Philinte vieillis tous deux...";[3] tantôt, il transforme Alceste en philosophe désireux de dialoguer avec La Bruyère, "moraliste trop tiède à ses yeux" (*Revue universitaire*, 1908); tantôt, enfin, l'imagination académique va jusqu'à la métempsychose dans le dessein d'illustrer l'universalité des défauts humains: "Imaginer que l'âme de Molière vient habiter la statue du grand écrivain" (*Annales du baccalauréat*, 1913). L'opposition systématique du couple Alceste/Philinte—Ditandy compare leur rapport à celui qui lie Don Quichotte à Sancho Panza (244)—a donné lieu à une multiplicité de sujets: "dans quelle société aimeriez-vous vivre, dans celle de Philinte ou dans celle d'Alceste?" [Paris, 1882] (Condamin 348); "A qui préférez-vous ressembler dans la vie, à Alceste ou à Philinte?" [1904] (Quentel 115);[4] "imaginez un dialogue entre le Misanthrope et le Philanthrope," et, enfin, ce sujet, à la limite du comique: "Voudriez-vous avoir un ami comme le Philinte du *Misanthrope?*" (*Enseignement secondaire des jeunes filles*, 1898).

De tels sujets de discours et de compositions visaient à ce que l'élève s'identifie à cette référence extérieure qu'est le modèle au détriment de ses qualités individuelles. On ne saurait trop insister ici sur la primauté du modèle, qu'il s'agisse de la récitation ou de la rédaction. Désireux de transformer l'élève en maître de la parole, l'enseignement rhétorique poussait ce dernier à recourir, à partir d'un canevas fourni par le manuel, au principe d'*amplificatio* afin de s'approprier le discours de l'écrivain. On a affaire à une pédagogie atemporelle qui véhiculait des modèles d'humanité abstraite, les sujets proposés en classe fournissant à l'élève une représentation symbolique du moi. Tout se passe comme si l'élève était amené à dissoudre la nature fictive des héros de Molière, à rendre réels des êtres imaginaires.

On ne s'étonne guère, dans cette pédagogie traditionnelle, que la mémoire occupe une place privilégiée. De la citation à la (ré)-citation, il n'y a en effet qu'un pas...littéralement réitéré. De là, le contenu fortement homogène sinon répétitif de ces "aide-mémoire" que sont les manuels scolaires—et l'on entend par là les traités de rhétorique et les livres d'histoire littéraire—qui devaient fixer dans la mémoire les connaissances nécessaires à une discipline donnée. Ainsi, selon ses conseils d'ordre méthodologique de P. Allain, il serait bon de confier des passages de Molière à la mémoire (39). Pour l'abbé Drioux, les pièces de ce dernier représentent des "comédies-proverbes" qui fournissent une multitude de formules piquantes se prêtant à la mémorisation (110). Plus on s'avance dans le cycle scolaire, plus on étudie les "grandes comédies" de Molière; cette promotion de la prose à la poésie, qui marque le passage de la classe de seconde à la classe de rhétorique, par exemple, accordait une place plus grande à l'emploi de citations qui, selon Ditandy, devaient faire l'objet même de la classe terminale (243). Il va de soi que la capacité de citer des vers de mémoire—"Madame, les rieurs sont pour vous," "Le temps ne fait rien à l'affaire," "Franchement, il est bon à mettre au cabinet"—constitue, au XIXème siècle, un signe d'appartenance à la culture, une sorte de ralliement à une classe lettrée. Fondée sur la notion de mémoire-dépôt, trouvant ses points d'ancrage dans les manuels, l'explication de textes en classe de rhétorique avait pour but, du moins jusqu'en 1880, la traduction pure et simple du texte, car on avait recours à une approche essentiellement philologique et grammaticale;[5] l'enseignement littéraire ne s'est pas encore dégagé d'un enseignement littéral. Quoique ses propos s'adressent à l'enseignement primaire, Lacabe-Plasteig souligne, dans cette même perspective, la "nécessité d'apprendre littéralement" un corpus de textes français: "Par là, on nourrit son esprit de fortes et grandes idées; on dépose dans sa mémoire des images et des constructions qui aideront à parler et à écrire."[6]

D'autre part, il est significatif que les manuels fonctionnent parfois à la manière des catéchismes, selon le schéma questions/réponses. La petite taille de certains livres scolaires, tel celui de Gasc-Desfossés (*Réponses aux questions du programme*) justifie l'étymologie du "manuel." La présentation lourdement didactique que l'on discerne dans les traités de rhétorique— véritables encyclopédies du savoir littéraire—privilégie les genres d'éloquence aux dépens de la littérature et, chose plus importante, envisage les divers genres littéraires sous forme de définitions fixes. A la "question sartrienne" "Qu'est-ce que la littérature?," qui se trouvait posée dès le départ dans plusieurs manuels, faisait réponse une classification systématique. Le théâtre de Molière se découpait génériquement en "comédies de caractère," "comédies d'intrigue," "divertissements," et "farces." A titre d'exemple, dans le *Cours complet de littérature...et de poétique*, datant de 1870 et dont l'auteur est anonyme, on trouve cette suite révélatrice de questions portant sur le genre comique, avec la réponse qui convient: 1) "Comment la comédie se distingue-t-elle de la tragédie?"; 2) "Quel doit être le but moral de la comédie?"; 3) "Ce but est-il toujours atteint?"; 4) "Dans quel sens les vices appartiennent-ils à la comédie?"; 5) "Qu'est-ce que le ridicule?"; 6) "Que faut-il penser de la farce?"; 7) "Que faut-il penser des effets des spectacles dramatiques?"; 8) "Citez quelques-un des auteurs qui condamnent le théâtre" (314-330). En somme, le souci de nomenclature fait partie intégrante d'une pédagogie qui valorise l'exercice de la mémoire, faculté maîtresse de l'élève; la valeur de la référence scolaire réside, en dernier ressort, dans sa fonction d'anamnèse, c'est-à-dire, de non-oubli, et il s'ensuit alors que la ligne de partage entre le mémoire et la mémoire n'est qu'une affaire d'article....

Un examen de la vaste majorité des manuels scolaires du XIXème siècle révèle qu'il existe une mise en place formelle des énoncés portant sur Molière, une véritable rhétorique de la présentation. Ce format archiconnu, qui s'est transmis d'une génération d'élèves à une autre, se ramène à une suite de considérations touchant la forme et le fond de diverses comédies ou bien de l'oeuvre complète; d'après la logique implicite de cette présentation, on passe de la valeur esthétique de l'oeuvre à un jugement sur sa portée proprement éthique, couronnement de toute l'entreprise critique. *Le Tableau d'histoire littéraire* de Bizeul et Boulay, par exemple, offre l'analyse suivante du "système dramatique" de Molière: après avoir traité, tour à tour, l'intrigue, les caractères, les situations, le domaine de sa comédie (c'est-à-dire, la peinture satirique de la bourgeoisie), la force comique et ses sources, les auteurs portent un jugement d'ensemble sur la morale de Molière, reprenant, en l'occurrence, les "justes réserves" à la Rousseau. Pour eux, Molière serait un "moraliste incomplet" qui s'ingénie à "trouver le mal," qui a donné un "tour gracieux au vice" et une "austérité ridicule et odieuse à la vertu" (*dixit* Fénelon).[7]

Comment s'expliquer cette valorisation de la dimension immorale ou bien, selon les cas, édifiante de l'oeuvre de Molière? D'abord, il est significatif qu'il n'existe aucune solution de continuité entre le contenu "intellectuel" et le contenu "moral" d'un discours au XIXème siècle; ils constituent une sorte de formule automatique dans le discours scolaire, et leur rapprochement évoque le rapport de complémentarité entre esprit et conscience. Ainsi, l'enseignement secondaire n'admettait aucune cloison étanche entre morale et littérature.[8] Des cours de morale faisaient partie intégrante du programme scolaire des jeunes lycéens, et cela notamment au niveau de l'enseignement secondaire des jeunes filles, nouvelle filière fondée en 1881. Cette mise en évidence d'une conception moralisante de la littérature du XVIIème siècle permet à l'Ecole d'extrapoler à partir de l'oeuvre de Molière, par exemple, des éléments éminemment enseignables, de la transformer en quelque sorte en machine pédagogique. La construction des poncifs scolaires véhiculant une image moyenne, terre-à-terre, empirique, bref, bourgeoise de Molière, s'explique, en partie, par la volonté de moralisation publique et même étatique propre à l'avènement de la Troisième République. L'impulsion profonde de l'Ecole républicaine consiste à remplacer l'education de l'Ecole libre par l'instruction morale et civique, au point de développer chez les élèves, pour reprendre le mot d'E. Maneuvrier, un véritable "dressage" moral (298).[9] Il n'est rien de plus évident, à cet égard, que la visée moralisatrice propre aux recueils de morceaux choisis à travers tous les niveaux du cycle secondaire.[10] P. Clarac, ancien inspecteur général, n'attribue-t-il pas à l'enseignement du français un idéal de perfectionnement moral (36, 58, 101, 110)? Tout se passe comme si l'on faisait confiance aux professeurs quant à la transmission des notions de morale. Héritiers d'une tradition fondée sur la lecture des classiques grecs et latins, ces derniers enseignaient avec la même volonté de simplification morale chère aux Anciens. Ils dispensaient, du haut de leur chaire, la bonne parole; fonction-naires de l'Ordre rhétorique, ils faisaient figure d'orateurs exemplaires. Les professurs de français, engagés, après 1870, dans le même processus de reconstruction nationale que les professeurs d'histoire et de philosophie, n'ont point répugné, comme on le verra, à fournir des exemples susceptibles de servir le cours de morale civique qui se constituait dans toutes les disciplines de l'Ecole républicaine.

Examiner l'évolution de la réception scolaire de Molière au XIXème siècle, c'est, d'abord, mettre en évidence une situation de porte à faux, car la difficulté d'introduire Molière dans l'enseignement tient à la perception morale et sociale du théâtre. Il suffit d'évoquer ici la persistance avec laquelle la critique cléricale, de Dupanloup à Veuillot, ainsi que les manuels de l'enseignement confessionnel, ont perçu dans l'oeuvre de Molière une école suprême d'immoralité, au point que le père Caruel estimait que la défaillance morale de Molière relèverait d'un anti-patriotisme de la part du poète comique (653).[11] Or, la seule façon de "récupérer" le théâtre comique, dont le statut en tant que genre était fort bas dans la hiérarchie implicite des manuels, c'était, en un mot, de le scolariser. S'interrogeant sur la légitimité de l'interprétation tragique du *Misanthrope*, G. Arnaud conclut que "le théâtre de Molière est comique à la représentation, tragique à la réflexion et à la lecture" (172)[12] et il justifie, par là, le plus grand dosage de solennité dans le traitement de Molière à l'Ecole. Dans cette perspective, on s'aperçoit de la fonction pédagogique des "matinées classiques," série de conférences publiques à l'Odéon qui, ayant servi de prélude aux représentations dramatiques des classiques, recoupent le discours scolaire. Institués dès les années 1880, de tels entretiens sur Molière, Corneille et Racine, attirant divers représentants du corps professoral, de Larroumet, Sarcey, Lintilhac et Doumic, jusqu'à Barrès, ne constituent-ils pas une incursion scolaire dans l'univers théâtral?

Loin de souscrire à cette division officielle entre l'Ecole et le Théâtre, certains critiques, tel E. Geruzez (un des auteurs de manuels les plus en vogue au XIXème siècle), envisageait la scène sous forme de tribune, de lieu de prédication susceptible de dépasser la vulgarité comique. Il traite Molière de "moraliste réformateur" et transforme, en l'occurrence, sa dramaturgie en pédagogie:

> Toutes les fois qu'il n'est pas obligé de divertir la cour par ordre, ou le peuple par nécessité, il moralise pour le siècle, il donne des cours, il tient école. *Le Misanthrope, Le Tartuffe, Le Bourgeois Gentilhomme*, et *Les Femmes Savantes* ne sont que des chapitres, et les plus importants, de ce cours de morale dramatique à l'usage des gens du monde. (164)

Cette tendance à privilégier la dimension instructive de l'oeuvre de Molière au détriment de sa dimension divertissante (cf. Henry 250-51; 258-59)—par le biais du moralisme bourgeois des porte-parole tels que les "raisonnables" Cléante et Chrysale, par exemple—sert non seulement à exalter la notion de correction morale et la primauté de la norme, mais encore illustre à quel point on a affaire à une exploitation, voire à un "détournement" du texte moliéresque vers des fins pédagogiques.

On aborde ici la problématique de la censure scolaire de Molière au XIXème siècle. Mettre en évidence, de manière générale, le travail de censure sur les classiques à cette époque, c'est en même temps évoquer une instance de régulation propre à l'institution scolaire. Si l'on admet que l'enseignement secondaire visait avant tout à la formation d'une élite, il va de soi que l'instruction littéraire constituait une entreprise d'acculturation, fonctionnant comme véhicule d'un discours normatif sur la société.[13] Le découpage officiel du corpus moliéresque aboutit à la revendication académique de Molière en tant que modèle de l'homme éternel, sujet transcendental dans un champ littéraire atemporalisé. Ce qui préside donc à la sélection des textes, c'est une volonté systématique d'exclure les parties de l'oeuvre jugées inassimilables par l'orthodoxie académique: en premier lieu, tout ce qui est bas— farces, scatologie, acrobaties, folies et névroses de certains personnages;[14] à cela s'ajoute toute la dimension aristocratique de l'oeuvre (les fêtes de cours, les comédies-ballets, etc.). Cette amputation des éléments farcesques et grotesques au profit d'une superficialisation de l'oeuvre contribue, de toute évidence, à la fabrication d'un Molière artificiel, créé de toutes pièces pour le baccalauréat. Les jeux de mots scabreux et les mauvaises images, le rire déchaîné de la farce ont été systématiquement refoulés par un académisme de bon ton, soucieux avant tout de créer un ensemble de banalités pseudo-morales. De même, le Molière satirique, iconoclaste, qui remet en question les "codes établis," a été occulté, voire châtré par l'enseignement officiel du XIXème siècle.

Mais c'est surtout en matière d'économie et de sexualité chez Molière que s'exerce la censure scolaire. Il suffit de mettre à l'évidence le décalage entre le portrait volontairement idéalisé d'une bourgeoisie immobile—on songe à l'idéal du pot-au-feu cher à Chrysale ou bien aux pratiques financières fort conservatrices d'un Harpagon ou d'un Orgon—et les problèmes réels auxquels les bourgeois français des années 1870-1914 devaient faire face dans leurs rapports quotidiens avec les ouvriers: formation des syndicats, grèves, anarchisme politique, etc. La bourgeoisie républicaine n'aurait-elle pas intérêt à cultiver une nostalgie à l'égard d'une société pré-industrielle, où règnent des valeurs paternalistes et où ses ancêtres ne sont point, comme elle, les détenteurs des moyens de production économique? N'est-elle pas éprise d'une idéologie qui offusque la notion de classe et même de tout contenu idéologique au profit d'un esthétisme humaniste dont l'idéal de "gratuité" sert à occulter son goût du lucre? Charles Péguy, dans ses souvenirs d'expérience scolaire à cette époque, fait état du rôle des professeurs du secondaire, qui exerçaient une sorte de sacerdoce de la culture. Armés du "vieux civisme classique et français," ils avaient pour mission de sauvegarder la culture antique, de la défendre contre les incursions de la culture contemporaine; à cet effet, il ne leur restait qu'à "ossifier, ...(à) momifier la réalité, les réalités qui leur (étaient) imprudemment confiées, qu'(à) ensevelir dans le tombeau des fiches la matière de leur enseignement" (*Notre Jeunesse*, cité par Bessière 106-07). Dans cette perspective, son adhésion inconditionnelle aux valeurs de culture dans l'enseignement secondaire et son activité scolaire comme représentation symbolique permettent à la bourgeoisie de se croire en quelque sorte hors-classe en occultant son argent.

L'image de la femme chez Molière, telle qu'elle a été véhiculée par les manuels scolaires, met en cause une même démarche lénifiante. A cet effet, les désirs sexuels de Célimène sont estompés au profit de la conception abstraite d'une coquetterie mondaine. La révolte sexuelle des femmes savantes est dévalorisée par le triomphe comique d'Henriette, qui se sauve grâce à la vertu de la modération. Si l'enseignement secondaire des jeunes filles fait une place exceptionnelle aux *Précieuses ridicules* et aux *Femmes savantes*, c'est pour proposer un idéal féminin propre aux futures maîtresses de maison, idéal qui exalte l'importance de la famille et des responsabilités conjugales, bref, de la respectabilité du mariage. Ainsi, dans un sujet de composition française proposé à maintes reprises, on note la nature tendancieuse de la question posée: "'Je consens qu'une femme ait des clartés de tout.' L'opinion de Molière sur l'éducation des femmes n'est-elle pas renfermée tout entière dans ce vers de Clitandre?" (Licence en lettres, *Revue universitaire*, 1892). Dans les manuels de Doumic (187-88), Lavrault et Ditandy (138), par exemple, le châtiment des pédantes parisiennes sert à définir les limites du savoir des femmes. Ils s'accordent tous pour reconnaître chez Henriette l'idéal féminin par excellence, et Ditandy précise que la satisfaction d'obligations morales aboutit à l'harmonie domestique aussi bien que sociale. Dugard, lui, dans un discours prononcé à l'occasion du vingt-cinquième anniversaire de l'enseignement secondaire féminin, laisse entendre que le lycée doit servir de lieu de fabrication des "Henriette du XXème siècle." Modèle accompli de la femme, l'héroïne des *Femmes savantes* en vient à incarner le bon sens français, voire la "parfaite santé morale": "c'est une figure essentiellement nationale, et que l'on retrouve dans la réalité quotidienne" (298).

De telles pratiques de censure trouvent un terrain privilégié d'expression dans les diverses adaptations scolaires de la série intitulée "Le Molière de la jeunesse." Destinées aux maisons d'éducation chrétienne, ces adaptations systématiques présentent des distributions de rôles dépourvues de tout personnage féminin, ceci afin de créer une absence totale de contenu sexuel. Ainsi, *Le Misanthrope* devient une comédie arrangée en un acte, où n'apparaît aucune trace, aucune mention ni de Célimène, ni d'Arsinoé, ni d'Eliante. D'après ce nouvel agencement dramatique, au dénouement parfaitement déféminisé, Alceste fait ses adieux à Philinte et au valet Dubois, et ces derniers tâchent de "rompre le dessein que son coeur se propose." Quel nouveau sens alors extraire après un texte à tel point tronqué? Bien que l'adaptation du *Bourgeois gentilhomme* dans cette édition accorde des rôles à Mme

Jourdain et à Nicole, il est révélateur que le projet de mariage conçu par M. Jourdain pour sa fille, ainsi que l'épisode de Dorimène, en soient exclus. Dans un recueil analogue (Perrault-Maynard), *Le Malade imaginaire* met Auguste, fils d'Argan, aux prises avec M. Belin, intendant sans scrupule qui a pris la relève de Béline; Antoine reprend envers Auguste le rôle que Toinette occupait auprès d'Angélique. La charmante "petite Louison" se transforme ici en "petit Louis," et l'interrogation que fait subir Argan à son petit fils élimine tout à fait l'équivoque sexuelle que l'on trouve chez Molière. Dans l'adaptation du *Médecin malgré lui*, fondée, elle aussi, sur une distribution de rôles exclusivement masculins, on remarque le couple fraternel Fagotin/Martin, en replacement du couple marié Sganarelle/Martine. S'étant chargé des enfants de Fagotin depuis la mort de leur mère, Martin présente tous les traits de la femme malmenée: Fagotin lui vend ses biens, ne cesse de boire, n'a pas de quoi nourrir les enfants. Et il lui administre même des bastonnades afin de le réduire au silence. Inutile de dire, enfin, que de telles éditions pudibondes ne font aucune référence au répertoire moliéresque où il est question de cocuage: *L'Ecole des Femmes*, *Tartuffe*, *Dom Juan*, *George Dandin*, *Amphitryon*. Au total, la déféminisation radicale de ces éditions scolaires, par le biais de personnages masculins sans passion et hors désir, vise à émasculer Molière, de peur qu'il ne corrompe la jeunesse.

Les diverses stratégies d'occultation que nous avons mises en évidence relèvent d'une entreprise de déconstruction scolaire de l'oeuvre de Molière. En fait, la production massive au XIXème siècle des recueils de morceaux choisis, régis par une démarche mutilante de cette oeuvre, aboutit à un démembrement total du corps en vue de la dégustation pédagogique. Pourtant, si "anthropophagie" il y a, celle-ci s'avère fort sélective, car on ne se nourrit à l'Ecole que des morceaux les plus nobles du "corpus" moliéresque. Ce parti pris institutionnel, consistant à privilégier certains textes canoniques tout en en rejetant d'autres, témoigne de l'envergure de l'humanisme classique dans l'Université française du XIXème siècle (Fayolle). L'affirmation triomphaliste du vrai, du beau et du bien, postulats de base de la trinité fondée par V. Cousin, se manifeste avec vigueur tant dans les manuels scolaires que dans les Instructions officielles.[15] Fondé sur une idéologie positiviste, l'humanisme traditionnel en vient à fournir la Somme des valeurs de référence; il contribue à développer la culture du commentaire et du goût intimement liée à la mise en extériorité du texte canonique. Des notions idéalistes telles que la beauté édifiante, la primauté absolue du modèle comme objet de délectation désintéressée, l'unité et l'universalité d'une culture désincarnée, coupée des réalités contemporaines, font partie intégrante du discours pédagogique classique. Qu'il s'agisse d'un enseignement secondaire fondé sur la rhétorique ou de celui qui, à partir des années 1880, accordera une place grandissante à l'histoire littéraire, on a affaire à un discours scolaire inspiré par les impératifs d'un humanisme militant.

L'instauration de l'histoire littéraire en tant que discipline moderne, ayant une légitimité scientifique dans l'Université française, entraîne, dans les années 1880, la disparition progressive de la rhétorique au niveau secondaire.[16] Supprimé au baccalauréat en 1881, le discours latin donne lieu à la composition française, exercice qui va, dès lors, établir son long règne. Les Instructions officielles de 1890 louent les mérites de l'explication de textes, deuxième exercice de choix dans la nouvelle pédagogie, dans la mesure où elle oriente l'élève vers l'analyse des faits concrets, où elle l'amène à cultiver l'esprit critique et le jugement aux dépens de la mémorisation, pratique de plus en plus désuète.[17] Cette mise en valeur de la méthode expérimentale relève d'une pédagogie qui se veut moderne. D'autre part, les nouvelles réformes accordent une place considérable aux auteurs français; L. Bourgeois, ministre de l'Instruction publique, précise que les exercices scolaires devaient constituer, par l'entremise des auteurs français, "une véritable leçon de choses morales, professée par des écrivains de génie" (Instructions officielles de 1890). Ainsi, si l'on admet que l'histoire littéraire vise à faire goûter les œuvres des classiques, il s'ensuit que ces derniers sont nécessairement envisagés comme des modèles éducatifs dont la partie centrale de leur œuvre est didactique. Dans cette perspective cartésienne, où l'éducation se ramènerait à une "conversation avec les plus honnêtes gens des siècles passés" (Descartes 43), les génies du patrimoine national prennent la relève des modèles antiques et, de la sorte, le rôle de véritables maîtres à penser de la jeunesse; l'humble tâche des professeurs consiste, dès lors, à exercer le rôle de médiateurs, d'interprètes officiels des œuvres classiques. Il va de soi, enfin, que certains manuels mettent les élèves en garde, par exemple, contre l'indépendance critique, leur conseillant de se plier aux jugements communément admis.[18] C'est ainsi que P. Clarac justifie un certain dogmatisme dans l'enseignement traditionnel du français, et il s'en prend à la liberté du jugement de l'élève qui, par faute de modestie devant le "grand texte," "prétend faire la leçon aux grands écrivains" (96).

La mise en place des nouvelles pratiques scolaires au niveau secondaire dans les années 1880—composition française, explication de textes, histoire littéraire—entraîne une évolution certaine du statut de Molière. C'est à partir de 1880, en effet, que Molière occupe la place qui lui revient dans les programmes: dans les classes de seconde (*L'Avare*, *Les Femmes savantes*) et dans celles de rhétorique (*Tartuffe*, *Le Misanthrope*), alors qu'on se contentait jusque-là d'offrir ou des "morceaux choisis" ou du "théâtre classique" sans préciser les pièces (Chervel).[19] Quant aux pièces de Molière devant servir aux questions des examens de licence, J. Ferry dresse, en 1880, une liste qui inclut *Dom Juan* et *Les Femmes savantes* (193). Mis à part l'enseignement secondaire des jeunes filles, dont l'orientation moderniste fait, on l'a vu, une large place à Molière, le programme de l'agrégation consacre, dès 1879, une place à *Dom Juan*, ainsi qu'à l'oeuvre de Rabelais, dont le rire subversif entre, à des degrés divers, dans le cadre de la politique laïque. Selon le classement établi par Thiesse et Mathieu, Molière figure treize fois parmi les sujets de l'Agrégation féminine entre 1890 et 1914; il apparaît seize fois dans les programmes d'Agrégation masculine pendant la même période (99).

La nouvelle place de Molière dans l'Ecole républicaine mérite, de toute évidence, une analyse attentive. Contentons-nous, en guise de conclusion, de présenter quelques-unes des directions d'un projet de recherche en cours. Grâce à la création d'un discours laudatif sur Molière au XIXème siècle, discours souligné par la fonction de célébration propre au livre scolaire, l'auteur comique en vient à incarner à la fois le théâtre universel et le génie national, et finit même par être l'objet d'une véritable idolâtrie.[20] Examiner le statut de Molière dans la "Troisième République des lettres," c'est d'abord faire ressortir la convergence de discours sur son œuvre, voire une sorte d'oecuménisme du texte. Ni l'otage du théâtre ni l'otage de l'Ecole, le "premier farceur de la France" est récupéré à la fois par la Gauche républicaine, qui voit en lui une filiation nettement progressiste, un ancêtre de la tradition laïque, et par la Droite, qui l'érige en porte-parole de son traditionalisme moral. Molière se trouve au centre d'une politique culturaliste dont le dessein principal consiste à s'incorporer des valeurs de l'héritage français, celles, plus conservatrices, de l'Ancien Régime, tout aussi bien que celles de la Révolution. Dans la mesure où elle se fonde sur une entreprise de nationalisation de la littérature française, où elle crée un Panthéon scolaire et laïque où vient prendre place chaque "grand" écrivain du passé, l'histoire littéraire relève d'un projet de constitution d'une culture nationale et, plus précisément, d'une volonté politique sous-jacente à une mise en place des valeurs culturelles du XVIIème siècle, valeurs qui procèdent d'un classicisme officiel. C'est là, en vérité, une des tâches principales que s'assigne l'institution scolaire au XIXème siècle et, notamment, l'enseignement secondaire et supérieur. L'Ecole républicaine, elle, prend en main le concept d'"esprit français," hérité de Nisard, au point de constituer toute une personnalité, une âme, bref, un fonds d'identité nationale inspirant une tradition académique parfaitement fixe: le "tendre" Racine, le "glorieux" Corneille, l'"aimable" Molière. C'est dans cette perspective qu'il convient d'envisager le sujet de composition suivant: "La comédie de Molière est à la fois humaine à un degré éminent, et une œuvre française par excellence, où se marquent les traits caractéristiques du génie national" [Montpellier, 1900; Nancy, 1904] (Quentel 139). Dans leurs *Etudes historiques et critiques des classiques*, Urbain et Jamey insistent sur l'ancienneté du poète comique, sur son rattachement aux sources de la tradition française, à savoir, l'esprit gaulois:

> Rabelais et Régnier lui ont fourni des caractères; Larivey, Boisrobert, Rotrou et Cyrano de Bergerac, des scènes. Mais surtout on peut dire qu'il s'est nourri de la substance et de la sève de nos vieux auteurs; par le caractère de sa raillerie et par sa manière d'envisager la vie humaine, il doit passer à bon droit pour un continuateur de l'esprit gaulois.

Citant Nisard et Sainte-Beuve, les auteurs de ce manuel discernent, dans la comédie de Molière, sous la voix des "aïeux," un surgissement de la conscience nationale (608, 610). Dans l'ensemble, divers critiques semblent vouloir rajouter à l'opinion admise en attribuant à Molière l'idéal *nec plus ultra* des traits de caractère français: il en est ainsi de Martel et Devinat ("Nul n'est plus Français, de la vieille race gauloise, par sa franchise et sa liberté d'allures" [255]), de G. Monval, chef de file des moliéristes, qui considère son idole comme "la plus complète incarnation du génie français" (39), et, enfin, de Lanson, qui voit chez lui l'auteur "le plus complètement français" (396).

N'y a-t-il pas lieu d'affirmer que le mythe scolaire du classicisme français et, plus particulièrement, le mythe Molière, participe d'une volonté d'affirmation, voire de reconstruction culturaliste coïncidant avec l'avènement de la Troisième République, d'une sorte de revanche imaginaire sur la défaite de 1870? Nisard, Sainte-Beuve et, plus tard, Brunetière, Faguet et Lemaître, n'ont-ils pas contribué à cette défense et illustration de la culture nationale au XIXème siècle, et à la valorisation des racines culturelles par le biais de l'histoire littéraire? Dans la mesure où le discours scolaire élabore un système cohérent de références culturelles, un classement qui s'avère, en fin de compte, ethnocentrique, ne finit-il pas par créer les valeurs symboliques de la culture?[21] L'ordre, la sagesse et la mesure en viennent, de la sorte, à incarner des valeurs françaises sûres et même monumentales. Le théâtre de Molière laisse transparaître souvent des leçons d'honnêteté, un rire de bonne grâce, de civilité, voire de correction. Epris de tolérance, de nombreux "raisonneurs" s'en tiennent aux principes d'une morale familiale "éminemment" moyenne. A cela s'ajoute une certaine image publique de Molière en tant que corpus de référence de la conversation, relais de divers points de vue critiques sur la médecine, l'hypocrisie ou bien l'arrivisme: un "M. Jourdain" ou un "Tartuffe" sont des appellations communément utilisées. Chose plus importante, peut-être, l'unité nationale, notamment après 1870, peut s'incarner au mieux dans ce théâtre qui évoque la totalité des classes sociales. Tout porte à croire, enfin, que l'exploitation de Molière au sein de la culture nationale tient lieu de référence globale, référence sur laquelle peut s'édifier une conscience civique, une volonté de consensus, un point d'équilibre nécessaire à la formation d'une morale. Etant donné le tohu-bohu de l'expérience politique des Français du XIXème siècle, ceux-ci étant, en l'occurrence, inexorablement attirés par diverses formes de démesure et, de la sorte, incapables d'arriver à un consensus politique, force était de miser sur une continuité plutôt culturelle qu'historique. L'enseignement orthodoxe français constituait ainsi, à l'instar des théâtres subventionnés et des matinées classiques, un appareil étatique de conservatisme.

Un dernier mot sur les déterminations idéologiques sous-jacentes à la mise en place de l'héritage culturel. Le développement de la conscience civique est intimement lié à l'essor politique de la bourgeoisie en France au XIXème siècle. La prise du pouvoir par cette classe entraîne l'autonomie de la littérature en tant que phénomène institutionnel.[22] Or, un des aspects essentiels de la vision républicaine de la modernité réside dans l'invention d'une transcendance bourgeoise: la sacralisation des arts, la valorisation de la culture comme succédané de la religion représentent des conséquences immédiates d'une idéologie laïque face au cléricalisme toujours menaçant. On comprend, dans cette perspective, le discours "parathéologique" d'un P. Clarac, qui sacralise l'héritage littéraire français en prônant une attitude de révérence à l'égard des textes canoniques: il s'agit de "... textes dont professeurs et élèves ne doivent s'approcher qu'avec respect et comme en tremblant" (44). La transformation du texte en monument scolaire et, de là, en icône culturelle, ainsi que la sublimation des "grands auteurs" en saints laïques, s'insèrent dans une politique qui permet à la bourgeoisie de chercher des brevets d'ancienneté dans la littérature classique. Si l'humanisme traditionnel représentait la voie royale des études secondaires au XIXème siècle, le véhicule de la haute culture, il est évident que l'enseignement littéraire permettait à la bourgeoisie de se concevoir comme classe éclairée, d'acquérir des titres de noblesse culturelle. Epris d'un idéal pédagogique marquant leur volonté d'appartenance au clan, les nouveaux privilégiés du XIXème siècle se faisaient fort, enfin, d'être les distributeurs officiels de la culture.[23]

Notes

[1]Selon J. Dubois, le jeu de consécration officielle de la littérature s'opère entre 1830 et 1850 (13; 37-56). Sur le nouveau statut de l'écrivain à l'époque romantique, voir P. Bénichou.

[2]Après avoir présenté la scène où Dom Louis fait des reproches à son fils ("Leçons d'un père à son fils, [IV, 5]), F-L Marcou fait ce commentaire à la suite de la réponse de Dom Juan ("Monsieur, si vous étiez assis, vous en seriez mieux pour parler"): "Cette impertinence froide n'est-elle pas plus coupable que la boutade de Cléante: 'Je te donne ma malédiction'—'Je n'ai que faire de vos dons' [*L'Avare*, IV, 5](208-210).

[3]"Vous composerez un dialogue entre Alceste et Philinte, vieillis tous deux. Philinte est dégoûté des hommes, qui ont abusé de son caractère conciliant...." quant à Alceste,"...les années lui ont appris combien est vrai le mot d'un stoïcien: *Qui vitia odit homines odit*; et il est désormais indulgent pour les faiblesses inhérentes à la nature humaine" [Baccalauréat classique: Montpellier, 1896] (Delmont 444).

[4]Dans sa réponse à cette question, Quentel conclut ainsi: "(Alceste) est donc le personnage qui a pour lui la raison et la justice, il est d'une très haute moralité." "Il convient donc de préférer Alceste. Ses défauts ne sont pas de ceux qui humilient et il est l'honnête homme personnifié "(116).

[5]Voir, à ce propos, A. Chervel, "Sur l'origine de l'enseignement du français dans le secondaire," 8.

[6]"Le français à l'école primaire," (Croiset 69). De plus, il convient d'évoquer les instructions officielles de V. Duruy qui, ministre de l'Instruction publique sous le Second Empire, souligne le rôle de la mémoire en tant que fondement de l'enseignement rhétorique:

> 'Le professeur lit lui-même à haute voix un fragment soigneusement choisi; il donne les explications propres à faire comprendre les idées de l'auteur et leur enchaînement; il signale les passages les plus importants. Le devoir est la reproduction par écrit et toujours de mémoire du morceau lu et expliqué (cité par V. Isambert-Jamati 28).

[7]Le manuel d'Urbain et Jamey illustre à merveille cette présentation typique du discours scolaire sur Molière au XIXème siècle. D'après le plan de ce texte, on passe de la vie de Molière à son œuvre, la biographie servant de grille explicative: "L'homme—I) Sa famille, sa jeunesse; II) Ses débuts: Molière en province, puis à Paris, sa mort; III) Portrait et caractère de Molière; IV) Adversaires et amis de Molière—L'auteur—I) Nature de son talent; II) Vues de Molière sur son art; III) coup d'oeil général sur son œuvre; sa variété, ses sources: l'observation et

l'érudition; son originalité; conduite de l'action dramatique; langue et style de Molière; de la mise en scène; la morale de Molière; IV) Molière et la critique." (571).

[8]Alors que la morale était perçue comme une donnée universelle, communément admise par le corps enseignant du XIXème siècle, il suffit de parcourir les Annales Vuibert de nos jours pour se faire une idée du caractère irréel de cette notion au sein du cycle secondaire actuel. D'où l'emploi des guillemets dans le sujet suivant: il s'agit de réfléchir, à partir d'une lecture de "L'Ivrogne et sa femme," à la "mise en œuvre dramatique d'une 'morale'" (Baccalauréat—Compositions françaises, 1981).

[9]L'absence de Dieu dans l'enseignement de l'Ecole laïque a pour contrepartie la mise en valeur d'un enseignement moral; on assiste, bref, à une sorte de compensation sinon de compromis politique, l'instituteur étant désormais le gardien des principes éthiques issus du républicanisme. Tout porte à croire que les professeurs du secondaire, à la différence de leurs collègues en histoire et en philosophie, recouraient à une approche oblique en discutant la valeur morale des auteurs français. La mise en garde de C. Benoist contre le danger d'abuser des sujets renfermant des leçons de morale est, à cet égard, révélatrice: "Je crois qu'il ne faut pas abuser des sujets de ce genre: à vouloir trop faire de morale aux enfants on risque de les en dégoûter; il faut tâcher de la leur suggérer plutôt que de la leur prêcher" (131).

[10]Il convient de citer, à ce sujet, le texte d'A. David-Sauvageot (v, vii), destiné aux classes de sixième et de quatrième: "Déjà nous pouvons faire plus large accueil aux pages abstraites, qui invitent à la réflexion...nous donnons la préférence aux récits touchants, aux pensées morales et en général à tout ce qui favorise l'éveil de l'imagination et du sentiment;" "... le but premier de tout recueil de morceaux choisis: offrir à la jeunesse de belles et bonnes pages, et cela moins pour la renseigner et l'instruire, que pour la former et l'élever;" ainsi que celui de C. Labaigue(5), qui s'adresse aux classes de seconde: "[tous les textes choisis]...peuvent être offerts comme de véritables leçons de littérature et de morale."

[11]Dans ce même ordre d'idées, on peut citer les réserves des pères S-J. Bizuel et P. Boulay dans un manuel destiné aux demoiselles de pensionnat. Les auteurs reprochent à Molière d' "*affaiblir dans l'esprit du peuple le respect pour la religion*, surtout lorsqu'elle est la base de la constitution nationale et de la tranquillité publique... Tartuffe est plus *odieux* que *ridicule*: de ses grimaces et de ses contorsions peuvent rire seulement les gens irréligieux et libertins...Quant aux spectateurs vraiment chrétiens... ils ne peuvent que ressentir la plus vive indignation à ce spectacle" (95).

[12]Le manuel de R. Doumic et de L. Levrault présente une opposition analogue entre le "sérieux" qui se dégage d'une lecture des comédies de Molière, et le "comique" qui ressort de la représentation sur scène (146).

[13]De même que les élites bourgeoises, dès le règne de Louis-Philippe, redoutaient la montée des "classes dangereuses" (voir L. Chevalier), Dupanloup, le célèbre évêque d'Orléans, signalait l'existence de "livres dangereux," qui n'étaient guère propres à l'enseignement (529). Dans cette perspective, le modèle scolaire répond parfaitement au modèle social.

[14]De nombreux auteurs de manuels, tels D. Bonnefon et H. Lucas, par exemple, dénoncent l'abondance des farces chez Molière; il s'agit, pour eux, d'une grossièreté indigne de la comédie. Ainsi, selon Bonnefon, "Il est à regretter qu'un grand nombre de comédies de Molière renferme des bouffonneries grossières, où la morale est trop souvent blessée et qui en rendent la lecture difficile" (130-131). Quant à H. Lucas, lui, il émet le jugement suivant: "Molière s'est souvent complu dans le détail des infirmités physiques et des fonctions de la vie animale: *le Médecin malgré lui, l'Amour médecin, le Malade imaginaire* contiennent à ce sujet des traits d'un goût peu délicat; c'est l'esprit de l'époque" (93). Du reste, ce sujet de composition française reflète un parti pris académique cherchant à justifier la démarche bien pensante de Boileau: "Boileau, après la première représentation des

Fourberies de Scapin , écrit à Molière pour l'engager à quitter la farce et à revenir aux comédies d'un comique noble et élevé, aux comédies de caractère dont il a donné de si brillants exemples dans le *Tartuffe"* (*Journal des élèves de lettres* , 1895).

[15]Voir, à titre d'exemples, les manuels de J. d'Arsac, de J. Chantrel et de C. Berville, qui véhiculent tous, à des degrés divers, l'idéologie humaniste. Les Instructions officielles de 1880 et celles de 1891 soulignent la primauté culturelle des humanités classiques. Quoique J. Ferry s'attache à moderniser les méthodes pédagogiques, force est de signaler que le nouveau plan d'études de 1880 prescrit presque trois fois plus d'heures pour les langues anciennes (cinquante-neuf heures au total) que pour le français (vingt et une heures).

[16]Voir l'analyse pertinente de l'émergence du lansonisme au sein de l'enseignement supérieur à cette époque par A. Compagnon.

[17]Selon les Instructions officielles de 1890: "(L'explication de textes)...ne fait que consacrer les progrès réalisés depuis plusieurs années, depuis qu'on ne se contente plus, comme autrefois, de lire et de commenter quelques pages de français apprises par coeur, mais que l'on veut connaître de nombreux morceaux et des ouvrages complets. Il est désormais entendu que l'explication française aura dans la classe autant d'importance que l'explication grecque ou latine."

[18]Voir E. Valton, qui fait la mise en garde suivante aux candidats à l'examen de licence: "Si vous ne vous sentez pas de disposition à approuver ce que d'autres approuvent, si vous n'êtes pas assez raisonnable pour chercher les causes de cette approbation, plutôt que de la combattre, tenez-vous au moins dans une respectueuse réserve, et ne vous faites pas étourdiment le champion d'une idée neuve, au risque de choquer à la fois vos juges et la vérité" (14).

[19]Il convient de préciser, toutefois, que *Le Misanthrope* apparaît dans les classes de rhétorique en 1803, 1831, 1841 et 1851. Au niveau des classes de seconde, cette pièce y fait une apparition en 1851.

[20]Voir, à ce sujet, notre article, "Lectures critiques de Molière au XIXe siècle."

[21]Il convient d'évoquer, à ce sujet, le propos de F. Ponge, qui souligne la valeur ethnologique des humanités, sorte de "substantifique moelle" dans l'expérience scolaire des Français:

> Et puis il se trouve que j'étais bon en latin et bon en français, d'une certaine façon, je veux dire que je suis quelqu'un de cultivé, j'ai des 'humanités' ...C'est-à-dire, que je considère qu'il est absolument impossible de barrer en nous, de refuser en nous ce qui nous vient de nos *Humanités*. Je considère que c'est une absurdité dans les termes, que ce qui nous vient de la bibliothèque, si vous voulez, de nos humanités, s'est intégré à notre nature profonde, à notre température, à ce qui est le plus subjectif en nous de façon matérielle, c'est dans notre physiologie" ("Entretiens," *Les Nouvelles Littéraires*, 30 déc. 1976, cité par J. Bessière 101).

[22]Voir, à ce propos, Sartre, *Qu'est-ce que la littérature?*, Barthes, *Le Degré zéro de l'écriture*, et plus récemment, J. Dubois. En ce qui concerne l'institution de l'enseignement de l'anglais au XIXème siècle, se reporter à T. Eagleton.

[23]Nous tenons à remercier Anne-Marie Wallace, Antoine Soare, et Dominique Chéenne d'avoir bien voulu nous faire bénéficier de leurs excellents commentaires d'ordre stylistique.

Ouvrages Cités

Albanese, R. "Lectures critiques de Molière au XIXème siècle." *Revue d'Histoire du Théâtre* 4 (1984): 341-361.

Allain, P. *Nouveau guide pour la préparation au baccalauréat ès lettres.* Paris: Delalain, 1850).

Arnaud, G. *Recueil méthodique de compositions françaises.* Marseille: Laffitte, 1896.

Arsac, J. d'. *Histoire de la littérature française.* Paris: Palmé, 1883.

Barthes, R. *Le Degré zéro de l'écriture.* Paris: Seuil, 1953.

—. "Réflexions sur un manuel." *L'enseignement de la littérature.* Ed. Serge Doubrovsky, et T. Todorov. Paris: Plon, 1971. 170-77.

Bénichou, P. *Le Sacre de l'écrivain, 1750-1830.* Paris: Corti, 1973.

Benoist, C. "De l'enseignement de la composition française dans les classes de Sixième et de Cinquième." *Revue universitaire* 14, 2 (1905): 131.

Berville, C. *Belles pages littéraires et morales à l'école.* Paris: Larousse, 1902.

Bessière, J. *L'Ecole.* Paris, Larousse, 1978.

Bizeul, Sévère-Jacques et P. Boulay. *Tableau d'histoire littéraire.* Paris: Poussielgue, 1885.

Bonnefon, D. *Les Ecrivains célèbres de la France.* Paris: Martin, 1871.

Caruel, le père. *Etudes sur les auteurs français.* Tours: Cattier, 1901.

Chantrel, J. *Nouveau cours de littérature.* Paris: Puttois-Crette, 1869.

Chervel, A. *Les Auteurs français, latins, et grec au programme de l'enseignement secondaire.* Paris: INRP et Ed. de la Sorbonne, 1986.

—. "Sur l'origine de l'enseignement du français dans le secondaire." *Histoire de l'Education* 25 (1985): 3-10.

Chevalier, L. *Classes laborieuses, classes dangereuses pendant la première moitié du XIXème siècle.* Paris: Plon, 1958.

Clarac, Pierre. *L'Enseignement du français.* Paris: PUF, 1964.

—. "Sur l'origine de l'enseignement du français dans le secondaire." *Histoire de l'éducation* 25 (1985). 3-10.

Compagnon, A. *La Troisième République des lettres.* Paris: Seuil, 1983.

Condamin, J. *La Composition française au baccalauréat.* Paris: Crovelle-Morant, 1884.

David-Sauvageot, A. *Nouveaux morceaux choisis des classiques français.* Paris: Colin, 1890.

Direction de l'enseignement supérieur. Règlements et circulaires. Paris: Imprimerie Nationale, 1880.

Ditandy, A. *Analyse explicative et raisonnée de cent morceaux choisis.* Paris: Belin, 1882.

Delmont, T. *Nouveau recueil de compositions françaises.* Paris: Poussielgue, 1911.

Descartes, René. *Discours de la méthode.* Paris, Editions sociales, 1950.

Doumic, R. et L. Levrault. *Etudes littéraires sur le auteurs français.* Paris: Delaplane, 1900.

Drioux, l'abbé. *Histoire de la littérature française.* Paris: Belin, 1850.

Dubois, J. *L'Institution de la littérature.* Bruxelles: Nathan, 1978.

Dugard, M. "L'Henriette du XXème siècle," *Revue universitaire* 22, 2 (1913): 292.

Dupanloup, F. *De la haute éducation intellectuelle.* Paris: Dounil, 1866.

Eagleton, T. *Literary Theory, an Introduction.* Minneapolis: U of Minnesota P, 1983.

Fayolle, R. "Les *Confessions* dans les manuels scolaires de 1890 à nos jours." *Oeuvres et critiques* 3, 1 (1978): 63-83.

Gasc-Desfossés, E. *Réponses aux questions du programme....* Paris: Crovelle, 1885.

Geruzez, E. *Histoire de la littérature française.* 2 volumes. Paris: Didier, 1861.

Henry, A. *Les Auteurs français de l'enseignement secondaire.* Paris: Belin, 1886.

Isambert-Jamati, V. "L'enseignement de la langue écrite dans les lycées du Second Empire et des premières années de la République." *Revue des Sciences humaines* 174 (1979). 20-35

Jauffret, M. *Le Molière de la jeunesse.* Paris: Maurras, 1830.

Labaigue, C. *Morceaux choisis de littérature française.* Paris: Belin, 1866.

Lacabe-Plasteig, M. "Le français à l'école primaire." A. Croiset, éd., *L'Enseignement du français.* Paris, Alcan, 1911. 51-85.

Lanson, G. *Histoire illustrée de la littérature française.* Paris: Hachette, 1923.

Lucas, H. *Histoire philosophique et littéraire du théâtre français.* Paris: Gosselin, 1843.

Maneuvrier, E. *L'Education de la république.* Paris: Cerf, 1888.

Marcou, F.-L. *Recueil de morceaux choisis du Moyen Age au XVIIIème siècle.* Paris: Garnier, 1892.

Martel, F. et E. Devinrat.*Théâtre classique.* Paris: Delagrave, 1894.

Monval, G. *Le Moliériste.* 4 (1882-1883).

Perez, B., E. Malvoisin, *et al.*, *La Composition de Rhétorique, recueil de tous les sujets de composition française donnés à la Sorbonne de 1893 à 1898.* Paris: Crovelle-Morant, 1898.

Perrault-Maynard, J. -A. *Le Molière de la jeunesse.* Lyon: Pelagaud, Lesne et Crozet, 1836.

Quentel, J. *La Composition française.* Paris: Lethielleux, 1910

Sartre, J.-P. *Qu'est-ce que la littérature? Situations II.* Paris: Gallimard, 1948.

Thiesse, A.-M. et H. Mathieu. "Déclin de l'âge classique et naissance des classiques. L'évolution des programmes littéraires de l'agrégation depuis 1890." *Littérature,* 42 (1981): 99.

Urbain, C. et Jamey. *Études historiques et critiques sur les classiques français.* 2 volumes. Lyon: Vitte et Perruel, 1884.

Valton, E. *Choix de sujets de compositions.* Paris: Delalain, 1861.

What *Was* French Classicism?

For Marc Fumaroli

Jules Brody
Stanford University

Définir le classicisme, ce sera en quelque sorte essayer de trouver le commun dénominateur d'oeuvres diverses, nées en un milieu non homogène, tantôt favorable, tantôt hostile, d'auteurs relativement isolés, guidés par des règles parfois ambiguës, souvent transgressibles, et dont les plus importantes ne sont pas toujours exprimées. TH. ARON (76-77)

In their bearing on French literary history, the words "classical" and "classicism" have, among others, these three characteristics and consequences: 1) "Classicism" designates the style that succeeded earlier styles called Renaissance, Baroque, Mannerism, Préciosité, etc.; as Valery has observed,"L'essence du classicisme est de venir après."[1] 2) "Classicism" owes this postpositive destiny to its inherently normative and corrective mission; as literary program, critical doctrine, and aesthetic value it opposes or restores discipline, order, simplicity, clarity, measure, etc. to a precedent situation governed, conversely, by freedom, exuberance, complexity, extravagance, excess, etc. 3) Since in literary history as in "real" history, nothing of any significance happens accidentally, the properties of "classicism"—like those of "baroque" or "romanticism"—are naturally taken to be the outgrowth of a spirit, the reflection of a *Zeitgeist*, a *Weltanschauung*, a *mentalité* or, as it is now more fashionable to say, an *episteme*.

From Voltaire onwards, critics have found it convenient to subsume the several features of French "classicism" and to recapitulate its historical uniqueness in the precise, referential notion of a "century" or "age" of Louis XIV. This is the tack followed by Roger Zuber and Micheline Cuénin in their elegant contribution to Artaud's revised *Littérature française*. Their volume, called *Le Classicisme* (1984), limits its actual coverage to the years 1660-1680, but its organizing principle and leading idea are rooted in the historical reality of a "Siècle de Louis XIV." It is this heading that presides over Zuber's "Première partie" (9-66) on the background to the century's literary production; his "Deuxième partie," labeled "La littérature," begins with a chapter that is entitled, in turn, "Une littérature royale." This nomenclature has the advantage of allowing critics and historians to describe and discuss literary works in terms of documentable realities, events and institutions—a Court, a leisure class, a *mécénat*, lavish entertainments—without always having to confront the vagueness and confusion that are instinct in abstractions like "classical" and "classicism." There is also the fact that an "Age of Louis XIV," thanks to its inevitable contradictions and infinite variety, can easily accommodate, along with all the canonically "classical" writers, the Pradons and the Quinaults, the Fontenelles and the Jean-Baptiste Rousseaus, without our ever having to say, on stylistic, aesthetic or doctrinal grounds, why they should be grouped in the same company or discussed in the same breath as Racine and La Fontaine. By its specificity and its dimensions, "The Age of Louis XIV" saves us the embarrassment of having to define *the* reigning mentality or the ideological climate that should by rights be manifest, if the *Zeit* is in fact inhabited by the *Geist*, in varying but appropriate proportions in writers as disparate as Madame de Lafayette, Molière and Pierre Bayle.

For here is the crux of the matter: the idea of a "classical" mind or *episteme* will fall flat on its face as soon as we try to use it to describe or explain the variety of styles, moods, philosophies and forms that are routinely consigned to the domain of French "classical" literature. I, for one, would be hard put to list the elements that link such obviously "classical" writers—if *they* are not "classical," who *is*?—as Pascal, La Fontaine, Bossuet, Mme de Sévigné and La Bruyère. The term "classical" remains meaningful, so it would seem, only as long as we refrain from using it too pointedly or too often.[2] This problem assumes altogether epic proportions, moreover, when we try to situate specific writers with respect to the so-called "classical" doctrine, a concept that began its currency in the critical idiom with the appearance of René Bray's *La*

Formation de la doctrine classique en France (1931). If this famous and influential thesis proves anything, it is surely that the "classical" doctrine, in the same way and for the same reasons as the word itself, is a complete epiphenomenon. Unlike the several "romantic" manifestoes—*Racine et Shakespeare*, the preface to *Cromwell*, *L'Art romantique*—written by real, live "romantic" authors and focused on specific works, problems and programs, the "classical" doctrine is a phantom theory abstracted and concocted from the writings of the ancient critics, as mediated, adapted, and distorted by imitators and epigonoi across the breadth of Europe, over a period of more than 150 years. The "doctrine" that is documented in the pages of Bray's book—compounded of a word in Aristotle, a Horatian hexameter, a paragraph from Castelvetro or Heinsius, a sentence by d'Aubignac, a couplet from Boileau, a snippet from one of Racine's prefaces—is so heterogeneous and dispersed in nature that it could never have been conceived or believed by any single, real human being or group of human beings. Because it is at bottom an after-the-fact *montage*, the "doctrine" has always been powerless to describe, let alone explain, the intricacies and subtleties of the creative works which are reputed to be the fair flower of its content. This failure, no doubt the most grievous and embarrassing one in the annals of French literary history, is easily understood: if we are unable to talk about typical "classical" works like a La Fontaine fable or a play by Molière in terms of the "classical" doctrine, this is because that doctrine is at best a crude, inorganic extrapolation of a neoteric, pseudo-Aristotelian theory of tragedy, modulated around such abstractions as imitation, reason, nature, unity, decorum, and verisimilitude, and designed to account teleologically for the mature production of Racine, the only "classical" writer, as it turns out, whose works betray any palpable connection with the doctrine. (Am I overlooking anyone?)[3] I would add this nice irony: Racine's own reading of *The Poetics* is far more informed, open, and sensitive than the neo-/pseudo-Aristotelian mishmash that he has been credited with having illustrated on the stage.[4]

In recent French literary historiography, the viability of the "classical" doctrine was dealt a crushing blow by Mornet's *Histoire de la littérature française classique* (1940, 3rd ed. 1947). This important synthesis depicts the predominance of "classicism" over certain precedent deviancies, notably *préciosité*, as the result of a slow, gradual negotiation whose total triumph was to be precluded, however, by what Mornet saw as the irrepressible *survivances* that continued quite late into the century to infiltrate and undermine the "classical" edifice. Mornet was also the first to acknowledge the presence and chart the inroads of another subversive element, the *je ne sais quoi*, a liberal, idiosyncratic tendency, which in the revisionist upsurge initiated by Borgerhoff's seminal *The Freedom of French Classicism* (1950) proved to be not a minority manifestation at all but, rather, a symptom of one of the most widespread and fundamental preoccupations of the so-called "classical" authors and their critics. It is highly significant in this regard that Zuber's chapter on "La Doctrine et l'esthétique classiques," which owes a large debt to Borgerhoff's perceptions, should invert the usual dosages and procedures, and that his sub-sections on "Le Goût et le Naturel" and "Le Sublime" should command as much space as the ones entitled "Nature et Raison, le Vrai et le Beau" and "Les Classiques et les Règles." In Zuber's revisionist perspective, the so-called "classical" doctrine reduces down in its simplest terms to the expression of a sustained, creative tension between the cult of energy and a countervailing rage for order, a tension that received its matricial formulation in Quintilian's opposition of *ingenium* and *judicium* (Zuber 105).[5]

It is at this point and on this note that I would like to enter the debate with the suggestion that one of the best places to start rethinking "classicism" is at the crossroads where, in recent years, critics like Bernard Beugnot, Hugh Davidson, Marc Fumaroli, and Roger Zuber have been inclined to situate the question: at that juncture where literary history intersects the history of rhetoric, displaces attention from biographical, factual and ideological concerns, and begins to center inquiry on the competing concepts of style and the philosophies of literary form that, as a matter of simple evidence, were the preponderant object of critical discourse during the French "classical" period.[6] More pointedly still, I would like to ask this practical question: when we get down to actual cases and take a hard, close look at the specific texts in which "classical" critics express their views and make their value-judgments, what is it, exactly, that we find them saying and doing?

What, for example, in plain descriptive terms is "classical" in Bouhours's *La Manière de bien penser dans les ouvrages d'esprit* (1687)?[7] To the extent that "classical" is a normative, meliorative term, attributed for the most part to such positive quantities as "economy," "simplicity," "rationalism," "equilibrium," etc., one might begin by observing that its functional equivalent is conveyed proleptically in Bouhours's title by the expression *bien penser* (="the right way") and opposed implicitly to an antithetical *mal penser* (="the wrong way"). This dichotomy is borne out and amplified, moreover, in Bouhours's opening sentence, where he names his two spokesmen in this book: "Eudoxe et Philanthe qui parlent dans ces dialogues, sont deux hommes de lettres que la science n'a point gâtês, et qui n'ont guère moins de politesse que d'erudition."[8] We learn from the name Eudoxe (<*eudoxía* =sound judgment), a personified variant of the adjective *orthodoxe*, that he is the *bien pensant*, the right-thinking critic, whose opinions are correct, whose taste is "classical," whereas Philanthe (*philein*=to love + *anthos*= flower), with his penchant for florid or flowery writing, is presented as a champion of the "manneristic" or "baroque." Bouhours makes all this clear at the outset; the group of dialogues that comprise his book will extend systematically the respective presuppositions of the names of his protagonists:

> Eudoxe a le goût très bon, et rien ne lui plaît dans les ouvrages ingénieux qui ne soit raisonnable et naturel. Il aime fort les Anciens, surtout les auteurs du siècle d'Auguste, qui selon lui est le siècle du bon sens. Cicéron, Virgile, Tite-Live, Horace sont ses héros. Pour Philanthe, tout ce qui est fleuri, tout ce qui brille, le charme. Les Grecs et les Romains ne valent pas à son gré les Espagnols et les Italiens. Il admire entre autres Lope de Vega et Le Tasse; et il est si entêté de la *Gerusalemme liberata,* qu'il la préfère sans façon à l'*Iliade* et à l'*Enéide.* A cela près, il a de l'esprit, il est honnête homme et il est même ami d'Eudoxe. (2)

La Manière de bien penser is built on the confrontation of two judgmental paradigms, the orthodox and the heterodox; its purpose and strategy are to show through a dialectical series of examples and arguments that Eudoxe is right and Philanthe is wrong in order, finally, to bring him around to his friend's way of thinking, and, in so doing, to celebrate the triumph of the "classical."

Within the sharply drawn confines of their antagonistic relationship, Eudoxe and Philanthe agree completely, however, on one fundamental issue: in *les ouvrages d'esprit* (what we would call "literature") such a thing as *bien penser* exists, in contradistinction to all opposite, lesser, or approximate phenomena; they disagree only as to the identity of those who attain this consummate level of literary performance. In the strictly binary universe of Eudoxe and Philanthe, *bien* and *mal penser* may be represented alternatively by the words *vrai* and *faux*, whose meanings are not to be confused— so Bouhours cautions his reader—with those that they enjoy in everyday language: "Tout ce qui paraît faux ne l'est pas, et il y a bien de la différence entre la fiction et la fausseté: l'une imite et perfectionne en quelque façon la nature; l'autre la gâte et la détruit entièrement" (13). The precious quality that Bouhours designates here by the vague, opaque word *nature*, he will describe a little further on, more usefully and meaningfully, as *l'essence des choses*: "le vrai doit se rencontrer dans les vers comme dans la prose. Par là je ne prétends pas ôter à la poésie le merveilleux qui la distingue de la prose la plus noble et la plus sublime: j'entends seulement que les poètes ne doivent jamais détruire l'essence des choses en voulant les élever et les embellir" (16-17).

This is what *La Manière de bien penser*, the quest for literary perfection, and the articulation of the "classical" are all about: the actualization of an inner essence which, when achieved by a writer and perceived by a reader, may be signalized, indifferently, by any one of a number of interchangeable metaphoric and tautological variants, such as *naturel, raisonnable, vrai*, etc.[9] The best writers, those whose thoughts impress us as being "true," "natural," etc. are the ones who succeed in extracting and communicating a latent, quasi-ineffable quality, which functions in a way that is curiously similar to what Riffaterre calls a "hypogram," that is, an unstated idea which constitutes, nevertheless, the central message in a literary text (*Semiotics of Poetry* 12-13 and *passim*). In a typical development, Bouhours reviews over the space of twenty pages a group of short passages, all of which illustrate the themes or actualize the hypograms: *survival-in-destruction* and *victory-in-defeat*. Eudoxe launches the discussion by quoting a Latin epigram by Giano Vitale on the paradoxical destiny of ancient Rome: "Regardez, dit-il, ces masses énormes de pierres, ces vastes amphithéâtres démolis et ruinés: voilà ce que c'est que Rome. Voyez comme le cadavre d'une ville si superbe [*ipsa cadavera tantae urbis*] a encore quelque chose d'impérieux et de menaçant" (119).[10] This vision of Rome as a living corpse reminds Philanthe of Tasso's characterization of a certain Saracen's courage: "Ce Sarrasin, dis-je, meurt de la main de Tancrède: mais il menace celui qui le tue, et veut même en mourant paraître n'être pas vaincu: *E vuol morendo, anco parer non vinto*." Eudoxe rejoins with a snippet from the historian Velleius Paterculus (ca. 19 B.C.-31 A.D.), and Philanthe follows up with Tasso's tribute to yet another dying Saracen: *E morto anco minaccia* (121). Florus and Sallust are then alleged by Eudoxe, parried by Philanthe with the words of an anonymous Spaniard on the death of the Duke of Burgundy, to which Eudoxe opposes a pungent epigram from Sidonius Apollinaris (5th century, A.D.). Philanthe then quotes from Florus, only to skip forward fourteen centuries to some other passages in Tasso "qui ont je ne sais quoi de bien héroïque" (122-123). It might appear from the proper names evoked in this citational sparring match that Eudoxe and Philanthe are squared away in an Ancient/Modern confrontation, but this is not the case at all. For Eudoxe will soon exalt the modern achievement by bringing to bear two quite disparate examples: an anonymous madrigal in praise of the Prince de Condé and a letter in Italian from Queen Christina of Sweden to the King of Poland (124-126). In the remainder of this development, the two friends quote their respective examples and authorities in this order: the madrigal and Italian letter remind Philanthe again of Tasso, Eudoxe brings in "un Panégyriste de Saint-Louis," Philanthe alleges Tasso once more, which prompts Eudoxe to cite Quintus Curtius whom he now advances as Tasso's source (126-130). This latter move elicits the following comment from Philanthe: "Si vous faites là-dessus le procès au Tasse, dit Philanthe, vous pouvez le faire à bien d'autres. Le malheur des modernes, ajouta-t-il, est de n'être pas venus les premiers; et tout leur crime souvent, c'est de penser comme les Anciens, sans les avoir lus" (130-131). Eudoxe agrees, and goes on to show that the reference to ancient Rome as a "cadaver," that had set their discussion in motion, actually had its source in a letter from Sulpicius to Cicero on the ruins of Carthage, which was also to crop up again in Tasso. At this point, Philanthe, somewhat exasperated, appears ready to give in, but not quite: "Comme si ces sortes de pensées, repartit Philanthe, ne pouvaient pas venir à tout le monde, et que le sujet ne les fournit pas de lui-même" (p. 133). Imitating Eudoxe's method and rivalling his learning, Philanthe then suggests, with a collection of apposite Latin texts arrayed in the margins, that the Rome-as-cadaver metaphor could be traced with equal probability to Florus, from him to Seneca and from Seneca to Cicero.

Eudoxe does not reply directly to this argument; rather, he moves the discussion to an adjacent terrain where he seems to be seeking a resolution to the question before them:

> Quoi qu'il en soit, reprit Eudoxe, Virgile a mieux pensé que les autres, en disant qu'il ne restait de Troie que la place où elle avait été: *Et campos ubi Troia fuit* [*Aen.* III, 11]. C'est aller plus loin que Lucain, qui fait mention de ses ruines, et que je ne sais quel autre poète qui parle de ses cendres. Par *les champs où a été Troie*, on n'a l'idée ni de ruines, ni de cendres, qui sont au moins les restes d'une ville détruite et brûlée: le lieu seul où fut cette ville, revient en l'esprit. (134-135)

Philanthe responds with the reminiscence of a sonnet on Rome by Girolamo Preti, but Eudoxe has struck gold with the Virgil passage and will take his last stand on it:

> Il y a de l'esprit, de la noblesse, et si vous voulez, de la magnificence dans le sonnet italien, repartit Eudoxe: mais à ne

> vous rien déguiser, ce seul mot de Virgile, *et les champs où a été Troie* me semble plus beau, et plus grand, tout simple qu'il est (136-137).

In a last try at advancing the discussion, Philanthe makes another pitch for Tasso, but the debate has become completely polarized; Bouhours has torn the contest down to its bare bones; it is now Virgil against Tasso:

> Faites valoir le Tasse tant qu'il vous plaira, dit Eudoxe, je m'en tiens pour moi à Virgile, et je vous déclare que je ne veux pas avoir plus d'esprit que lui. Ce n'est pas que je méprise le poème du Tasse; il a de grandes beautés, et du sublime en plusieurs endroits: mais c'est que j'estime plus *l'Enéide* qui n'a rien dans les pensées que de noble et de régulier. (137-138)

In closing, Eudoxe disclaims any blind attachment to the Ancients, insisting that Italian, Spanish and French writers can be favorably compared even to those of the "Siècle d'Auguste."   Philanthe concurs:

> Pour moi, je suis un peu de l'avis du Chancelier Bacon, qui croit que l'antiquité des siècles est la jeunesse du monde, et qu'à bien compter nous sommes proprement les anciens. Je ne sais, reprit Eudoxe, si la pensée de Bacon n'est point trop subtile: mais je sais bien que sans décider si nous sommes les anciens ou non, nous avons du bon sens, de l'élévation, et de la justesse pour le moins autant que les Grecs et que les Romains. (138-139)

The handful of operative, value-laden terms that undergird Bouhours's comparison of Virgil and Tasso (*beau, grand, simple, noble, régulier,* etc.) tell us little more about the nature of French "classicism" than can be gleaned from the standard text-book treatments of the subject. These two nuances, however, are worth retaining: 1) Bouhours's judgment remains flexible and relative in that he considers Tasso's performance not so much deficient as intermittent ("il a de grandes beautés, et du sublime *en plusieurs endroits*"), whereas Virgil's qualities are everywhere sustained ("*rien* dans les pensées *que* de noble et de régulier"); 2) the beauty and poetic power of the Virgilian example is inversely proportional both to its size and its degree of stylistic elaboration ("plus beau, et plus *grand*, tout *simple* qu'il est").

What is most striking in Bouhours's procedure is his supreme indifference to considerations of *race, milieu,* and *moment.* In their joint quest for "classical" perfection, that is, the optimal rendering with respect to a given subject of "l'essence des choses," Eudoxe and Philanthe skip and dart from contemporaneous French poet to

Roman historian, to neo-Latin epigrammatist, to Italian "Renaissance" sonneteer, as if the known frontiers of time and place, language and genre, did not exist. The undifferentiated synchrony in which Bouhours situates his inquiry into *La Manière de bien penser* is rooted in a conception of "literature" that has become as odd and foreign to us as it once was natural and familiar to him and his readers. The apparently arbitrary and random forays of Eudoxe and Philanthe over the glut and gamut of occidental writing are inscribed in a mental universe where *before* and *after* do not count. The dialogue between Eudoxe and Philanthe takes as its milieu and its object a self-contained, self-sufficient community of writers and readers, French and Roman, Spanish and Greek, old and recent, who might be pictured as if sitting around one large table, bound together in a feeling of total, exemplary comity, their collective energies marshalled in the pursuit of a quintessential literary quality that may be found anywhere or everywhere in a sprawling, polyglot *res literaria*. This vision of a timeless, egalitarian corporation of convergent minds, focused on a unitary object, builds on the far-reaching and—for the modern reader— altogether radical assumption that the study and appreciation of "les ouvrages d'esprit" or "literature," in the same way and for the same reasons as essentialistic subjects like morals and theology, have no place whatever among the historical disciplines.

Although *La Manière de bien penser* and Perrault's *Le Siècle de Louis le Grand* came out in the same year, 1687, the conceptual underpinnings of these two works lie centuries apart. Perrault's assertion of progress in the arts could never have been made in the absence of a prior view of history as linear development in time, at- tuned to a constant rhythm of differentiation, opposition, and change. Bouhours and his functional belief in the absolute parity of all writers whatever their dates and provenance, looks back, *mutatis mutandis*, to a rival view of history as *tradition*, in the etymological sense of that which is "handed down" over the span of time from generation to generation, from writer to writer and reader to reader.[11] This history-*qua*-tradition, unlike the modern progressive version, is concerned not with providing a chronological, factual description of what has happened, but with maintaining and explaining a qualitative record of what has survived. It is the first of these conceptions, of course, that has shaped the linear, vertical model on which modern, "scientific" literary history constructs its surveys and catalogs of the events and crises, the attitudes and ideals that seem to have governed—sometimes causally, sometimes reactively or correctively—the successive phases and stages in the production of literary works. The ultimate concern of this history—our own—is with literature as symptom and index of periodic and, usually, determining changes in sensibility and ideology; literary history according to this conception is first and foremost the locus and the focus of a *process*.

The divisions that structure the Castex-Surer *XVIIe Siècle*, to cite a random but typical example, provide a suitable case in point: *L'Age du romanesque et du baroque (1598-1661)* is followed by *La Génération classique (1661-1685)*, which gives rise in turn to *L'Eveil de l'esprit philosophique (1685-1715)*. These time-frames and their content are certainly not meant to be immovable or watertight, nor do the words *baroque* and *philosophique* preclude such alternatives as *maniérisme* and *scientifique*. Individuals may quibble about the terminology, but no one today would dream of denying that between 1600 and 1700, give or take a decade here and there, some such development or progression as the one proposed by Castex and Surer certainly did occur. From the firm ground on which we stand—"we" being right-thinking, critical-minded, sophisticated, relativistic onlookers—it is a self-evident truth that Time, along with the complex of human activities—politics, religion, economics, literature, science—that are caught up in it and co-extensive with it, is always and has always been going *somewhere*. As partners in the cult of progress, and believers in the progress of culture, we share a natural desire and a visceral need to ascertain what and where that "somewhere" is and how the phenomena on which we happen to center our attention—the advent of "classicism," the romantic rebellion, the *nouveau roman*—got there. We may not always or even often agree with the answers that are proposed, but we devoutly believe in the present instance that "le classicisme," "les grands classiques," their doctrine and their aesthetic, like the Age of Louis XIV in which these items are temporally ensconced, all belong integrally and inalienably to one global, many-faceted, epoch-making cultural event that came after one thing and before something else.

Over and against the sequential, vertical literary history that we find it so natural and necessary to cultivate, there is another that I have elsewhere called "naïve," a literary history built on a static, horizontal model, which takes as its object and proper study not process but product, not movement but duration, not external or contingent reference but absolute and anachronic immanence.[12] The naïve view of French "classicism," that is, the one that was espoused and expounded by its artisans and apologists, rests *sine qua non* on three axioms or articles of faith: 1) an ideal literary quality, appropriate to every domain and form of expression, exists, objectively; 2) it and it alone is the ultimate target of creative effort and the primary concern of critical judgment; 3) this ideal may be manifested and apprehended in the works of all writers irrespective of time, country, language or genre. During the French "classical" period a profound, widespread belief in what Fumaroli aptly calls the "universalité de l'éloquence" (19) motivated a sustained, passionate quest in all the areas of "literary" production for the *optimus stylus dicendi*; and it was this quest, rather than any theory or doctrine, any regime or *episteme*, that constituted the overriding, often exclusive preoccupation of the naïve literary history to which I have referred.[13]

In the eyes of their "classical" successors, the theoretical preoccupations and practical experiments of the Pléiade group initiated, but did not bring to its appointed conclusion, a heroic and historically decisive rivalry with the poets of Antiquity; it remained for Malherbe, his associates, and his disciples to stabilize and naturalize this incipient commerce between the burgeoning vernacular literature and Graeco-Roman culture. Within the purview of naïve literary history, the space enclosed between Ronsard's "Le premier en France j'ai pindarisé" and Boileau's "Enfin Malherbe vint" was the locus of a momentous *agon* and, finally, of a triumphant progress from groping apprenticeship to independence and maturity. In a later amplification of the implicit message of his "Enfin Malherbe vint," Boileau insisted that the fate of Ronsard and his school was to be seen as identical with that of their ancient counterparts, Naevius, Livius Andronicus and Ennius:

> il ne faut point s'imaginer que la chute de ces auteurs, tant les Français que les Latins, soit venue de ce que les langues de leur pays ont changé. Elle n'est venue que de ce qu'ils n'avaient point attrapé dans ces langues le point de solidité et de perfection qui est nécessaire pour faire durer et pour faire à jamais priser des ouvrages.

In keeping with this very same model of cyclical replication, the mission of Malherbe and Racan, identical with that of their respective ancient counterparts, Cicero, Horace and Virgil, was to have discovered and consecrated the *optimus stylus* for all time to come, "ayant attrapé dans le genre sérieux le vrai génie de la langue française, qui bien loin d'être en son point de maturité du temps de Ronsard... n'était pas même encore sortie de sa première enfance" ("Réflexion VII," 523-24).[14]

Aetas augustalis rediviva. As we enter the "classical" age, a relationship with Antiquity that had begun in the pre-Malherbian and pre-Bolevian time as subalternate and vertical, becomes horizontal and egalitarian. When Thomas Sébillet brought out an art of poetry in 1548, it was written in prose and given a title, *L'Art poétique français*, in which the last word conveyed both the newness of the undertaking and its implicitly humble status with respect to the "real" one composed by Horace in elegant Latin hexameters. When in 1674 Boileau published his *Art poétique*, it was written in alexandrines and received by its first readers not merely as the local counter-part, but as the French equivalent of Horace's *Ars poetica*. "Horace ou Despréaux l'a dit avant vous. —Je le crois sur votre parole mais je l'ai dit comme mien" (La Bruyère, "Des ouvrages de l'esprit," no. 69). This famous pronouncement takes for granted that Horace, Boileau, and *mutatis mutandis*, Jean de La Bruyère himself were all laboring in a unique dispensation and a common cause as equal members of a homogeneous, atemporal, humanistic confrerie.

In Boileau's case this conviction is so intense and deeply rooted that it permeates his most innocent and casual remarks. In the following couplet, for example,

> Si je pense exprimer un auteur sans defaut,
> La raison dit Virgile et la rime Quinault.
> (*Satire* II, 19-20)

one has every reason to wonder why Boileau should speak of "Virgile" in a line where, from the metrical standpoint, the names of Corneille, Molière or Racine would have fit just as well and where, with respect to context and content, any of the three as writers for the stage would have made a more suitable foil for the dramatist, Quinault. However arbitrary or inappropriate the Virgil-Quinault confrontation may seem to the modern reader, it makes eminent sense in the essentialistic purview of naïve literary history, in which these two proper names function as symbolic entities rather than referential signifiers, one representing hyperbolic greatness and the other hyperbolic mediocrity. In the same way and for the same reasons, Horace and Voiture make easy and natural company in the following passage that Boileau addressed to his "Esprit" or alter ego:

> Qui vous a pu souffler une si folle audace?
> Phébus a-t-il pour vous applani le Parnasse?
> Et ne savez-vous pas, que sur ce mont sacré,
> Qui ne vole au sommet tombe au plus bas degré?
> Et qu'à moins d'être au rang d'Horace ou de Voiture
> On rampe dans la fange avec l'abbé de Pure?
> (*Satire* IX, 23-28)[15]

Within the closed, ahistorical, value-oriented "classical" system, writers are routinely grouped and compared with complete indifference to considerations of time and place, mutability and contingency; critical judgments and the taxonomies that they generate observe a solitary criterion: the degree to which literary works contribute to the achievement of the *optimus stylus dicendi*, a point of fullness and perfection that insures survival and commands incorporation into a comprehensive, authoritative *res literaria*.[16]

The very freedom of a Bouhours or a Boileau to treat Tasso and Virgil, Voiture and Horace, as if they were contemporaries, presupposes between them and their implied readers a shared sense of cultural community and continuity, which rested in turn on a prior equation of literacy with Latinity, and, more fundamentally still, on an abiding belief in the permanent relevance of the Encyclopedia of Graeco-Roman letters.[17] When modern discussions do not absolutely ignore the powerful antiquarian component of French "classicism," they routinely subordinate it to the innovations, the "original," "creative" triumphs of the *grands classiques*. Naïve literary history, in sharp contrast, reveals a picture in which presumed boundaries and antagonisms between "Classicism" and a precedent "Humanism" are absorbed in a vision of the harmonious fusion of old and new, learning and worldliness, tradition and invention. If we were to pay strict attention to the linguistic skills, literary awareness, and cultural breadth that a critic like Bouhours or a poet like Racine brought to his craft and presupposed in his reader, it would appear that Montaigne's *Essais*, rather than Aristotle's *Poetics*, were the actual breeding place and cradle of French "classicism."

For what was French "classical" literature, after all, what did the "classical" generation in fact achieve, if not the artistic transposition and aesthetic enactment of that stupendous merger of cultures—the Ancient and the Modern, the erudite and the mundane, the pagan and the Christian—of which the *Essais* of Montaigne remain still today the most dramatic and persuasive example? As a purely visual specimen, almost any random page in Montaigne, with its strands of italicized Latin interlaced typographically with the preponderant French, testifies eloquently to the extensiveness and vitality of this cultural symbiosis. More often than not, Montaigne will neglect or refuse to identify his Latin authors, and, again, more often than not, refrain even from translating or paraphrasing them, as if to say by his deliberate, sustained bi-lingualism that he assumed, or, ideally, wanted to be able to assume in his readership a "classical" background commensurate with his own. We have a vivid case in point

in the opening of *De l'experience* (III, 13), whose first sentence —
"Il n'est desir plus naturel que le desir de connoissance"—turns out
to be an opaque paraphrase of the *incipit* to Aristotle's
Metaphysics.[18] In the immediate sequel, a rambling survey of the
paradoxical vicissitudes in human affairs of art and nature, similarity
and difference, Montaigne quotes, alleges or otherwise invokes in
conjunction with his own words the opinions of Manilius and
Cicero, Luther and Calvin, Justinian, Tacitus, Seneca and
Quintilian, but without identifying a single one of them. This
striking procedure, which did not escape comment and criticism in
its day, carries with it an unstated message.[19] By appropriating the
writings of his predecessors obliquely, without naming them or their
books, without giving a clue as to their origin or historical situation,
Montaigne was rendering them, their works, and their words
timeless; he was using anachronism and anonymity to assert the
lasting relevance of their ideas. Montaigne's cavalier treatment of
ancient writers, who still tended to be viewed by his more
conventional contemporaries as "sources" and "authorities," had the
further effect of removing them from their traditionally vertical,
hierarchical relationship to the reader, and of reestablishing them in a
horizontal, egalitarian, dialogic connection.[20] Montaigne, and
through him his reader, speaks about and with the ancients at no
greater distance and with no more ceremony than if they were in fact
moderns. In the absence of such indications as "in the immortal
words of Cicero" or "as Plutarch so aptly put it," in the further
absence of marginal "footnotes" or references, the examples and
opinions that Montaigne weaves into his discourse are demoted,
functionally, from the rank of testimony or evidence to the lesser but
more humane status of idea or opinion. Aside from the language of
his quotations, most of which are in Latin, the authors whom
Montaigne alleges in his essays are presented as voices parallel and
in fact equal to his own and to our own.

   The monumental task, so brilliantly executed by Montaigne, of
acclimatizing and adapting the Graeco-Roman Encyclopedia to the
articulation of modern concerns was to traverse two subsequent,
equally crucial stages before the "classical" synthesis could be
realized. The first of these thresholds was marked by the so-called
"reforms" of Malherbe, whose rejection of Pléiade poetic practice—
"illustration" through imitation of ancient models—quickened the
pace of the secularization and socialization of "Renaissance"
humanism. Aiming beyond what seemed to him the derivative,
pedantic antiquarianism of Ronsard and his followers, Malherbe
called for the creation of a new, more natural and more national

poetic manner, compounded of an abstract, Latinate, neo-Virgilian diction and a stately, elegiac, neo-Stoical tone. These were the chief elements in the elaboration of the indigenous courtly atticism—"une éloquence française et royale," in Fumaroli's phrase (29)—that was to enable French poets for the first time to speak with the same linguistic autonomy and stylistic authority as their ancient forebears. This, at least, is the meaning attributed retrospectively to the Malherbian *œuvre* by figures like Boileau and La Bruyère, who perceived Malherbe's rise to prominence and subsequent influence as coeval and continuous with a parallel ascendancy of the French language itself.[21] It was this new conviction on the part of the "grands classiques" of the inherent self-sufficiency and superiority of literary French that made possible the various definitional formulas and enabling cultural myths —the equality of Ancients and Moderns, the *Siècle de Louis le Grand* as a new *Siècle d'Auguste*— which, from Perrault and Voltaire to Nisard and Brunetière, became the natural, indispensable vehicle for the idea and the ideal of French "classicism."[22]

A further, even more decisive step in the assertion of this pivotal Ancient/Modern parity, was taken in the wake of the Quarrel of the *Cid*. This controversy widened the breech and, in some respects, signaled a violent break between the new, mundane, egalitarian Malherbian poetics and the academic, normative Renaissance Humanism that had survived alongside the flexible example and eclectic message of Montaigne. By its modern, Spanish theme and setting, its structural openness and lyric flavor, *Le Cid* constituted a powerful, calculated assault on the prevailing neo-Aristotelian, pseudo-Sophoclean—and proto-Racinian—dramatic model against which Corneille's critics were prepared to measure his ambitions and accomplishments.[23] The condemnation of *Le Cid* was perceived by Corneille, his defenders, and immediate posterity as a crude, unpopular, unjustified, and, in the last analysis, ill-conceived show of critical force, rooted in retrograde ideological and authoritarian motives. In the history of criticism, the Quarrel of the *Cid* stands out as a prophetic example of the potential vanities and inanities of literary theory when it succumbs to its often irresistible and always myopic craving for autonomy. It was Boileau, the forward-looking, modern-minded critic/poet and partisan of the Ancients, who, as spokesman for *la Cour et la Ville*, had the last word against Corneille's detractors:

> En vain contre *Le Cid* un ministre se ligue.
> Tout Paris pour Chimène a les yeux de Rodrigue.
> L'Académie en corps a beau le censurer,

Le public révolté s'obstine à l'admirer.
(Satire IX, 231-234)

An essential distinction is in order here. Corneille's stance with respect to academic literary Aristotelianism was not adversative, but competitive, even cooperative, to the extent that he had no wish, any more than Boileau did in celebrating Corneille's victory, to institute or exploit an Ancient-Modern antagonism. Throughout his extended debate with the critical establishment, Corneille's exclusive concern was for the right of modern dramatists to experiment and invent on an equal footing, with the same freedom and, ultimately, with the same authority as their ancient counterparts.[24] It was, moreover, this freedom that Montaigne and Malherbe, and, after their example, Boileau, La Fontaine, Racine, and La Bruyère required for themselves. If a *Zeitgeist* or governing creed prevailed over the flourishing of what I would call "classical" Humanism—bounded *grosso modo* by Malherbe at one end and La Bruyère at the other—it was surely this or some close variant of it: it had become possible during these years for a majority of professional writers and critics to believe that their language and the literary works for which it was the vehicle had achieved an eminence and a brilliance worthy of the accomplishments of Greece and Rome. Marc Fumaroli has described this condition with exemplary clarity: "Les chefs-d'œuvre que nous qualifions de 'littéraires' illustrent cet anoblissement de la langue vulgaire enfin devenue capable, à l'exemple du latin classique, de la 'pleine éloquence'" (29). Owing above all to a reigning belief in this parity, it remained possible during the brief period with which we are concerned to think of Ancients and Moderns, indifferently, as inhabitants of one unchanging mental universe and as partners in One Culture.

In reality, of course, there already existed two cultures, the very same two that C.P. Snow has since identified as the Humanistic and the Scientific; very few people, however, knew much about the second, and, of the handful that did, not many had reason to care much about it. In the forefront of those who did know and care was René Descartes who, within a year of *Le Cid*, brought out *Le Discours de la méthode*, which marked *inter alia* an aggressive rejection of the working assumptions and effective content of the "classical" Humanism that had produced both Corneille and himself. At the heart of Descartes's dissatisfaction, was the linguistic and literary emphasis of the education he received from the Jesuits at the Collège de la Flèche. In the sentence that opens his extensive critique of 17th-century pedagogical practice, "J'ai été nourri aux lettres dès mon enfance..." (Gilson, *editio minor* 48), the word "lettres" designates the *literae humaniores* or *res literaria*, a curriculum consisting of books of poetry, rhetoric, criticism, history, fiction, philosophy, and including works that would now be consigned to science or medicine, all of them written in Latin or translated into Latin from the Greek. Although Descartes granted the continuing need to learn these languages, "pour l'intelligence des livres anciens" (50), he no longer recognized their traditional hegemony. Whence this disappointed but momentous decision: "C'est pourquoi, sitôt que l'âge me permit de sortir de la sujétion de mes précepteurs, je quittai entièrement l'étude des lettres. Et me résolvant de ne chercher plus d'autre science que celle qui se pourrait trouver, en moi-même, ou bien dans le grand livre du monde, j'employai le reste de ma jeunesse à voyager" (55).[25] Descartes's consignment of the "livres anciens" and "l'étude des lettres" to the graveyard of the Past, eventually to be subsumed and amplified in the grandiose figure of the *tabula rasa*, was anchored in the conviction of a radical discontinuity between the Old and the New, specifically between the humanistic and scientific cultures, and of an equally radical superiority of the one over the other. For Descartes's immediate contemporaries the historical implications of the *Discours* were clear. On May 31, 1637 Chapelain urged Guez de Balzac to send "un mot de conjouissance à M. Descartes sur le succès de la publication de ses ouvrages," adding that if Balzac failed to do so he would resort to another intermediary in the elite Cartesian circle, "pour l'exhorter ... à nous donner moyen d'être plus savants que toute l'Antiquité aux choses naturelles, sans avoir besoin de grec ni latin" (*Lettres* 1:152-153).

In the clear light of history, Descartes's break with the past was less programmatic and complete, to be sure, than he himself wanted to have it appear; in the eyes of his intellectual heirs, however, he stood out as the architect of a decisive cleavage and the herald, if not the actual instigator, of the formal quarrel between the Ancients and the Moderns. From the earliest stages in this controversy, no argument in support of the Modern position could be complete without some variant of the proposition: *Enfin Descartes vint.* Fontenelle, in his *Digression sur les anciens et les modernes* (1688), praises Descartes as the agent of an irreversible historical divide between Before and After, Then and Now: "Avant M. Descartes, on raisonnait plus commodément; les siècles passés sont bien heureux de n'avoir pas eu cet homme-là. C'est lui, à ce qu'il me semble, qui a amené cette nouvelle méthode de raisonner" (6: 207ff).[26] It was Descartes's mission and destiny to have ushered in a brave new world marked by "une précision et une justesse qui, jusqu'à présent, n'avaient été guère connues" (224). In a word, as Foucault has since reminded us (60-75), history, no longer as before a tale of Continuity and Resemblance, is perceived in the post-Cartesian era as the record of the march of Progress and the assertion of Difference: "nous serons quelque jour anciens," proclaims Fontenelle; "et ne sera-t-il pas bien juste que notre postérité, à son tour, nous redresse et nous surpasse...?" (224-225). Just as in our time we continue to outdistance the ancients and one another, the Romans in their time were already overreaching the achievements of the Greeks: "Selon mon goût particulier," Fontenelle goes on, "Cicéron l'emporte sur Démosthène, Virgile sur Théocrite et sur Homère, Horace sur Pindare, Tite-Live et Tacite sur tous les historiens grecs" (227).   In its presuppositions, this comment stands light years apart from the naïve literary history of Boileau and Bouhours, studded and structured as it was by cyclical, renewable moments of qualitative transcendency.   In Fontenelle's neo-Cartesian scheme, writers are bunched together in sympathetic groupings and self-delimiting time blocks, according to considerations of nationality, profession, genre, and language; as their collective creative energies are used up, they distinguish themselves from those belonging to earlier and later "periods": "Les meilleurs ouvrages de Sophocle, d'Euripide, d'Aristophane, ne tiendront guère devant *Cinna*, *Horace*, *Ariane*, *Le Misanthrope*, et un grand nombre d'autres tragédies et comédies du bon temps, car il en faut convenir de bonne foi, il y a quelques années que ce bon temps est passé" (243-244). With this extraordinary statement— specifically with Fontenelle's trenchant redundancy "du bon temps," "ce bon temps"—the idea of a French "classical" period is formulated. Fontenelle, too often dismissed as a marginal latecomer and/or a half-baked forerunner, has given us, with respect to his two essential claims, impeccably accurate literary history: 1) in the wake of Descartes's challenge to traditional humanistic education and to the hegemony of ancient learning, it had become impossible for an important minority of responsible intellectuals to believe any longer in the myths of creative imitation and symbiotic connivance with Greece and Rome that buttressed the pro-Ancient position; 2) as of the publication of the *Digression* in 1688, the magnificent flowering of the *grande génération classique* was in fact over.

As we move deeper into the next century the configurations and consolidations that Fontenelle, as a close contemporary, could only glimpse and hint at began to take on greater consistency and to invite more elaborate and reflective description.   In Rémond de Saint-Mard's *Lettres sur la naissance, le progrès et la décadence du goût*

(1735), we find an expansive rewriting of Fontenelle's *Digression*, which both announces and preposterously complements the message of Voltaire's *Siècle de Louis XIV* (1751):

> Enfin arriva le règne de Louis XIV où le grand goût qui avait déjà éclaté en Italie parut en France dans tout son lustre. Vous eussiez dit...que tous les esprits s'étaient donné le mot pour briller tous ensemble: ...il nous vint surtout en ce temps-là un homme dont nous avions grand besoin: ce grand homme s'appelait Descartes, et comme si ç'avait été sa mission de venir nous éclairer il dessilla nos yeux, nous fit honte du respect que nous avions pour Aristote et porta dans la philosophie... une manière de raisonner, qui jusque-là avait été peu connue, ou qui du moins avait été peu cultivée... Aussi quel nombre prodigieux de bons livres n'eûmes-nous point dans ces temps-là? Quel éclat et quelle ordonnance dans tous les ouvrages? (3: 227-279)[27]

Fontenelle's personal conviction that he was witnessing the end of an era—"il en faut convenir de bonne foi, il y a quelques années que ce bon temps est passé"—assumes here the authority of historical, objective fact. With the statement: "Enfin arriva le règne de Louis XIV" (read: *Enfin Descartes vint, Enfin Racine vint*), Rémond affirms the teleological fulfilment of a development that he sees as having been set in motion in the wake of the Cartesian revolution and in the light of the Cartesian revelation (*il dessilla nos yeux*). The nostalgic exclamation that rounds out Rémond's observation— "quel nombre prodigieux de bons livres n'eûmes-nous point dans ces temps-là?"—looks back to a time gone by so rich in achievement that, although just a generation distant from him, it bathes already in a mythic aura. Rémond goes on: "Tel fut... notre état de splendeur, tels furent les beaux jours de la république des lettres; jours qui, comme ceux des Romains, furent bientot passés et qui, faits comme nous sommes, ne pouvaient pas longtemps durer" (3: 280).

The Age of Louis XIV, a supreme moment of cultural ascendancy carried with it the seeds of what in the title of his essay Rémond calls its *décadence*. There were three chief reasons for this falling away from "classical" splendor, all of them tributary to the epigonoi of Descartes. Rémond identifies the first of these as an abuse of "la précision," and the second as "le mépris qu'on nous donna pour les anciens"; most damaging, however, was the false assumption that, because Nature is perfectible, it was possible in the arts as well to surpass "ces prétendus grands hommes dont on faisait tant de bruit" (280). Rémond appears to be suggesting that if Fontenelle, La Motte and their followers had been less doctrinaire and shortsighted things might have turned out differently. But as his argument develops, it becomes clear that he situates the real problem elsewhere. Rémond believed, as Fontenelle had suspected fifty years earlier, that the resounding triumph of French "classical" writing—"les beaux jours de la république de lettres"—having become as much a part of history as the golden age of Latin literature was now beyond recall except as an object of curiosity, veneration and contemplation. The grands classiques, those privileged spirits who had dwelled in such intimacy with the Ancients, were now ancients in their own right, not only in the temporal sense, but more pointedly in Rémond's view, because to the "modern" mind their achievement no longer seemed commensurate with legitimate or realistic expectation. Rémond is aware of addressing a phenomenon that is all but enshrined in a mythical past, outside the flow of time, suspended in a state of transcendental plenitude:

> Le parfait a un point fixe, en-deçà ou en-delà on n'y est plus. Ces grands hommes du siècle passé, les Corneilles, les Molières, etc. avaient attrapé ce point de perfection, et une seule chose raisonnable restait à faire à leurs successeurs, c'était de les imiter et de tâcher de les égaler: mais cette opération était difficile. D'ailleurs, quand ils auraient réussi dans une entreprise aussi délicate, il y avait toujours à perdre pour eux: le mérite de la nouveauté leur manquait, il fallait qu'il leur en coutât pour être venus trop tard... (3: 286-287)

Here is the stuff that literary history is made of! Rémond's commentary illustrates in spectacular fashion the essential difference between what French "classicism" was and what it has since been made into. The nomenclature has yet to surface, but all the attributes of an exceptional, unique "école," "génération," or "époque classique" are already in place; in Rémond's proto-Lansonian description, the creative energies of a clearly circumscribed period are subsumed in the work of a stellar, élite group, whose collective, definitive conquest of perfection in the *grands genres* sets them apart for all time as canonical, inimitable models.[28] With a factual finality typical of modern scientific literary history, Rémond singles out from the roster of a vast, atemporal Republic of Letters a handful of proper names, destined to figure in the progressively more radical reductions of Voltaire and the Romantics as the exemplary incarnation of an historically delimited *esprit classique*. The polyglot *res publica literaria* that had been for Bouhours and Boileau the natural locus of the quest for the *optimus stylus dicendi*, has been made over into a national Pantheon.

How different in spirit and direction is the naïve literary history in which the *grands classiques* felt and saw themselves involved as actors and witnesses! In the first preface to *Britannicus* (1669), Racine opposes his own essentialistic, neo-Sophoclean manner to the increasingly popular, modern, action-packed Cornelian dramaturgy that he feels is being urged upon him by his critics:

> Que faudrait-il faire pour contenter des juges si difficiles? La chose serait aisée pour peu qu'on voulût trahir le bon sens. Il ne faudrait que s'écarter du naturel pour se jeter dans l'extraordinaire. Au lieu d'une action simple, chargée de peu de matière, telle que doit être une action qui se passe en un seul jour,... il faudrait remplir cette même action de quantité d'incidents qui ne se pourraient passer qu'en un mois, d'un grand nombre de jeux de théâtre d'autant plus surprenants qu'ils seraient moins vraisemblables, d'une infinité de déclamations où l'on ferait dire aux acteurs tout le contraire de ce qu'ils devraient dire... Mais que dirait cependant le petit nombre de gens sages auxquels je m'efforce de plaire? De quel front oserais-je me montrer, pour ainsi dire, aux yeux de ces grands hommes de l'antiquité que j'ai choisis pour modèles? Car, pour me servir de la pensée d'un ancien, voilà les véritables spectateurs que nous devons nous proposer, et nous devons sans cesse nous demander: Que diraient Homère et Virgile s'ils lisaient ces vers? Que dirait Sophocle s'il voyait représenter cette scène?[29]

In this eloquent defense of "classicism," Racine is asserting four central truths: 1) less is more; 2) authentic literary quality is a distillation of "l'essence des choses" as opposed to their fortuitous external trappings; 3) this transcendent immanence was perceived and actualized centuries ago by Homer, Virgil, and Sophocles with whom the best writers of today and tomorrow remain leagued together in an anachronic polity; 4) it is in the nature of things that the Search for the Absolute to which Racine and his fellow "classiques" are committed should go on forever.[30]

It is this last assumption that Perrault, Fontenelle, La Motte and Rémond de Saint-Mard, wedded as they were to a linear, progressive vision of history, had no choice but to reject. Not only could the Search for the Absolute not go on forever, but by the last decade of the seventeenth century it was already a thing of the past. That privileged group of writers who had dwelled in such intense intimacy with the Ancients, had now become ancients themselves. What the *grands classiques* had regarded as the timeless aspiration after an Idea, Fontenelle and Rémond describe as the final materialization of an entity; what in the naïve view had been an open-ended anachronic transcendency emerges in the modern, scientific view as a historical period.

It could be argued—in terms that are perhaps unconventional, but still as valid historically as the ones to which we are usually regaled—that French "classical" literature was the victim of its own success. When French became the literary equivalent of Latin, and Molière at least the equal of Plautus and Terence, when Corneille and Racine were judged to be the peers of Seneca, it was no longer necessary to read Seneca and Terence or even to know the language in which they wrote in order to participate in high culture. French "classicism" self-destructed, it sundered itself from its vital, creative impulses and shed its life-blood, at that point in history when Molière and Racine succeeded in becoming "classics."

Foreigners are always surprised to learn that it is possible for students in contemporary France to acquire the *baccalauréat* without having read a play of Corneille or Racine. If, as seems to be the case, the *grands classiques* are indeed too remote and irrelevant to be taught or studied with intelligence and enjoyment, if French theater audiences cannot be shown *Tartuffe* and *Phèdre* without the benefit of outrageous modernization and directorial intervention—à la Planchon, à la Vitez—this is surely not because the world is in disarray and civilization in decline; nor is it possible to accuse any vulgar democratic plot against the True and the Beautiful. It is simply that, with the passage of time, French "classical" writing has come to look more patently and starkly like what it was from the start: a naturally archaic, deliberately abstract, inalienably Latinate clone of the "classicism" of Antiquity. The language of Racine is, right now, fast on its way to becoming the Latin of French culture, just as in Racine's time the idiom of Rabelais and Montaigne was fast on its way to becoming its Greek.

In closing, I would like to stress that I have not been attempting here to describe "reality" as an historian of events or ideas might want to do. As a reader of 17th-century texts, as a philologist and psychologist of style, I have been interested rather in probing the latent content of certain striking formulations —"l'essence des choses," "j'ai quitté l'étude des lettres," "ce bon temps est passé"— in assessing their historical and cultural impact and, at times, in speculating on the process by which certain attitudes and judgments were formed and propagated, how they were received and perceived, how they changed or disappeared, were superseded or replaced by others that have since become exclusively familiar and comprehensible to us.

Notes

[1]Paul Valéry, "Situation de Baudelaire," (Œuvres, 1:604): "Tout classicisme suppose un romantisme antérieur. Tous les avantages que l'on attribue, toutes les objections que l'on fait à un art 'classique' sont relatifs à cet axiome. L'essence du classicisme est de venir après. L'ordre suppose un certain désordre qu'il vient

réduire. La composition, qui est artifice, succède à quelque chaos primitif d'intuitions et de développements naturels. La pureté est le résultat d'opérations infinies sur le langage, et le soin de la forme n'est autre chose que la réorganisation méditée des moyens d'expression. Le classique implique donc des actes volontaires et réfléchis qui modifient une production 'naturelle' conformément à une conception claire et rationnelle de l'homme et de l'art" (italics in the text). Let us not be seduced too easily by the solemnity and elegance of Valéry's rhetoric, which does no more than transpose into a poetico-aesthetic code the *poncifs* of Lansonian literary history.

[2]On the problem of classifying authors within the "classical" canon, see Robert J. Nelson, "Modern Criticism of French Classicism: Dimensions of Definition." René Wellek has mapped the fortunes of "classicism" on a European scale: "The Term and Concept of 'Classicism' in Literary History."

[3]Nelson, *loc. cit.*, speaks persuasively to the dominance of a Racinian "teleology" in modern treatments of French "classicism."

[4]One is reminded of the heroic but—so these things go—catastrophic attempt by Bernard Weinberg to read Racine through the lens of an eclectic/amended Aristotle: *The Art of Jean Racine* . See Ronald Tobin's evaluation of this ill-fated effort in *A Critical Bibliography of French Literature* (3A: 6992). For Racine's own subtle and elegant reading of the *Poetics* see *Principes de la tragédie.*

[5]On the matricial role of the *ingenium/judicium* antinomy in the European fortunes of "classicism," see Brody, "Constantes et modèles de la critique anti-'maniériste' à l'âge 'classique'."

[6]Marc Fumaroli's *L'Age de l'éloquence: rhétorique et "res literaria" de la Renaissance au seuil de l'époque classique* will remain for years to come a *summa* of work in this field; see in particular the section of his bibliography entitled: "Points de repère pour une histoire de la rhétorique dans l'Europe moderne" (801 ff.)

[7]The discussion that follows complements and extends the treatment of Bouhours in Brody, "Constantes," (10-17). In the tradition that Voltaire fashioned and then bequeathed to French literary historiography, Bouhours's *Manière de bien penser* and *Remarques sur la langue française* "seront toujours utiles aux jeunes gens qui voudront se former le goût: il leur enseigne à éviter l'enflure, l'obscurité, le recherché, et le faux." "Catalogue de la plupart des écrivains français qui ont paru dans le siècle de Louis XIV, pour servir à l'histoire littéraire de ce temps," (*Le Siècle de Louis XIV*, 2: 202).

[8]I quote *La Manière de bien penser* in the second edition.

[9]Bouhours's quest for "l'essence des choses" puts him squarely in the Platonic tradition of aesthetic inquiry that Fumaroli (340) illustrates with the following text from Charles de Saint-Paul Vialart, *Tableau de l'éloquence française où se voit la manière de bien écrire* (Paris, 1632): "Le style a sa beauté essentielle, aussi bien que le reste des êtres, et si nous voyons que l'or a des qualités qui lui donnent le premier rang entre les autres métaux, il se trouve certaines grâces excellentes dans le style qui donnent cette beauté excellente" (84). We owe to Jean Mesnard a luminous study of the *vrai/faux* antithesis: "Vraie et fausse beauté dans l'esthétique du XVIIe siècle."

[10]The theme of Rome-surviving-its-ruins was a commonplace in neo-Latin and vernacular poetry of the early modern period; in our day, students of French literature are likely to know it only in Du Bellay's famous variant (*Antiquités de Rome*, Sonnet 3): "Nouveau venu, qui cherches Rome en Rome/Et rien de Rome en Rome n'aperçois, etc." There is a remarkably learned and insightful study of this topic and the fortunes of Vitale's epigram by Roland Mortier: *La Poétique des ruines en France*, 46-53.

[11]On history-as-tradition see Brody, "Constantes," 28-29.

[12]For the further implications of the "naïve" view of literary history, see "Constantes," 9-10.

[13]The quest for the *optimus stylus dicendi* is one of the great unifying themes of Fumaroli's *L'Age de l'éloquence.*

[14]Cf. La Bruyère, "Des ouvrages de l'esprit," no. 42: "Ronsard et les auteurs ses contemporains ont plus nui au style qu'ils ne lui ont servi: ils l'ont retardé dans le chemin de la perfection; ils l'ont exposé à la manquer pour toujours et à n'y plus revenir. Il est étonnant que les ouvrages de Marot, si naturels et si faciles, n'aient su faire de Ronsard, d'ailleurs plein de verve et d'enthousiasme, un plus grand poète que Ronsard et que Marot; et, au contraire, que Belleau, Jodelle, et du Bartas, aient été sitôt suivis d'un Racan et d'un Malherbe, et que notre langue, à peine corrompue se soit vue réparée." The Malherbe/Ronsard comparison, often in the very language used by Boileau and La Bruyère, was a standard topic of 17th-century criticism; see Claude Faisant, "Lieux communs de la critique classique et post-classique."

[15]I have discussed the implications of this passage and the critical stance subjacent to it in "Boileau et la critique poétique."

[16]Boileau's outlook is typical in this respect; he is, in fact, the only French "classical" critic to have articulated and popularized the equivalence, that had become central to the rhetorical tradition, between the Sublime and the *optimus stylus dicendi*, on which, see Fumaroli (164-168, 177-178). At the uppermost reach of the *altitude/platitude* structure that informs Boileau's judgmental scheme, he situates what he was the first to call in its substantivized, hypostasized form, "le Sublime," as opposed to the *genus grande* or "style sublime": "cet extraordinaire et ce merveilleux qui frappe dans le discours, et qui fait qu'un ouvrage enlève, ravit, transporte" ("Préface," *Traité du sublime* 338). Boileau's discussions of the Sublime illustrate with particular clarity his view of literary quality as an atemporal transcendency: "Longinus" had given the *Fiat lux* in *Genesis* as an examplar of sublimity (*Peri Hupsous* IX, 9); alongside this capital instance, Boileau alleges as French equivalents the *Qu'il mourût* in Corneille's *Horace* ("Préface," *Traité du sublime* 340) and the "Moi!" of his *Médée* ("Réflexion critique X," 549), as if Corneille and the author of *Genesis* were contemporaries.

[17]In the 17th century there was nothing at all special or original in this belief; it was, on the contrary, part and parcel of an unquestioned and unquestionable critical *koine* as is illustrated by the following entry (s.v. "Poète") in Furetière's *Dictionnaire universel* (1690): "Homère et Virgile ont été de grands poètes épiques, Sophocle et Corneille de grands poètes dramatiques, Térence et Molière de bons poètes comiques, Horace et Malherbe grands poètes lyriques." On the broader implications of this passage see Fumaroli, 26-28.

[18]This remarkable intertextual connection was pointed out by Michael A. Screech, "Commonplaces of Law, Proverbial Wisdom and Philosophy: Their Importance in Renaissance Scholarship (Rabelais, Du Bellay, Montaigne)."

[19]In my *Lectures de Montaigne* I have dealt in detail with the early reception of Montaigne's *Essais*; for reactions to what Jean-Pierre Camus calls "sa mode de citer sans citer," see 23-27.

[20]This achievement on Montaigne's part has been described with particular elegance by Marc Fumaroli: "en l'absence d'interlocuteurs capables et dignes d'entrer dans le dialogue libéral, Montaigne se rejette vers les seules âmes fraternelles qui soient à sa portée, les grands Anciens. Le monologue des *Essais* n'est pas seulement dialogue de Montaigne avec les 'grandes âmes' de Rome et de la Grèce, il est aussi le lieu d'un vaste *Dialogue des morts*. Et c'est peut-être l'aspect le plus étonnant de ces inépuisables *Essais*: cet homme qui prétend ne pas aimer les livres, à moins d'y avoir trouvé réponse à une des postulations de sa nature, se montre capable d'animer un immense débat où, prêtant sa voix aux diverses écoles d'âmes et de sagesse, il les fait tenir ensemble et dialoguer, dans un acte d'interprétation dramatique..." ("Michel de Montaigne ou l'éloquence du for intérieur," 38).

[21]See above, note 14.

[22]See Franco Simone's learned and penetrating treatment of this subject: "La Storia letteraria francese e la formazione e dissoluzione dello schema storiografico classico."

[23]Corneille's *Oedipe* (1659) is by far the most flagrant example of his challenge to traditional readings of Aristotle; see his "Au lecteur" to the play itself and his further remarks in the *Trois Discours* (*Œuvres*, 1:31-32, 56-57, 61, 98-99). On the implications of *Oedipe* for Corneille's innovative "esthétique ouverte," see Alain Viala, *Naissance de l'écrivain*, 224-230.

[24]On Corneille as a proto-modern, see the article by Alain Niderst, "Corneille et les commentateurs d'Aristote." A similarly "modern" attitude motivates La Fontaine's famous statement in the *Epitre à Huet* (1687): "Souvent à marcher seul j'ose me hasarder/On me verra toujours pratiquer cet usage;/Mon imitation n'est point un esclavage."

[25]According to Nicolas Faret it is more profitable "d'étudier dans le grand livre du monde que dans Aristote" (*L'Honnête homme ou l'art de plaire à la cour* 26.) Jean Mesnard sees this opposition as correlative with Descartes's modernist position ("Vraie et fausse beauté").

[26]On the revolutionary impact of Descartes's influence see Perrault's article, "René Descartes, philosophe": "Ceux qui ont eu la force de faire changer de face aux choses qu'ils ont trouvé établies dans le monde, ont toujours été considérés comme des hommes extraordinaires... Il eut pour amis tous les savants hommes d'un mérite distingué, à la réserve de ceux que sa manière nouvelle de philosopher souleva contre lui; car la hardiesse qu'il eut d'établir des maximes contraires à celles des anciens lui suscita des ennemis..." (123-24). Hugh Davidson has discussed with his usual subtlety and clarity the "enormous change in perspective" that Descartes brought to bear on humanistic study ("Disciplinary Options and the Discussion of Literature in Seventeenth-Century France" 123-124).

[27]On Rémond's role in the Ancient/Modern controversy and his position in the history of criticism, see Arnaldo Pizzorusso, "La 'Poetica arbitraria' di Rémond de Saint-Mard" and Robert L. Myers, *Rémond de Saint-Mard: a Study of His Major Works.*

[28]Rémond's use of the expression "avaient attrapé ce point de perfection" levies openly on the language of Boileau and La Bruyère (above, pp. 58-59 and n.14). Note, however, that his usage institutionalizes and historicizes what for his predecessors had been a dynamic process of cyclical renewal.

[29]The "ancien" to whom Racine refers here is "Longinus," *Peri Hupsous* XIV, 2.

[30]I borrow the expression "Search for the Absolute" from Hugh Davidson, "Yet Another View of French Classicism" (60), who uses it to characterize the gist of my essay: "Platonisme et classicisme," In this study I argue that the major values and tenets of French "classicism"—its preoccupation with form, universality, perfection, etc.—should be regarded as coded variants in the Platonic-Platonistic paradigm of the Good. If I may say so without exceeding the bounds of modesty, I would judge from recent work in the history of French "classical" aesthetics that this is an idea, as they say, whose time has come. I refer, in particular, to the powerful confirmation of my views in the thesis of Annie Becq, *Genèse de l'esthétique française moderne: de la raison classique à l'imagination créatrice, 1680-1814* (1: 91-94). I find further fuel for my fire in Jean Mesnard's impressive study of "L'Esthétique de La Rochefoucauld" soon to appear in the Acts of the 1987 meeting of the North-American Society for 17th-Century French Literature; Professor Mesnard demonstrates that the views of La Rochefoucauld were grounded in the same neo-Augustinian Jansenistic circles to which I trace the Platonic strain in French "classical" criticism.

Works Cited

Aron, Th. "Le Classicisme." *Manuel d'histoire littéraire de la France*. Ed. Annie Ubersfeld and Roland Desné. Tome II: 1660-1715. Paris: Editions Sociales, 1966. 76-77.

Becq, Annie. *Genèse de l'esthétique française moderne: de la raison classique à l'imagination créatrice, 1680-1814*. Pisa: Pacini, 1984.

Boileau, Nicholas. *Œuvres complètes*. Ed. by Antoine Adam and Françoise Escal. Paris: Bibliothèque de la Pléiade, 1966.

Bouhours, Dominique. *La Manière de bien penser*. 2nd edition. Paris: chez la Veuve de S. Mabre-Cramoisy, 1688.

Brody, Jules. "Boileau et la critique poétique." *Critique et création littéraires en France au XVIIe siècle*. Paris: Editions du CNRS, 1977. 243-250.

—. "Constantes et modèles de la critique anti-'maniériste' à l'âge 'classique.'" *Rivista di letteratura moderne e comparate* 40 (1987): 5-31.

—. *Lectures de Montaigne*. Lexington: French Forum, 1982.

—. "Platonisme et classicisme." *Saggi e ricerche di letteratura francese* 2 (1961): 7-30. Repr.with additions and corrections in *French Classicism: a Critical Miscellany*. Ed. Jules Brody. Englewood Cliffs: Prentice-Hall, 1966. 186-207.

Chapelain, Jean. *Lettres*. Ed. Ph. Tamizey de Larroque. Paris: Imprimerie nationale, 1880.

Corneille, Pierre. *Œuvres*. Ed. Charles Marty-Lavaux. Paris: Hachette, 1910.

A Critical Bibliography of French Literature. Ed. by H. Gaston Hall. Volume 3A: The Seventeenth Century (Supplement). Syracuse: Syacuse UP, 1983.

Davidson, Hugh. "Disciplinary Options and the Discussion of Literature in Seventeenth-Century France." *New Literary History* 17 (1985-1986): 288-290.

—. "Yet Another View of French Classicism." *Bucknell Review* 13 (1965) 5-62.

Faisant, Claude. "Lieux   communs de la critique classique et post-classique." *Etudes Françaises* (Montréal) 13 (1977): 143-162.

Faret, Nicolas. *L'Honnête homme ou l'art de plaire à la cour*. 1630. Ed. Maurice Magendie. Paris: Alcan, 1925.

Fontenelle, Bernard Le Bouvier de. *Œuvres diverses*. Paris: Brunot, 1715.

Foucault, Michel. *Les Mots et les choses: une archéologie des sciences humaines*. Paris: Gallimard, 1966.

Fumaroli, Marc. *L'Age de l'éloquence: rhétorique et "res literaria" de la Renaissance au seuil de l'époque classique*. Geneva: Droz, 1980.

—. "Michel de Montaigne ou l'éloquence du for intérieur." *Les Formes brèves de la prose et le discours discontinu (XVIe-XVIIe siècles)*. Ed. Jean Lafond. Paris: Vrin, 1984. 27-50.

Furetière, Antoine. *Dictionnaire universel....* The Hague and Rotterdam: Leers, 1690.

La Bruyère, Jean de. *Caractères*.

La Fontaine, Jean De. *Epitre à Huet*.

"Longinus," *Peri Hupsous*.

Mesnard, Jean. "L'Esthétique de La Rochefoucauld." *Acts of the 1987 Meeting of the North-American Society for 17th-Century French Literature*. (In press)

—. "Vraie et fausse beauté dans l'esthétique du XVIIe siècle" *Convergences: Rhetoric and Poetic in Seventeenth-Century France—Essays for Hugh M. Davidson*. Ed. David Lee Rubin and Mary B. McKinley. Columbus: The Ohio State UP, 1989 [tent.].

Mortier, Roland. *La Poétique des ruines en France: ses origines, ses variations, de la Renaissance à Victor Hugo*. Geneva: Droz, 1974.

Myers, Robert L. *Rémond de Saint-Mard: a Study of His Major Works*. Geneva: Institut et Musée Voltaire, 1970.

Nelson, Robert J. "Modern Criticism of French Classicism: Dimensions of
    Definition." *Bucknell Review* 13 (1965): 44-48.
Niderst, Alain. "Corneille et les commentateurs d'Aristote." *PFCSL* 14 (1987):
    733-743.
Pizzorusso, Arnaldo. "La 'Poetica arbitraria' di Rémond de Saint-Mard." *Rivista
    di letterature moderne* 15-16 (1954): 5-25.
Racine, Jean. *Principes de la tragédie.* Ed. Eugène Vinaver. Paris: Nizet,
    1951.
Rémond de Saint-Mard. *Œuvres mêlées.* Nouvelle édition augmentée. The
    Hague: Naulne, 1742.
Riffaterre, Michael. *The Semiotics of Poetry.* Bloomington: Indiana UP, 1978.
Screech, Michael A. "Commonplaces of Law, Proverbial Wisdom and
    Philosophy: Their Importance in Renaissance Scholarship (Rabelais, Du
    Bellay, Montaigne)." *Classical Influences on European Culture, A.D.
    1500-1700.* Ed. R.R. Bolgar. Cambridge: Cambridge UP, 1976. 127-134.
Simone, Franco. "La Storia letteraria francese e la formazione e dissoluzione
    dello schema   storiografico classico." *Rivista di letterature moderne* 4
    (1953): 5-22, 169-178.
Valéry, Paul. "Situation de Baudelaire." *Œuvres.* Ed. Jean Hytier. Paris:
    Bibliothèque de la Pléiade, 1957. 1:604.
Viala, Alain. *Naissance de l'écrivain.* Paris: Editions de Minuit, 1985.
Vialart, Charles de Saint-Paul. *Tableau de   l'éloquence française où se voit la
    manière de bien écrire.* Paris: 1632.
Voltaire. *Le Siècle de Louis XIV.* Ed. Antoine Adam. Paris: Garnier-
    Flammarion, 1966.
Weinberg, Bernard. *The Art of Jean Racine.* U of Chicago P, 1963.
Wellek René."The Term and Concept of 'Classicism' in Literary History."
    Aspects of the Eighteenth Century. Ed. Earl R. Wasserman. Baltimore: The
    Johns Hopkins UP, 1965). 105-128.
Zuber, Roger and Micheline Cuénin. *Le Classicisme.* Vol. 4 of *Litterature
    française.* Paris: Arthaud, 1984.

French Classicism:
Dimensions of Application*

Robert J. Nelson
University of Illinois

I

For about two centuries now, "French Classicism" has operated as the "invisible hand" regulating the exchange of French literary commodities offered not only in the blue chip stocks marketed for the first time in the second half of the 17th century but of those offered ever since. The bluest of the chips on this literary Dow-Jones Index has been Racine, proleptically and paradoxically raised to his market-leverage by Voltaire in his *Commentaires sur Corneille*. Stintingly commenting on his eponymous subject along lines derogating Cornelian excess in the light of Racinian concision—the Voltairean Corneille reads like Shakespeare, whose "unruly" and "English" genius Voltaire ever abides with difficulty—the commentator at once set up and provided the solution to a problem of definition and inclusion for future literary historians. How could one leave out the prodigious Corneille, who sat astride the seventeenth century with perhaps even more impact than would Voltaire astride the eighteenth, Hugo the nineteenth or Sartre the twentieth? How to inscribe Corneille into "French Classicism?" As we well know, the solution has been to "enRACINate"—or, more exactly—to "pre-enRACINate" Corneille. Following the invisible hand of the Racinocentric market index of French literary history since Voltaire, Corneille has come to be understood as the author primarily of four plays more predictive than representative of concision and clarity in the tragic mode defined as "Racinian": *Le Cid, Horace, Polyeucte*, and *Cinna.*

That the "fit" of this solution has not been without its problems is obvious in the very play, *Le Cid*, with which literary history has found Corneille "founding" French Classical Tragedy and thereby consecrated him as "le Père de la tragédie française." Given his obvious dissent, both creatively and theoretically, from at least Aristotelian conceptions of tragedy, one suspects that the author himself might have been happier to be remembered as the Father of the genre under whose rubric he first denominated *Le Cid*: "tragicomédie." Moreover, the Cornelian "dissent" from Racinian as well as Aristotelian conceptions of tragedy is sharp enough to cast doubt on the appropriateness of "fitting" each of the remaining plays of Corneille's Classical tetralogy into a "Racinian" or "pre-Racinian" mold. Each, finally—and, unlike *Le Cid*, unambivalently— vindicates its "hero" in the most un-Racinian fashion. Nevertheless, the doubt is overcome. It may be the source of learned, ingenious, compelling and, for some, convincing doctoral dissertations, but, in the broad historiographical enterprise of transmitting "French Classicism" from one generation to the next, it is overcome: Corneille continues to be inscribed within the Racinocentric conception of that moment of French Literature for students of that literature at home and abroad.

At home: in France, primarily in French schools from elementary through university levels (but not exclusively by them alone, of course, given the suffusiveness of Literature and other forms of "High Culture" in the French polity); *abroad*: probably primarily in schools and, even more probably, primarily in some secondary but mostly college and university curricula in literature— particularly French Literature—like those which I and many of the contributors to this volume have taken as students and offered as teachers. That the problem—contradictions, ambiguities, puzzles— of definition that I have briefly sketched thus far with respect to but one writer should be underplayed if not programatically resolved in France is not irrelevant to my concern with "applications" of the concept here. I shall suggest some political and psychoanalytic perspectives on the matter later, but suffice it to say now that each polity presents its literary tradition to its members, particularly its young, as part of a process of "socialization" or "inscription" into its mores and values.

My greater concern is with this process in the "transmission" of the concept of "French Classicism" *abroad*, primarily in American Higher Education. In that context I shall rely on "secondary sources" of commentary rarely evoked by scholars in the matter: (1) students to whom we scholars/teachers transmit the concept of "French Classicism;" (2) scholars and thinkers either concerned tangentially, if at all, with the concept or concerned with it in a defensive and, at times, adversarial mode. Given the ignorance (by which I do not mean: stupidity) of American students, the perspectives of my first "source" of commentary might be described as "pre-critical," that of my second as "meta-critical." On the other hand, as far apart as these sources may be (first of all, obviously, by dint of formal education), they do share a common ground of knowledge-as-information as to just *who* are the major authors making up "French Classicism." Given a wide-spread American isolation of the "aesthetic" or, in literary terms, the "belle-lettristic" from the "practical-real" or the "practical-cognitive," playwrights and at least one poet and one novelist "belong" to this "literary" moment almost encyclopedically": Corneille, Racine, Molière, La Fontaine and Mme de Lafayette. In a subset underscoring this logic, a number of other "writers," primarily of "philosophical" texts, are (ar)ranged within the moment in a supportive or infrastructural light: Descartes, Pascal, Boileau, La Rochefoucauld and Bossuet. For "specialists" of "French Classicism" it may seem odd to range Boileau within the "philosophical subset" of the moment, but from the American perspective which is my focus here, I trust that this arrangement is as appropriate as my exclusion of such writers as La Bruyère and Mme de Sévigné. In the logic of much American literary criticism and theory of the past fifty years—from the "New Criticism" to "Structuralism"—literary criticism and epistolary writing (especially when it constitutes the entire canon of the "writer") as well as theological discourse (including that of a *roman à thèse* like *Télémaque*) are not "literary genres."

This logic has come under scrutiny, much of it very adversarial, in the present "post-structuralist" moment. However, there is a lag between theory and practice. Departments of Language-and-Literature continue to "transmit" the concept of French Classicism in the mode I have outlined above. For some of these Departments the "lag" is a deliberate defense of the "tradition," a programmatic rejection of criticism and theory (post-modern or modern), an instance of what Paul De Man has called the "resistance to theory." Other departments - including some at the cutting edge of theory in their scholarship but aware of the "balkanization" of theory in this "post-structuralist" moment - tend to play it "safe." At least at the pedagogical level they hew to the "tradition" more on pragmatic than on theoretical or, more polemically as the case may be, anti-theoretical grounds.

Now, these pragmatic grounds could be said to be buttressed, in part, on "linguistic" grounds. Undergraduate and, increasingly, graduate student "majors" in French are incompetent and ignorant (again, not stupid) both linguistically and culturally. On this, at this early point in this essay, I offer a special *caveat* on two counts. First, I am aware as any teacher of French at the university level of the difficulty most French "majors" have in achieving linguistic competence in the language exclusively through academic means. Over the past forty years, the plethora of "methods" to remedy this situation is largely a record of successive failures. The failures seem to me to be rooted in the second count I offer in a cautionary spirit at this point and in anticipation of the primary metacritical perspective I shall develop at a later point in this essay. The widely noted American inability to achieve linguistic competency in a foreign language is rooted in an American diffidence before the fact of language, including the English language. Even those Americans who achieve competency in a foreign language (usually through a combination of academic and "in-country" learning) bring to that language, as to their own, a diffidence, a suspicion before the fact of language. This is as true, in Riffaterian terms, of the cultivated "lecteur moyen" who has "mastered" French as it is of those students who, in many institutions, can be "exempted" from the "Foreign-Language Graduation Requirement" on grounds of an attested learning disability. In this connection, a pedagogical, self-serving myth bears strongly on my concerns here: scientific linguists notwithstanding, it is a commonplace, particularly with the French but with most Americans as well, that the French language is a more exact (and exacting) instrument of communication than English. For example, the great American novelist, Willa Cather, sees French as having two polarized attributes lacking in the English language: "sympathetic criticism" and "the fatal attribute of perfection." Taking Cather's ambivalence as emblematic of the American attitude, it seems to me that "French Classicism," the moment when the French language is said to have been "fixed" in its alleged perfection, is thus a most paradoxical moment through which to transmit to Americans the "French Tradition," literary and other.

Yet, it is also a "site" potentially rich in new ways of "rethinking French Classicism" itself. In the following pages, elaborating the theoretical perspectives outlined above, I shall consider at some length the appropriateness of applying the concept of "French Classicism" to three patently "belletristic" authors "encyclopedically" ranged under the concept—Corneille, Racine and Molière—and to one "philosophical" author ranged under the concept infrastructurally—Pascal. My strategy will be to accept the Racinocentric "definitions" which have dominated the concept since Voltaire. I do so fully aware of such ingenious protestations as Stendhal's re-definition of the author of *Phèdre* as a "Romantic" and Roger Caillois' despairingly corrective assertion that Corneille is by far a greater writer than Racine. Stendhal and Caillois are "commentators" casting "internal" doubts on the validity of the concept of "French Classicism" itself. They thus differ from recent commentators who attack the sacrosanct status if not the validity of the concept by "external" stratagems—for example, Joan de Jean's displacement of "les grands classiques" as the principal legacy of sevententh-century French literature through her brillant study of *libertinage*. For my part, more in the manner of Caillois than of Stendhal, I shall here attempt further and more extensive "internal displacements" arrived at, for the most part, through non-French critical and metacritical perspectives themselves "external" to French Literature and its scholarly commentary.

II

Like Emerson for Americans, according to Harold Bloom, Pierre Corneille may be seen as the "father of [us] all" in the French literary tradition. He is a prodigious playwright (thirty-five plays in forty-five years); a poet in several forms (amounting to one tenth of his canon); a provocative literary presence (a "recalcitrant" among the celebrated "Cinq Auteurs," thereby earning himself Richelieu's reproach of not having enough "esprit de suite"); the first great "creative" French writer to produce an extensive body of criticism and theory. In Bloomian optics, his famous three *Discours* on dramatic art are a frontal defense of his own practice as a dramatist, an Oedipal rebellion against Aristotle and his French adepts in the first third of the seventeenth century (and beyond). Corneille-the-critic escapes the Bloomian indirect "ratios" of the revolution he proposes so directly that one is tempted to add to Bloom's six ratios the seventh non-ratio of sheer apodixis (*apo* plus *deiktos*: show forth clearly). For all but possibly his last plays (*Pulchérie* of 1672 and *Suréna* of 1674), Corneille's theater is a celebration of the power of language to create its own world. His is a dramaturgy stressing, as Georges May showed us forty years ago, "curiosité" and "nouveauté." These are, we might say, the esthetic expression of humanity's possibility and variety stressed by Sartre in his correction of La Bruyère's famous assertion that Racine paints humankind as it is, Corneille as it ought to be.

Possibility/curiosity and variety/novelty express, in Bloom's terms, the "primordial" energies which the sublimating tendencies of the nascent Classicism of the critics of *Le Cid* will eventually contain in a concept of Classicism exalting the Superego through the agencies of *vraisemblance* and *bienséance*. In Bloom's terms, such a concept veers, understandably, towards the introjective and metonymizing Racine; such a concept withdraws from the existentialistic implications of Sartre's (and, later, Doubrovsky's) conception of the Cornelian universe. Like their creator before the "facts" of history, of consecrated mythology and of Aristotle's poetics, Corneille's heroes and heroines flaunt circumstantial evidence to declare their own sense of self and circumstance, manipulating self and other to realize their own history.

In defense of that manipulation, Corneille turns critic, taking up his pen to assert his priority and independence from "classicizing" critics from Aristotle to Scudéry.

> Bien que, selon Aristote, le seul but de la poésie dramatique soit de plaire aux spectateurs, et que la plupart de ces poèmes leur aient plu, je veux bien avouer toutefois que beaucoup d'entr' eux n'ont pas atteint le but de l'art. Il ne faut pas, dit ce philosophe, que ce genre de poésie nous donne toute sorte de plaisir, mais seulement celui qui lui est propre; et pour trouver ce plaisir qui lui est propre et le donner aux spectateurs, il faut suivre les préceptes de l'art, et leur plaire selon ses règles. Il est constant qu'il y a des préceptes, puisqu'il y à un art, mais il n'est pas constant quels ils sont. On convient du nom sans convenir de la chose, et on s'accorde sur les paroles pour contester sur leur signification.

Thus begins Corneille's *Discours de l'utilité et des parties du poème dramatique*. Noting Aristotle's (as well as Horace's) greater "étude et spéculation que d'expérience du théâtre," Corneille uses primarily his own plays to demonstrate the futility of such an Aristotelian notion as the therapeutic value of the theater, morally and psychologically. On the contrary, "la poésie dramatique a pour but le seul plaisir du spectateur." It is thus left to the sublimating Racine of the preface to *Bérénice* to extend this pleasure in such a way as to allow re-entry of Aristotelian and Horatian psycho-ethical perspectives: "la seule règle est de plaire *et toucher*" (my emphasis).

These are perspectives Corneille will have already elsewhere mocked. In his *Discours de la tragédie et des moyens de la traiter selon le vraisemblable ou le nécessaire*, he doubts whether purgation *à la Aristote* ever takes place. He specifically denies the philosopher's very attribution of a fault to be "purged" in the paradigmatic tragic hero, Oedipus. His own *Oedipe* of 1659 is, of course, really an heroic comedy in which, as Nadal has noted, the hero blinds himself not in self-punishment but in challenge that the heavens justify themselves. Again, in his "Au Lecteur" on *Nicomède* of 1651, to Aristotle's "pity and terror" as the hallmarks of tragedy Corneille opposes "la fermeté des grands coeurs, qui n'excite que l'admiration." How far we are from that "tristesse majestueuse" which Racine, again in the preface to *Bérénice*, will see as the hallmark of tragedy! In his "tragédies" as in his *Discours de la tragédie*, the "Father of French Classical Tragedy" flies in the face of an esthetic which is really an ethos whereby the *vraisemblable* is assimilated into the *bienséant*. For Corneille, the *vraisemblable* is to be stretched to the needs of the poet, not tailored to the centralizing, domineering imperatives of a state seeking to create submissive citizens conducting themselves in a "well-fitting" manner. As the "Founding Father" of the "Constitution" of "French Classicism," Corneille is a very "loose Constructionist" indeed!

Not surprisingly, then, he anticipates the position and many of the specific objections to the "classical rules" that Hugo will voice in the *Préface de 'Cromwell'* two centuries later. In his *Discours des trois unités d'action, de jour, et de lieu*, Corneille stresses that faculty suspect to infrastructural French Classics as different as Descartes and Pascal: the imagination. For Corneille, the spectator's imagination is as free as that of the poet. More accommodating in this *Discours* than in the others, Corneille peppers his reflections with wry but no less effective criticism of the ancient philosopher. Aristotle's "unity of time" oppresses many writers and they would soon be done with it "si elle n'était fondée que sur l'autorité d'Aristote; mais ce qui la doit faire accepter, c'est la raison naturelle qui lui sert d'appui." However, the sly creator-critic then stretches his own "rule" that natural reason would dictate that plot-time and running-time coincide. Rather, he goes on, let us not be slavish in the matter and "si nous ne pouvons la renfermer dans ces deux heures, prenons-en autre, six, dix, mais ne passons pas de beaucoup les vingt-quatre, de peur de tomber dans le dérèglement et de réduire tellement le portrait en petit qu'il n'aie plus ses dimensions proportionnées et ne soit qu'imperfection." In sum, be relaxed, not tense and defensive - for, after all, the sole purpose of the theater is to please the spectator: "surtout je voudrais laisser cette durée à l'imagination des auditeurs et ne déterminer jamais le temps qu'elle emporte, si le sujet n'en avait besoin, principalement quand la vraisemblance y est un peu forcée comme au *Cid*, parce qu'alors cela ne sert qu'à les avertir de cette précipitation."

Rebelliously rejecting Aristotelian (and other) "influence," Corneille strikes us, in Bloom's categories, not as "belated poet" suffering an "anxiety of influence" but as a "Founding Father" against whom what we might call the "belated creator-critics" of the French tradition struggle unto our own day. French writers suffer, as Sima Godfrey has perceptively put it, from an "anxiety of anticipation" affecting French literary thought since Boileau, the "powerful father figure of modern French poetry [whose] strength is derived not so much from his role as a poet, which he was, as from his role as a critic." For Godfrey, Boileau thus becomes that "giant" whom Bloom finds lacking in the French poetic tradition compared to the English and American with their plethora of "giants" (Chaucer, Spencer, Shakespeare, Milton, Wordsworth, Whitman, Dickinson).

In fact, Godfrey's valence of anxious anticipation is perhaps metacritically even more widely applicable to French poetry than she heuristically suggests in her acknowledgement that Boileau is not the first patriarch anxiously preoccupied with earlier patriarchs. The line goes back in poetry at least to Ronsard and, in other genres, perhaps earlier but at least to Montaigne (Emerson's mentor and thus, in Bloom's optics, it is the great French essayist who is the "Father of us all," French and American!). If formal criticism by the French "creative writer" and its attendant "anxiety of anticipation" is not in and of the literary work itself before Boileau, it is very much next to it not only then but throughout the last four centuries of French literature: from the Pléiade's *Deffence et illustration de la langue françoise* and Ronsard's own *Art poétique* through Malherbe's *Commentaires sur Desportes* onto Corneille's *Trois Discours* and Racine's *Préfaces*, followed by Voltaire's *Commentaires sur Corneille* and Rousseau's *Lettre a d'Alembert*, onto Stendhal's *Racine et Shakespeare*, Hugo's *Préface de 'Cromwell*,' Baudelaire's art and literary criticism, Flaubert's corresondence through, in this century, Valéry's criticism, Gide's *Journal* and *Journal des 'Faux Monnayeurs*,' Proust's *Contre Sainte-Beuve*, Sartre's *Qu'est-ce que la littérature* and his *Flaubert*, Queneau's contributions to *Histoire des littératures*. These dialectics within and between French writers bid to constitute an intertextual dialogue between "art" and "critique" which converts French Literature into a near synchronous intratextuality. Bloom notwithstanding, there thus occurs far earlier within the French tradition that "achieved dearth of meaning" that he finds "accomplished more powerfully by Wordsworth and Whitman... than by Eliot and Pound." In this connection, it is useful to remember that Bloom's assessment of the French poetic tradition as "weak" is set in the ascendancy of "deconstruction" in contemporary French thought. This very ascendancy emerges, as Bloom sees it, from the absence of a "poetic giant." In this light, the stress in post-structuralist thought on "absence," on logophobia and intertextuality as evidences of an "anxiety of anticipation" only realizes what has been virtual in the French tradition for more than four centuries.

And yet, as I have indicated, before Boileau and after Ronsard or Montaigne or whomever one wishes to posit as the "Founding Critical Father" bequeathing the legacy of anxious anticipation to French Literature, there was and is the *unanxious* Corneille. In Sartrean terms, this is a "Father" (at least of French Classical Tragedy) bequeathing a legacy of possibility/curiosity and variety/novelty. However, that this is not the legacy "transmitted" either by the majority of French scholars (or of *françisants* in their wake elsewhere) is undeniable. It is, rather, the "enRACINated" Corneille of the famous tetralogy whom this scholarship has bequeathed. Sartre (and, later, Doubrovsky) notwithstanding, this Corneille "fits" better into the process of "socialization" or "inscription" to which I alluded in Part I of this essay. The Sartrean Corneille smacks too much not of a "Founding Father" but of a refractory "Founding Son" for a Racinocentric concept of French Classicism designed to "inscribe" a nation's subjects into "good citizenship." This is so, in fact, whether we are talking about the nascent royal nation-state of the France of Richelieu and Mazarin, the embryonic monarchist-Republican or simply Republican nation-states of nineteenth-century and twentieth France or, in my Americanist perspective here, the centrist Constitutional Republic of the United States of America, where, to however limited an extent, "French Classicism" is a staple of curricula interpreting the French tradition.

In this connection, there is a curious philosophical and historical irony: the "existentialist" Corneille is a misinterpreted Corneille. As we have noted, Corneille writes for himself and his audience, representing to them heroes and heroines who become what they are bound to become as they dramatically realize that which is virtual in themselves in relation to their conditions of birth and genius (their *ingenium*—i.e., their "nature"). More appropriate than Hegelian notions of "becoming" or Sartrean concepts of "being-for-itself" and "being-in-itself" is, ironically enough for Corneille-the-critic, the Aristotelian essentialistic notion of "entelechy," the realizaiton of that which is formally virtual. Those who might be thought of as representatives of libidinal or, in Bloom's terms, "primordial" energies—the "people"—hardly exist in Corneille. Such energies are not absent in Corneille, of course, but they are eschatologically linked to the aristocratic ethos of his universe. Unrequited love and inappropriate ambition among the "principal" actors is rare: moral, psychological and political mutuality dictates who loves whom and who allies with whom —kings-queens, princes-princesses, dukes-duchesses, counts-countesses, marquis-marquises, etc. (such that, were there a *un boulanger* in Corneille, he would inevitably fall in love with and marry *une boulangère*). His "heroes" and heroines" are aristocrats and they appeal to an aristocratic audience.

For all the flexibility, ingenuity, openness, assertiveness of these characters (and of their creator as a critic) it is a mistake to read them, anticipatively, as critics themselves of the politically and psychologically constricted universe of Racinian drama. With rare exception (*Suréna*, for example), dramatic "conflict" in Corneille revolves around situational, not characterological impediments (e.g., the famous "tragic flaw") to predetermined destinies. The impediments removed or overcome, the no-longer-impeded characters resume their well-intentioned steps toward these destinies —kingships and marriages, usually. Restored or reaffirmed or, in the case of royal scions, newly-crowned kings and queens, loyal princes and princesses, the gratulatory courtly retinue all con-cele-brate the removal of the impediments that had created "dramatic interest."

The "con-celebratory" aristocratic atmosphere of Cornelian denouements is an index to the oligarchic and, especially, non-revolutionary politics of Corneille's theater: it is the atmosphere of "La Fronde," of a feudal compact of noble peers in which none is "first among equals" in the governance of lands long-held or lands newly available or allied through conquest or marital alliance. Had Corneille been widely accessible academically to pre-Civil War Americans, his expansionist imperialism might well have appealed to them more than the "defeatist" outcome of Racinian drama. Cornelian drama is, usually, an infinitely expanding "West of the mind;" to paraphrase a famous fragment of the *Pensées*, "*beyond* the mountains" (Appalachians, Rockies), there is the same truth as *before* them. Little wonder, then, that Pascal could write: "COMMINUENTES COR, saint Paul: voilà le caractère chrétien. ALBE VOUS A NOMME, JE NE VOUS CONNAIS PLUS, Corneille: voilà le caractère inhumain. Le caractère humain est le contraire" (fr. 499, Sellier edition). Predestination in Corneille is not the harrowingly aleatory and selective supra-human event it is in Pascal; it is stably, universally and thus reassuringly intra-human.

This is the spirit of Cornelian drama in all but a few of the final plays. *Sertorius, Pulchérie* and especially *Suréna* are subliminally Racinian. The aged Corneille seems to have suffered the anxiety of influence in reverse, what might be called a "Laius complex" in which the father fears the son's "castration threat" and thus identifies with his offspring "subliminally" or, in Bloom's optics, "sublimationally" as a way of relieving the anxiety. Yet, this is not too-surprising a Cornelian solution. From Rodrigue who could not rebel against his father to Suréna who cannot fully believe that the "king-father" has betrayed him, all of Corneille's sons are more royalist than the king, more paternalistic than the father. Looking more at the surface structure than the deep-structure of Corneille's famous tetralogy, literary history has cast their maker as the "precursor" of Racine. To have achieved this, scholarship on "French Classicism" need not have truncated the Cornelian to less than an eighth of its length. With respect to the "spectator dynamics" of the royal audience first addressed, Cornelian as well as Racinian dramaturgy is basically a tri-partite structure of pre-dialectical thought: A-B-A, an evenemential dialogue in which an initial situation (usually, the first of the five acts) is conflicted (Acts II-IV) and then restored (Act V). The differences are, of course, in the moral and psychological "lessons" conveyed in the outcomes through the process by which, formalist theoreticians notwithstanding, the average spectator "identifies" with the protagonists. Corneille typically produces an ultimately reassuring pattern which we might represent as (+)-(-)-(+), Racine typically an ultimately disspiriting pattern of (-)-(+)-(-). However, looking at the structure of Corneille's final plays, we have a paradoxical instance of Bloom's ratio of "kenosis," the "emptying of the self." Essentially an author of heroic comedy (or, in his own first rubric for *Le Cid*, "tragi-comédie"), the aged Corneille empties himself of the very aspects of his art which paradigmatically ill-fits him for inscription into a concept of "French Classicism" whose core is Racinian tragedy.

III

Legend has it that, in a conversation between an aged Louis XIV near the end of his long reign as "Le Roi Soleil" and an aged Boileau near the end of his "reign" as "Le Législateur du Parnasse," the latter was asked by his royal interlocutor: "Qui était le plus grand écrivain de mon règne?" The critic is said to have replied unhesitatingly: "Molière." The king is said to have retorted as unhesitatingly: "Tiens, je ne l'aurais pas pensé." The king's instant literary history strikes me as proleptic of the even greater difficulty of situating Molière than Corneille as a figure of the Racinocentric concept of "French Classicism" I have elaborated in Parts I and II of this essay.

The difficulty is especially apparent in the American classroom. In works like this scholarly collection we scholars address each other "horizontally" on the "what" of our subject. In the classroom our address to our students is "vertical:" from the heights of knowledge on which we are perched, we speak "down," hoping that our students will "come up" at least to the levels of knowledge-as-information (and-as-judgment) that their own commitment and abilities will permit. In this pedagogical transaction, the "who" and the "whom" are as important as the "what:" who applies and for whom is the "transmission" of the concept of "French Classicism" being applied? As I indicated in Part I, over three decades now but especially in the past decade or so, in my own classrooms I have been aware of the American diffidence before the fact of language itself which makes the teaching of literature and especially of "Classical" Literature difficult. In this part of my essay, then, the "meta-critical" perspectives in which I shall "rethink French Classicism" are crucially linked to the "pre-critical" perspectives provided by "vertical" transactions with my students. Hoping for a controlling if necessarily limited illustrativeness to my speculations here, I address, as concretely as space allows, three plays: *L'Ecole des femmes*, *Le Tartuffe*, *Le Malade imaginaire*.

With its concision, its clarity, its *vraisemblance* modelled on *la nature*, and its *bienséances* modelled on *le naturel* of *l'honnête homme*, *L'Ecole des femmes* proposes itself as a worthy stone in the vault of a French Classicism as defined, say, by Henri Peyre in a correction of René Bray. Now, this definition would include as well Racine's admittedly less comic strictures on obsessive passion of the kind afflicting Arnolphe and Pascal's incisive exposure of the Arnolphian masks such obsession assumes. Of course, in a Racinocentric conception of "French Classicism," to fit that other major stone of seventeenth-century French Literature, Corneille, into the "Classical Ceiling," that writer's prodigious canon has to undergo the kind of "critical surgery" I reported earlier here. Yet, a restoration of the entire Cornelian canon—"baroque" extravagances and all—suggests a rethinking of the concept of "French Classicism" as "Molierio-centric." With the Molière of *L'Ecole des femmes* as the keystone of the "Classical Ceiling," the "upbeat," tragi-comic Cornelian stone would support one side of the Molierian keystone, the "downbeat," tragic Racinian stone the other side. Of course, in its ultimately comic thrust, the weight of the keystone is thrown more to the Cornelian than to the Racinian side. Nevertheless, is there not enough Racinian sense of "volonté corrompue" in the unreformed Arnolphe to support adequately the other side of the vault?

As for *Le Tartuffe*, along these lines I here adapt from Bénichou's *Morales du grand siècle*, it might be situated in the vault of French Classicism in a "mirror effect:" the part in Molière's hair is on the other side of the head, the Racinian side, as it looks out at us. This tragifying ambivalence would be especially true of what might be called the *ur-Tartuffe*, the three-act version of 1664 which concluded with Tartuffe in full possession not only of Orgon's household (including his daughter prospectively) but of Orgon's soul and even, possibly, of his body. In this connection, I would modify to a certain extent a contention in my article of 1959 on the "Unreconstructed Heroes of Molière." I then maintained that the balletic, festival setting in which the three-act version was first played for the court and not the town gainsays this ominous dénouement. I would now say that the King's presence and his laughter may show *too few* of the players secure from Tartuffe's insidious confidence game. One need not be of "la cabale des dévots" to recognize the tragic frustration of good intentions as represented by every member of Orgon's household except himself and his mother at this point in the action. This being so, the comedy is not so universal as my earlier interpretation implied. Only the King and his playwright are "comically" free and secure. Indeed, from a Marxist perspective, one might well sense in the King's offstage laughter at the end of the three-act version the historically inevitable oppressive power of the mercantilist state in its class struggle with the nascent bourgeoisie represented by Orgon's household. For that matter, this power is less derisively but no less in fact reified in the speech of the Exempt in the definitive version of the play. I suggest this perspective not to enlist Molière, as Goldmann would Pascal, in the historical dialectic leading—presumably—to the eventual withering of the state. Rather, in the

synchronics of something we have come to call French Classicism
along ethical, socio-political and esthetic axes of definition, we see
how Molière-as-keystone would be supporting more the
Racinian/Pascalian side of the vault than the Cornelian. The "happy
ending" of the members of the household restored to each other
might easily be judged as tacked-on, even as that of *L'Ecole des
Femmes* is for many readers of that play who stress the tragic deep
structure of Molière comedy.

And yet... the center will not hold—which is to say that *L'Ecole
des Femmes* and *Le Tartuffe* may not be sturdy enough to hold the
Classical Ceiling in place. Along the very ethical and political
paradigms of French Classicism I have used thus far, one can
stumble over the block of these two plays as one makes one's way
through a French Classicism which has traditionally contained
Corneille, Racine and Molière. For one thing, in *L'Ecole des
Femmes*, the valence binding *la nature* and *le naturel, le vraisemblable* and *les bienséances* differs radically from that of the Racinian
universe.

In the tragic ethos of the Racinian universe (as in much of the
formal theory of the century, starting with the critics of *Le Cid*) *le
vraisemblable* is a dependent of *les bienséances, la nature* of *le
naturel*, the id of the superego. Phèdre's early surrender of her
natural love for Hippolyte to the dictates of conscience (the incest
tabou, marital fidelity, other symbolic proscriptions) is relieved by
chance—the report of her husband's death. But happy chance is out
of place in a tragic universe: Thésée has not died; he returns; Phèdre
learns of Hippolyte's love of Aricie and jealously lets the father
condemn his son; Hippolyte dies; Phèdre repents; she renounces the
vraisemblable in the name of *les bienséances*. More exactly, she
returns to the *bienséances* in whose name she had earlier, hidden
herself—however ambivalently—in the forests in order to escape *la
nature*. Abetted by Oenone's own casuistic linkage of *la nature* and
les bienséances (permitted by the report of Thésée's death), Phèdre
had—erroneously, she finally realizes—assimilated the *bienséances*
into the *vraisemblable* in surrending to her incestuous passion.

In the comic ethos of the Molierian universe, *la nature* and *le
naturel, le vraisemblable* and *les bienséances* are coextensive rather
than hierarchical. Agnès forfends Arnolphe's *bienséances* through
natural wile—a wile born, as Barbara Johnson perceptively shows,
through the very dialectic of *la nature* and *le naturel*. The pattern is
the same in *Le Tartuffe*. *Les bienséances* represented in the
prescriptive and proscriptive codes of Tartuffe are the utter
expression of the symbolic order of the society and they are

suspended by the *vraisemblable* - the likeness to truth - of the King, even as the wily *naturel* represented in the hypocrite's seduction of Elmire is suspended by the King's nature.

The King's likeness to which truth? To God's truth, as I argued in the 1959 article I adduced earlier here. I would now elaborate that conflation of the divine and the kingly by saying that the truth which the King represents is supernatural truth. Still more precisely for my purposes here, the King's truth is SUPER natural—i.e., utterly natural, even as Tartuffe's codes are, as I have said, utterly *séant*, codes of *le naturel* understood as the expression of the society's values. More crucially, the King's super-natural truth is reported as having been exercised prior to and without language (he leaves such "linguification" and legislation to people like L'Exempt). The natural is intra-human (that is, not supernatural in the theological sense) even as *le naturel* is language-bound—which is to say: anything but natural. It is hypocritical, in fact, in the etymological sense of that word: a play-acting, an illusion, a construct. To frustrate the maleficent gaze of language through which Tartuffe looks out on the world, one needs the pre-linguistic beneficent gaze of the super-natural King.

Expressing such a non-linguistics in both *L'Ecole des Femmes* and *Le Tartuffe*, Molière, it seems to me, fits poorly into either Racinian or, for that matter, Cornelian definitions of French Classicism. Like Joyce three centuries later, Corneille is a writer who believes that he can do anything he wants with language—with text in its narrow sense of "words" and "style" as well as in its broader sense of dramaturgical, narratological and other syntagmatic signifying systems. Thus, though Corneille has lots of fun with language, he always takes it seriously. On the other hand, in Bloom's terms, Racine, supposed son of Corneille rising against the father, is like Beckett, supposed son of Joyce. Like the twentieth-century son of the linguistically confident father, the seventeenth-century son of the linguistically confident father (each a superb writer of and on language) lacks the father's faith in language. For Racine and for Beckett, language is all we have—and it is not much.

Molière too, has his doubts about language. The fabric of language through which Tartuffe would order the world proves to be the gauze of language consumed in the pure fire of the super-natural gaze of the Sun King, "un prince dont les yeux se font jour dans les coeurs" (*Le Tartuffe*, V, 7, 1907). In making "raison de tout," the King's nonlinguistic and pre-linguistic power shows the limits of "impudence" to which language can go in Tartuffe's resort to legal tricks and pseudonymity or in the papers Orgon has hidden for his friend. The King's para-linguistic power also shows the instability of language as a ground for truth: it is as easily the instrument of wicked Tartuffe as it is of the good Orgon in the word he has faithfully kept with his friend, author of the rebellious papers, and in the word he has foolishly given to Tartuffe in signing over his worldly goods to him. The King makes it clear that Tartuffe is no better than his word, but words are not good enough to "faire raison de tout".

Obviously, this solution of the play's plot differs from the solution of the plot of *L'Ecole des Femmes*: there chance proves to be destiny, language to be law. Agnès and Horace have been vowed to one another by their fathers and this verbal contract abridges Arnolphe's efforts to evacuate language, as Barbara Johnson shows, by teaching ignorance through language. The solution is intralinguistic in the earlier play, paralinguistic in the later. Nor will Moliere rest with the paralinguistic solution of *Le Tartuffe*. In *Le Malade Imaginaire* the neologistic exuberance of the final "Intermède" suggests that though Molière may have lost faith in paralinguistic guarantees of value, he has not returned to the intralinguistic confidences of *L'Ecole* in his continuing reflections on the status of language.

In the final Intermède of *Le Malade Imaginaire* —his last "act" as a playwright—Molière plays with language in a way suggesting that resistance to language itself which Paul De Man sees at the heart of what he calls the "resistance to theory" in contemporary literary studies. As rhetoric inherently destabilizes grammar for De Man, so in *Le Malade Imaginaire* language inherently destabilizes codifications in language—those of Arnolphe in his "Maximes de mariage," Tartuffe in his catechetical precepts, Argan in his medical prescriptions. Maxims and catechisms and doctor's prescriptions work *and* at the same time do *not* refer to something beyond themselves.

Both dramaturgically and linguistically, the "Troisième Intermède" provides an open closure to Molière's canon. It is actually "inter" something and—nothing. There is no return after it to a post-frame which, like the previous "Interemèdes," returns us to the "real" world of the portions of the act preceding it. In that "real" world, language prioritizes the signified: it performs its role referentially, In the final "Intermède," the interaction is reversed: the signifier is prioritized. The prescriptive function of language which Argan had found in doctor's prescriptions is subsumed into the rhetorical function of language.

In Demanian terms, the dialectical and neologistic instability of language in this final "Intermède" destabilizes not only the signified but the signifier as well:

> Vivat, vivat, vivat, vivat, cent fois vivat
> Novus doctor, qui tam bene parlat!
> Mille, mille annis, et manget et bibat
> Et seignet et tuat!

I translate these very last words of the play as

> Qu'il vive, vive, vive, vive, cent fois vive
> Nouveau docteur, qui tant bien parle
> Mille, mille annees, qu'il mange et boive
> Et saigne et tue!

Or should I translate this very last verse as:"et signe et tue!"? In the text, *seignet* is spelled: s - e - i - g - n - e - t. In the polyglot dialectics and neologistics of the entire third"Intermède," one can thus see and hear two spellings: s - a- i - g -n - e and s - e- i - g - n - e. The first, *saigne* as "that he bleed" or "that he let blood, " is straightforward enough, but the second is less so. It evokes the infinitives of both *signer* and *enseigner*, suggesting a synomy of the two rendered ominous by the conclusion of the verse : "et tuat." To "teach" is to "sign," to "undersign," to "sign on " or to "sign up". The conflation in the text's *seignet* of blood (*saigner*) and sign (*signer*) also suggests that teaching is bleeding. As schol-ars/teachers, we might just wonder whether the act is transitive or intransitive; whose blood is being let and who is doing the bloodletting in the interaction between teacher and student? That is an issue we can meet—or, more likely, moot—in a possible future number of *Continuum* on "rethinking" *this* number.

For now, let us consider the last verse of the play in the setting of the play as a whole. Read as either "bleed" or "sign," this final verse could be seen as returning us to the "lesson" about language in the formal three acts of the play itself. There, too, Molière can be seen to demonstrate that, in its prescriptive and referential use, lnaguage is unreliable, not the stable and subordinate agent we take it to be when we prioritize the signified. Nevertheless, this attack upon language differs from the one in the final "Intemède."

Now, in the "real" world of the formal acts of *Le Malade Imaginaire* Molière attacks faith in language satirically—as he had, for example, in a previous play about medicine, *Le Médecin malgré lui*. Satire is essentially reformist in nature, it presupposes a stable signified from which that which is being satirized has strayed and to which the satire will restore the universe of the play. But in the polyvalent last verse of *Le Malade Imaginaire* (as in the whole last "Intermède," in fact) rhetorical uncertainty is extended not only to the profession of medicine but also to the profession of signing in each of the senses allowed by the bivalence I have found in "seignet." Rhetorical uncertainty attaches to "signing" as the pedagogical enterprises of satire or of institutionalized teaching; it also attaches to that "signing" which is writing itself—the writing of this verse, for example, or, more broadly, of this "Intermède" which is a "play within a play," perhaps the most "writerly" expression of dramatic writing. Form calls attention to form here with an utterness emphasizing the dubiety of making differences between the "real" world of the formal acts of the play, on the one hand, and, on the other, the "illusory" world of all three "intermèdes" in the play. The last "Intermède" in particular insists on this dubious difference: in the "real" world of the third Act, at whose end Béralde invites all to join in the final "Intermède," Argan is no more "real" a doctor than he is in the "Intermède" itself. In each world it is only a matter of putting on an "habit", of being certified through conventional signs. Is, then, the art of the last "Intermède" true to life, as true as life? Or is it as untrue as life, suggesting that signing in art (that is, the writing of texts of art) kills as surely as prescribing in medicine (that is, the writing of prescriptions)?

A Romantic interpretation of this final moment of Molière's canon might see Molière as telling us that writing may indeed kill, but that Molière's art cannot be limited to his writing. The play does not actually end with the verse, "Et seignet et tuat!" It actually ends with a

Quatrième Entrée de Ballet

Les médecins, les chirurgiens et les apothicaires sortent tous, selon leur rang, en cérémonie, comme ils sont entrés.

The fourth ballet is not only still another intercalated structure—a play within a play within a play—it also turns on itself in its very form, suggesting a kinesthetic circle, or in dance terms, a "round." It is, then, in this final "act"—really "action"—that we are to look for the meaning of the play. This romantic hypothesis sems to me to raise the same problems as my attention to the play's language.

In John T. Irwin's terms, is Molière showing the superior communicative power of the "pictographic" over the "phonetic"— the phonetic being verbal language in either spoken or written form? If the last ballet of the play is a pictograph, what does it depict ? Is it the priority of the art of dance over the art of words? Even in this light, do we not remain within a frame of reference in which the choices remain rhetorical? If the last ballet is a "round"—a circular form—can we forget what the kinetic round of the form contains— the verse ending with "Et seignet et tuat!"? Does, then, the whole round of the ballet comport the priority of the esthetic over the satiric? But this interpretation only returns us to the interaction of the non-verbal signifiers—the medical corps doing the dancing— and the signified of the dance they perform. The dancers are "real" doctors from the "real" world of the formal acts of the play. Is Molière then telling us that non-verbal forms of the art are more reliable signifiers for conveying the satiric message of his play, that "literature" is subordinate to "theater" in dramatic art in depicting the "signifed" of the "real" world? But then how reliable, how stable as signifer is "theater"? A given play or dance varies, in its rhetorical terms, from one performance to the next at least as much as any given word or text of words. Yet, more pertinent to my inquiry here is that, wherever we locate the greater stability—in verbal language or non-verbal gesture—we are still debating an unstable relation between two signifying systems pointing primarily at themselves and at each other. The shaping power of language, Molière tells us in the last act of his canon, leads neither to the infinitely reconstructive confidence in word and self informing the Cornelian universe nor to the deconstructive despair of word and self de- forming the Racinian universe. It leads to the instructive skeptical self-reflexivity of the speaking being—the "parle être" of Lacanian discours who can "be" only "par lettre."

"Self-reflexivity" is, of course, a very "American" notion. However, in its American expression, the notion is practiced more by the "parle" than by the "lettre." Indeed, American suspicion of the well-spoken is almost as great as it is of the written, well-done or not. It is, then, as my fellow contributors can testify, hard enough talking to American students about Molière, not to speak of attempting to present him to them as a representative of something called "French Classicism." In this connection, however, I advise my readers that it is not my intention here to echo former Secretary of Education Bennett and other recent critics of the contemporary educational scene in their lament about the flight from basics which has brought us to the pass in which "Classicisms" of any kind are unknown to today's students. Again, it is not my intention to bewail here the influence of television, film, rock music, Reaganian affluence or, more closely, to our curricualr concerns, the student flight from French Studies to colleges of Business Administration and, even more closely, to options in Commerical French Studies within French Departments like my own. The "ignorance" of the Classics and thus of configurations like "French Classicism" seems to me to be paradigmatically located deeper in the American structure than such laments suggest. It seems to me to be located in an American "resistance to language"—a suspicion of language in spoken or wrtten form that John T. Irwin has discerned in the luminous book to which I have already alluded, *American Hieroglyphics*, his study of the impact of Champollion's deciphering of the Egyptian hieroglyphics on major writers of the American Renaissance. Subsuming, as I indicated earler, both speech and writing under the rubric of the "phonetic," Irwin illustrates a paradigmatic American tropism to the "pictographic" - to the unspoken and unwritten - and a rejection of the "phonetic." Springing off Irwin's penetrating study here, I can only stress the problem of trying to make American readers of any age deal with a literature so resolutely "phonetic" as the literature of French Classicism.

It also seems relevant to me that the literature is deeply rooted in a religious culture, Catholicism, which, in spite of the syndrome of the "melting pot," is still very much at odds with the Protestant heritage of American culture with its paradigmatic suspicion of "mediating" structures, be they ecclesiastical, social, political or linguistic. (There is, to be sure, an "American Catholicism," nominally making up a quarter of the citizenry, but it is conservative, "fundamentalistically" so, it seems to me, in almost Jansenistic terms). More than six decades ago, in the "Foreword" to his *Studies in Classic American Literature*, D. H. Lawrence posited that "the furthest frenzies of French modernism or futurism have not yet reached the pitch of extreme consciousness that Poe, Melville, Hawthorne, Whitman reached." In "The Spirit of Place," the first chapter of the book, the English novelist posited a religious base for the intensely self-conscious "freedom" which he saw as the great theme of American Literature: "men are free when they are obeying some deep, *inward* voice of religious belief" (my emphasis). Believing that Americans had not yet "discovered America and their own wholeness" because they were still "chained " to "old things," he went on to say:

> Which will win in America, the escaped slaves, or the new whole men? The real American day hasn't begun yet. Or at least, not yet sunrise. So far it has been the false dawn. That is, in the progressive American consciousness there has been the one dominant desire, to do away with the old thing. Do away

with masters, exalt the will of the people. The will of the people being nothing but a figment, the exalting doesn't count for much. So, in the name of the will of the people, get rid of the masters. When you have got rid of masters, you are left with this phrase of the will of he people. Then you pause and bethink yourself, and try to recover your wholeness. So much for the conscious American motive, and for democracy over here. Democracy in America is just the tool with which the old mastery of Europe, the European spirit, is undermined. Europe destroyed, potentially, American democracy will evaporate. America will begin.

"Destroy...undermine... do away with... get rid of the masters"— the Lawrentian and Protestant ground of American culture hardly a fertile one in which to (im)plant the masters of a "French Classicism" whose "freedom" E. B. O. Borgerhoff sees as a kind of balancing act between conscience (social or individual) and consciousness. What then to make of, how to "situate" not only a particular writer within French Classicism, but how to transmit to Americans a Classicism which itself "mediates" an earlier Classicism?

It woud require at least another volume like this one for us to explore this bi-cultural tension. Here, I can only suggest that, foregrounding the problematic of language through which I have "de-situated" Molière within French Classicism, we might begin "teaching French Classicism" not as a coherent moment but as a fractionated and fractious moment of French literary history. And where better to begin than with Molière for students who are themselves paradigmatically fractionated and fractious before the fact of language? For them, at least, and perhaps for us finally, Molière might best serve as the "lodestone" of that cluster of writers whom French literary history has called "les grands classiques." Molière is a magnet in ways that, I suspect, would lend even more ironic force to Boileau's reply to his royal interlocutor's question and even greater surprise to that interlocutor's reaction to the reply in their legendary colloquy near the end of their lives.

IV

As much scholarship (some of it my own) has demonstrated, the Racinocentric model of "French Classicism" from which I have dissociated Corneille and Molière in the preceding pages might as easily be described as a "Pascalocentric" model. There are, to be sure, Pascal's disclaimer in *Les Lettres provinciales* ("je ne suis pas stronghold (where he had been raised) at least in his "pagan" plays (the occasion of his quarrel with Nicole about the morality of the theater). However, theologically as well as biographically, as especially Goldmann has maintained, each has a "Jansenist" outlook. Yet, even within this "Pascalo-Racinocentric" model, the separate textualizations of the model pose problems of definition as disturbing as those posed by the traditional inscriptions of Corneille and Molière into the model. With respect to the Pascal canon, the inscription has been, as in the case of the Corneille canon, at the expense of a significant truncation: the "Classical" hallmark has been imprinted onto the *Pensées* transmitted in their entirety (in whatever "edition"), while *Les Lettres provinciales*, like certain shorter writings, are either "etched out" of the canon altogether or reduced to an emblematic few (usually, in curricular offerings, the fifth and seventh letters). The ironies are enormous here on various counts.

It is a commonplace in the teaching of "French Literature" to say that, in *Les Lettres provinciales*, Pascal "founds modern French prose." That prose is thus understood to have, in the context of persuasively well-organized "essayistic" texts, the virtues of clarity, concision, sobriety and purity—no mistaking, presumably, the denominative rapport between "signifier" and "signified." This description of Pascal's provocative letters is, of course, that which has been more broadly assigned by literary history to "French Classicism." However, that this description is, on the whole, not that of the *Pensées* is obvious. In that work, perhaps only "concision" survives as "Classical" hallmark, but its communicative function in a near-chaotic "con-text" of assaultive fragments designed as much (if not more) to obscure than to clarify suggests how little "Classical" even this stylistic trait is.

Certainly, within the framework of the texts of those writers whom I earlier described as "infrastructurally" classical, the *Pensées*, rhetorically to begin with, makes for a poor "fit." The cool if cruel *Maximes* of La Rochefoucauld, with their syntactic elegance and epigrammatic equilibrium; the ponderous geometricity (as in "esprit de géométrie") of Bossuet's sermons; the narrative cohesion of La Bruyère's *Caractères* —none of these is "Pascalian." As for La Fontaine and Boileau, Pascal is too suspicious of poetry (as we know from the eleventh *Lettre*) for a direct contrast on generic grounds. However, assuming some "apologetic" intention for the *Pensées* (in, again, whatever "edition"), does not Pascal's masterwork in its very public address (of the kind *Les Lettres* represents as well) violate that "separation of powers" (religious and artistic, in this instance) which is a key tenet of *L'Art poétique* and which earned the Corneille of *Polyeucte* the great critic's reproach?

"Rhetorically to begin with," I noted in setting up these distinctions between Pascal and the infrastructural classical cohort. Yet, the "beginning" of these "signifiers" has fundamental implications for the "signifieds" not only in this cohort but in the Classical writers of "belles lettres," including Racine. As I indicated earlier, Racine's confidence before the fact of language is nowhere so great as that of Corneille. Nevertheless, Racine has at least the confidence that it is through language that he will signify the tragic frustrations of language. In his assault on language in the *Pensées*, Pascal signifies that tragedy as being **beyond** language. The fragmentedness of the *Pensées* is a fragmenting of language, an assault on the reader's confidence in language (including Pascal as reader of his own text, as the fragment on "ecrivant ma pensée," Sellier fr. 540, linked to that on "L'écoulement," Sellier fr. 625, shows). *Les Pensées* records the fall not only **into** language, as Sara Melzer puts it in her *Discourses of the Fall*, but through and out of language. As I argued in my *Pascal: Adversary and Advocate*, Pascal's masterwork shows not a "Classically" integrated architecture but an "*anarchi*-tecture," the appropriate composition of the lesson it seeks to re-present.

Extending that interpretation here, I would say that editions of the fragments which do not preserve juxtapostions of the different "styles" (the"apodictic" or "geometrical" and the "aporetic" or "fin," as I discussed them in my book) misread the lesson about language both by and within the disorder of Pascal's own language. For example, an editor's presumption that, had Pascal "finished" the projected *Apologie*, he would have "revised" in the direction of the apodixis of *Les Lettres provinciales* is a misunderstanding. Similarly, the contrary presumption—admittedly less likely to be made in view of an inherent tendency of editors to "rationalize" the text—is a misunderstanding: that Pascal would have "revised" in the direction of the aporesis so widely found in the fragments (and considered by Louis Marin and others as paradigmatic). The inherently unstable combination of syntaxis and asyntaxis, of apodixis and aporesis, of sentence and ellipsis is, rhetorically, *the* "rhetorical mode" paradigmatically enfiguring the inherent instability of the human condition before the *Deus absconditus*. The *Pensées* is a work which dictates an "arrangement" of its parts as necessarily a "dis-arrangement." To ignore that disarrangement is to refuse the lesson of moral and psychological disarray that the work is designed to drive home: in that disarray, the reader has the best chance, God willing, to concede to "abêtissement" as a "state of being" which is a state of "being without language"—such that, again (given Pascal's theological exactitude) *God willing*, grace can be received. The lesson is hardly "Classical." Indeed, in terms of the economic metaphor with which I began this essay, it is the "Great Crash" of the "Market" of "French Classicism."

V

I have, then, "rethought" the Racinocentric concept of "French Classicism" without Corneille, without Molière and without Pascal. I have been guided by a compulsion within French culture since the eighteenth century to define the literature of the second half of the preceding century as "Classical," with Racine posited as the emblematic "grand Classique." Along political, economic and psychoanalytical axes which might well be the subject of still another essay of this length, I have here only hinted at possible grounds for these choices. Why, indeed, has almost every major French "creator-critic" from Voltaire to Roland Barthes felt compelled to inscribe Racine into his or her usually very different theory and practice? It seems to me that such "extra-literary" perspectives should themselves be subjected to the test of language which has been my chief concern here.

In conducting that test on key texts of "French Classicism" itself, I have concentrated on linguistic and cultural parameters of the concept as it brings its language and culture into the language and culture which I and my "concitoyens et concitoyennes," especially students, bring to it. Both practically and theoretically, to particularize the problematic in this way seems to me to be advantageous to each of the languages and cultures on the ground that particular "cases" test general "laws." To draw on American institutions one last time in concluding here, the "decisions" in this "case" depend, of course, on the compostion of the "Court:" "strict Constitutionalists" will read my "brief" one way, "loose Constructionists" another. My "appeal" has obviously been addressed to the latter. In conclusion, I offer them one final case for their docket: in "rethinking French clasicism" along the Racinocentric lines on which I have "made my case," is it unthinkable to wonder if Racine is as "Racinocentric" as literary history has made him? What of such Racinian "romantic dramas" as *Alexandre Le Grand, Andromaque, Mithridate, Esther*?

*My title echoes one I used for an earlier essay on the subject: "Modern Criticism of French Classicism: Dimensions of Definition." As with work on the subject by other scholars and critics which I evoke here, bibliographical detail is to be found in the section, "Works Cited," at the end of this essay. That section serves at once as the source of quotations from specific commentators as well as of postions of other commentators to whom I refer. Moreover, except for Pascal for whom the status of the test is so much at issue, I have assumed that my readers know my "source" and, thus, I have not provided bibliographichal reference for the works of "Les Grands Classiques." In addition, there are no footnotes, annotative or expository. I trust that these procedures enable my reader to attend as undistractedly as possible to the text of my essay itself.

Works Cited

Bénichou, Paul. *Morales du Grand Siècle*. Paris: Gallimard, 1948.
Bloom, Harold. "The Breaking of Form." Ed. Harold Bloom, Paul De Man, Jacques Derrida, Geoffrey H. Hartman, J. Hillis Miller. *Deconstruction and Criticism*. New York: The Seabury Press, 1979.
Borgerhoff, E. B. O. *The Freedom of French Classicism*. Princeton: Princeton University Press, 1950.
Bray, René. *La Formation de la doctrine classique en France*. Paris: Hachette, 1927.
Caillois, Roger. "Un Roman cornélien." *Nouvelle Revue Francaise* I (1938): 477-482.
Cather, Willa. *The World and the Parish: Willa Cather's Articles and Reviews, 1893-1903*. Ed William M. Curtin. Lincoln: U of Nebraska P, 1973.
DeJean, Joan. *Libertine Strategies*. Columbus: Ohio State UP, 1981.
DeMan, Paul. "Resistance to Theory." *Yale French Studies* 63 (1982): 3-20.
Doubrovsky, Serge. *Corneille ou la dialectique du héros*. Paris: Gallimard, 1963.
Godfrey, Sima. "The Anxiety of Anticipation: Ulterior Motives in French Poetry." *Yale French Studies* 66 (1984). 1-26.
Goldmann, Lucien. *Le Dieu caché: étude sur la vision tragique dans les Pensées de Pascal et dans le théâtre de Racine*. Paris: Gallimard, 1959.
Johnson, Barbara. "Teaching Ignorance: L'Ecole des femmes." *Yale French Studies* 63 (1982). 165-82.
Lawrence, D. H. *Studies in Classic American Literature*. New York: Viking Press, 1923. Rpt. Anchor Books. Garden City, N. Y.: Doubleday, 1953.
Marin, Louis. *La Critique du discours: sur la Logique de Port Royal et les Pensées de Pascal*. Paris: Minuit, 1975.
May, Georges. *Tragédie cornélienne, tragédie racinienne: étude sur les sources de l'intérêt dramatique*. Urbana: U of Illinois P, 1948.
Melzer, Sara E. *Discourses of the Fall: A Study of Pascal*. Berkeley: U of California P, 1986.
Nadal, Octave. *Le Sentiment de l'amour dans l'œuvre de Pierre Corneille*. Paris: Gallimard, 1948.
Nelson, Robert J, ed. . *Corneille and Racine: Parallels and Contrasts*. Englewood Cliffs, N.J..: Prentice-Hall, 1966. Contains portions of Sartre entry, below.
—. "Night unto Day unto Night: Racinian Tragedy." *La Cohérence intérieure*. Ed. Jacqueline Van Baelen and David Lee Rubin. Paris: J.-M. Place, 1977. 95-112.
—. *Pascal: Adversary and Advocate*. Cambridge: Harvard UP, 1981.

—. "The Unreconstructed Heroes of Molière." *Tulane Drama Review* 4(1960): 14-37. Rpt. in *Molière: A Collection of Critical Essays.* Ed. Jacques Guicharnaud. Englewood Cliffs, N. J.: 1964. 111-35.

—. *Willa Cather and France: In Search of the Lost Language.* Urbana: U of Illinois P, 1988. Contains extensive comment on Cather entry, above.

Pascal, Blaise. *Pensées: nouvelle édition établie pour la première fois d'après la copie de référence de Gilberte Pascal.* Ed. Philippe Sellier. Paris: Mercure de France, 1976.

Peyre, Henri. *Qu'est-ce que le classicisme?* . Ed. rev. et augmentée. Paris: Nizet, 1965.

Sartre, Jean-Paul. "Forgers of Myths: The Young Playwrights of France." *Theater Arts* 30 (1946). 324-335.

Stendhal. *Racine et Shakespeare.* Ed. Bernard Drenner. Paris: J.-J. Pauvert, 1965.

Voltaire. *Commentaires sur Corneille. Œuvres Complètes.* Ed. Louis Moland. Paris: Garnier, 1885-1887.

Les Classicismes:
les mots et les choses

Alain Niderst
Université de Rouen

Classique est un mot, qui comme tous les mots, renvoie à une réalité. Ou, si l'on préfère, un signifiant qui a son signifié (ou ses signifiés). Cela est évident, et il est également évident que les rapports du signifant et du signifié sont pour ce mot particulièrement complexes. Les Romantiques se sont voulus romantiques et ont produit des manifestes pour expliquer ce qu'ils entendaient par là; il ne reste plus qu'à comparer leurs théories et leurs pratiques, à suivre les ruptures et les réconciliations des unes et des autres; les poètes de 1865 se sont voulus parnassiens; des romanciers se sont prétendus naturalistes, et d'autres poètes symbolistes ou romans. Même les précieuses ont proclamé qu'elles étaient précieuses. Personne n'a jamais osé se dire "classique." Ni "baroque " peut-être? Mais le mot (sinon la réalité) baroque est finalement bien moins compliqué, situé dans moins de domaines différents, que le classicisme.

Le plus simple est d'étudier successivement le mot et l'histoire, ce qu'on a voulu dire et quelles réalités ont pu souffrir ce discours.

I

Pour étudier le mot, il est des dictionnaires, des gloses, des essais. Comme l'a expliqué Pierre Moreau (1-8), le *classique* latin, qui signifiait "excellent", ou, selon la définition de Richelet, digne "d'être pris pour modèle", s'est marié avec le *classique* bas-latin, qui signifiait "scolaire" ou "adapté à des classes d'écoliers". Mariage qui n'était guère naturel, car le *classique* scolaire n'était pas trop éloigné du "pédant." A quoi s'est venu ajouter le *classique* anglo-allemand, qui signifie "antique".

En *classique* se découvrent donc trois orientations. L'une purement normative: est *classique* ce qui mérite l'admiration et l'imitation. La seconde pédagogique : un texte est *classique*, s'il convient à l'enseignement. La troisième historique : *classique* est synonyme de grec ou gréco-romain.

La fusion en un mot de ces significations différentes suppose trois postulats:

1. Il existe entre les écrivains une échelle incontestable. Il en est de bons, de médiocres, d'exécrables.
2. Les meilleurs écrivains doivent être présentés et expliqués aux écoliers.
3. Ces écrivains, qui sont à la fois les meilleurs et les plus utiles aux enfants, sont les auteurs antiques.

Toutes ces affirmations sont évidemment discutables, et même arbitraires. Elles supposent une philosophie très particulière de l'histoire et de la beauté. L'histoire ne semble qu'une dégradation progressive de l'Idéal, qui s'est incarné au temps de Périclès. La Beauté est évidente; elle s'impose à tous, même aux enfants et aux adolescents, qui ont besoin de cette délectable nourriture.

Cette philosophie a trouvé sa forme définitive en accueillant d'autres notions qui la complètent. Les écrivains classiques n'auront pas seulement le plus beau talent; ils manifesteront aussi les plus grandes qualités morales et intellectuelles. Dans leurs œuvres, le Beau, le Bon et le Vrai se trouvent réunis, comme dans le système de Victor Cousin. On admettra, d'autre part, l'existence d'un classicisme italien, anglais, espagnol. On en vient ainsi à l'école de 1660, qui offrira à la France des modèles aussi prestigieux qu'Homère et Virgile chez les anciens, et, dans les autres nations modernes, Shakespeare, Dante, et Cervantès. En étudiant les anciens et ces grands modernes, l'enfant s'abreuvera aux sources éternellement pures de l'intelligence, de l'harmonie et de la morale.

Cette conception, nourrie de postulats et d'inductions hâtives, ne va pas sans contradiction. Shakespeare est classique, puisque les Anglais l'admirent et l'imitent, mais, en France, ce sont les Romantiques qui se réclament de lui, et l'on exalte les classiques du XVIIe siècle contre Dumas, Hugo et aussi Shakespeare. C'est-à-dire que les sources mêlées, où le mot *classique* a pris sa naissance, ne se sont pas parfaitement fondues, que la synthèse éclate par moments et découvre des apories.

En France, c'est l'époque des *Causeries du lundi*, et le classicisme de Sainte-Beuve, avec sa volonté de rabaisser le drame et le lyrisme de 1830, son effort pour accorder les valeurs esthétiques, les valeurs morales et les valeurs intellectuelles, sa prudente acceptation d'un très partiel renouvellement des formes et des idées, n'est évidemment qu'une projection de la politique: haïssant le républicanisme et le socialisme auxquels peuvent céder les Romantiques, refusant l'implacable réaction des ultras, le centre-droit se veut à la fois conservateur et presque tolérant. Il sait ce qui est le mieux—Boileau, Racine, parfois Corneille. Il ne refuse pas totalement l'histoire, et accepte quelques mutations, sûr qu'elles ne pourront s'imposer qu'en rejoignant les éternels principes de la Vérité et de la Beauté.

Vers 1920, Gide, Valéry et leurs émules promurent un néo-classicisme, dont l'idéologie et les buts n'étaient pas tellement éloignés de ce qu'on avait vu au XIXe siècle. Qu'est-ce que *La Porte étroite*, sinon une réécriture un peu modernisée de *La Princesse de Clèves*? Qu'est-ce que *La Jeune Parque*, sinon une imitation, proche parfois du centon, de *l'Adonis* de La Fontaine, et de quelques grandes tirades de Racine? Il n'est pas certain que ces pastiches aient toujours été heureux. Le néo-classicisme est ce qu'il y a de plus éloigné du classicisme, et *La Porte étroite*, et *La Jeune Parque*, avec leurs archaïsmes, leur pompe, leurs palimpsestes, peuvent être regardées comme des œuvres alexandrines ou rococo, en tout cas comme des exercices décadents.

Mais l'esthétique de Gide et de Valéry reproduit, dans une forme hautaine, voire épigrammatique, celle de la Monarchie de Juillet. La pure beauté suppose des règles, la contrainte, la domination de la spontanéité. Le classicisme succède au romantisme et le dompte. Il chérit la litote au lieu de l'hyperbole, et nous émeut d'autant plus qu'il est plus discret et plus modeste (Gide 37-40). Le message philosophique ou moral n'est pas oublié. Même si la morale de Ménalque est plus hardie que celle de La Fontaine. C'est à de grandes vérités éternelles, ou à de graves problèmes éternellement insolubles, que l'œuvre, parfaite dans sa discrétion, difficile et pourtant accessible aux plus studieux des adolescents, doit nous conduire. Conservatisme assoupli, comme celui de la Restauration. C'est celui des "ralliés", ainsi que l'écrivait Sartre dans un article célèbre. La haute-bourgeoisie admet la république; elle élève la morale et les lois artistiques comme une digue devant les innovations qu'acceptent les radicaux, et que souhaite la Gauche. La démarche est toutefois plus subtile qu'au siècle précédent. On commence par le nihilisme: tout est fini, tout est ruines; dans cette universelle déperdition, pourquoi ne pas se fier à des œuvres, dont les conventions s'accommodent si bien avec le désespoir? Il en sera de même en morale et en politique. Les règles, qui se justifiaient jadis par une volonté de réalisme, sont maintenant fondées sur le renoncement à tout réalisme. Les formes classiques deviennent les principes d'un jeu qui frôle l'absurdité totale, et ne suppose, au fond, qu'un conservatisme désolé.

L'essentiel demeure: condamner le drame et le lyrisme romantiques. On procèdera avec adresse. On ira jusqu'à saluer le classicisme de Baudelaire, et même les splendides cataractes des derniers grands poèmes de Victor Hugo (Valéry, "Situation de Baudelaire" et "Victor Hugo créateur par la forme").

Le grand artiste est celui qui achève ce que les autres ont entrepris, et souvent raté. Mais comme les hommes mûrs renoncent aux folles espérances de leur jeunesse, les arts, dans leur maturité, renoncent aux audaces intempérantes, et reviennet au Temple, toujours overt, où Ingres et Poussin, Racine et Homère, les attendent avec un sourire bienveillant mais un peu ironique. Celui que les parents, dans les romans bourgeois des années 1930, réservent aux enfants prodigues, qui, après avoir couru le monde ou connu la débauche, acceptaient de reprendre la fabrique fondée par leurs ancêtres.

Ce sourire désabusé, c'est le classicisme même, et il s'agit avant tout de nier l'histoire. Aucune prévision n'y est possible et aucune intentionnalité, surtout aucun progrès, ne s'y découvre. Et, comme en esthétique et en morale l'universelle facticité étaie les conventions et leur assure une sorte de survie, le noir tourbillon de l'histoire sauve le passé et suggère, malgré tout, une irrémédiable décadence.

L'histoire du mot *classique*, de la doctrine *classique*, n'est, au fond, qu'une histoire politique. On a l'impression que les œuvres, antiques ou louis-quatorziennes, sont à peine lues (ce qui suscitera plaisamment *Le Romantisme des Classiques* et *Le Classicisme des Romantiques*). On chercherait en vain les œuvres judicieuses et raffinées qu'invoque Valéry. Nous sommes en plein idéalisme. Il convient donc de retourner vers le réel et de chercher le classicisme dans les faits, au lieu d'inventer des faits pour étayer une théorie.

II

En réintroduisant le réel, on réintroduit l'histoire—ou plutôt les histoires. Le classicisme n'est plus une réalité fondamentale, qui parvient presque à se passer de preuves ; il est un mot fait, comme tous les mots, pour accélérer un peu le raisonnement, concentrer des similitudes qu'on a observées.

Assurément l'histoire n'est pas innocente. D'ailleurs, nous avons dit les histoires. Tout dépend de ce qu'on cherche dans le passé.

Si l'on tente une histoire générale de l'art, ou plutôt de l'esthétique, on peut selon la tradition germanique ou anglaise, appeler classique ce qui est grec. C'est le choix de Hegel.

Si l'on se limite à une histoire des arts plastiques,on peut appeler classique ce qui fut produit au temps de la Renaissance, en somme entre 1480 et 1580. C'est le choix de Wölfflin. Dans une histoire de la littérature, le classicisme est le style des grandes écrivains du régne de Louis XIV. C'est évidemment ce que veulent les Francais, et surtout les universitaires.

Hegel appelle l'art primitif ou oriental *art symbolique*, l'art grec *art classique*, l'art chrétien *art romantique*. Les termes choisis assurent évidemment le glissement de l'histoire à la philosophie, ou plutôt affichent la fusion du réel et du rationnel.

L'Idée, qui pour apparaître doit, dans l'art symbolique, broyer et mutiler le réel, et produit ainsi tous les colosses et les monstres de Crète, d'Egypte et de Chaldée, va dans l'art romantique, refuser la matière, et, comme il n'est pas possible de s'en passer, la refuser en jouant avec elle et en disant à travers ce jeu la subjectivité et la souveraine liberté de l'artiste. Au-delà du symbolisme, en decà du romantisme, se dresse l'art classique, insuffisant comme pensée, mais parfait comme art, puisque la matière et l'idée sont intimement fondues. Les beaux corps que cisèle le statuaire, sont l'incarnation même, parfaitement plausible et parfaitememt signifiante, de l'Amour, de la Force, de la Puissance.

Hegel semble donc partir des chefs d'œuvre des musées, et très vite accéder au développement rationnel, qui les englobe et les justifie. Après tout, il est plus proche du réel que les idéalistes français de la Restauration et de la Troisième République. Il décrit bien la surhumaine sérénité des statues grecques et les complications alexandrines, qui doivent succéder aux harmonies classiques. Comment nier qu'en passant des monstres érotiques de l'Orient à Vénus, on passe d'un amour qui cherche son incarnation, à un amour qui l'a trouvée, et quand on quitte les éphèbes et les belles femmes de Phidias, n'accède-t-on pas bientôt à des sophistications fleuries, avant d'atteindre les emblèmes modernes de l'amour qui échappent difficilement aux nostalgies et aux allégresses personnelles de l'artiste?

L'esthétique de Hegel est aussi adaptée au réel qu'il était possible en son temps. On sait maintenant que le marbre des temples grecs était badigeonné d'ocre et d'azur, et que les statues, avec leurs violentes couleurs, étaient peut-être plus terrifiantes que belles, et plus proches de l'expressionnisme baroque que de la sérénité classique. Mais ces objections ne sont pas les plus fortes. L'esthétique de Hegel nous conduit trop vite du concret à l'idéal. Elle n'explique pas assez comment les sculptures d'Athènes ont incarné l'idéal. On cherche—à un niveau qui serait proprement celui de l'esthétique, et non immédiatement de la métaphysique—les principes qui assurent la fusion de l'Idée et de la Matière. La sculpture est peut-être l'art essentiel du classicisme, mais, s'il y eut une peinture et une littérature grecques, s'il y eut, de toute facon, des peintres et des poètes qui se voulurent classiques, on ne peut les analyser et les apprécier qu'en dégageant et en transférant à d'autres arts les principes grâce auxquels les sculpteurs antiques parvinrent à la perfection. Synthèse richement informée et admirablement rigoureuse. Vraie donc, mais rapide, et qui laisse des blancs entre le réel et le rationnel.

La démonstration de Wölfflin est étayée d'une foule d'exemples, et au lieu de nous porter des chefs d'œuvres aux idées, elle met systématiquement en évidence les procédés et les méthodes classiques, qui ne se peuvent définir qu'en superposant et en confrontant les réalisations des artistes.

Cette fois, ce sont les arts plastiques entre 1480 et 1580 qui ont incarné le classicisme. Si l'on confronte *La Pêche miraculeuse* de Raphaël et celle de Van Dyck, une femme nue de Dürer et une femme nue de Rembrandt, une princesse de Bronzino et une infante de Vélasquez, on discerne cinq domaines où l'art classique et l'art baroque sont opposés.

L'art classique est linéaire, et l'art baroque pictural. L'un procède en juxtaposant des plans parallèles, l'autre en créant par les obliques une profondeur. L'un cherche une clarté totale, l'autre se contente d'une clarté partielle. La forme, chez l'un, est fermée, chez l'autre, ouverte. L'unité classique résulte d'un ensemble, et la multiplicité préexiste, l'unité baroque est immédiate.

Ce qui signifie, en tout cas, que le classicisme est intellectualiste, analytique, et foncièrement optimiste: il est persuadé que le réel, s'il est limité à un aperçu précis et parfaitememt éclairé (le reste étant nié ou laissé dans l'ombre), s'il est décomposé en éléments distincts, que la ligne isole nettement, est accessible, à l'intelligence. Négligeant les ombres et les reflets, les déformations que le soleil et la distance imposent aux objets, l'artiste classique représente le réel tel qu'il est. L'espace est discontinu comme le temps. L'harmonie générale suppose la coïncidence de l'esprit et de la matière. Coïncidence fondamentalement théologique, car il faut que la même lumière divine illumine l'esprit humain et organise la matière, et que les mêmes mathématiques règnent dans notre intelligence et dans le réel. L'homme baroque ne sait plus. Fils de Montaigne, il voit crouler toutes les organisations et toutes les connaissances. Il sait que ses aperçus sont incomplets, et mangés d'ombre et d'illusion. Il va vers des totalités immédiates, sans passer par la décomposition intellectuelle et sans parvenir à la recomposition intellectuelle. Il dit, comme Shakespeare, qu'il y a plus de choses dans le monde que dans toute notre philosophie, et qu'on ne peut représenter que des aspects. Le scepticisme et l'empirisme ont donc succédé aux sereines certitudes de l'âge précédent. La physique aux mathématiques, les expériences aux perspectives, et un Dieu de surprise et d'effroi à un Dieu d'ordre et de lumière.

Beau système appuyé de maints exemples convaincants et finalement en accord avec l'histoire de l'esprit européen au XVIe et au XVIIe siècles. Il demeure difficile, mais peut-être pas impossible, d'appliquer ces principes à la littérature. Ils sont, en tout cas, bien plus tangibles que la sublime métaphysique hégelienne. Encore que quelque flottement dans la chronologie se découvre, et que Poussin, au XVIIe siècle, nous paraisse assurément un classique, ayant des procédés plus proches de Raphaël que de Rubens ou de Guido Reni.

Les analystes de notre littérature du XVIIe siècle sont plus décevants. Ils savent assurément nuancer ou même renouveler l'interprétation traditionnelle de la doctrine de Boileau, montrer qu'elle était plus originale et plus cohérente qu'on ne le pensait d'ordinaire (Brody *passim*), et que le satiriste et les grands auteurs du règne de Louis XIV montrèrent une audace, une liberté, qui compte peut-être davantage que la soumission aux règles (Borgerhoff *passim*). Mais ces remarques restent partielles. Elles ne débouchent pas sur une théorie du classicisme francais. Comment généraliser? Y eut-il une école, un groupe cohérent? Personne ne croit plus que les quatre amis de *Psyché* aient été La Fontaine, Racine, Molière et Boileau. Cette belle tétrade, que le ciel nous aurait envoyée pour nous enseigner les chemins du bon sens et de la vraie beauté, n'a jamais existé. Racine et Boileau furent amis—

et encore... La Fontaine et Molière furent liés. Mais jamais entre ces poètes aucune théorie commune, et *l'Art Poétique*, qui devrait boucher ce trou, ignore la fable et méprise les farces de Molière.

Si Hegel limite le classicisme à la statuaire grecque du cinquième siècle, si Wölfflin le borne à la peinture et à la sculpture européennes du XVIe siècle, nos historiens ont choisi la littérature française des années 1660-1690. Et que n'ont-ils écrit pour justifier, voire sacraliser, ce choix! Que de lignes, que de livres, pour expliquer "le milieu et le moment" du classicisme français—milieu et moment exceptionnels et qui suscitent d'éternelles nostalgies!

Toutefois, dans ce terrain béni, bien des mauvaises plantes ont poussé, et il faut éliminer (on se demande pourquoi) Quinault et Thomas Corneille, dont les pièces firent salle comble pendant vingt ans, Pierre Corneille, qui écrivit jusqu'en 1674, le jeune Fontenelle, Donneau de Visé, Mme de Villedieu, Catherine Bernard. Restent— et rien n'est moins historique que ce choix—Racine, Molière, Boileau, La Rochefoucauld, Mme de Sévigné, La Bruyère, Mme de Lafayette. Pourquoi? Personne ne nous le dit clairement. Si encore on osait dire que tous les écrivains des années 1660-1690 ne furent pas "classiques," qu'il exista deux courants—celui des Anciens et celui des Modernes—et que seuls les Anciens peuvent être regardés comme des classiques. Cela serait un peu plus raisonnable. Mais l'époque choisie perdrait son exceptionnel prestige. Et d'ailleurs il n'est pas sûr que Molière, Mme de Lafayette, Mme de Sévigné, La Rochefoucauld, aient été des Anciens—quel sens pour un auteur de farces italiennes, pour une romancière, ou pour un moraliste? On peut enfin nous dire que seuls les grands auteurs, les gloires qui ont franchi les siècles ont été considérés. Mais est-ce vraiment leur valeur qui les a conservés? Ne sont-ce pas d'abord les habitudes des écoles et des théâtres subventionnés? Ce n'est pas forcément parce qu'ils ont duré qu'on peut les dire classiques. C'est peut-être parce qu'ils furent classiques (au sens scolaire du terme), qu'ils ont duré. Et d'ailleurs leur éclat connut, au cours des siècles, bien des vicissitudes, et Boileau, en notre temps, n'a plus guère de lecteurs.

Consentons, malgré tout, à limiter notre étude à Racine, à Molière, à Boileau, à La Rochefoucauld, à Mme de Sévigné, à La Bruyère, à Mme de Lafayette. Quels traits va-t-on retrouver chez ces sept auteurs, qui définiront le classicisme? L'intellectualité, c'est-à-dire "l'exploration par la clarté et l'ordre de l'intelligence des (...) mystéres du subconscient et de l'inconscient" (Peyre 59)? Cela ne signifie pas grand chose: il n'y a ni subconscient ni inconscient au XVIIe siècle, et croit-on que les *Fables* de La Fontaine ou *La comtesse d'Escarbagnas* soient destinées à sonder les mystères de l'âme humaine? Même La Bruyère: ses fats et ses sots n'ont pas une psychologie bien compliquée, et ne sont d'ailleurs pas présentés selon un ordre didactique. L'impassibilité et l'universalité? Mais La Fontaine est souvent lyrique, et le Racine de *Bajazet*, de *Mithridate*, d'*Athalie*, n'a nullement négligé "la couleur locale"; on peut dire, au contraire, qu'il a voulu l'approfondir autant qu'il était possible, et qu'elle est la clef de la psychologie et de la métaphysique de chacune de ses pièces. La nature, c'est-à-dire le refus de la caricature burlesque et du maniérisme précieux? Mais *Le repas ridicule* est-il moins caricatural que *Le roman comique*? Troïle que Matamore? Et *Clélie* est-elle moins réaliste que *La Princesse de Clèves*? Restent les règles, mais on sait que la règle des règles est de plaire. Corneille méprise la vraisemblance; Molière n'est presque jamais vraisemblable, ni bienséant.[1] Et d'ailleurs y a-t-il des règles pour la fable, pour le roman, pour la lettre, pour le portrait, pour la maxime? Quant à unir l'art et la morale, les poètes de 1670 n'ont montré aucune originalité en y prétendant. C'est ce que disait Térence, et c'est ce que dira Zola.

Si toutes ces conceptions sont décevantes, c'est parce que nos historiens, au lieu d'étudier les auteurs qu'ils ont choisi d'étudier, tiennent, à tout prix, à retrouver dans leurs œuvres les principes de Boileau:

> "La raison pour marcher n'a ouvert qu'une voie (...)
> Quoi que vous écriviez, évitez la bassesse (...)
> Une merveille absurde est pour moi sans appas (...)
> Que la nature donc soit votre étude unique...."
> (*Art poétique*, 1. 48, 79; 2. 49; 3. 359)

Une mauvaise méthode ne peut donner que de mauvais résultats. On commence par mutiler l'objet qu'on étudie (en éliminant la plupart des auteurs de la période choisie), puis on plaque sur cet objet quelques maximes si vagues et si générales, qu'elles signifient ce qu'on veut. Un empirisme aussi incomplet et aussi tendancieux ne peut mener bien loin.

Faut-il abandonner tout espoir, et conclure qu'il y eut un classicisme grec, dont Hegel a exprimé la métaphysique, un classicisme renaissant, dont Wölfflin a dégagé les principes essentiels, et que cette notion n'est qu'un mythe, ou comme le disait Valéry, un calembour, quand on l'applique au XVIIe siècle? Mais deux classicismes, celui de Hegel et celui de Wölfflin, c'est peut-être trop, et, si l'on pouvait n'en faire qu'un, il ne serait pas interdit, à la limite, de le chercher dans quelques œuvres écloses au temps de Louis XIV.

La statuaire grecque était classique, car elle incarnait dans des corps humains, plausibles, et pour ainsi dire, réels malgré leur pureté, des idées qui semblaient ainsi tombées du ciel. La peinture de la Renaissance se propose aussi de représenter le réel, mais en l'harmonisant de manière à le rendre significatif, et non comme un symbole qui implique une distance, significatif comme un mot dont les phonèmes et l'idée se saisissent en même temps et paraissent indissolublement liés.

Le classicisme est un langage parfait. Les significatifs, c'est-à-dire le corps et l'espace, ne doivent pas sembler arbitrairement choisis ou déformés pour permettre l'éclosion de l'Idée. Poussin, au long de ses promenades dans la campagne romaine, ramassait des cailloux et des ramures pour les représenter fidèlement sur sa toile. Comment donc l'idée apparaissait-elle? Par la composition, ce qui suppose d'abord l'isolememt linéaire des éléments, ensuite la production de plans parallèles, enfin la construction d'une unité avec cette multiplicité. Tout cela suppose l'intelligence de l'artiste, et donc la promotion de la matière à un ordre rationnel et à une dimension significative. Le spectateur reconnaît la nature et la sent pénétrée d'un sens, qui n'est pas toujours évident.

Cette fusion de la Nature et de l'Esprit n'est pas simple. Elle est même paradoxale, ou entièrement fausse, à nos yeux, car nous croyons que les données immédiates de l'expériencc scnsible sont fondamentalement rebelles à la systématisation intellectuelle. Les classiques sont plus optimistes que nous. Ils croient que tout est rationnel. Ils croient à un Dieu architecte et mathématicien.

Y a-t-il un classicisme dans la littérature française du XVIIe siècle? La première exigence demeure le réalisme. Comme les cailloux et les ramures des mythologies de Poussin sont vrais, Hermione doit paraître une véritable amante. Cette exactitude est souvent baptisée "naïveté", ce qui signifie le naturel dans l'élocution, une sorte de coïncidence entre le langage et l'objet dont on parle. La Bruyère, quoi qu'on ait dit, n'a jamais songé à inventer "l'écriture artiste". La composition et le style de *Mopse* et de *Cydias* sont d'abord destinés à incarner Mopse et Cydias, à nous les rendre présents, à nous faire dire, comme Mme de Sévigné: "Cela est peint".

"Les plus belles scènes," écrit Racine dans le préface de *Mithridate*, "sont en danger d'ennuyer, du moment qu'on les peut séparer de l'action et qu'elles l'interrompent au lieu de la conduire vers sa fin." L'ensemble l'emporte donc sur les éléments, mais ceux-ci sont clairement circonscrits et isolés: chaque acte, chaque scène, chaque tirade, voire chaque vers, affirment d'abord leur indépendance en affichant leur plénitude interne, leurs symétries, leur beauté particulière. Prologue, noeud, dénouement, divisent le drame. Exorde, développment, péroraison, rythment les tirades. Dans le développement des parties se succèdent. Pour que chaque élément affirme son autonomie, il faut évidemment qu'il soit aisément reconnaissable, donc qu'il se conforme à un code. Ce qui suppose, d'une certaine manière, l'empire de la rhétorique.

Même la *Princesse de Clèves* s'analyse aisément en chapitres, en scènes, en discours. Ainsi pouvons-nous discerner treize parties: la Cour, le Mariage de Mlle de Chartres, la Rencontre de M. de Nemours et de Mme de Clèves, la Découverte de l'Amour, la Mort de Mme de Chartres, les Déclarations de M. deNemours, les "Déclarations" de Mme de Clèves, la Lettre perdue, l'Aveu, les Conséquences de l'Aveu, la Mort de Henri II, la Jalousie et la Mort du prince de Clèves, le Dénouement. Dans la plupart de ces parties se discerne une action essentielle, que précèdent des préparations (ou des explications) et que suivent des conclusions. D'autre part, les grands discours, celui de Mme de Chartres à sa fille avant d'expirer, l'aveu de la princesse à son époux, les adieux que celui-ci fait à sa femme sont nettement composés: d'évidents arêtes séparent l'introduction et la conclusion de reste de la tirade, qui peut lui-meme se découper aisément (Niderst, *La Princesse de Clèves*).

Cette discontinuité est comparable à celle ce la peinture. Les chapitres du roman, les actes des tragédies, peuvent être assimilés à des plans, les scénes et les discours aux objets qui peuplent ces plans.

Les *Maximes* de La Rochefoucauld et les *Caractères* de La Bruyère ne sont apparemment que des amas d'atomes. Chaque réflexion, chaque portrait, chaque maxime, paraissent isolés. Cependant, de même qu'au théâtre les actes recomposent des ensembles et l'intrigue générale une unité, de même que les morceaux du roman forment finalement un puzzle cohérent, on peut discerner dans les ouvrages de La Rochefoucauld ou de La Bruyère des séquences et, par delà de ces séquences, un ordre général. Prenons par exemple le chapitre *Du Mérite personnel* de La Bruyère: les trois premières remarques soulignent la variété des valeurs mondaines, les fragments 4 à 12 indiquent toutes les difficultés à parvenir, les fragments 13 à 24 définissent l'homme de mérite. Les morceaux 25 à 28 marquent un retour aux jugements des hommes, qui sont en général erronés. De 29 à 34 la définition du véritable mérite est approfondie. De 35 à 40 sont à nouveau indiquées toutes les apparences qui perturbent les jugements des hommes. Les fragments 41, 42, 43, 44, donnent enfin le tableau du véritable mérite. Ainsi, bien loin de son apparent désordre, ce chapitre contient un plan qui n'est pas trop caché, mais qui est plutôt dialectique que déductif. Dialectique du faux et du vrai mérite, culminant dans l'opposition du dérisoire Ménippe et de l'homme héroïque et parfait qui ressemble au Christ (Niderst, "*Du Mérite personnel*" 333-34).

On pourrait dire que chaque œuvre classique est susceptible de deux lectures opposées, qui sont également fausses. C'est une erreur de n'être sensible qu'à la discontinuité, aux brillants et aux harmonies de détail. Mais c'est aussi une erreur de ne s'arrêter qu'aux mérites d'ensemble et de simplifier à l'excès l'architecture générale. Le classicisme réside dans cet irritant et au fond sécurisant paradoxe: le morceau est un tout et est un morceau; les individus se suffisent et ne suffisent pas à eux-mêmes; le fragment peut être lu isolément: il a sa beauté et son ordre propres; mais, lu comme un fragment, il acquiert une nouvelle résonnance qui prolonge ce qui précède et annonce ce qui suit.

Imitation de réel, unité construite à partir d'une multiplicité d'éléments, qui avouent chacun leur autonomie; ce n'est pas assez. Encore faut-il que l'architecture générale soit logique et achevée. A la fin tout est réglé: le sujet, clairement circonscrit qu'a traité l'écrivain reçoit une solution convaincante:

> Par cette fin terrible, et due à ses forfaits,
> Apprenez, roi des Juifs, et n'oubliez jamais
> Que les rois dans le ciel ont un juge sévère.
> L'innocence un vengeur, et l'orphelin un père."
> (*Athalie* 1813-16)

En ce sens, Racine, Mme de Lafayette, La Rochefoucauld, La Bruyère, sont classiques. Molière beaucoup moins, car il sacrifice souvent la pièce à la scène, et l'effet d'ensemble aux effets de détail: ainsi les fameux portraits que brosse Célimène à l'acte II du *Misanthrope*, ne sont nullement indispensables à l'intrigue de la comédie. On sait d'ailleurs que l'intrigue générale est parfois boiteuse, et les dénouements bâclés. La Fontaine est-il classique? Il est permis d'en douter: les fables sont trop fluides pour être rigidement composées; d'un vers à l'autre nous passons du style familier à l'élégie ou à la parodie d'églogue; le poète ne se sacrifie jamais à son sujet; il ne cesse de se rappeler à nous par sa désinvolture et surtout par le jeu des styles, qui exclut finalement tout réalisme. Pour Boileau, le problème ne paraît guère se poser, ou serait bien plus difficile à résoudre. La satire est, aux yeux de Hegel, une dégradation du classicisme, et les discours de morale ou de poétique, que propose Boileau dans ses épitres et son *Art poétique*, ne seraient classiques, que si leur signification, incarnée dans la composition générale, dépassait toutes les significations particulières de ses maximes et de ses couplets.

Il ne serait d'ailleurs pas impossible, mais cela nous entraînerait trop loin, de marquer les limites du classicisme de Mme de Lafayette, car la *Princesse de Clèves* compte des épisodes (l'histoire d'Anne Boleyn, celle de Mme de Tournon, par exemple) qu'il n'est pas toujours facile d'intégrer dans le tout, même de Racine consentant souvent aux "morceaux de bravoure" (les grandes récits d'Arbate, d'Ulysse, de Théramène), de La Bruyère, et surtout de La Rochefoucauld, dont la composition est souvent trop subtile ou même discutable.

Quant au classicisme du XIXe et du XXe siècles, il doit exister, mais certainement pas chez les néo-classiques, qui interposent toujours leur culture. Ce n'est pas quand La Fontaine joue avec les apologues d'Esope qu'il est classique. La Bruyère n'imite presque jamais Théophraste. Racine traduit Sénèque dans *Phèdre*, mais comme il traduisait Tacite dans *Britannicus* et Virgile dans *Andromaque*, pour profiter de leurs thèmes et de leur poésie, et les fondre en un ensemble neuf, pas du tout pour faire un palimpseste sérieux ou ironique.

Semblons-nous retrouver les formules de René Bray et d'Henri Peyre? Mais ce sont plutôt ces formules, apparemment convenues et un peu naïves, qui peuvent retrouver, une fois purifiées et approfondies, celles de Hegel ou de Wölfflin. Une autre intellectualité et une autre nature se découvrent. La morale n'est pas la morale, mais l'idée, et il ne faut la chercher ni dans ce que disent les personnages, ni dans ce qui leur arrive, seulement dans la compositon.

Il n'y eut peut-être pas beaucoup plus d'œuvres classiques au temps de Louis XIV qu'au temps de Louis-Philippe ou d'Albert Lebrun. Mais ce serait long et malaisé de les chercher d'un siècle à l'autre. Il demeure que notre XIXe siècle, avec sa subjectivité, ses paysages qui sont "des états d'âmes," ses *Souvenirs de Morte-fontaine*, ses *Impressions d'Italie*, est nourri de ce que Hegel appelait romantisme. Il demeure aussi que le roman moderne, de Proust à Nathalie Sarraute, avec ses profondeurs à l'infini, qui exclut toute discontinuité, ses imparfaits aperçus du réel, son ouverture vers autre chose, correspond assez bien au baroque de Wölfflin.

Note

[1]On sait que René Bray dans *La formation de la doctrine classique en France*, voit dans la vraisemblance et les bienséances les règles essentielles des auteurs classiques.

Ouvrages cités

Boileau, Nicolas. *Œuvres complètes*. Ed. F. Escal. Paris: Gallimard, 1966.
Borgerhoff, E.B.O. *The Freedom of French Classicism*. Princeton: Princeton UP, 1950.
Bray, René. *La formation de la doctrine classique en France*. Paris: Nizet, 1951.
Brody, Jules. *Boileau and Longinus*. Paris: Droz, 1958.
Gide, André. *Incidences*. Paris: Gallimard, 1924.
Hegel. *Esthétique*. Paris: Aubier-Montaigne, 1964.
Moreau, Pierre. *Le classicisme des Romantiques*. Paris : Plon, 1932.
Niderst, Alain. "'*Du Mérite personnel*': remarques sur la composition d'un chapître des *Caractères* de La Bruyère." *Approches des lumières—Mélanges offerts à Jean Fabre*. Paris: Klincksieck, 1973.
—. *La "Princesse de Clèves": le roman paradoxal*. Paris: Larousse, 1973.
Peyre, Henri. *Qu'est-ce que le Classicisme?* Paris: Droz, 1933.
Racine, Jean. *Œuvres complètes*. Ed. Raymond Picard. Paris: Gallimard, 1960.
Sartre, Jean-Paul. *Situations II*. Paris: Gallimard, 1948.
Valéry, Paul. *Œuvres*. Ed. Jean Hytier. Paris, Gallimard, 1957.
Wölfflin, Heinrich. *Principes fondamentaux de l'histoire de l'art*. Trans. Claire et Marcel Raymond. Paris: Club des Editeurs, 1961.

Monchrestien's *Aman* and Racine's *Esther*:

Toward a Game-Theory Definition of French Classicism

Herbert De Ley
University of Illinois

Despite general theorizing since the publication of Huizinga's *Homo Ludens* in 1938, few scholars have tried to apply the notion of games and play to specific texts. And despite considerable theorizing about real strategic scenarios since Von Neumann and Morgenstern's *Theory of Games and Economic Behavior* of 1944, even fewer scholars have tried to apply the insights of mathematical game theory to specific works of literature. A recent notable exception has been Steven J. Brams's *Biblical Games*, which analyzes a variety of biblical stories in terms of extended-form and normal-form matrices, dominant and dominated strategies, and the like. Brams laments, however, that the Bible typically provides only sparse information on personages' motivations and preferences, thus severely limiting the range of game theory concepts that can be applied. Other types of literature give considerably more such information, however, and therefore lend themselves more readily to game-theory analysis.

Using methods like Brams's I have lately tried to apply such concepts as payoffs and utilities, extended-form and normal-form game matrices, dominant and dominated strategies, the formation of coalitions, the optimum of Pareto, and the minimax to a variety of

French literary texts—first, in an article in *Substance* and later, in a book, *Le Jeu classique*. In a period marked by methodological complexity in literary studies, game-theory analysis can produce results that are unexpectedly—or disarmingly, or disappointingly, or refreshingly—simple. Applied to the literature of the *Grand Siècle* it can express a great deal about a given text, or texts. In particular, it can distinguish between different versions of the same story. Sometimes it highlights differences which are time-specific to the French classical period, thus offering something like a game theory definition of French classicism. As examples one might study any number of stories existing in versions written before, during and after the classical period: the Phaedra legend, the tribulations of Sophonisbe, or others. One other such possibility is the biblical story of Esther.

The biblical version of Esther has been analyzed in game-theory terms by Brams in *Biblical Games*. Another version, Montchrestien's *Aman*, dates from 1601 or 1604. The best known French version is Racine's *Esther* of 1689. To some extent the later versions, providing more information on personality and motivation than the laconic biblical text, amplify and confirm Brams's analysis of the biblical version of the story. At the same time, they present differences from the biblical story—differences which game-theory analysis may be able to distinguish.

According to Brams the biblical story of Esther offers, among other examples of royal conflicts, "a quieter kind of heroism" (139), in a conflict that is not "a challenge to a king by either God or a human competitor" (139). Instead the story of Esther presents "machinations and legerdemain in the royal court by an ambitious courtier determined to destroy his enemies" (139). When this courtisan, offended by the Jew Mordecai, seeks to destroy the whole Jewish people, Mordecai asks queen Esther to intervene in their favor. Mordecai points out to Esther that, a Jew herself, she risks perishing with the others if she does not. For her part, she reminds him that no subject of king Ahasuerus is allowed to appear before him unless invited. If anyone ignores this rule, and if the king does not hold out his golden scepter as a sign of pardon, the offending subject is immediately executed. Despite all its biblical seriousness, this situation can be modeled as a game, a game whose payoffs are summarized in the normal-form matrix appearing in Figure 1 (Brams 139).

Esther's game might be modeled in "extended form," that is, as a tree-like diagram in which each fork represents a strategic choice to be made and each branch represents a strategic alternative. More widely used in game theory, however, is the "normal-form" matrix. A normal-form matrix presents the overall, final result(s) of each possible series of moves and countermoves by the players. Figure 1, adapted from Brams, models the biblical Game of Esther and Ahasuerus in normal form. The Game of Esther and Ahasuerus in the Bible has only one move by each player: Esther intervenes or does not, and Ahasuerus supports Aman or does not. The normal-form matrix of Figure 1 presents each player's strategic alternatives in this given situation and, in each box representing the intersections of the players' possible strategic choices, shows the resulting payoffs. By tradition, the game-theory normal-form matrix presents the payoff of the player on the left (Esther, in this case) first in the parenthesis; the payoff of the player at the top of the figure (Ahasuerus) is presented second in the parenthesis, within each box in the figure. It is most important to note that in this game—as in a great many others presented in literature—there is no "winner" or "loser" but rather degrees of gain or loss for each player— something like the "score" each player can expect from the result of given strategic choices by each one. The Game of Esther and Ahasuerus, therefore, is not a "zero-sum" game. Rather it is a "non-zero-sum" game—one in which the players' interests are partially in conflict but also partially cooperative. Like politicians in loyal opposition or merchants involved in price wars, they may thus achieve a larger or smaller collective payoff depending on whether they can cooperate to optimize the result.

Since biblical personages generally—and Esther and Ahasuerus in particular—typically offer little quantitative information concerning their preferences, Brams, *faute de mieux,* simply attempts to deduce their order of preference for various alternatives. The payoff numbers, therefore, are not cardinal numbers but ordinal numbers—orders of preference, with the highest preferences numbered highest (first choice among four possible results is four, second choice three, etc.). As always in game-theory analysis, if the reader questions the assumptions informing the game model, s/he is invited to vary the assumptions and study their effects on the payoffs—and hence on the normal-form matrix of the game.

Figure 1.
The Game of Esther and Ahasuerus (adapted from Brams)

AHASUERUS

	Arrest Haman	Support Haman
Intervene	(4, 3)	(3, 1)
ESTHER		
Abstain	(2, 2)	(1, 4)

In (x, y), x = Esther's payoff; y = Ahasuerus' payoff
4 = first choice; 3 =second choice, 2 = third choice, 1 = fourth choice

According to Brams's analysis of the payoffs, as expressed in Figure 1, Esther understands that she may win everything but also risks everything—or almost everything—if she appears before the king unbidden (4 or ?, depending on Ahasuerus' response). However, even if she loses, she will be a martyr for her people, so the consequences of intervention are perhaps not actually her worst alternative (3). On his side, if Ahasuerus is obliged to execute her, he thereby loses a second queen, having already divorced queen Vashti (1). On the other hand, if Esther does not intervene, she risks disgrace as the executioner of her people (1), or else—perhaps less terrible but more ironic—disgrace as a lazy and ineffective person, if her people are indeed saved without her help (2).

In these circumstances, as Brams puts it, "Esther's stoicism...is not untouched by logic" (141). In Brams's view, Esther's preparations and precautions before intervening seem to confirm that analysis. In any case, it is interesting to note that in this game Esther possesses a dominant strategy—that is, a strategy offering better payoffs than any other, no matter which countermove Ahasuerus chooses. Ahasuerus however, despite his superior rank and power, does not possess a dominant strategy in the Game of Esther and Ahasuerus. Also interesting is that the solution actually adopted achieves the optimum—that is, the highest total value of the payoffs of the game actually obtainable. Brams concludes by observing that "There is no Moses in Esther's story, nor any mean spirited or vindictive God, either. Instead, there is the female embodiment of beauty and charm—and tact and daring as well." Brams suggests further that, as regards royal conflict in general, this sort of conflict is different than others because it is "more consequential than ordinary conflicts, which impinge on fewer people. That is why I think it [royal conflict] is worth distinguishing, even if it is just another manifestation of the common struggles all people have" (147). Significantly, therefore, Brams's game-theory analysis coincides with a doctrine of Aristotle's *Poetics* (Brams 141, 147).

If Esther's problems may appear exemplary in the Bible according to Brams, the game of Esther and Assuérus takes a very different form in Montchrestien's play *Aman*. When he sees Esther about to appear before him without permission, the king decides to "play" with her. This will be, he thinks, an educational game:

> Mais la voici venir, il faut un peu me feindre,
> Afin qu'à l'advenir elle apprenne à me craindre:
> Elle vient sans mander et permis il ne l'est;
> Je veu faire semblant que cela me deplaist. (Act IV)[1]

But before the king can begin his game, Esther faints from fear: "Hà Rachel soustien moy, soustien moy je me pâme." Assuérus's game breaks down before it even begins, and the king adopts an almost burlesque style, certainly a familiar style, as he tries to comfort his royal spouse:

> Hà ma fille qu'as tu! qu'as tu ma petite ame!
> Je suis ton cher espoux; ma belle ne crain pas,
> Tu ne dois pour ta faute encourir le trépas.
> Pour le commun sans plus est faite l'ordonnance:
> Esther approche donc, change de contenance:
> J'esten sur toy mon sceptre, appaise appaise toy;
> Reine de mes desirs baise un petit ton Roy. (Act IV)

The difference is significant. Throughout *Aman* games tend to be over before they begin. In Montchrestien's play Mardochée doesn't preach to Esther: he doesn't need to. Esther sees him passing, she sends her servants to ask what's troubling him, and without dialogue or debate she is ready to do her duty. Before Mardochée arrives, she apostrophizes him in her monologue:

> O vieillard abusé tu ne me connois pas,
> Encores qu'on me vint presenter cent trépas,
> Pour divertir l'amour si constante et si forte,
> Qu'à toy mon Nourrissier dés l'enfance je porte:
> Certes je les voudroy moins que rien estimer,
> Pourveu qu'on me permist en mourant de t'aymer. (Act III)

Elsewhere she explains that the other possible payoffs of her game are worth exactly zero to her:

> Ni de mon cher Espoux les douces mignardises,
> Ni de ses Boufonneurs les folles gaillardises,

> Ni ces habits royaux d'or canelé frangeé,
> Ni ce long train de gens à ma suite rangés (Act III),

and so on, in a long baroque enumeration of advantages which are worth, precisely, nothing to her in comparison with her love of God (Montchrestien 100, 102).

Thus in Montchrestien games either break down rapidly or are played against nature. Neither Mardochée nor Assuérus nor God is truly a player. Esther earns her payoff by doing the will of Mardochée, by doing the will of God. She does so, however, without question, without even considering the possibility of choice. At the beginning of the following act, still without debate, she explains precisely that without balancing, without hesitating, her mind is made up: "Y deussé-je mourir, dit-elle, j'en courrai le danger" (Montchrestien 120).

The same is true in the only explicit challenge, the only explicit bet in the play. In Montchrestien's text, God does not play either for or against Esther; Aman, on the other hand, plays explicitly against God. God, he declares, will not listen to the grief of the Jews:

> Ils ont beau dans le Ciel espandre des sanglots,
> Pour ne les point oüir son oreille il a clos:
> Forment tant qu'ils voudront des piteuses complaintes,
> Les Ames n'en seront à la pitié contraintes:
> Quoy qu'ils tendent en haut leurs suppliantes mains,
> Pour faire rengainer les glaives inhumains,
> Nul touché de leurs maux nul ne leur fera grace.
>
> . . . .
>
> Et qu'un peuple exilé par le Monde espandu,
> Pour la faute d'un seul a tout esté perdu. (Act I)

Racine's *Esther*, finally, lends itself to a much more ample analysis, a description which illuminates and confirms in several respects that of Brams. Game-theory analysis of Racine's text also produces results which differ significantly from Brams's, however. It seems, moreover, that games and festivals are preoccupations for Racine himself. According to his preface, the first representations of the play were a sort of private royal fête. According to Racine "le Roi lui-même, qui en avait été touché" could not "refuser à tout ce qu'il y a de plus grands seigneurs de les y mener." The King had the "satisfaction de voir, par le plaisir qu'ils y ont pris, qu'on se peut aussi bien divertir aux choses de piété qu'à tous les spectacles profanes." For the young ladies of Saint Cyr, the message was similar: Esther was an educational spectacle—since it was one of "plusieurs moyens qui, sans les détourner de leur travail et de leurs exercices ordinaires, les instruisent en les divertissant. On leur met, pour ainsi dire, à profit leurs heures de recréation."[2]

Thus according to Racine *Esther* is a pastime like the seventeenth-century *Jeu des Rois de France* or any other educational variant on the Game of Goose: for these players, Esther mixes the useful and the pleasurable. In the text of the play, moreover, Racine alludes further to "vos jeux innocents." And he speaks in several places of celebrations, whether the unfortunately interrupted "fêtes" of Israel or the "fêtes criminelles" of the Persians or the "horrible fête" organized by Aman. Aman himself, complaining of the good treatment given to the Jew Mardochée by Assuérus, cries out against this "Roi cruel" and adds: "ce sont là des jeux où tu te plais" (III, l). When Esther explains the machinations of that same Aman to Assuérus, his reaction takes a characteristic form: "Tout mon sang de colère et de honte s'enflamme./ J'étais donc le jouet . . . Ciel, daigne m'éclairer" (III, 4). Festivity and play thus form in Racine's play something like a leit-motif, one of those characteristic "metaphors" of the theater of the *Grand Siècle*. The metaphor of game and festivity is reflected, moreover, in the strategic choices faced by the personages of the play.[3]

In the first scene of Esther the queen herself describes her situation in terms of a contest, the beauty contest she won to become the royal spouse. Her speech expands upon the laconic biblical account:

> De l'Inde à l'Hellespont les esclaves coururent.
> Les filles de l'Egypte à Suse comparurent.
> Celles mêmes du Parthe et du Scythe indompté
> Y briguèrent le sceptre offert à la beauté. (I, 1).

This wife-hunt, in the Assuérus version, quickly becomes a sort of judgment of Paris:

> Chacune avait sa brigue et de puissants suffrages:
> L'une d'un sang fameux vantait les avantages;
> L'autre, pour se parer de superbes atours.
> Des plus adroites mains empruntait le secours.
> Et moi, pour toute brigue et pour tout artifice,
> De mes larmes au ciel j'offrais le sacrifice. (I,1).

Amply expressing its personages' motivations, Racine's *Esther* tends to confirm certain of Brams's conclusions—sometimes a little tentative in the absence of explicit information in the Bible. Thus in her first scene with Mardochée, Esther develops the argument that she herself will perish if she appears unbidden before Assuérus. Mardochée's response is stinging:

> Quoi! lorsque vous voyez périr votre patrie,
> Pour quelque chose, Esther, vous comptez votre vie.
> Dieu parle, et d'un mortel vous craignez la courroux!
> Que dis-je? Votre vie, Esther, est-elle à vous?

Mardochée also brings up the possibility of disgrace as he preaches:

> Songez-y bien. Ce Dieu ne vous a pas choisie
> Pour être un vain spectacle aux peuples de l'Asie,
> Ni pour charmer les yeux des profanes humains (I,1).

This last remark, however, while it confirms Brams's intuition, also points up a fundamental difference between the biblical version and Racine's—a difference clearly reflected in the structure of Esther's game in the Racinian text. For Racine, perhaps expressing a Jansenist notion, Esther plays less against Assuérus than against God himself. Esther suggests this in her very first scene when she explains how she won the beauty contest. According to Esther, "Dieu tient le coeur des rois entre ses mains puissantes." Thus Assuérus fixed her with his gaze and "le ciel, qui pour moi fit pencher la balance,/ Dans ce temps-là sans doute agissait sur son coeur" (I,1).

This idea, which clearly differs from Brams's interpretation of the biblical version, returns as Esther debates with Mardochée. Even as he insistently demands Esther's help, Mardochée points out that her intervention is not at all indispensable. God really does not need her to accomplish His goals:

> Et quel besoin son bras a-t-il de nos secours?
> Que peuvent contre lui tous les rois de la terre?
>
> . . . .
>
> Et les faibles mortels, vains jouets du trépas,
> Sont tous devant ses yeux comme s'ils n'étaient pas (I, 3).

If God has chosen Esther, this is only "Sans doute qu'il voulait éprouver votre zèle." For Mardochée continues that:

> . . . s'il faut que sa voix frappe en vain vos oreilles,
> Nous n'en verrons pas moins éclater ses merveilles.
> Il peut confondre Aman, il peut briser nos fers
> Par la plus faible main qui soit dans l'univers.
> Et vous, qui n'aurez point accepté cette grâce,
> Vous périrez peut-être, et toute votre race. (I, 3)

Thus even as he confirms the notion that Esther should worry about being left out of the game, Mardochée evokes something like the inexorable God of the Jansenists. Esther's game thus becomes, in Racine, a game against God as a hostile player. This game is modeled in Figure 2. As in Brams's model, the strategy of intervention is dominant for Esther. But Assuérus' choices no longer play any role in the situation. And God's payoffs do not change, whatever Esther's choice. Under these conditions the Game of Esther and God resembles less the corresponding game in Brams than it does Brams's game between God and Pharaoh—a game conducted through the intermediary Moses, as this one is conducted through the intervention of Mardochée. And the object of the game, if it is not simply to test Esther's soul, is to reveal the power of God.

Figure 2. The Game of Esther and God (adapted from Racine)

| | GOD | |
	Triumphs using Esther	Triumphs without
ESTHER Intervenes	(4, 4)	(3, 4)
Abstains	(2, 4)	(1, 4)

To better reveal God's power in the Game of God and Pharaoh, God is obliged to "cultivate" Pharaoh's stubbornness. God's purpose is not served if Pharaoh behaves reasonably and surrenders "too soon." In the Game of Esther and God, Esther may hesitate but she is not obstinate. If there is an evil force in Racine's play, a force charged with maintaining a potentially disastrous situation, it can only be found in the activity of Aman. However Aman himself, a "plaything" of fortune (that is, of God), plays a game of imperfect information. He does not know that the queen is Jewish. And he does not know it is Mardochée that the king wishes to honor. Most especially, he does not know that his own fortunes are about to change drastically. In these circumstances, moreover, those close to him give him only partial advice about the payoffs of his game. His confidant Hydaspe—unlike-Aman's confidant in Montchrestien's play—counsels prudence and suggests that "Un si faible ennemi" cannot "troubler la paix" of so glorious a life as his own (II, 1). Aman's wife Zarès also counsels prudence, and indeed she gives him a lesson in courtly wisdom, reminding him of his own judgment that:

> Quiconque ne sait pas dévorer un affront,
>
> . . . .
>
> Loin de l'aspect des rois qu'il s'écarte, qu'il fuie.
> Il est des contretemps qu'il faut qu'un sage essuie.
> Souvent avec prudence un outrage enduré
> Aux honneurs les plus hauts a servi de degré (III, 1).

Thus both confidant and spouse counsel a maximin strategy, one which will minimize loss. Zarès even suggests that, Aman's fortunes possibly being about to change, they should flee. "Osez chercher ailleurs un destin plus paisible," she suggests, "Regagner l'Hellespont." She offers finally to ensure their escape:

> Nos plus riches trésors marcheront devant nous.
> Vous pouvez du départ me laisser la conduite;
> Surtout de vos enfants j'assurerai la fuite (III, 1).

As things turn out, of course, this maximin strategy is revealed to be the correct one. Not only is Aman himself executed, but his goods are confiscated and his sons killed by Assućrus's men.

Aman, however, prefers the opposite strategy. He hopes to maximize his gains, to strike a decisive blow. Indeed he declares he wants the punishment of the Jews to be disproportionate to the crime. Observing that "La vengeance trop faible attire un second crime," he adds that he wants the universe to tremble at their punishment, and that "on tremble en comparant l'offense et le supplice" (II, 1). This way of reasoning recalls curiously another celebrated seventeenth-century text on games: the *pari* of Pascal. Whatever the error in judgment of Aman—and whatever the mathematical problems in Pascal—these two ideas have in common the classic opposition of proportion and disproportion.

Modeled simply, the Game of Mardochée and Aman—or, perhaps, the Game of Aman against the Jews—is represented in Figure 3. If some of the suppositions implied by this figure appear arbitrary, the reader is again invited to arrange them differently. However that may be, these suppositions, much more than those Brams finds in the Bible, appear clearly proposed by the text. And in this special context, Aman's and Mardochée's thought "becomes rational," becomes thought that seems normal and acceptable, given the assumptions of the game.

Figure 2. The Game of Aman and Mardochée
(as imagined by Aman; adapted from Racine)

MARDOCHEE

		Bows down	Declines to bow
	Punishes	(2, 1)	(4, 4)
AMAN			
	Doesn't	(3, 2)	(1, 3)

In this game, what are Aman's preferences? If one believes
Aman himself, the past actions of the Jews against Aman's own
people play only a minor role in his thought. When Hydaspe asks
him if "Ce n'est donc pas, Seigneur, le sang malécite/ Dont la voix
à les perdre en secret vous excite?" Aman answers clearly:

> . . . crois-mois, dans le rang où je suis élevé,
> Mon âme, à ma grandeur tout entière attachée,
> Des intérêts du sang est faiblement touchée.
> Mardochée est coupable, et que faut-il de plus ? (II, 1)

One might suppose, therefore, that Aman's utilities would be
those implied by Figure 3: since Mardochée has offended him,
Aman wants to destroy him; indeed he wants his punishment to be
exemplary, thus disproportionate (4). One might suppose that
Aman is so evil that he wants to destroy the Jews at any price; the
Racinian text does not seem to support such an idea, however.
Consequently, Aman may prefer that Mardochée bow down to him,
and thus that everyone honor his authority (3). Certain of Aman's
remarks suggest moreover that it is to destroy Mardochée that he
wants to destroy the Jews, rather than the opposite. However, even
if Mardochée makes amends, Aman is perhaps mean enough,
having gained the essential, to punish Mardochée anyway (2). The
worst, obviously, would be for Mardochée to defy Aman without
being punished (1).

Mardochée's priorities are different, of course. For Mardochée,
saving the Jewish people and manifesting the greatness of God are
most important (4). Mardochée does not suggest, however, that the
Jews might be saved by denying God. Indeed Jewish history, as
presented in *Esther*, clearly suggests the opposite. Thus Mardochée
must prefer a challenge which may manifest the greatness of God
(3) to obeying and seeking compromise (2). In any case, the worst

would be that the Jews be lost for nothing, without God's greatness being manifested (1).

In this situation Mardochée possesses a dominant strategy, and Aman does not—another example in which an apparently superior power does not carry with it real strategic superiority. Nevertheless Aman appears able to avoid the worst by punishing Mardochée, whatever the latter may do. In reality, however, the payoffs of Aman's game are not what he believes. As a victim of imperfect information, Aman plays in reality a different game than that of Figure 3. Given Esther's intervention and Assuérus' favorable reaction, Aman's only viable strategy is to swallow his pride—to use his wife's expression—and hope to avoid the worst. Any strategy of punishment is dominated in the real Game of Aman. The unfortunate courtier can only hope that Mardochée will not challenge him—and even this modest hope is not realized in the text of *Esther*.

Thus, three versions of the story of Esther lend themselves, each in its own way, to game-theory analysis. Whatever simplifications, whatever reduction such analysis may entail in each text, game theory nevertheless points up certain significant differences between them—not only in the incidents of their plot structure but also in the underlying "deep structure" of each text. Of the three texts, Racine's probably lends itself the best, gives the most information, and organizes that information most clearly in terms of strategic choices. Comparative strategic analysis, moreover, might be applied with similar results to a great many texts of the *Grand Siècle*. I have suggested elsewhere that this method may be applied profitably to Corneille's *Le Cid* and its source, Garnier's *Bradamante*.[4] One might also study the diverse Don Juans, the diverse Amphytrions, the diverse Roman emperors, and their adaptations in Molière and Corneille. As if the classicist esthetic, celebrated for its supposed rationalism and more recently accused of irrationalism, does indeed possess some quality, some tendency to select structures which finally are rational—the structures of diverse games.

This last point requires some clarification, however. Generations of commentators have found it reasonable that in *Le Cid* a hero and heroine might have to choose between true love and family honor—or that in *Cinna* a Roman emperor might choose between power and repose, between judgment and clemency—or that in *Bajazet* a sultan's brother might have to choose between love and simple survival. Yet in dozens or indeed hundreds of other plays the issues are completely different. Bajazet, for example, can hardly afford to be concerned about the sticky points of family honor. And the sultan Amurat shows lofty unconcern for the burdens of power—or indeed the possible benefits of clemency. In *Bajazet* the issues which seem so crucial in *Le Cid* or in *Cinna* simply do not arise—or may even arise in reverse form, with Amurat something like a negative image of Auguste, Atalide something like a negative image of Esther. Thus each play creates— as the game theoreticians love to say—its own special game. Where the name of the game is love versus duty, Rodrigue, Chimène, the Infante and Don Sanche fall into line and play the Game of the Cid. Where the name of the game is power and clemency, Auguste, Cinna, Maxime, and Emilie choose up sides and play the Game of Cinna. Where the name of the game is risk-taking to gain some great benefit, Esther, Ahasuerus, Mardochée and Aman take their places and play the Game of Esther. Within each of these situations the characters understand their choices and make reasonable decisions. Their play, in the language of game theory, is rational. It is thus within the sometimes rather special structures of these games—and perhaps only within them—that the sometimes obsessive or megalomanic classic personages "become rational," that they achieve something like "la raison classique."

Curiously, however, such a comparative strategic approach is applicable also to comparisons of so-called "later baroque" plays with their sources. Thus one might also profitably apply the method to comparison of Rotrou's *Veritable Saint Genest* or Corneille's *Le Menteur* or some others to their Spanish sources. Any game-theory definition of French classicism may thus be more period-specific than "period-style-specific"—emphasizing, like some of the oldest and most "Lansonian" definitions, the similarities rather than the differences between such plays as *Polyeucte* and *Saint Genest*, between *Rodogune* and *Venceslas*, among others. As Jean Rousset wrote—also years ago—"On dit: ordre, mesure, raison, règle et c'est le classicisme. On dira donc: désordre, outrance, fantaisie, liberté, et ce sera le Baroque....C'est vrai et c'est faux" (Rousset 242). Rousset concludes, just as the preceding analysis would have the reader do, that classicism and baroque style are not opposites, but rather partially overlapping, partially complementary aspects of the literature of the *Grand Siècle*. In particular, the well-known later baroque plays, divergent from classicist contemporary texts with respect to the famous "rules," nevertheless are convergent in their characteristic preoccupation with strategic choice.

Notes

[1]Montchrestien's text exists in two versions, 1601 and 1604. For this purpose, the differences do not appear to be significant.
[2]Henceforth in text as act/scene references.
[3]See J. D. Hubert, *Essai d'exégèse racinienne.*
[4]H. De Ley, *The Movement of Thought.* Arguing from very different premises, this book suggests that an early baroque (*Bradamante*) and mannerist literature preceded a later baroque (*Le Cid? Le Menteur?*) and classicist literature.

Works Cited

Brams, Steven J. *Biblical Games.* Cambridge, Mass.: MIT Press, 1980.pp. 141, 147.

De Ley, H. *Le Jeu classique: jeu et théorie au Grand Siècle.* Tübingen: Biblio 17, 1988.

—. *The Movement of Thought.* Urbana: U of Illinois P, 1985.

—. "The Name of the Game." *Substance* 55 (1988). 34-46.

Hubert, J. D. *Essai d'exégèse racinienne.* Paris: Nizet, 1956.

Huizinga, J. *Homo ludens. Essai sur la fonction sociale du jeu.* Trans. C. Seresia. Paris: Gallimard, 1951.

Monchrestien. *Aman.* Ed. George O. Siever, Philadelphia: U of P Press, 1929.

Racine, Jean. *Théâtre complet.* Ed. Maurice Rat. Paris: Garnier, 1953.

Rousset, Jean. *La littérature de l'âge baroque en France.* Paris: Corti, 1954.

Von Neumann, John and Oskar Morgenstern. *Theory of Games and Economic Behavior.* Princeton: Princeton UP, 1944.

Classical Uncertainties

Barbara Woshinsky
University of Miami

"It is hard to be sure of anything among so many marvels. The world is all grown strange. Elf and Dwarf in company walk in our daily fields; and folk speak with the Lady of the Wood and yet live; and the Sword comes back to war that was broken... How shall a man judge what to do in such times?" "As he ever has judged," said Aragorn. "Good and ill have not changed since yesteryear; nor are they one thing among Elves and Dwarves and another among Men. It is a man's part to discern them, as much in the Golden Wood as in his own house." J.R.R. TOLKIEN, *The Two Towers* (49-50).

I

The last twenty years have witnessed a vast and thoroughgoing re-examination of classical literature and thought—so thoroughgoing, indeed, that its results can overwhelm the reader. It almost seems as though recent incursions of "theory" into the seventeenth century have created a whole new classicism—as if the *pays du tendre* had changed its familiar shape and taken on, say, the contours of the *cinquième arrondissement*. In this upheaval, not even the reassuring certainties of Cartesianism have remained inviolate. According to Pierre-Alain Cahné, the Descartes we thought we knew is really an ideological invention of later readers:

... pendant longtemps... la pensée de Descartes [a été] tronquée et présentée comme un pur rationalisme....symptôme d'une mutation brutale de l'Occident qui, se sentant menacé dans son existence même par l'événement spirituel dont la sensibilité baroque était le document, s'est défendu en la refusant en bloc, au profit d'une nouvelle foi dont il fallait inventer le prophète. (162)

Whether we find the fact exciting or daunting, the "classical moment" can no longer be regarded as given or immutable; from its origins, it now appears as evanescent, as dependent on our engendering act as is the literature of today.

In a more general way, these interpretive revisions raise basic philosophical and critical questions which will be, in part, the subject of this essay. What, for example, is the relation between text and interpretation? What is the historical role of criticism? At the same time, these questions, by their very nature, affect the way in which my own text can be written. In this quandary, I could see no better strategy than to adopt a Cartesian autobiographical "discourse", tracing my own methodical itinerary from skeptical questioning to possible reconstructions, moving back and forth between general considerations and concrete analysis, review and criticism, text and thought.

II

If intellectual history is anything, it is a history of the situated uses of language constitutive of significant texts. DOMINICK LACAPRA, *Rethinking Intelllectual History* (19)

The title of *Continuum's* inaugural issue brings to mind that of Dominick LaCapra's recent book. It is on these, or analogous, issues, that my own "rethinking" has focused for the last fifteen years or so. In particular, I have tried to clarify the relation between intellectual history and literary expression. Traditionally, intellectual history has been viewed as the "history of ideas": what people have thought about various questions at given moments in the past. The problem arises in trying to connect these "ideas" to the self-contained, yet open, creation which is a literary text. In a study of *La Princesse de Clèves*, I attempted to make this connection by juxtaposing Lafayette's vision of social life against the social views of major thinkers of the period. But this approach, to my thinking, raised more questions than it answered. For example, how could I move, by ordinary comparison or juxtaposition, from "text" to "thought" and back again? How, in so doing, could I avoid a circular application of theory?[1] What precise statements could I make about the connection between work and context, without falling into question-begging generalities on "influence," "climate of opinion," or the "spirit of the age?"

While still in the throes of these skeptical musings, I was excited to discover a mode of thought which seemed to throw a new light on the problematic relations between intellectual and literary "history." The central development which made this critical "rethinking" possible was the borrowing, from linguistics, of the concept of discourse, in the broad sense of the communicative and symbolic systems which underpin social acts. Instead of examining what people think, the student of discourse tries to understand how, at a given period, thought was possible; to elucidate the unconscious preconditions for knowledge which are linked to, and discernible through, language. This central role afforded to language has important implications for literature. As a verbal medium, it exists on the same plane of reference as other representative systems and can be compared to these systems across the board. According to LaCapra,

> nothing is seen as being purely and simply inside or outside texts. Indeed the problem becomes one of rethinking the concepts of 'inside' and 'outside' in relation to processes of interaction between language and the world. . . . to see how the notion of textuality makes explicit the question of the relationships among uses of language, other signifying practices and various models of human activity that are bound up with processes of signification (26-27).

Touching the specific problem that concerned me, it seemed that this approach radically altered the old relation between literature and thought. If the unconscious preconditions of thought are present in language in general, they should also be present, and discernible, in literary language in particular. Thus, philosophy is not something which must be "related" to literature; to paraphrase LaCapra, it is "in" literature already. And intellectual history is no longer a matter of opinion or influences, but of words.

The linguistic model, I discovered, also fostered a new approach to periodization which changed my traditional picture of the seventeenth century. A number of philosophers, linguists and critics now consider the classical period as a threshold between linguistic views. According to this theory, before the late sixteenth century, the world was perceived as a chain of resemblances reaching from the Creator down to the humblest of his creation. At that point, a major change is presumed to have taken place in the epistemological outlook. Through a process of secularization whose causes are unexplained—or inexplicable—God was brusquely separated from the world. The divine order still existed on high, but for practical purposes it was removed from human ken. The old hierarchical order was shattered, leaving in its place not yet the radical relativism of modern times, but an array of discrete moral/verbal principles—

shards of belief. At this point vision is no longer whole, not yet wholly subjective: it is prismatic. This is the age of the "perspective mind."[2]

According to Sylvie Romanowski, the resulting qualitative gap between medieval and modern thought cannot be overemphasized:

> Aucune commune mesure entre les deux mondes scolastique et galiléen: la destruction des ressemblances illusoires a fait place à un monde divisé entre perception et réalité. Ainsi la vérité se trouve dans la différence, qui, rappelons-le, est un trait opposé à la ressemblance, l'une des deux composantes de l'illusion. (26)

The effects of this division can be felt across the spectrum of discourse, from art to philosophy to science to metaphysics. But the religious and scientific crisis of the classical age is also, and above all, a crisis of the word. Before the classical age, language partook of a cosmic analogy: as Michel Foucault puts it, words and things resembled one another (*Les Mots*, ch. 2). But since the early seventeenth century, language has no longer been considered part of the created universe; it simply represents that universe, like a grid of street names laid over a map. This shift from revelation to representation changes, but does not destroy, the power of language. In fact, the notion of representation, which runs through all classical discourses, affords us a new entry into their interrelations, similarities and differences. These interrelations, and the central position occupied by representation, are illustrated in the following diagram:

Figure 1.

DISCOURSE	EPISTEMOLOGICAL OPPOSITIONS	
Art/Esthetics	Mimesis/Versimilitude/	Illusion
Science/Philosophy	Representation	Error
Metaphysics	Truth	Falsehood
Theology	Perfection (divine)	Flaw (human)

As Foucault and Derrida, among others, have asserted, classical epistemology is reality- or truth-centered, and it is the aim of classical discourse to convey this reality. The central column of Figure 1, with its changes in terminology, expresses the various means by which reality can be represented through discourse. The right-hand column indicates the failure of accurate representation. These categories, far from being exclusive, display much overlap and ambiguity. For example, "illusion" can be considered either as flawed mimesis (as in *invraisemblance*) or as a necessary concomitant to mimesis (as in *illusion dramatique*). This relation, however, is not reciprocal: a work of art, which imitates reality, rather than making true claims about it, cannot logically be accused of "error." In the central column, there is also continuity between metaphysical truth and divine perfection, but representation, in its primary sense, must cease at the divine (transcendent) level. In a secondary sense, discourse can be said to represent (*figurer*) God, as in Biblical texts.

It is the term "representation" itself, however, that is the most ambivalent and all-encompassing. It cuts across several categories since it can signify either artistic portrayal (in the sense of *figurer*) or philosophical conceptualization (in the sense of *représenter à l'esprit*). These complex interconnections require a diagram to themselves:

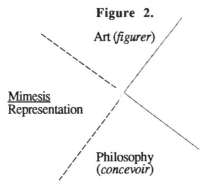

Figure 2.

Art (*figurer*)

Mimesis
Representation

Philosophy
(*concevoir*)

Representation, in its dual sense of mental concept and esthetic portrayal, thus finds itself at the intersection between art and philosophy.

III

> ...the dilemma of contemporary criticism arises not because inquiry, particularly into a past poetics and literature, is inventional but because we attempt to conceal and deny that fact.
> ADENA ROSMARIN, "Hermeneutics versus Erotics," (24).

The theories of Foucault and his followers have, not surprisingly, given rise to much philosophical controversy. For example, in an article in the *London Review of Books,* David Hoy calls Foucault's early work relativist and structuralist, terms which, in his usage, appear equally and synonymously damning:

> Where Foucault's thinking becomes particularly difficult to
> understand is not so much in his social criticism as in his
> conceptions of knowledge and truth. During his earlier,
> structuralist phase he seemed to be relativising knowledge to
> whatever discourse happened to be spoken at a particular time,
> and to be denying the possibility of serious truth (18).

Foucault indeed posits the existence of an underlying system of
assumptions that constitute the conditions of meaning: in Daniel
Stempel's formulation, "the given becomes significant only through
its participation in the order of representation" (389). In that sense,
perhaps, Foucault may be called a "structuralist." However, his
theory seems to me to be less relativist than relational: in Foucault's
own words, he seeks to define "the total set of relations that unite, at
a given period, the discursive practices that give rise to
epistemological figures, sciences and possibly formalized systems"
(*Archeology of Knowledge,* p. 191). For Foucault, certainly,
knowledge is tied to discourse and both change through time; but
does truth have to be divorced from history and language to be
"serious," as Hoy seems to imply? And how would such a truth be
either measurable or comprehensible?

The question of intellectual change leads to another controversial
point in Foucault's theory: instead of viewing thought in terms of
continuity and evolution, he speaks of upheaval and rupture. Like
Thomas Kuhn and Charles Taylor, Foucault asserts that ideas can
take sudden, qualitative leaps: "the conceptual mutations in human
history can and frequently do produce conceptual webs which are
incommensurable, that is, where the terms can't be defined in
relation to a common stratum of expressions" (Taylor, 49). In *The
Movement of Thought,* Herbert De Ley attempts to reconcile the two
apparently antithetical models of rupture and evolution by applying
"various sorts of empirical tinkering" to Foucault's concepts (150).
De Ley's attempts at reconciliation are not wholly successful,
perhaps because theoretical concepts do not respond well to
"tinkering". For my part, I find the discomfort caused by the notion
of discontinuity neither surprising nor disturbing. When rethinking
our intellectual history with the mental apparatus inherited from our
own culture, it is inevitable that we arrive at certain concepts that are
not totally clear, and feeling uncomfortable is, colloquially speaking,
part of the deal. Further, it seems to me that Foucault offers his
concept of sudden epistemic shifts not as a definitive solution, but as
an acknowledgement of the poverty of previous solutions. What
Paul de Man calls the "genetic" concept of history—"a temporal
hierarchy that resembles a parental structure in which the past is like

an ancestor" (164)—is now recognized as part of our intellectual inheritance from nineteenth century science. It is difficult to see how nineteenth century notions of "history" and "evolution" can help us, in the twentieth century, to elucidate seventeenth century thought: if anachronistic we must be, at least let our anachronisms be modern.

What is more troubling to me than the notion of discontinuity is the corollary, less present in Foucault than in his followers, that an abrupt change in mind set gave rise, in the early seventeenth century, to a coherent, "dominant" world view based on accurate representation. Timothy Reiss, in *The Discourse of Modernism*, makes a forceful, if extreme, argument for this view.[3] In my own work on the classical period, I have found that "new" linguistic views do not totally abolish the old, and in fact the most illuminating insights can come from the interplay of both.[4] For all its trappings of modernity, Reiss' holistic image of the classical period bears an ironic resemblance to the "Age of Reason" long propounded by the literary orthodoxy. In my view, neither the traditional nor the "modernist" interpretation really addresses the unsettling questions posed by contemporary criticism and philosophy: questions about how social history works, how language works, and, how minds work. All these questions are provocatively raised by Richard Rorty.

Rorty's contribution to seventeenth century studies, notably in *Philosophy and the Mirror of Nature*, is both considerable and double-edged. On the one hand, his repeated, and emphatic, tributes to classical thinkers would warm any *dix-septièmiste'* s heart:

> We owe the notion of a 'theory of knowledge' based on an understanding of 'mental processes' to the seventeenth century, and especially to Locke. We owe the notion of 'the mind' as a separate entity in which 'processes' occur to the same period, and especially to Descartes (3-4).

Rorty concurs with Foucault and Reiss that representation has been the dominant model of thought since the seventeenth century: "To know is to represent accurately what is outside the mind. . . . Philosophy's central concern is to be a general theory of representation" (Rorty, 3). However, seventeenth century chauvinism quickly fades when we realize that Rorty is raising up classical representation only in order to demolish it: "... the notion of knowledge as accurate representation, made possible by special mental processes, and intelligible through a general theory of representation, *needs to be abandoned*" (6, emphasis mine).

Rorty's attack on representation is not, or is only secondarily, historical: his real target is contemporary philosophy. He indeed points out that the notion of philosophy as a discipline centering on epistemology as a foundation for the sciences, and the notion that the sciences need such an epistemic foundation, are creations of the seventeenth century: "since the period of Descartes and Hobbes, the assumption that scientific discourse was normal discourse and that all other discourse needed to be modeled upon it has been the standard motive for philosophizing" (387). But he makes this observation in order to argue that these notions are 300 years out of date. Leaving the philosophers to defend themselves—which they are certainly well equipped to do—I will concentrate on the dilemma posed to criticism: it would be ironic indeed if literary theorists, seeking a more solid, "scientific" basis for their work than that afforded by post-Kantian esthetics were to find they had borrowed a concept of science which is even more outdated. In a fittingly Cartesian way, however, this undermining of previous certainties may yet supply a point of departure for the reorganization of literary knowledge. To make this point, I will need to examine in greater detail Rorty's attack on representation.

IV

...for words are but the images of matter. FRANCIS BACON, *The Advancement of Learning* (26).

It is pictures rather than propositions, metaphors rather than statements, which determine most of our philosophical convictions. *Philosophy and the Mirror of Nature* (12).

It is both paradoxical and revealing that Richard Rorty's indictment of representation draws its ammunition not from philosophy, but from criticism. He claims that the whole basis of Western rationalism—the human mind contemplating, and reflecting, truth, and thereby creating a foundation for knowledge—rests on a misplaced "ocular metaphor": the eye in the mirror. The eye Rorty refers to is the Greek "eye of the mind," the mirror Shakespeare's "Glassy Essence," both of which are given a renewed philosophical form in the late seventeenth century. With a relativism more radical than Foucault's, Rorty asserts that there is no particular reason why this ocular metaphor seized the imagination of the founders of Western thought:

> The notion of "contemplation," of knowledge of universal concepts or truths as *theoria* makes the Eye of the Mind the inescapable model for the better sort of knowledge. But it is fruitless to ask whether the Greek language, or Greek economic conditions, or the idle fancy of some nameless pre-Socratic, is responsible for viewing this sort of knowledge as looking at something (rather than, say, rubbing up against it, or crushing it underfoot, or having sexual intercourse with it). (38-39)

As Rorty would have it, the long search for philosophical certainty is the result of an arbitrary, almost accidental turning, not of thought, but of phrase—a rogue metaphor that we should henceforth purge from our intellectual vocabulary.

Rorty's refreshingly outrageous relativism is full of fascinating contradictions. On the one hand, by implying that representation is not "seriously" philosophical because it is not an idea but a metaphor, he appears to rejoin philosophers like Paul Ricoeur who show a Platonic suspicion of the figurative. In *The Rule of Metaphor*, "Ricoeur is himself concerned with the excessive encroachment of the poetic on the philosophic. . . " (LaCapra, 143). But at the same time, Rorty's intellectual sympathies clearly lie with those thinkers who, like Thomas Kuhn, challenge the distinctions made by analytic philosophy:

> To sum up the line I am taking about Kuhn and his critics: the controversy between them is about whether science, as the discovery of what is really out there in the world, differs in its patterns of argumentation from discourses for which the notion of 'correspondence to reality' seems less apposite (ie. politics and literary criticism) (332)

Rorty, thus, seems to be sitting on the disciplinary fence: he willingly adopts methods from literary analysis, but uses them in order to discredit philosophy for being—horror—too "literary" and imagistic.

To a literary critic, however, this dominance of imagery comes as no embarrassment. *Au contraire*, it may supply the missing link we were seeking, the nexus and point of intersection between philosophy and art on the one hand and representation and mimesis on the other. To the diagram proposed above (Figure 2), it is now possible to add a new element:

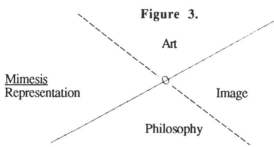

Figure 3.

Imagery is an inseparable part of philosophy as it is of language: it is through the image that representation, in thought and in art, takes its form. Before continuing to pursue the general implications of intellectual imagery for literature and philosophy, it is time to turn to a concrete instance drawn from a classical master of such imagery: Corneille.

V

Polyeucte and the Sovereign Image

Corneille's *Polyeucte* takes place on the Cornelian fringes of the Roman empire, in a kind of political no-man's-land. Unlike *Nicomède*, which is also set in one of those backwater provinces dear to the playwright, Polyeucte's kingdom does not even have a king. "Pour donner plus de dignité à l'action," Corneille tells us in the *Examen*, he was obliged to promote Félix from mere official-in-charge to governor, but nothing like a real ruler ever appears in the play. That is why *Polyeucte* is a particularly pure environment for studying the image of the sovereign. A work may be monarchical without the actual presence of a monarch; in the case of *Polyeucte*, while the sovereign is physically absent, politically and morally the whole text is permeated by an absolutist vision, a vision conveyed through language. Thus in order to see where political and ideological sovereignty really lie, it is necessary to examine the word and the notion of sovereignty as they appear in Corneille's text.

Interestingly, the word *souverain* appears in *Polyeucte* only in metaphorical contexts:

> Tant qu'ils ne sont qu'amants nous sommes *souveraines*.
> (Pauline, I, 3, v. 133)

> Pourrai-je voir Pauline, et rendre à ses beaux yeux
> L'hommage *souverain* que l'on va rendre aux dieux?
> (Sévère, II, 1, vv. 366-7)

These examples are derived from the "courtly" tradition in which love exercises sovereignty—supreme authority—over the lover, preempting both political and religious obligations. In the next examples, love (control over the love object) and self-control (dominion over one's own passions) are shown to be interrelated:

> Et sur mes passions ma raison souveraine
> Eût blamé mes soupirs et dissipé ma haine.
> (Pauline, II, 2, vv. 477-8)

> Ainsi de vos désirs toujours reine absolue...
> (Sévère to Pauline, v. 481)

> Ma raison, il est vrai, dompte mes sentiments;
> Mais quelque autorité que sur eux elle ait prise,
> Elle n'y règne pas, elle les tyrannise.
> (Pauline, vv. 500-503)

For Pauline and Sévère, the characters in the play who are primarily concerned with private lives and feelings, it is not surprising that the *souverain empire* is psychological. Littré's fifth definition of *souveraineté* contains a similar metaphor, indicating its currency in the language: "Il se dit de *l'empire* que l'on a sur ses passions, sur son âme, sur le coeur d'un autre" (emphasis mine).

Beyond this psychological sense of the term, where in the play is sovereign power perceived to lie? Not in the political sphere, where authority is severely fragmented. Félix, who nominally represents the Emperor, is a weak power broker who fears Polyeucte, Sévère, the gods, and his own shadow. Polyeucte, descendant of local kings, poses a political as well as a religious threat to imperial rule. Sévère, the victorious Roman hero, might decide to reign in his own right. This dispersion of power creates a vacuum which will be filled by the dynamic new force of Christianity. From the outset, the Christian religion is accorded the supremacy political institutions lack. In the original etymological sense of the term, it is above (*superamus*) all other values and obligations. Speaking of baptism, Polyeucte uses the word *suprême*, etymological double of *souverain*:

> Bien que je le préfère aux grandeurs d'un empire,
> Comme le bien suprême, et le seul où j'aspire,
> Je crois pour satisfaire un juste et saint amour,
> Pouvoir un peu remettre, et différer d'un jour.
> (I, 1, ll. 49-52)

Baptism is *le bien suprême*, but it is paramount in a hierarchical structure which reserves space for other obligations. Néarque's reply, while more extremist, still maintains this hierarchical view:

Nous pouvons tout aimer, il le souffre, il l'ordonne;
Mais, à vous dire tout, ce Seigneur des seigneurs
Veut le premier amour et les premiers honneurs.
Comme rien n'est égal à sa grandeur suprême,
Il faut ne rien aimer qu'après lui, qu'en lui-même,
Négliger, pour lui plaire, et femme, et biens, et rang,
Exposer pour sa gloire et verser tout son sang. (ll. 70-76)

This speech displays an interesting ambivalence. The first part, with its noble vocabulary (*seigneur*, *grandeur*) evokes the image of a feudal monarchy in which the ruler is supreme but not absolute. The last three lines, however, initiate a movement from a multivalent, hierarchical system to a unitary, absolutist one: *après lui* is supplanted by *en lui-même*, which is then reinforced by *négliger . . . verser tout son sang*. For Néarque, Christianity's sovereignty is not total: one neglects other loves, but one does not abandon them. It will be Polyeucte's destiny to take this further, radical step.

Absolute sovereignty: three variations on the Credo

Polyeucte contains three passages which outline the tenets of the Christian faith. These share as subtext the Credo of the Latin mass, universally familiar to French audiences from Corneille's time well into the twentieth century. But a comparison between the French and Latin texts reveals major shifts of emphasis. In the first passage (III, 2) Stratonice recounts Polyeucte's desecration of the temple and reports his words:

Le Dieu de Polyeucte et celui de Néarque
De la terre et du ciel est l'absolu monarque,
Seul être indépendant, seul maître du destin,
Seul principe éternel, et souveraine fin.
C'est ce Dieu des chrétiens qu'il faut qu'on remercie,
Des victoires qu'il donne à l'empereur Décie;
Lui seul tient en sa main le succès des combats;
Il le veut élever, il le peut mettre à bas;
Sa bonté, son pouvoir, sa justice est immense..... (844-51)

Certain of Stratonice's terms, like *bonté*, *pouvoir*, *justice* are common in Biblical and liturgical usage, but others, like *l'absolu monarque* and *maître du destin*, apply more aptly to a political ruler than a divine one.

This tendency towards politicization continues into the second passage (IV, 6), where Sévère comments, as an impartial outside observer, on the characteristics of Christianity. Like Polyeucte (as quoted by Stratonice), Sévère offers a gloss on the first line of the

Credo (*Credo in unum Deum, patrem omnipotentem/Les chrétiens n'ont qu'un Dieu, maître absolu de tout*); and like Polyeucte's, his version changes the paternal to the monarchical (*patrem omnipotentem>maître absolu*). He also asserts that the strength of Christianity lies in its monotheistic premise: one absolute God ruling the universe, as opposed to a mob of weak and warring deities. Finally, Sévère places a greater emphasis on divine will than one finds in the liturgical text: "De qui le seul vouloir fait tout ce qu'il résout" (1430). Thus, the language of these two preliminary *credos* creates a monarchical image of God, in which the divine becomes a representation of the royal, rather than the (expected) reverse.

These tendencies come to full fruition in Polyeucte's *credo* (V,3) which, not incidentally, also marks the dramatic high point of the play—a real "show-stopper." At last, Polyeucte speaks in his own voice about the attributes of God and his own relation to Him. Polyeucte's speech reiterates the alterations we have already found in the earlier passages (emphasis on monotheism, secular *maîtrise* of God, etc.) while adding important new elements. For one thing, Corneille floods the text with emotive, even passionate vocabulary. "Je n'*adore* qu'un Dieu," cries Polyeucte, twice echoed by Félix's *adore les [idoles]* (vv. 1675, 6; cf. also 1659-61). Such language transfers the dominion of passion from the human to the divine level. It is only fitting at this point for Polyeucte to say his last earthly farewells: "Chère Pauline, adieu, conservez ma mémoire." But the most thrilling (sublime) moment of the scene comes with the repeated affirmation, "Je suis chrétien." This line contains no hint of Christian abnegation: by uniting with God, Polyeucte is not diminishing but aggrandizing himself to become all-powerful, autonomous, self-sustaining—the divinized image, in fact, of the Cornelian hero "de qui le seul vouloir fait tout ce qu'il résout." At this moment, the audience enjoys a kind of vicarious "power trip": we share Polyeucte's excitement as he gleefully hooks himself into the source of cosmic potency.

In conclusion, our examination of *Polyeucte* has revealed that a pervasive politicization extends into all aspects of the play. By gradual linguistic accretions, Corneille transforms the spiritual God of the Credo into an absolute monarch, *un portrait du roi*. But our analysis has unearthed a further curious twist: both God and monarch are representations of the hero. Or more precisely, God, king and hero are subsumed under a structure of global oppositions which constitutes, in my view, the ideological core of the play:

Figure 4.

LEVELS OF ACTION	WEAKNESS	STRENGTH
Religious (God)	Polytheism: weak and fragmented divinity (broken idols)	Monotheism: one powerful deity
Political (King)	Political Division	Political Unity and absolutism
Individual (Hero)	Psychological and moral weakness, indecisiveness, corruption	Moral strength, integrity

With a kind of circular reflexivity, God, at first image of the King, in turn becomes a reflection of the autonomous (sovereign) will. And Polyeucte's heroic monotheism reveals itself as a form of narcissism, even to the tautological form of the enunciation, *je suis chrétien*. Whether the classical sign, as Jay Caplan suggests, "necessarily acts out an eucharistic scenario" (811), it does have a doubly absolute meaning here: *je suis chrétien=je suis moi=je suis Dieu*. But this transcendent absolute, in turn, is revealed as a projection of the individual's yearning for absoluteness. *Portrait du roi, portrait du moi*: Polyeucte's *credo* is a tribute to the sovereign ego, his kingdom, the dominion of the self.

VI

> Reason in language—oh, what an old deceptive female she is! I am afraid we are not rid of God because we still have faith in grammar. NIETZSCHE, *Twilight of the Gods*, III, 5

What connections can be drawn between this analysis of Corneille and the philosophical issues raised earlier? Or, as LaCapra asks, "What is the relationship between metaphor and model or between model and mathematics" (108) or, for that matter, between philosophy and criticism? As a limited answer to these questions, I would suggest that the relation is partly in the eye of the beholder. Literary analysis reveals different things about texts than philosophical analysis because the literary analyst seeks to elucidate meanings rather than test claims. Not only are critics—perhaps—more comfortable with contradictory, or at least coexisting, meanings, but they have elaborated techniques to unearth and deal with them. Thus, for example, in the preceding analysis of *Polyeucte*, I used etymology and contextual reading to unravel the varied senses in which one could say that "the sovereign" is represented; and, in the process, the hidden interrelations between these senses came a little more clearly into view.

While Rorty also uses the concept of figurative language, his method and aims are quite different. He holds up his metaphorical mirror to prove a point, and picks his examples accordingly: a practice certainly not limited to philosophers. But in skipping from the Greeks to the seventeenth century, Rorty fails to see, or at least to mention, the other glass that flashes its occult light through Western thought—*per speculum in ænigmate*, the clouded mirror of Scriptural epistemology. In her scholarly study of medieval thought, *The Mirror of Language,* Rosamund Colish points out that the "dark glass" of 1st Corinthians is not a *visual* image but a *verbal* one: in the original Greek, *ænigma* ("allusive or obscure speech,") is a rhetorical device involving the use of subtle and puzzling discourse. Augustine, himself trained as a rhetorician, defines the *ænigma* as "a kind of simile but obscure and hard to understand" (*de Trinitate*, XV, ix, 15-16). For Augustine any theological statement is an *ænigma*—a kind of riddle—because God is unspeakable and yet spoken of.

This verbal image passed from Augustine into medieval philosophy, becoming a kind of model for theological knowledge. According to St. Anselm, "We know and express God. . . *through words*, as through a reflection in a mirror" (Colish, 137). Anselm's own language on this point is itself "enigmatic" in the rhetorical sense: "And in this way, we often express and yet do not express, see and yet do not see, one and the same object, we express it and see it through another; we do not express it, and do not see it by virtue of its own proper nature" (quoted in Colish, p. 138.) This view of language, assimilated by Scholasticism, became part of Descartes' philosophical heritage. It would be the task of another scholar, more philosophically qualified than I, to see to what extent, and in what form, these ideas persist in modern thought. The least one can say, however, is that in place of one mirror, we have two: Rorty's intellectual glass, doubling reflection with double clarity, and Augustine's rhetorical one, connoting not just obscurity, as is commonly thought, but indirection; knowledge conveyed through the distorting mirror of language.

In these two examples—my study of Corneille and Colish's of Augustine and Anselm—the use of methods associated with literary, rather than philosophical, analysis, gives rise to an "archeology of knowledge" different from Foucault's. For the critic, language cannot be split into geological layers; its meanings continue to persist, to a greater or lesser degree, throughout time. Semantics is an aggregate of which the writer is only partly in control: above and beyond her individual choices, conscious and unconscious, language continues to *mean through*, and to enrich, her text. Thus, rather than the image of an archeological artifact, cut off in its own space/time layer, I prefer to think of the word as a piece of antique furniture which, in the phrase of the Maine auctioneer, "has some age on it," which carries with it the patina of previous lives. Hence criticism, like furniture restoring, should be both innovative and preservative. As Steven Marcus has said, it entails a *refabrication* of the text by epoch and reader, and the greatness of certain texts lies both in their power to attract this refabrication, and in their strength to persevere, even as we force ourselves upon them again and again. In that spirit, let us welcome with open arms—and eyes—modern endeavors to link literature and history, language and thought, with the uncertainties these explorations inevitably create.

Notes

[1]La Capra makes this criticism of *Wittgenstein's Vienna* (Allan Janik and Steven Toulmin [New York: 1973]): "The paradoxes and silences of the text are not questioned precisely because they are filled in or smoothed over by generous helpings of context, and the paradoxes of the context itself are transcended through a methodology that ties everything together" (*Rethinking* 88).
[2]See Timothy Reiss's introduction to *Yale French Studies* 49, *Science, Language and the Perspective Mind.*
[3]Cf. La Capra's extremely interesting criticism of Reiss (*Rethinking,* 69 -71, n. 24).
[4]See my article on *Dom Juan,* p. 49.
[5]This argument is made by André Lefever in *Literary Knowledge.*

Works Cited

Augustine. *De Trinitate.* In *Patrologia latina cursus completus,* 42. Paris: Migne, 1945.
Bacon, Francis. *The Advancement of Learning.* Ed. Arthur Johnston. In *The Advancement of Learning and New Atlantis.* Oxford: Clarendon Press, 1974, 1-212.
Cahné, Pierre-Alain. *Un Autre Descartes: Le Philosophe et son langage.* Paris: J. Vrin, 1980.
Caplan, Jay. "Vicarious *jouissances*: on reading Casanova." *Modern Language Notes,* 100 (1985):803-814.
Colish, Rosamund. *The Mirror of Language.* New Haven and London: Yale UP, 1968.
Corneille, Pierre. *Polyeucte. Oeuvres complètes.* Paris: Classiques Garnier, 1960.
De Ley, Herbert. *The Movement of Thought.* Urbana and Chicago: U of Illinois P, 1985.
De Man, Paul. *Insight and Blindness.* Minneapolis: U of Minnesota P, 1983.

Foucault, Michel. *Les mots et les choses*. Paris: Gallimard, 1966. Eng. trans.
    The order of things. New York: Pantheon Books, 1970.
—. *L'Archéologie du savoir*. Paris: Gallimard, 1969. Eng. trans. *The
    Archaeology of Knowledge*. New York: Harper & Row, 1972.
Hoy, David. "Foucault's Slalom." *London Review of Books*, 4-17 November
    1982, 18.
LaCapra, Dominick. *Rethinking Intellectual History*. Ithaca and London:
    Cornell UP, 1983.
Lefever, André. *Literary Knowledge*. Assen/Amsterdam: Van Gorcum, 1977.
Marcus, Steven. Quoted at a *Partisan Review* conference held at Boston
    University, September 14, 1979.
Nietzsche, Friedrich Wilhelm. *Twilight of the Gods*. In *The Portable
    Nietzsche*. Trans. Walter Kaufmann. New York: Viking Press, 1954.
Reiss, Timothy. *The Discourse of Modernism*. Ithaca: Cornell UP, 1982.
Romanowski, Sylvie. *L'Illusion chez Descartes*. Paris: Klincksieck, 1974.
Rorty, Richard. *Philosophy and the Mirror of Nature*. Princeton: Princeton UP,
    1979.
Rosmarin, Adena. "Hermeneutics versus Erotics: Shakespeare's Sonnets and
    Interpretive History." *PMLA*, 100, (1985), 20-37.
Science, Language and the Perspective Mind. Yale French Studies 49 (1973).
Stempel, Daniel. "Blake, Foucault and the Classical Episteme." *PMLA*, 96,
    (1981), 388-407.
Taylor, Charles. "Interpretation and the Sciences of Man." *Metaphysics*, 25,
    (1971), 3-51.
Tolkien, J.R.R. *The Two Towers*. New York: Ballantine Books, 1965.
Woshinsky, Barbara R. *La Princesse de Clèves: the Tension of Elegance*. The
Hague: Mouton, 1973.
—. "Two Concepts of Language in Molière's *Dom Juan*," *Romanic Review*,
    72, (1981), 401-408.

Classical Discourse:
Gender and Objectivity

Erica Harth
Brandeis University

By 1643 the discourse that Timothy J. Reiss has called "analytico-referential" and that I will call "objective" or "scientific" was in force if not yet hegemonic. When in that year Descartes and Princess Elizabeth of Bohemia began what was to be a six-year correspondence on natural and moral philosophy it was against the background of a "new science" inscribed in this new discourse. The discourse promised immediate signification: through the transparency of the word, the thing (referent) would be apparent. The new science promised mastery over a nature traditionally represented as female and which now became an object of conquest by methodical investigation. Evelyn Fox Keller and Carolyn Merchant, among others, have discussed the androcentricity of the new science. There is nothing to indicate that Elizabeth, as a woman, could have had anything to contribute to the development of its discourse. Yet, I will argue, there was a "Cartesian moment" in which women did not so much help to consolidate the discourse as to keep open the various possibilities of its elaboration. The rage for Descartes's philosophy in the salons was symptomatic of a discursive openness that prevailed from the 1640s to the 1660s. It was as if women provided a "different voice," one that commanded and received attention in these years. Princess Elizabeth was one such voice, to which Descartes was particularly attentive.

By 1686, when the original edition of Fontenelle's *Entretiens sur la pluralité des mondes* (lacking the sixth *entretien*) appeared, that other voice seems to have been silenced or driven underground. Fontenelle and his fictitious Marquise may be seen as emblematic of a moment of discursive dominance. The Marquise's status as a pupil marks the triumph of a definitively male objectivity. Her voice is indeed different, but its difference is subordinated to and used as a foil for the objective truth spoken by Fontenelle. By contrast, I hesitate to characterize the relationship of Descartes and Elizabeth as one of mentor to disciple. At times, allowing for the compensatory value of Elizabeth's rank, their relationship verges on one of equality.[1]

It may be objected to my comparative scheme that the Marquise was Fontenelle's fictional creation, whereas Descartes did not after all create Elizabeth. To this double antithesis—fictional woman/real woman (male created voice/genuine female voice)—I would bring several qualifications. Elizabeth addresses herself to philosophical questions posed by Descartes; within the limits of their correspondence his philosophy sets the conditions for her voice. She adopts the discourse of objectivity, which still retained some of the polyphony of its formative phase, in order to speak to and against it. On the other hand, Fontenelle may have modelled his Marquise on a real woman (Mme de la Mésangère? Mme de Lambert?) with whom he may have had real conversations. In both cases, the discursive conditions are established by men; men set the limits within which the other voice speaks. Descartes could have responded differently to Elizabeth. Something in his letters, however, allowed enough play for a true exchange to take place. Fontenelle and his Marquise do not speak the same language; she stands outside the discourse, which is now resolutely his. Her resistance merely highlights his power. My choice of a "real" and a "fictional" pair underlines the problematic nature of discourse, at once concrete and abstract.

What happened between 1643 and 1686 was the flourishing of a literature that has subsequently been called "classical," Louis XIV's assumption, with his personal rule, of ambitious political and economic goals, and the founding, in 1666, of the Académie des Sciences—events which are not unrelated. Like Charles II's incorporation of the Royal Society of London four years earlier, the founding of the French scientific academy institutionalized the compact between power and science. Although the informal academies, such as Mersenne's and Montmor's, had been male preserves, the establishment of the Académie des Sciences marked an official exclusion: science was for men only. Unlike the *ruelle*, the academy now meant serious business. The distance between academy and salon is signalled by the degradation of the verbal exchange of the salon to "ridiculous" *préciosité* and the simultaneous elevation of the discourse of objectivity to a place of sole epistemological authority. As Louis XIV co-opted scientific and technological expertise for the greater glory of the monarchy, science became the very model of truth. At the same time, classical literature elaborated a model of reason that was meant to be universally valid. Classical discourse, a variant of the discourse of objectivity, derived its legitimacy from its alliance with an official culture that now saw itself as hegemonic.

Paradoxically, at the very moment that Louis claimed science as a necessary adjunct to his mercantilist program and the Académie des Sciences shut its doors to women, science breathed a democratic message of accessibility to all. The early works of the Académie are written in deliberately limpid, jargon-free language. The official natural histories were comprised of taxonomies aimed above all at intelligibility. Similarly, classicism claims universality: its truths are to apply equally to everyone. In reality, of course, science was open only to the educated (male) few, and the works of French classicism were addressed to a literate elite. Androcentric objectivity became dominant at precisely the moment when democratic claims of universality were officially incorporated into its discourse. The decades intervening between Descartes's correspondence with Elizabeth and the creation of the paradigmatic pair of male master and female pupil in Fontenelle and the Marquise mark the consolidation of objectivity into a hegemonic male discourse. "Classicism," as the esthetic deployment of objectivity, contributed to the promotion of what Evelyn Fox Keller has called the "objectivist illusion" (70): the concealment of subjectivity in scientific pursuit of the object. The "different voice" in objectivity's formative phase, however, was that of the subject, who had not yet lost what Reiss calls the "responsibility of enunciation" (Reiss, *Discourse* 42).

In the pages that follow, I will attempt to delineate the trajectory of objectivity through its classical phase. The relationship between Descartes and Elizabeth on the one hand and that of Fontenelle and the Marquise on the other will represent not so much "real" gender relations of the time (although they may also have such representational value) as discursive patterns and possibilities. The two relationships will serve, respectively, as the *terminus a quo* and the *terminus ad quem* of the passage from a discourse that still admitted of another voice to one that was sealed in its own androcentricity.

I

Although Elizabeth of Bohemia was not French and did not live in France, she, like her friend Anna Maria van Schurman, participated from afar in a moment of extraordinary intellectual ferment among both the women and men of the French elites. From the mid-seventeenth century, public lectures in French began to proliferate, offering a refreshing alternative to the Latin of the university. Women may have attended Renaudot's lectures at the Bureau d'Adresse (1633-42); they certainly went to the "conférences académiques et oratoires" of Richesource in the 1650s, and, in 1655, to the "Palais Précieux," or hôtel d'Anjou, rue Béthisy, where they found a mixture of lectures and polite entertainment. Lecturers spoke on a wide variety of subjects, especially at the Bureau d'Adresse, but the preferred topics fell within the province of moral or natural philosophy. Louis de Lesclache's lectures on moral philosophy (1635-69), for example, enjoyed great popularity. His attempt to accommodate a female audience is captured by the title of one of his courses, "Les Avantages que les femmes peuvent recevoir de la philosophie et principalement de la morale, ou l'Abrégé de cette science" (Paris, 1667). Women attended Lémery's courses on chemistry and lectures on natural science given by the Cartesians Rohault and Régis. Descartes was at once a catalyst and a symptom of expanding intellectual horizons. With the new science and the exhilaration of intellectual discovery came a new openness, a sense that nature was accessible, even to women. Knowledge could, as it were, go public, appear in salons in the vulgar tongue. So it is understandable that in the general flush of excitement over Cartesian philosophy, Elizabeth should have initiated a correspondence with its author in May of 1643.

The princess's erudition and intelligence are reflected in the fact that her very first question to Descartes called attention to one of the weakest links in his deductive chain, his dualism. How, she wanted to know, can body and soul be separate and yet united (Descartes, *Lettres* 3-4)? This inquiry drew a respectful, serious reply from Descartes, and the exchange set the tone for their entire correspondence.

Although initially Elizabeth makes some modest references to her "stupidité," she does not hesitate to question even Descartes's most definitive statements. She tenaciously pursues the matter of dualism through two more of her letters, suggesting that the *Méditations* leave important questions unanswered. As the correspondence unfolds, an authentic dialogue develops that problematizes the relationship of the writers. Elizabeth's impressive solution to the problem of the three circles (one so difficult, said Descartes, that it would take a miracle for an angel to be able to solve it) and the evident intellectual challenge that she consistently posed to the philosopher suggest that he could treat her neither as a pupil nor as a patron. Descartes's dedication of the *Principia philosophiae* (1644) to Elizabeth could have signified an expression of his gratitude for her intellectual companionship as much as a politically motivated compliment. Gender does not seem to have been a serious issue between the correspondents. Although in his first letter of May 21, 1643 Descartes did try out one courtly compliment to the princess in speaking of her "discours plus qu'humains" emanating from her "corps si semblable à ceux que les peintres donnent aux anges" (5), he quickly abandoned the genre. And although Elizabeth makes some infrequent references to the physical weakness of her sex, she mentions received ideas on women only once in passing. In her letter of December 4, 1649, she says that she is happy to have gotten a glowing description of Queen Christina of Sweden from Descartes because the image of such a talented woman "affranchit notre sexe de l'imputation d'imbécillité et de faiblesse que MM. les pédants lui soulaient donner" (223).

The best word that I can find to characterize the tone of the epistolary relationship between Descartes and Elizabeth is "complicity." Perhaps the two exiles, one voluntary, the other involuntary, were uniquely qualified to understand one another. Their letters seem to project an early dawn of enlightenment, limited for the moment to the small corner of the earth that these two inhabit. The philosopher and the princess share a scorn for "préjugés" and recognize in one another the intellectual liberation of the exceptional individual. Descartes tells his correspondent what "extraordinary joy" he feels in reading her letters because "il m'arrive si peu souvent de rencontrer de bons raisonnements, non seulement dans les discours de ceux que je fréquente en ce désert, mais aussi dans les livres que je consulte" (114). Elizabeth writes from Crossen about nearby villagers who believe that a terrible plague of flies is a result of witchcraft. She, however, attributes it to an overflow of the Oder (185). She sympathizes with Descartes's dismay at the incomprehension and backbiting with which his ideas have been greeted in scholarly quarters. The correspondents sometimes resort to cryptic language or code to protect themselves, and in her letter of December 7, 1645, Elizabeth worries that her last (rather daringly irreverent) letter to Descartes may have fallen into the wrong hands: "Je serais fâchée qu'elle vienne entre les mains de quelqu'un de ces critiques, qui condamnent pour hérésies tous les doutes qu'on fait des opinions reçues" (123).

The attraction of Descartes's philosophy in these years must have resided partly in his methodical doubt, which had the effect of lifting the veil of received wisdom. Timothy J. Reiss, correctly, I believe, sees Descartes's appeal for women in the concept of a reason that—at least as far as we can tell—knows no distinction of sex (Reiss, "Corneille" 10). The other side of that reason, methodical doubt, aside from raising the hackles of the orthodox, must have had the effect of opening a discursive space for previously silent voices to test out their opinions. It is into this space that Elizabeth so eagerly steps.

Because the bright side of Descartes—overwhelming confidence in the power of his method to attain certainty—is so prominent in his letters, the space may not be immediately visible. Despite the complaints about his detractors, Descartes's communications to Elizabeth are filled with the optimism of the *Discours de la méthode* : universal human reason is the source of our greatest and most available contentment. The moral precepts that he derives from this variety of stoicism have the democratic connotations of "bon sens": in following them, anyone will find happiness (Descartes, *Lettres* 62). The universal applicability of Descartes's moral rules and scientific method, both informed by a "democratic" principle of accessibility to all, constitute perhaps the firmest commitment to date in France to objectivity.

Descartes positions himself as if somewhere in outer space and points to truth and certainty for all to see. Such abstraction of the subject has been variously called "the view from nowhere" (Nagel) and "the angelic eye"—or "I" (Harries). For Descartes, science has above all heuristic value, yet there are times when he comes dangerously close to reifying it. In one letter, he draws a comparison between the possible adulteration of chemically prepared medicine by a change of formula and the adulteration of *science* by the ignorant. This knowledge sounds suspiciously like an already established corpus of wisdom: "Il en est quasi de même de la Science, entre les mains de ceux qui la veulent débiter sans la bien savoir; car, en pensant corriger ou ajouter quelque chose à ce qu'ils ont appris, ils la convertissent en erreur" (168).

As the relationship between the two correspondents deepens, Elizabeth takes charge of her subjectivity and introduces it as a counterpoint to what begins to sound more and more like axiomatic pronouncement on Descartes's side. When in the first several letters the discussion centers on mathematics and natural philosophy, this subjectivity takes the form of well-placed substantive doubts about the validity of Descartes's theories (how can the soul be immaterial and impart movement to the body?). But when in May of 1645 Descartes and Elizabeth move into the realm of moral philosophy with a discussion of Seneca, she begins to reflect on her subjectivity and in effect proposes an alternative epistemology.

Descartes's neo-stoicism rests on the major epistemological premise that *res cogitans* has a reflexive capacity to disengage itself from the body (to which, we remember, it is attached while nevertheless distinct), to view it and all that befalls it, and, consequently, all accidents that befall *res extensa* with the bemused detachment of a spectator at the theater. Developing a spectacular image that he had used in the *Discours de la méthode*, which expresses a theme that he would develop further in the *Passions de l'âme*, Decartes writes of "les plus grandes âmes" that:

> se considérant comme immortelles et capables de recevoir de très grands contentements, puis, d'autre part, considérant qu'elles sont jointes à des corps mortels et fragiles, qui sont sujets à beaucoup d'infirmités, et qui ne peuvent manquer de périr dans peu d'années, elles font bien tout ce qui est en leur pouvoir pour se rendre la Fortune favorable en cette vie, mais néanmoins elles l'estiment si peu, au regard de l'Eternité, qu'elles n'en considèrent quasi les événements que comme nous faisons ceux des Comédies. Et comme les Histoires tristes et lamentables, que nous voyons représenter sur un théâtre, nous donnent souvent autant de récréation que les gaies, bien qu'elles tirent des larmes de nos yeux; ainsi ces plus grandes âmes ...ont de la satisfaction, en elles-mêmes, de toutes les choses qui leur arrivent, même des plus fâcheuses et insupportables. (Descartes, *Lettres* 42)

I cite this passage at length because it illustrates precisely how in Descartes's case dualism leads logically to an epistemology of the spectacular, to the "angelic eye (I)." Reason and will can then dominate the passions, because, as properties of the impassive spectator, they are so distant from passion that the thinking subject all but withdraws into that contemplative eye.

Elizabeth resists Descartes's invitation to apply this epistemology to a stoical acceptance of the misfortunes attendant on her exile. A comparison with Freud irresistibly suggests itself when Descartes tries to persuade her that a fever she develops is a result of melancholia and that she is capable of rising above it all to attain the contentment of a "grande âme." She counters that her body, specifically, her female body, exercises too great an influence on her soul for her to reach this degree of detachment. In a vein quite consistent with her initial doubts about Descartes's dualism she writes, "Sachez donc que j'ai le corps imbu d'une grande partie des faiblesses de mon sexe, qu'il se ressent très facilement des afflictions de l'âme, et n'a point la force de se remettre avec elle ..." (44-5). She refuses the spectacular image by objecting that she is unable to view the misfortunes of her family as anything other than a "mal" (45).

The facts of Elizabeth's continuing debility and family problems inspire her to pursue the subjectivist alternative. To Descartes's emphasis on the will, she counterposes the power of the involuntary: what happens to will and reason when they are eroded by disease or distracted by personal cares (65-6)? Descartes, whose position on free will brought him in any case perilously close to heterodoxy, is obliged to reply that he intended his notion of beatitude to apply only to the mentally sound. That is, he is obligated to qualify a universal statement and therefore to modify the objectivist stance: "...ce que j'avais dit généralement de tous les hommes ne doit être entendu que de ceux qui ont l'usage libre de leur raison...." (79).[2]

The question remains as to how correct judgments—those that will ultimately bring the contentment that comes with the conquest of passions—are formed. Descartes's reiteration that knowledge and memory of truth are all that is required takes on the character of a tautology under Elizabeth's insistent questioning, and his final recourse to God begins to look like little more than the escape hatch that some critics thought it was. For Elizabeth, the thinking subject is grounded in materiality: imagination and the senses as well as reason have their part. She does not, in other words, understand the effacement of the subject behind an abstract reason, or the bracketing of subjectivity. She sees language itself as a materiality in which subjectivity is embedded:

> Mais j'avoue que je trouve de la difficulté à séparer des sens et de l'imagination des choses qui y sont continuellement représentées par discours et par lettres, que je ne saurais éviter sans pécher contre mon devoir. Je considère bien qu'en effaçant de l'idée d'une affaire tout ce qui me la rend fâcheuse (que je crois m'être seulement représenté par l'imagination), j'en jugerais tout aussi sainement et y trouverais aussitôt les remèdes que je fais avec l'affection que j'y apporte. Mais je ne l'ai jamais su pratiquer qu'après que la passion avait joué son rôle. Il y a quelque chose de surprenant dans les malheurs, quoi que prévus, dont je ne suis maîtresse qu'après un certain temps, auquel mon corps se désordonne si fort, qu'il me faut plusieurs mois pour le remettre, qui ne se passent guère sans quelque nouveau sujet de trouble. (52-3)

Elizabeth, who was suspected of complicity with her brother in the murder of a Frenchman, punctuates her communications with allusions to family problems and responsibilities. She did not have the male prerogative, which Descartes exercised to the best of his ability, of roaming about alone, relatively free from domestic care. Her illness and misfortune constantly remind her of the concrete conditions of subjectivity. Although Descartes brings her "consolation" and a buoying confidence in the powers of her own rational faculties, her admiration for his philosophy remains tempered by the "responsibility of enunciation" which she takes so seriously. Descartes's methodical doubt has a welcoming effect and generates the mutual respect of two intellects for whom *science* is the antidote to "prejudice." In this Cartesian moment the subjectivist strain enhances the heuristic value of science and knowledge and counterbalances tendencies toward their reificaton. When Descartes invites Elizabeth to discuss Seneca with him, he lets her know that her comments will be instructive and helpful to him: "outre qu'elles serviront de beaucoup à m'instruire, elles me donneront occasion de rendre les miennes plus exactes...." It is this space of doubt and exploration that allows their dialogue to unfold.

II

It was undoubtedly the Cartesian in him that led Fontenelle to adopt the opera as his central metaphor in the *Entretiens sur la pluralité des mondes*.[3] In Fontenelle's hands Descartes's spectacular image undergoes significant development. Nature is now a fully mechanized spectacle with no one to get it going. When the prime mover is taken out of the picture, the important agents become explanatory ones. It is the philosopher sitting in the audience with his understanding of the "derrière du Théâtre" who counts. Fontenelle all but apotheosizes Descartes (along with "quelqu'autres Modernes"), whose role it was to dispel ancient myths about what was going on behind the scenes (17-20). Fontenelle does not place himself in the pit with the audience, but rather at an unspecified vantage point from which he can reveal the spectacle to the Marquise: "je n'ai qu'à tirer le rideau, et à vous montrer le Monde" (21). His persona is a kind of superspectator, a master of ceremonies or tour guide who can induct the Marquise into the mysteries of the performance.

Fontenelle externalizes Descartes's image of the spectator, literally pushing the viewer into outer space. As Descartes invites

Elizabeth to join him in viewing the human comedy from a moral elevation, so Fontenelle invites the Marquise to view our planet from the heavens. "Il faudrait être simplement Spectateur du Monde, et non pas Habitant," he tells her (51). Interestingly, her response to this invitation is similar to Elizabeth's. She remains emotionally rooted in her own planet, unable to shake off the mentality of the earthling. This strong identification with her native globe may be taken as a metaphor for subjectivity. The Marquise's language, like Elizabeth's, is colored by the emotion of the subject; Fontenelle's pupil refuses "scientific" detachment. Fontenelle, in contrast with Descartes vis-à-vis Elizabeth, does not engage in a true intellectual exchange with the Marquise. As her mentor, he aims to change her perspective and to introduce her to a new mode of thought.

The gap between the subjective immanence of the Marquise and the transcendence of her feelings toward objectivity that Fontenelle demands of her may be measured by their respective use of the pronoun "nous." Fontenelle's first person plural has the ambiguity of the shifter, which Philip Lewis has so perceptively discussed in connection with La Rochefoucauld. It is an ambiguity, as I will argue below, that is fundamental to "classicism." Fontenelle says: "Nous voulons juger de tout, et nous sommes toûjours dans un mauvais point de vûë. Nous voulons juger de nous, nous en sommes trop près; nous voulons juger des autres, nous en sommes trop loin" (50). Fontenelle's subject pronoun, at once subject of the utterance and subject of the enunciation, conceals this basic split in its identity by explicitly counterposing itself to the object pronoun "nous," which is on a level with the other objects, "tout" and "les autres." In order to judge ourselves we must alienate our subjectivity, somehow remaining impassive before the self as object. The subject pronoun is drained of subjectivity as it claims the power of reflexivity, which grants to the self the status of pure object, or object of disinterested judgment and scientific investigation. The Marquise, responsible for her enunciation, identifies both herself and Fontenelle with a resolutely earthbound "nous": "Je ne me consolerai jamais, dit-elle, de l'injustice que nous faisons à la Terre et de la préoccupation trop favorable où nous sommes pour la Lune [in thinking it alone is luminous], si vous ne m'assurés que les Gens de la Lune ne connoissent pas mieux leurs avantages que nous les nôtres, et qu'ils prennent notre Terre pour un Astre, sans sçavoir que leur habitation en est un aussi" (51).

In consistently assuming the earthbound condition of her subjectivity, the Marquise humanizes Fontenelle's astronomy lessons. Of the Copernican system she says, "Cela est assés plaisant...la Terre prend tout sur soi, et le Soleil ne fait rien" (34). Into her "nous," which contrasts comically with Fontenelle's detached subject, she pours the partisan feeling of embattled geocentricity. Fontenelle, on the other hand, wishes that he had the perspective of a lunarian in which an ideally detached subject could observe its alter ego, the objectified "nous":

> S'il se pouvoit faire que nous eussions de la raison, et que nous ne fussions pourtant pas Hommes, et si d'ailleurs nous habitions la Lune, nous imaginerions-nous bien qu'il y eût ici-bas cette espece bizarre de créatures qu'on appelle le Genre humain? Pourrions-nous bien nous figurer quelque chose qui eût des passions si folles et des réflexions si sages?...Il faudroit que les Gens de la Lune eussent bien de l'esprit, s'ils devinoient tout cela. Nous nous voyons incessamment nous-mêmes, et nous en sommes encore à deviner comment nous sommes faits. (66-7)

The Marquise's response is devoid of reflexivity. Her "nous" defines itself against the lunar Other in a kind of Cold War mentality: "Nous voilà donc bien en sûreté du côté des Gens de la Lune...ils ne nous devineront pas; mais je voudrois que nous les pussions deviner; car en vérité cela inquiete, de sçavoir qu'ils sont là-haut, dans cette Lune que nous voyons, et de ne pouvoir pas se figurer comment ils sont faits" (67).

In the context of the new science, the Marquise's subjectivity and consequent humanization of the world become categorized as mythical thought. The famous elephants that Fontenelle's pupil needs to support the earth in celestial matter are borrowed from Bernier's report of an Indian myth. In response to the Marquise's idea that the Indians would have doubled the number of elephants had they known that the earth was "en péril de se mouvoir," Fontenelle merely laughs (37-8). This laughter, which recurs (e.g. 72), seems to echo the Olympian laughter of the gods contemplating their creation of humanity, which the philosopher invokes in his speculations on the inhabitants of the moon (67). Elsewhere he subtly suggests that the Marquise's is a "savage mind," anchored in primitive patterns of thought. He scoffs at her scepticism about the possibility of interstellar travel and visitors from outer space, likening it to the ignorant surprise of the American Indians at the arrival of the Europeans on their shores (70-2).

The Marquise's need for design in the universe, for security and certainty—"j'ai besoin de croire," she says (78)—place her in the realm of the prescientific, the mythic and the primitive. Fontenelle's task as her mentor is to draw her into the modern world, to convert her to the discourse of objectivity. To this end, the "soirs," or lessons, get progressively more difficult, so that by the sixth and last the teacher can congratulate his pupil on having achieved the ability to reason (although he must warn her about premature systematizing): "Voilà, Madame, . . . un petit commencement de Sistême que vous avés fait assés heureusement" (176). Unable to free herself sufficiently from the archaic need for security to be able to tolerate the uncertainty of competing hypotheses on the habitability of the moon, the Marquise at least learns how to ask "pourquoi non?" (91). She is brought, in other words, to the point at which Elizabeth begins, the moment of doubt and suspension of judgment, the necessary precondition for the development of objectivity.

In this parable of enlightenment it is highly signifcant that the pupil is female and that the many layers of her metaphorical meaning specify different aspects of femininity. It is she who speaks for the realm of the concrete—"Allons au fait," she says (77)—and for the imagination and the senses. Like those for whom Copernican theory was unacceptable because unconfirmed by sensory evidence, she says of the plurality of worlds: "Ma raison est assés bien convaincuë, mais mon imagination est accablée..."(95). Her attachment to the concrete, the sensory, and the mythic link her to nature; and, in her encounters with Fontenelle, it is tempting to see the meeting of Nature and Reason. But Fontenelle, in his prefatory letter to Monsieur L., explicitly links her to the goddess Wisdom. Although less learned than Minerva, she is the very figure of *docta ignorantia*, her native *bon sens* receptive to the training of a master: "Ne croyés-vous pas que si la Sagesse elle-même vouloit se présenter aux hommes avec succès, elle ne feroit pas mal de paroître sous une figure qui approchât un peu de la Marquise? . . . Pour moi, je la tiens sçavante, à cause de l'extrême facilité qu'elle auroit à le devenir" (11). At the same time her charming naïveté and the historical association of women and children lend her the guise of a child. Fontenelle likens her to a child when he chides her for her fear of comets: "ils ne font peur qu'aux Enfans . . ." (145-46).

In its classical form, her many-layered femininity is enveloped in *agrément*. She is the component of pleasure, as Fontenelle's prefatory remarks inform us, in the classical formula of pleasure and instruction: "J'ai mis dans ces Entretiens une Femme que l'on instruit, et qui n'a jamais oüi parler de ces choses-là. J'ai crû que cette fiction me serviroit...à rendre l'Ouvrage plus susceptible d'agrément...." (5). The principle of textual embellishment embodied in the Marquise is not the proverbial coating of the pill in what has commonly been seen as an effort at scientific popularization. She is as it were the soul of Fontenelle's scientific discourse, with her message that science is pleasurable—so pleasurable and so easy that even a woman can learn it. The occasional *compliments galants* which Fontenelle intersperses in his lessons remind us of the pleasure that should inhere in the educational enterprise. Fontenelle underscores this pleasure by advising his female readers that the *Entretiens* are just as accessible as *La Princesse de Clèves* (6), and he compares mathematical reasoning to the casuistry of love:

> Vous ne sçauriez accorder si peu de chose à un Amant, que bientôt après il ne faille lui en accorder davantage, et à la fin cela va loin. De même accordés à un Mathematicien le moindre principe, il va vous en tirer une consequence, qu'il faudra que vous lui accordiés aussi, et de cette consequence encore une autre; et malgré vous-même, il vous mene si loin, qu'à peine le pouvés-vous croire. (138)

The suggestion that the language of mathematics can be translated into the langugage of love is no mere conceit. Like the French of the *Discours de la méthode*, it expresses the Cartesian project of sweeping away the obfuscations of antiquated erudition with the clarity and familiarity of a native language. The *Entretiens* open with a conundrum about translation: Cicero resolved his problem about a readership for his philosophical translations from the Greek by ultimately appealing to everyone, but Fontenelle in wanting to write unphilosophically about philosophy fears that he will alienate both "gens du monde" and "sçavans." What he wants is "un milieu où la Philosophie convînt à tout le Monde" (3-4). As a figure for the "tout le monde" to whom Fontenelle's unphilosophical philosophical language is directed, the Marquise is at once a pretext for and principle of newly intelligible scientific discourse. She is also the Other (child-woman) against whom the power of the discourse is tested.

A woman was of course the logical choice of figure for a "tout le monde" that was largely uninitiated into the mysteries of science and philosophy. This choice was, nevertheless, problematic. In his preface, Fontenelle tells us that he means the Marquise as an encouragement and example to ladies who would like to acquire some learning (5). Her intellectual journey, as he writes to Monsieur L..., supposedly culminates in her conversion to "le parti de la Philosophie" (10-11), a signal victory for her mentor and for scientific discourse. Yet what are we to think of the concluding sentence of the *Entretiens*, which sends the Marquise right back to her separate sphere and seems to exclude her from the very territory that she was finally able to enter? Fontenelle, in speaking of a European "génie" which extends beyond the "sciences" and "spéculations séches" to "choses d'agrément," says to the Marquise of the latter: "Ce sont celles-là, Madame, ausquelles il vous appartient de vous occuper, et qui doivent composer toute votre Philosophie" (179).

The richly metaphorical inclusion of the Marquise in the scientific discourse of objectivity and her ultimate exclusion from it at the very moment of her "conversion" reproduce the complexities in the usage of the first person plural pronoun as it appears in the *Entretiens*. At the center of the philosopher's didactic "nous" ("Nous voulons juger de nous") is a fracture: subject confronts object. It is difficult to pin down the identity of the abstract subjectivity in Fontenelle's "nous": who judges whom? But it is less difficult to locate the Marquise among the judged. In the gesture of reflexivity, the addressee belongs on the side of the object, for the addresser is after all trying to inculcate in her (them) the self-consciousness that he already possesses. Although Fontenelle's subject pronoun would seem generously to include his interlocutor, it establishes a false complicity that is denounced by the Marquise's earthbound "nous." Fontenelle's bracketed subjectivity speaks from on high to the Marquise who remains firmly on the ground, loyal to her earth.

If Fontenelle's goal is to convert the Other to the "party of philosophy" this other must remain forever convertible for the *Entretiens* to retain its effectiveness as instruction. If he wishes to show the accessibility of the new discourse, its access must be always about to open in order to allow entrants the foretaste of victory. Accessibility is after all only a potentiality inscribed in closure. The Marquise, then, must ultimately remain outside the discourse of objectivity, hovering at its periphery. Fontenelle's falsely inclusive "nous" in fact objectifies the Marquise, conferring on her prescientific, mythic subjectivity the status of object of scientific examination. But in this moment her subjectivity is cancelled. Extinguished by the clear light of reason, the "préjugés" that her thinking represents are nullified by the science that preempts them. That Cartesian doubt which was fundamental to the process of discursive construction has become absorbed as scientific certainty in an already constructed discourse. The discursive space opened in the correspondence between Descartes and Elizabeth now appears closed.

III

The problem of what I will call the spectatorial subject, encapsulated in Fontenelle's ambiguous use of the first person plural subject/object pronoun, underlies the discourse of French classicism. By creating the persona of a cosmic master of cermonies who shows an objectified Marquise the earth in perspective, Fontenelle in a sense "solves" this problem, which remains implicit in other literature of the period. Ultimately, of course, the objectification of the Marquise and the concealment of the narrator's identity behind a façade of omniscience defer the responsibility of subjectivity. The identity and relationship of addresser and addressee are put most acutely in question by the manipulation of perspective. Critics have commonly formulated the problem in Pascal's "Disproportion de l'homme" as that of the interlocutor's identity: was it the *libertin* to whom Pascal addressed his summary of the human condition? Yet the questions "Qu'est-ce qu'un homme dans l'infini?" and "Car enfin qu'est-ce que l'homme dans la nature?" immediately implicate the spectatorial subject (the addresser in this case), who is after all a man in nature. It is interesting that Pascal in the "Disproportion" initially uses "l'homme" and the third person singular to paint his picture of human suspension in infinity, switching to "nous" in a reflective moment ("Nous avons beau enfler nos conceptions au delà des espaces imaginables, nous n'enfantons que des atomes, au prix de la réalité des choses"); and "on" to mark the passage to a higher order ("Quand on est instruit, on comprend que la nature ayant gravé son image et celle de son auteur dans toutes choses, elles tiennent presque toutes de sa double infinité") (no. 199). In his objectification of both "man" and nature, Pascal problematizes the relations of spectator to what is viewed and addresser to addressee, leaving us uncertain as to just how inclusive the universals "on" and "nous" may be.

The spectatorial subject is at home in a shifting perspective that invites the addressee to cast a critical eye on him/herself and to play catch-as-catch-can with the addresser, who may or may not be within the perspective surveyed. La Rochefoucauld is perhaps the perfect exemplar of French classicism's construction of a perspective of objectivity. "Les hommes et les affaires ont leur point de perspective. Il y en a qu'il faut voir de près pour en bien juger et d'autres dont on ne juge jamais si bien que quand on en est éloigné" (La Rochefoucauld, no. 104). Here, as in Pascal's "Disproportion," there is no reason to believe that the addresser should not be included among "les hommes," yet disengagement grants to the spectatorial subject (what Philip Lewis calls the abstract subject in the case of La Rochefoucauld) a certain specular immunity. The play of identification and distantiation between addresser and addressee, which Lewis sees as ideological (179-83), forms a universality of what it does not abstract from the purview of the subject.

The spectatorial subject also implicates the object (when object coincides with addressee) in its deferral of responsibility. For to the extent that the subject abstracts itself from its gender, class, or race, for instance, it abstracts the addressee, with whom it claims solidarity, from these same conditions. The example of Fontenelle is instructive, because while he specifies his speaker of another discourse as female, he also designates her as a representative of "tout le monde." Just how accessible did he want the new discourse to be, we may ask, if, finally, women and "tout le monde" stand outside it? In a letter to the *Histoire des ouvrages des savans* (1699), Fontenelle reveals that "les ignorans" were his "veritables Marquises" (416). Like other scientifically minded men of his time, Fontenelle stumbled over the problem of accessibility. In a society where not much important information was accessible to anyone, it became important to view science as open to all. In reality, however, science created its own educated initiates. By the time of Fontenelle's nomination to the post of secretary of the Académie des Sciences in 1697, this tension had materialized in the establishment of a power elite of official scientists who nonetheless conserved the ideal of a vast diffusion of knowledge. In the preface to the *Histoire de l'Académie Royale des Sciences* for the year 1699, Fontenelle writes, first: "On a tâché de rendre cette Histoire convenable au plus grand nombre de personnes qu'il a été possible," and then, "Telle est la destinée des Sciences maniées par un petit nombre de personnes; l'utilité de leurs progrés est invisible à la plûpart du monde...."

When he founded the Académie des Sciences in 1666, Louis XIV officially recognized scientific and technological expertise as a source of power. I have elsewhere discussed the crucial importance of the Académie for Colbert's program of mercantilist expansion (Harth, 225-32). This new collusion of science and power in the furtherance of Colbert's economic goals was bound to contradict the Cartesian aims of universal accessibility to scientific method and the use of science for the betterment of humanity. It was a contradiction that Descartes dimly foresaw when he recorded, in the sixth part of the *Discours de la méthode*, his struggles with the problem of whether or not to publish his treatise on *Le Monde*. Descartes was aware of the potentially vexing consequences not only of publishing geocentric theory, but also of looking to the state for support in conducting the many experiments necessary to his enterprise. His conclusion, a declaration of independence from the state (a declaration which, when compromised by his service to Queen Christina led tragically to his death in Stockholm), represents not so much his individual idiosyncrasy as his distance from the following generation of men of science.

The institutionalization of science in France marks a moment of rupture. Science linked to economic policy takes on the character of a state secret. Although the *Journal des Savants* served as an official organ of publication for the Académie, and although from 1667 on, academic findings were published, the public was not admitted to the regular meetings of the scientific body. By 1699, when the Académie underwent major reorganization, this body had gained control over all kinds of scientific activity in France. It was only after its inspection of machines sent by the Crown, to cite one of the most significant instances of the Académie's authority, that a royal *privilège* was granted (Hahn, 16-18; 59-60). Nothing in the rhetoric of the Académie's official publications, however, suggests that its members abandoned the democratic vision of a method that anyone could ply in order to uncover the truths of nature. Yet the fact remains that behind the closed doors of the Académie an elite group wielded considerable power.

The all-male composition of the Académie des Sciences lent added weight to a distinction between salon and academy, which by 1666 had become familiar. The *cercle* and the *ruelle*, dominated by women, paled in importance before the informal academies that housed male erudition and expertise. Samuel Chappuzeau dramatized this distinction in two plays, *Le Cercle des femmes* (1656) and *L'Académie des femmes* (1661). Although Chappuzeau presents *préciosité* with some sympathy, the frivolity of the "cercle" contrasts with a certain dignity surrounding the project, which he presents in the later play, of founding an academy for women. In *L'Académie des femmes*, the character Emilie sees the academy as yet another institution of male power:

> Ils [men] ont pour s'établir Senats, Academies
> Cours, Dietes, Conseils; Nous seules endormies,
> Nous seules sur le point de nous voir accabler,
> Ne songeons point qu'il est tems de nous assembler.
> (III, 3, 741-44).

The prospect of founding a female academy challenges the male power structure. It is of course this challenge that makes Molière's "femmes savantes" so formidable. Unlike his *précieuses*, who are merely silly, these ladies threaten the male alliance of knowledge and power. Philaminte's true fault is not her enthusiam for Plutarch and astronomy. It is, as her husband tells her, that "le raisonnement bannit la raison" (*Les Femmes savantes,* II, 7, 598). The reasonable Henriette makes it clear that her mother's unreason is her will to power: "C'est elle qui gouverne, et d'un ton absolu/ Elle dicte pour loi ce qu'elle a résolu" (I, 3, 209-10).

For contemporaries, female was to *cercle* as male was to *académie.* But this equation is only an approximation, since men frequented the *cercle* , whereas the *académie* was closed to women. As the informal scientific academies gained in prestige, the *cercle* was feminized and trivialized. After the founding of the Académie des Sciences, this process had advanced to the point where Poullain de la Barre could designate the *cercle* as a kind of second-class academy where there reigned a specifically feminine language: "Les bals, les comédies, les modes font le sujet de leurs [women's] entretiens: elles regardent les cercles, comme de celebres Academies, où elles vont s'instruire de toutes les nouvelles de leur sexe" (Poullain, *Egalité,* 211). This inequality, which Fontenelle as a member of three official academies took for granted, became for Poullain the basis of an agenda of change. Having frequented Richesource's informal Académie des Orateurs (Alcover, 14-15), which offered public lectures open to both men and women, Poullain, writing in the 1670's, saw the institutionalization of academies as a decisive step in the exclusion of women from a dominant culture: "On fit des Académies, où l'on n'appella point les femmes; et elles furent de cette sorte excluës des sciences, commes [sic] elles l'étoient du reste" (*Egalité* 28).

Women, then were left with the discourse of polite society: "...il y a des sciences dont on n'entend point parler les femmes, parce que ce ne sont point des sciences de mise ni de societé. L'Algebre, la Geometrie, l'Optique, ne sortent presque jamais des cabinets ny des Academies sçavantes, pour venir au milieu du monde" (*Egalité* 57-8). In contrast to the final picture of Fontenelle's Marquise, presiding over the feminine domain of *agrément,* Poullain envisions a dismantling of institutionalized androcentric discourse: "Si les Cercles estoient changez en Academies, les entretiens y seroient plus solides, plus agreables, et plus grans. Et chacune peut juger de la satisfaction qu'elle auroit à parler des plus belles choses, par celle qu'elle ressent quelquefois, à en entendre parler les autres" (*Egalité* 173-74).

In terms of his relation to the discourse of objectivity, the true heir to Descartes was of course not Fontenelle but Poullain. Like

Elizabeth's correspondent, Poullain rejects the language of *galanterie*, as he tells us in the preface to *De l'Egalité des deux sexes* (1673). He intends to speak "en Philosophe," and views the two languages as incompatible: "On ne peut gueres éclairer l'Esprit et l'égayer par la même voye." In shunning the classical pairing of pleasure and instruction, Poullain avoided the trap into which Fontenelle later fell: the feminine, as a principle of *agrément* in the *Entretiens*, is ultimately excluded from the discourse it is meant to embellish. I do not claim that Descartes's use of the discourse of objectivity was not androcentric. The philosopher who could dream of science as enabling its practitioners to become "maîtres et possesseurs de la nature" (*Discours* 128), as Carolyn Merchant has pointed out (188), was speaking as a man. Descartes may even have subscribed to a theory of female inferiority (Alcover 71-3). But his methodical doubt made possible a modification, if not a transformation, of androcentricity.

It is therefore of capital importance that Poullain seizes on Cartesian doubt as a first principle in his feminist apologies. Like Descartes and Elizabeth, Poullain saw himself as the embattled spokesperson for unprejudiced reason. His militant feminism, as he announces in the preface to *De l'Egalité des deux sexes*, begins with a rejection of custom and authority. Although his program is authentically democratic—a "science universelle" embracing both sexes and all classes—it is spearheaded by an enlightened vanguard. We have found this inevitable elitism of the enlightened in Fontenelle and Descartes also. Fontenelle, however, speaks to the Marquise from within a citadel of knowledge; between master and pupil there is a language barrier that is largely inoperative for Descartes and Elizabeth. Descartes's radical doubt opens on to a future of truth which is always under construction. Poullain would construct a feminist counter-discourse based on his own doubt that androcentric discourse is true. His figure of the enlightened man refuses the master-pupil relationship that Fontenelle was to adopt with the Marquise. "Je hay le mot de maistre," Stasimaque says to Eulalie in *De l'Education des dames* of 1674 (191). Such a refusal effectively excludes the possibility of male dominance.

In this connection it is significant that the spectatorial subject all but disappears from Poullain's writings. That subtle and problematic fracture of the first person plural pronoun does not occur. Poullain is quite self-conscious in his polemical use of "nous." In *De l'Egalité des deux sexes* it designates either the men whom Poullain wishes to persuade that women are intellectually equal to "us" or else a genuinely inclusive human community: "En effet nous avons tous hommes et femmes, le même droit sur la vérité, puisque l'esprit est en tous également capable de la connoistre, et que nous sommes tous frappez de la même façon, par les objets qui font impression sur le corps" (142). In *De l'Education des dames* Poullain sketches a gesture of reflexivity that unites male and female in an attempt to overcome the "préjugés," chief among which is gender, that impede the exercise of human reason: "...nous sommes nous mesmes le livre où il la [la science de nous mesmes] faut étudier: il s'y agit de sçavoir, non pas ce qui arrive ailleurs en des Provinces éloignées, mais ce qui se passe en nous cent fois le jour..." (246). Eulalie learns the lesson of reflexive thought quite easily. Unlike Fontenelle's Marquise, she does not speak from the other side of a linguistic barrier masked by a deceptive first person plural pronoun. Agreeing with the epistemology of Stasimaque (represented as the author of *De l'Egalité des deux sexes*), she says:

> Il n'y a, comme vous dites, qu'à faire reflexion, sur ce que nous faisons, pour le connoistre. Et je voy bien presentement que je n'auray besoin que d'attention, pour sçavoir, par exemple, ce que c'est que douter, se resoudre, vouloir avoir faim [*sic*], et soif, sentir de la douleur et du plaisir. Et cela acheve de me persuader, de ce que vous prouvez dans le livre de l'Egalité, qu'il n'est pas si mal-aisé de devenir Philosophe que Tapissier. (*De l'Education* 240-41)

In urging such reflexivity upon his addressee, Poullain takes responsibility for his subjectivity. Implicitly he, like everyone else, must undertake to examine the conditions of his reasoning. Poullain therefore draws his spectacular image from a different perspective than does either Descartes or Fontenelle. His subject, at once spectator and participant, is inside the theater of the world on a quest for an empirical truth based on self-knowledge:

> ...Autre chose est de voir les hommes au naturel, et de ne les regarder qu'en perspective dans une Bibliothèque. Il faut que l'usage du monde acheve ce que les bons livres ont commencé; Et l'on s'instruit bien plus solidement, quand on voit les choses en grand sur le Theatre du monde, que lorsqu'on ne les voit qu'en petit dans un écrit. Cette bizarrerie que l'on peut remarquer dans la conduitte des hommes...et la maniere dont chacun condamne ce qui le choque et approuve ce qui luy plaist, donnent lieu à un esprit bien tourné de faire sans sortir de son païs des reflexions aussi importantes et aussi capables de détromper, que si, ayant voyagé par toute la terre, il avoit médité sur la diversité des humeurs, des coutumes, des opinions, des Religions de tous les peuples qui l'habitent. (*De l'Education* 315-16)

Although Poullain was not self-conscious in his use of the masculine universal "les hommes," he wished to speak as both a man and a human. His "esprit bien tourné" carries a nuance of elitism, but it also marks an educative horizon for everyone. It is only in the "theater of the world" that reflexivity can form the mind. In this theater, where androcentricity was on stage, to be both actor and audience was a precondition for changing the program.

Poullain strove for a discourse that would overcome the puzzle of objectivity, the abstraction of the subject. Yet his polemic signals that he too, like Elizabeth, was already speaking within and against the discourse of objectivity. His desired transformation of *cercle* into *académie* would after all only further diffuse the discourse spoken within the academy. Poullain nevertheless clung to a vision of universally self-conscious subjects whose discourse would abolish the barriers of gender and class. Can we say that in the 1670s his was as large as even a minority view? It has taken until our own day for him to gain some measure of recognition. Fontenelle, speaking the dominant discourse, advertised the universality of classicism: an objective truth that effaces the conditions of its construction: "Il n'y a que la vérité qui persuade, même sans avoir besoin de paroître avec toutes ses preuves. Elle entre si naturellement dans l'esprit, que quand on l'apprend pour la premiere fois, il semble qu'on ne fasse que s'en souvenir" (Fontenelle 75).

Descartes's correspondence with Elizabeth figures prominently in the list of recommended readings that Poullain appended to his *De l'Education des dames* (309). But by the 1670s the Cartesian moment had passed. The appeal that Descartes held for women of the salons may be partially explained by the emancipatory possibilities of a methodical doubt calling for critical scrutiny of all received ideas, a scrutiny that could eventuate in female empowerment. The year 1666, however, closed off that route by reserving for men a scientific knowledge that was to serve the interests of the regime in the corridors of political power. Henceforth "objective" truth was determined by and for men within limits set by the state. It was only a few years later that Molière had the reasonable Clitandre say:

> Je consens qu'une femme ait des clartés de tout;
> Mais je ne lui veux point la passion choquante
> De se rendre savante afin d'être savante;
> Et j'aime que souvent, aux questions qu'on fait,
> Elle sache ignorer les choses qu'elle sait;
> De son étude enfin je veux qu'elle se cache,
> Et qu'elle ait du savoir sans vouloir qu'on le sache,

Sans citer les auteurs, sans dire de grands mots,
Et clouer de l'esprit à ses moindres propos.
(*Les Femmes savantes*, I, 3, 218-26)

Notes

[1]My chronology, which is not meant to be strictly linear, agrees roughly with that outlined by Timothy J. Reiss in his "Corneille and Cornelia," although there are important substantive differences in our respective notions of the various moments involved.
I am indebted to Joan B. Landes's *Women and the Public Sphere in the Age of the French Revolution* (Ithaca: Cornell University Press, forthcoming) for providing me with much food for thought on the relations of discourse, gender, and French classicism. Although I am in agreement with some of Ruth Perry's basic points about women's relation to the new learning, I do not find this learning quite as liberating for women as she does.
[2]My use of the terms "subjective," "objective," "subjectivist," "objectivist," is specified to this discussion and is not to be confused with their strictly philosophical sense. By "subjective" I mean the discourse that emanates from the self-consciously individual thinking and feeling subject; by "objective," the discourse that brackets individual subjectivity in claiming to apply neutrally to everyone or to speak a general truth about nature as object (what Evelyn Fox Keller calls "static objectivity"). Cf. Keller, pp. 116-17.
[3]Alexandre Calame, in his critical edition of Fontenelle's *Entretiens sur la pluralité des mondes*, follows the edition of 1742 but gives variants for earlier editions. Because I focus on Fontenelle's connection with classicism, I omit any reference to the fable of the bees, which appeared only in the edition of 1742. For the purposes of this discussion, other variants of the 1686 and 1687 editions have no great significance.

Works Cited

Alcover, Madeleine. *Poullain de la Barre: Une aventure philosophique.*
    Tübingen: *Biblio. 17-1 [Papers on French 17th-Century Literature]*, 1981.
Chappuzeau, Samuel. *Le Cercle des femmes et L'Académie des femmes.*
    Ed. Joan Crow. University of Exeter, 1983.
Descartes, René. *Discours de la méthode.* Ed. Etienne Gilson. Paris: Vrin,
    1966.
—. *Lettres sur la morale.* Ed. Jacques Chevalier. Paris: Hatier-Boivin, 1955.
Fontenelle, Bernard Le Bovier de. *Entretiens sur la pluralité des mondes.* Ed.
    Alexandre Calame. Paris: Didier, 1966.
Hahn, Roger. *The Anatomy of a Scientific Institution: The Paris Academy of
    Sciences, 1666-1803.* Berkeley: University of California Press, 1971.
Harries, Karsten. "Descartes, Perspective, and the Angelic Eye." *Yale French
    Studies* 49 (June, 1973). 28-42.
Harth, Erica. *Ideology and Culture in Seventeenth-Century France.* Ithaca:
    Cornell University Press, 1983.
Histoire de l'Académie Royale des Sciences (1699). 2nd ed. Amsterdam: Pierre
    Mortier, 1734.
Histoire des ouvrages des savans (Sept. 1699).
Keller, Evelyn Fox . *Reflections on Gender and Science.* New Haven: Yale
    University Press, 1985.

Landes, Joan. *Women and the Public Sphere in the Age of the French Revolution.* Ithaca: Cornell UP, 1988.

La Rochefoucauld, François duc de. *Réflexions ou Sentences et Maximes morales.* Ed. Jacques Truchet. Paris: Garnier, 1961.

Lewis, Philip E. *La Rochefoucauld: The Art of Abstraction.* Ithaca: Cornell University Press, 1977.

Merchant, Carolyn. *The Death of Nature: Women, Ecology, and the Scientific Revolution.* San Francisco: Harper and Row, 1980.

Molière. *Les Femmes savantes.* In *Théâtre complet.* Vol. 2. Ed. Robert Jouanny. Paris: Garnier, 1962. 677-749.

Nagel, Thomas. *The View from Nowhere.* New York: Oxford, 1986.

Pascal, Blaise. *Pensées.* In *Œuvres complètes.* Ed. Louis Lafuma. Paris: Seuil, 1963.

Perry, Ruth. "Radical Doubt and the Liberation of Women." *Eighteenth-Century Studies* 18 (1985). 472-93.

[Poullain de la Barre, François]. *De l'Education des dames pour la conduite de l'esprit dans les sciences et dans les moeurs. Entretiens.* Paris: Antoine Dezallier, 1679. 2nd. ed. Reprinted by Université de Toulouse Le Mirail, n.d.

—. *De l'Egalité des deux sexes, discours physique et moral, où l'on voit l'importance de se défaire des préjugez.* Paris: Jean Du Puis, 1673.

Reiss, Timothy J. "Corneille and Cornelia: Reason, Violence, and the Cultural Status of the Feminine. Or, How a Dominant Discourse Recuperated and Subverted the Advance of Women." *Renaissance Drama* 18 (1987), 3- 41.

—. *The Discourse of Modernism.* Ithaca: Cornell University Press, 1982.

The Singular Voice:
Monologism and
French Classical Discourse

Nicholas Cronk
St Edmund Hall, Oxford

Il faut en tout dialogue et discours qu'on puisse dire à ceux qui s'en offensent: de quoi vous plaignez-vous? PASCAL, L. 669

Interrompez-moi donc, si vous voulez. Je ne saurais disputer, si l'on ne m'interrompt. Vous vous taisez exprès, et me laissez parler par belle malice. *Dom Juan*, III, 1.

Familiarity breeds incuriousness, and it is easy to overlook just how peculiar a phenomenon French classical discourse is. What are we to make, for example, of Bouhours's apparently serious suggestion in the *Entretiens d'Ariste et d'Eugène* (1671) that "le beau langage ressemble à une eau pure et nette qui n'a point de goust" (37)? Even more extraordinary is a passage later in the same work, in which the prestige of the French language becomes indistinguishable from that of the French monarch; Bouhours is describing how certain individuals at Court manage to be masters of the language without ever having studied it:

> Mais sçavez-vous bien que nôtre grand Monarque tient le premier rang parmi ces heureux genies, et qu'il n'y a personne dans le Royaume qui sçache le François comme il le sçait. Ceux qui ont l'honneur de l'approcher, admirent avec quelle netteté, et avec quelle justesse il s'exprime. Cét air libre et facile dont nous avons tant parlé, entre dans tout ce qu'il dit; tous ses termes sont propres, et bien choisis, quoy-qu'ils ne soient point recherchez;

toutes ses expressions sont simples, et naturelles: mais le tour
qu'il leur donne est le plus delicat, et le plus noble du monde.
[...] Enfin pour tout dire en un mot, il parle si bien, que son
langage peut donner une veritable idée de la perfection de nôtre
langue. Les Rois doivent apprendre de luy à regner; mais les
peuples doivent apprendre de luy à parler. (91-92).[1]

Tasteless water, spouting from the lips of the King—it sounds more
like a plan for a piece of baroque statuary than the ideal model of
literary discourse which Bouhours intends. Barthes hints at the
problem, though without elucidating it further, when he writes that
"l'autorité politique, le dogmatisme de l'Esprit, et l'unité du langage
classique sont donc les figures d'un même mouvement historique"
(84). This essay will try to account for Bouhours's model by
considering the language of French classicism in the light of
Bakhtin's theory of discourse.

I

Bakhtin and French Classicism

Central to Bakhtin's theory of discourse is a concern with the
means by which voices permeate literary language, and in
elaborating his ideas about the dialogic or plurivocal text and in
describing the resultant tensions between dialogism and
monologism, he has frequent recourse to examples from the French
seventeenth century. The germ of this theory is to be found in the
pioneering critique of Saussure made in *Marxism and the
Philosophy of Language* and in the distinction there drawn between
two basic trends of thought in the philosophy of language.
Dialogism is founded on the idea, deriving from Humboldt, that
linguistic study should begin with "the individual creative act of
speech" ("individualistic subjectivism"); opposed to this is the idea
of language as "a stable, immutable system [...] which the
individual consciousness finds ready-made" ("abstract objectivism")
(*Marxism* 48, 57).[2] This last view of language, epitomized for
Bakhtin by Saussure, is traced back to seventeenth-century rationalism: "There can be no doubt that the second trend has profound
inner connection with Cartesian thought and with the overall world
view of neoclassicism and its cult of autonomous, rational, fixed
form" (*Marxism* 57).[3] Classical discourse is essentially monologic
in its belief that all utterances derive from a single, impersonal, linguistic system:

> For classicism, only the word of language exists, "no one's
> word," a material word which is part of the poetic lexicon, and
> this word passes directly from the treasurehouse of poetic
> language into the monologic context of a given poetic utterance.
> Thus a stylistics nurtured on the soil of classicism recognizes
> only the life of a word in a single self-enclosed context. [...] It
> recognizes only those changes that come about when a word is
> transferred from the system of language into a monologic poetic
> utterance. (*Dostoevsky* 200)

Bakhtin also highlights the political dimension to monologism,
linking "the Cartesian poetics of neoclassicism" with what he calls
the "centripetal forces" of absolutism: "A unitary language gives
expression to forces working toward concrete verbal and ideological
unification and centralization, which develop in vital connection with
the processes of sociopolitical and cultural centralization" (*Dialogic
Imagination* 271). But just as the absolutism of Louis XIV was
achieved in the face of internal conflict, so monologism is
meaningful here only in the context of a struggle against dialogism.
"A unitary language is not something given," writes Bakhtin, "but is
always in essence posited—and at every moment of its linguistic life
it is opposed to the realities of heteroglossia" (*Dialogic Imagination*
270).

Related to this idea of heteroglossia is another central Bakhtinian
concept, that of carnival. Bakhtin singles out the seventeenth-
century writers who perpetuate, albeit in an adulterated form, the
carnivalesque tradition embodied by Rabelais: comic novelists such
as Sorel and Scarron, libertine poets like Saint-Amant, Théophile de
Viau and Dassoucy (*Rabelais* 103-07). These authors all belong of
course to the pre-classical period, and Bakhtin's view that the folk
culture which supported carnival goes into decline during the
seventeenth century is supported by recent historical research
(Bercé, Temple), and by Domna Stanton, who notes the ambivalent
status of carnival under the *ancien régime*. Classicism emerges
therefore just at the moment when carnival is waning. "Until the
second half of the seventeenth century," writes Bakhtin, "people
were *direct participants* in carnivalistic acts and in a carnival sense of
the world; they still *lived* in carnival" (*Dostoevsky* 131).

There are evident dangers in sifting through Bakhtin's writings
in order to turn him into a literary historian of the French
seventeenth century, not least because one runs the risk of
monologizing his own discourse. But the striking frequency of his
references to the seventeenth century and to classicism suggests, as
Joan DeJean has said, that 1650 marks for Bakhtin an
epistemological break. The advent of classicism—and of absolutism

—coincides both with the disintegration of the folk culture which had supported carnival, and with the prevalence of monologism over the warring voices of dialogism. In a late essay, Bakhtin writes elliptically of

> Ideas about the magicality of the word. The word as action. The entire about-face in the history of the word when it became expression and pure (actionless) information (the communicative function). The sense of one's own and another's in the word. Later, the origin of authorial consciousness (*Speech Genres* 115).

The change which Bakhtin is gingerly evoking here recalls the shift which Foucault describes from a Renaissance to a classical episteme—but with the important difference that Bakhtin places the emphasis squarely on the sense of the voice behind the word.

II

The Classical Shift to Monologism

The literature of the pre-classical period abounds in overtly dialogic works: Béroalde de Verville's *Le Moyen de parvenir*, for example, a menippean satire in which a series of voices, some identified and other anonymous, vie with each other to debate a willfully bewildering and scabrous range of topics, or Cyrano de Bergerac's *L'Autre Monde*, with its depiction of a moon-world in which all earthly values are turned upside-down. Cecilia Rizza speaks of "the variety of tones" as a characteristic of French baroque poetic theory; and the burlesque writing of, say, Scarron, with its juxtapostion of discordant linguistic registers, provides a text-book example of dialogic discourse.[4] Jean-Pierre Camus deliberately draws his reader's attention to the dialogic interplay of voices in his *Diversitez*, describing his work as a cento,

> qui admet toute sorte de contexture, soit polie, soit entrecouppee, or je produits mes imaginations avec peu d'auctoritez, au rebours quelques fois j'entasse et fagotte un bon nombre de traicts ramassez et pillotés ça et là, sans ordre presque, unison, et liaison, selon le rencontre casuel et fortuit, ou de ma memoire qui en enfante et entrelasse quelques uns, soit de mes brevets et catalectes. Ils serviront à l'adventure aux esprits qui ayment ces fricassées et salades de meslanges: tant y a que c'est tousjours diversité par laquelle seule je desire et essaye de plaire. (6: 151-52)

As we move into the second half of the century, there is a clear shift away from the dialogic and towards the monologic. This can be seen, for example, in the hostile reaction of classical critics to the burlesque, and in their singling out for opprobrium precisely those features of burlesque writing, such as the use of popular, regional and archaic terms, which reinforce its dialogic impact. The change can be traced too in the evolution of the various genres of the anthology. Genres such as the cento and the *florilège*, which are composed of a variety of fragments from different (and sometimes unattributed) sources and so characterized by multiple and interlocking voices, had flourished during the Renaissance and early part of the seventeenth century, but they vanish with the advent of classicism (Lafond; Beugnot "Florilèges"). At the moment of their disappearance there emerges a new genre, however, the *ana*, which is a collection of anecdotes in which the fragments are all drawn from a single (identified) author and so speak with one voice (Beugnot "Forme"). The monologic genre of the *ana* was evidently more suited to classical tastes than the dialogic genres of the cento and the *florilège*.

The monologic drift of classicism is well exemplified in two contrasting descriptions of the literary language from either end of the century. Writing in 1621, Du Pré defends the use of literary digression as a means of providing necessary variety of tone:

> Je ne me rangeray du costé de ceux qui blasment les digressions en l'oraison, ainsi que les similitudes et les inductions qu'on tire des fables. Qui sçait que l'estomach s'ennuye d'une mesme viande, l'oreille d'un mesme son, et l'oeil d'un mesme objet, celuy-là comprend combien à meilleure raison nostre esprit se plaist qu'on luy donne le change, et qu'on le pourmene sur diverses matieres. [...] Je ne desapreuve non plus [...] qu'on se serve des belles inventions de nos Poetes, qui sont entre-tissues d'une vray semblance d'histoire à guise de quelque trame de fil couverte de soye par dessus, où ce qu'on nous baille pour vray a pour la plus part sa chaine ourdie de fictions. (100-04)

Du Pré recalls here Camus's aesthetic of "diversité," and his image of poetic discourse as a piece of fabric woven from different threads, and even from threads silk-covered so as to conceal their real natures, is a graphic assertion of dialogism which stands in stark contrast to this account of the French language written in 1696:

> C'est encore une des proprietez de nostre Langue, de ne souffrir rien de vuide ni d'entr'ouvert; sur tout dans le stile oratoire, où il faut que tout se suive, que tout soit lié, que toutes les periodes paroissent, pour ainsi dire, enchaisnées, et toutes les pensées enchassées les unes dans les autres: de sorte neanmoins qu'on

n'apperçoive rien de forcé dans les liaisons, ni de trop recherché
dans les transitions. (Gillet 236-37)

That literary discourse came to be perceived differently in the
wake of classicism is clear. But to what extent did writers of the
period address the concept of dialogic writing at a theoretical level?
There is an abundant contemporary literature concerned with the
French language: Brunot lists over 40 works concerned with
grammar and vocabulary published during the period 1660-1680
alone. The path from Malherbe via Vaugelas to Bouhours and
Ménage is well known, and the preoccupation with the ideals of
clarté, netteté and *pureté*, which grows more marked as the century
advances, suggests growing intolerance of dialogic discourse. To
insist so emphatically on clarity is to assert one right way of
expressing an ideal, to offer, in other words, a monologic model.
Jean d'Aisy's *Le Génie de la langue françoise* (1685) marks the
culmination of this prescriptive grammatical tradition; it is in effect a
cento consisting of no more than an orderly compilation of the
various remarks of Vaugelas, Bouhours and Ménage, and with the
author/compiler intruding only in the "Avertissement." Vaugelas's
much-vaunted criterion of "usage" necessarily privileges one voice
at the expense of many others; and Marie de Gournay points to the
impoverishment which such a monologic model entails:

> Quelle apparence y auroit il, si les choses qu'on exprime en Vers
> ou dans les discours Politiques et Philosophiques, sont hors
> l'usage des muguets de Cour, reconneus tres-ignorans pour la
> pluspart; que les dictions à les exprimer n'en osassent estre
> aussi? Comment exprimerions nous au language de ceste espece
> d'hommes et de femmes, des choses qu'elle n'a jamais dites, ny
> conceuës, ny pensées? (115)

Opponents of Vaugelas such as La Mothe Le Vayer and Dupleix
sought to mitigate the monologic stance of the prescriptive
grammarian, arguing that alternative forms of expression could be
equally valid: "On parle toujours bien quand on se fait entendre";
but a generation later, Vichard de Saint-Réal is scathing about such a
view, setting against it the opinion of Patru (the first lawyer to be
elected to the Académie française, and a supporter of Vaugelas):
"C'estoit un principe excellent de Patru, que quelque également
bonnes que paroissent deux manieres de parler, il est impossible
qu'elles le soient, et il y en a toujours une meilleure que l'autre" (79,
84). The philosophical interest in optics in this period had helped
foster the view that there was one "right" way of picturing reality
(Siguret) and in the same way classical critics typically argue that

there is only one "right" way of giving verbal expression to reality. This monologic view of language is at the heart of the classical theory of discourse and is memorably expressed by La Bruyère:

> Il y a dans l'art un point de perfection, comme de bonté ou de maturité dans la nature. [...]
>
> Entre toutes les différentes expressions qui peuvent rendre une seule de nos pensées, il n'y en a qu'une qui soit la bonne. On ne la rencontre pas toujours en parlant ou en écrivant; il est vrai néanmoins qu'elle existe, que tout ce qui ne l'est point est faible, et ne satisfait point un homme d'esprit qui veut se faire entendre. (69, 71)

The classical genre of the dialogue might at first seem to give the lie to this monologism. The seventeenth century actually uses the word *dialogisme* (first attested in 1557) to describe writing in dialogue form; Camus entitles a chapter on the dialogue "Dialogisme problématique de l'éloquence" (*Diversitez* 6: 457), while La Mothe Le Vayer speaks of Plato as "le Père du Dialogisme" ("Platon" 5-6). Although rare in the first half of the century, the dialogue, or *entretien* as it was more usually known, found increasing favour among writers after 1650.[5] Earlier in the century, readers had been suspicious of the genre, as La Mothe Le Vayer and Sorel both acknowledge. They seek to defend the dialogue by pointing to its classical pedigree, and Sorel further argues that, far from being the unnatural form of writing which many contemporaries believe, the dialogue is the most natural, for if writing is no more than the record of speech, then the first and simplest form of writing must be the dialogue ("Des dialogues"). Sorel distinguishes between the two different types of dialogue, those from which the author is entirely absent, where two or three interlocutors speak on their own account and those in which the author sets the scene and describes his characters, whose words are then relayed in indirect speech— another writer of the period, Caillières, labels these "dialogues recitez" ("Le Libraire au lecteur"). It is to Pellisson, however, that we owe the most extended analysis of the dialogue, which he divides into three types. The first he calls "Didactique," dialogues which are designed purely to inculcate certain facts; the second are "les Dialogues de raillerie qui ne prennent que la fleur des choses, qui n'instruisent jamais qu'en riant"; and the third, a compromise between the previous two types, are dialogues which are both instructive and entertaining (10-14).

There is no doubting classical awareness of the dialogue as a genre. But it is clear that the classical view of the dialogue is not a dialogic one. Theorists may discuss the extent of the narrator's presence in the dialogue, or the degree to which the didactic content should be given a pleasing wrapping, but that the dialogue does straightforwardly communicate to the reader the unmediated opinion of the author is never even questioned. Classical *dialogisme* is distinctly unBakhtinian, and we begin to wonder indeed whether the particular attraction of the dialogue to classical writers was not precisely that it lent to monologic discourse the flattering illusion of an open-ended form. "C'a esté encore pour le divertissement du Lecteur, que j'ay choisi le Dialogisme, qui est le genre d'escrire le plus ancien, le mieux authorisé, et le plus agreable," writes Le Moyne (*Peintures*, sig.⅂ iv r); but the pleasing facade of the dialogue masks an entirely systematic exposition: "Tout le fond et toute la méthode d'une dissertation s'y doit recontrer," declares Fleury, "et cependant, il ne faut pas qu'on y voie aucune affectation de dogmatiser" (73). The classical *entretien* is perhaps no more than the acceptable face of monologism.[6]

III

The *Querelle des citations*

It is in fact in discussing the legitimacy of quotation that the seventeenth century comes face to face with the fact of dialogism. The recourse to frequent quotation, especially of classical texts, is a natural product of humanist scholarship, and the practice finds its most sophisticated literary manifestation in Montaigne. In the seventeenth century there is a marked trend against the use of learned quotations, both in legal oratory (Holmès 32-33), and in pulpit oratory, where there is a shift away from what Peter Bayley calls the "thesaurus style" (36-37). These developments are obviously of consequence for literary discourse generally, and seventeenth-century reactions to Montaigne demonstrate vividly the growing intolerance of mutivocal and self-consciously dialogic discourse (Brody, "Montaigne"; Compagnon 306-313).

It is with respect to legal oratory that the question of the abusive use of quotation is initially broached. The first to speak out against what Fumaroli calls "la rhétorique des citations" (466 *et passim*) was Pasquier, who in 1586 criticized the speeches of his friend and fellow lawyer Loisel for their abundant use of Latin and Greek quotations: "Nous seuls entre toutes les autres nations faisons profession de rapiecer, ou pour mieux dire rapetasser, nostre eloquence de divers passages" (*Lettres* 100). This view is given greater prominence a few years later by Du Vair's *De l'éloquence francoise* (1594), which is severly critical of lawyers whose speeches are larded with otiose quotations. "Ces discours estoient si remplis de passages d'allegations et d'authoritez", he writes of one colleague, "qu'à peine pouvoit-on bien prendre le fil de son oraison. Car vous sçavez combien cela l' interrompt" (136). The debate continued to simmer: in 1602 Loisel retorted to Pasquier that the judicious use of quotation was admissible (123), prompting Pasquier to return to the subject in 1607 (*Recherches* 628-33).

Then, in 1610, there appeared a full-length *Discours contre les citations*, which, though still immediately concerned with legal rhetoric, had obvious wider implications for poetic theory. The author, Filère, insists that French eloquence will triumph if it can be freed from its subservience to the ancients, and he suggests that since the ancients themselves did not normally quote, we do not best imitate them by quoting them. Most interesting of all, Filère argues strenuously for "un language rond et uny" (38), and is disparaging of "ces discours marquetez et rioliez de divers jargons" and of "ces centons et ramas de passages Grecs et Latins" (31, 62). This work was published in the same year as Deimier's *Académie de l'art poétique*, the work which marked the growing ascendancy of Malherbian literary values, and Filère's criticism of multivocal texts is one which Malherbe would have well understood:

> Car un parler pur, simple, uny, esgal par tout, et coulant tout à l'aise, est mille fois plus doux plus delicat et plus ravissant que celuy qui est embrouillé d'un divers language. L'harmonie nombreuse, qui naist de ceste agreable façon de parler sans citations, Grecques ni Latines flate sans doubte, et chatoüille avec plus de plaisir l'esprit et l'oreille d'une attentive assemblée. [...] La plus haute et divine façon de discourir est celle qui n'est entrecoupée de passages d'autheurs ny d'allegations ramassees. (26-27)

Filère does allow allusion to other authors, but only when they are unobtrusively translated into French, and as if to exemplify his point, he himself borrows from Du Vair without ever mentioning him by name. Compare the passage quoted above from Du Vair ("Ces discours estoient...") with Filère's demand for the rejection of "toutes ces allegations, qui arrestent la fluidité d'un discours, qui luy desrobent sa grace, et qui empeschent le plus souvent qu'on ne peut *bien prendre le fil d'une Oraison*" (60, emphasis mine)—the quotation of Du Vair is discreet, but undeniable. On the other hand, when writers pile up unconnected Latin and Greek citations, "c'est du sable sans chaux, comme on disoit des escrits de Senecque" (28)—the quotation, this time, is overt, but translated and introduced in a way which does not disrupt the essential unity of discourse. The constant recourse to learned quotations is in Filère's view merely a facile diversion from the prime task of creating a unitary language:

> Nous prenons plaisir d'estonner le monde à force de citations de Grec et de Latin, ce sont des espouvanteaux pour les ignorans, la seule prolation de ces langues leur faict peur, ils se laissent esbloüir à cest eclat, et ravir à ceste fastueuse parade. Mais les hommes de sçavoir et de jugement, sçavent bien que ces espouvantaux sont faciles à trouver, que ces discours enflez d'une multitude de passages, sont des corps bouffis et non pas sains, et qu'il est plus aisé de rapporter les lieux entiers de cent Autheurs, que de faire un discours qui soit tout à nous, où les conceptions et les paroles reluisent à l'egal et à l'envy l'un de l'autre. Il n'est rien si facile que de paroistre docte, sans toutesfois l'estre. (55-57)

Filère's work provoked an instant reply from a fellow lawyer, Antoine de Rambaud, who the following year published his *Discours parénétique aux advocats pour l'usage des citations du grec et du latin*. Hitting out at "ces nouveaux censeurs" (9) who wish to overturn "l'ordre de nostre republique" (11), Rambaud defends stoutly the traditional humanist practice of quotation, "la cause generalle, cause saincte, la cause de nos peres" (11-12), which in his view is essential to eloquence and which does no more than acknowledge out debt to the ancients. He argues against Filère that if the ancients do not themselves quote, that is because their situation is different, and in any case they do not expressly forbid the practice of quotation. But at the heart of Rambaud's difference with Filère is a quite distinct linguistic aesthetic, and his advocacy of the highly ornate style which had been customary in legal oratory since the time of Président de Thou amounts to a rousing defence of dialogic discourse:

> Un riche plaidoyé, n'est autre chose, qu'une pyramide Royalle, pour servir de base, et fondement à loger une belle pomme d'or (le Symbole de la Justice) qui puisse reluire de tous costez: ou bien, comme une tour sur le bord de la mer, pour y servir de Phar aux mariniers, l'Arrest qui s'en ensuit après la plaidoyerie, est ceste belle pomme d'or [...]. Mais qui a jamais dit, voire pensé, qu'un Phar ou une piramide fussent desembelis, par le meslange des pierrres esclatantes en diverses couleurs, par la diversité de leurs roches? C'est chose dont l'usage des anciens et modernes nous monstre le contraire, et nous donne à cognoistre que le meslange des langues (principallement des

riches et polies) apporte autant de lustre, et de magnificence aux
plaidoiés, que ces diverses pierres aux bastimens. (14-16)

Rambaud argues that a translated quotation often lacks the force of
the original; citing in the original offers moreover the best means of
enriching the French language; and the judicious use of quotations
by certain authors can enhance the expressivity of their writing—
Montaigne is singled out as an example (64-67). The keyword of
Rambaud's aesthetic, already familiar from Camus, is "diversité":

> La citation des bons Autheurs apporte de l'ornement, de la force,
> et de l'authorité, en nos discours: de vouloir dire que la diversité
> des langues, efface cest ornement, affoiblisse la force, et
> diminuë l'authorité, cela seroit bon au Royaume des aveugles,
> ou des ignorants: car tout ainsi que l'œil se plaist à la diversité
> des couleurs: et l'aureille des sons, diversement entremesles,
> par une musique bien ordonnee; pourquoy non, une ame plaine
> de sçavoir ne se plaira t'elle, à la docte varieté d'un discours
> entremeslé de divers langages? Il n'y a point de doute que
> l'esprit n'en reçoive d'autant plus de contentement, qu'il en est
> plus capable que le sens: car à la verité, la tisseure des graves
> sentences, raportees en l'esclat, et vigueur que chaque langue
> leur a donné, n'est autre chose qu'un amas de diverses pierres
> precieuses artistement enchassees dans une coronne d'or. (39-
> 41)

The "modern" view of Du Vair and Filère was beginning to
prevail over the baroque aesthetic of dialogic *diversité*, and many
writers on eloquence ritually repeat their arguments. In 1619,
Caussin for example, quotes Du Vair explicitly (530), while in
1632 another rhetorician, Vialart, follows Du Vair without citing
him when he urges restraint in the use of quotations. "Il est bien
permis de se rendre propres les pensées des autres, et de dire mesme
qu'elles sont deux, rapportant fidelement le sens de leurs paroles
sans y rien alterer," writes Vialart, but this all within the context of
"un discours d'un style continu" (190): his model remains
essentially monologic.

Much more difficult is to find anyone to argue the opposing
case. The only serious attempt after Rambaud to defend *la
rhétorique des citations* is that of La Mothe Le Vayer in his
Considérations sur l'éloquence françoise of 1638.[7] He too notes
that quotations lose force in translation; and he considers it absurd
for any author to believe all his thoughts to be original, so why
should he not acknowledge his authorities? But his central argument
is simply that eloquence should not be "uniforme", a word which
could be translated here as *monologic*; discourse should rather
reflect the reality of ""diversité":

> Mais pour venir à ce qui nous touche, il me semble qu'il faut considerer, que l'eloquence n'est pas uniforme, et n'a pas tousjours un mesme visage. Elle en change au contraire, et paroist toute autre, selon la diversité des matieres, des tems, des lieus, et des personnes. (145)

This defense of dialogism is notably more muted than that of Rambaud, and it is interesting that even La Mothe Le Vayer, though later an outspoken opponent of Vaugelas's purism, draws the line at a cento such as Lipsius's *Politica* : "Un tel travail ne pourroit pas passer pour une piece d'eloquence," he writes. "Il y a de la retenuë, et quelque bien-seance à observer en cela" (152). Le Moyne, writing in 1640, shows himself sensitive to these conflicting pressures in the preface to his *Peintures morales*; he wishes to record his use of classical sources, yet realizes that his contemporaries are increasingly intolerant of intrusive quotation:

> Quoy que je n'aye pas embarassé mon Discours d'allegations Grecques et Latines, j'ay crû neantmoins estre obligé de les mettre à la marge; et en cela je pense avoir fait une action de civilité et de justice; il estoit de la civilité, que je reconnusse les magnifiques Morts, qui sont les Bienfaiteurs communs de tous les Vivans: et il estoit de la justice, que je ne me fist point le proprietaire d'un Bien que je n'ay que d'emprunt, et que ma pauvreté ne fust point confonduë avec les richesses de ces grands Hommes. (sig. ꭲ iv r)

By the time of the classical generation there is virtual unanimity: "Les Pedants sont sujets à faire beaucoup de *citations* inutiles, et par pure ostentation," remarks Furetière in his *Dictionaire universel* (1690). "Les *citations* ne sont plus guere à la mode dans les discours oratoires." Even so, Claude Fleury goes to the lengths of composing a two-part dialogue to demonstrate that quotations in judicial eloquence are superfluous and ineffective (Hepp). The *Dialogues sur l'éloquence judiciaire: si l'on doit citer dans les plaidoyers* were written in 1664; they remained unpublished during Fleury's lifetime, but circulated in manuscript, prompting a reply in 1666 from Gabriel Guéret .

Guéret dismisses as inaccurate Fleury's contention that the ancients do not quote, and argues that we should anyway temper respect of the ancients with reason. He favours a very selective use of quotations, and it is a mark of how far opinion has evolved since the beginning of the century that Guéret invokes Du Vair and Pasquier in *support* of his views. Notwithstanding his modest endorsement of the practice of quotation, Guéret is clearly hostile to anything which smacks openly of dialogism: "Un Plaidoyé qui doit estre un corps parfait, et composé de parties jointes ensemble, n'est qu'un assemblage confus de plusieurs pieces, on n'y voit rien de lié" (152). Bernard Lamy, in *De l'art de parler*, is close to Guéret in his cautious advocacy of the use of quotations, and he, too, is anxious that the essential unity of style should be preserved; excessive quotation "gâte un stile, et empêche qu'il ne soit net et coulant." The multi-coloured texts beloved of Rambaud are now seen as bearing the mark of sickness (recalling Filère's imagery earlier): "La nature aime la simplicité, c'est une marque de quelque fâcheuse maladie que d'avoir la peau marquée de taches de differentes couleurs" (216). Even the classical champions of quotation can muster only lukewarm enthusiasm. When Richelet writes in his *Dictionnaire* that "une sentence est pour ainsi dire en saillie, et sort du corps du discours", his disapproval of such dialogism can be taken for granted.

The debate continued to provoke ripples well into the following century,[8] but its climax as far as the classical period is concerned comes in 1668 with Racine's *Les Plaideurs*. In his extended plea in defence of the dog Citron (III, iii), l'Intimé commits every known solecism, clumsily inserting into his speech inapposite Latin quotations at every turn. His absurd condition is analysed a few years later by La Bruyère:

> *Hérille*, soit qu'il parle, qu'il harangue ou qu'il écrive, veut citer: il fait dire au Prince des philosophes que le vin enivre, et à l'Orateur romain que l'eau le tempère. S'il se jette dans la morale, ce n'est pas lui, c'est le divin Platon qui assure que la vertu est aimable, le vice odieux, ou que l'un et l'autre se tournent en habitude. Les choses les plus communes, les plus triviales, et qu'il est même capable de penser, il veut les devoir aux anciens, aux Latins, aux Grecs; ce n'est ni pour donner plus d'autorité à ce qu'il dit, ni peut-être pour se faire honneur de ce qu'il sait: il veut citer. (371; cf. 93, 174)

For the generation of Racine and La Bruyère, the *citation* has become an object of ridicule. "Il n'y a que la fausse érudition, et l'esprit de polymathie qui ait pu rendre les citations à la mode comme elles ont été jusqu'ici," declares Malebranche (437) in 1674 —a far cry from Erasmus's *De copia* (1512), which had devoted an entire chapter (I, 66) to the enumeration of some twenty-six different formulas for citing an author.

IV

The Speaking Subject

The *querelle des citations* brings out into the open classical mistrust of multiple and intrusive voices (Beugnot "Aspect textuel"; Kapp). Antoine Compagnon has spoken of the beginnings in the classical period of "une modalité de l'écriture où l'auteur, sujet singulier et autonome, et non plus avatar d'une lignée ou d'une tradition, sera pleinement partie prenante" (305). In stark contrast, Bakhtin's theory of discourse is founded on the idea of language as living dialogue:

> The word (or in general any sign) is interindividual. Everything that is said, expressed, is located outside the "soul" of the speaker and does not belong only to him. The word cannot be assigned to a single speaker. (*Speech Genres* 121)

Bakhtin rejects out of hand the idea—which has its roots in the Cartesian theory of mind—of "one single language and a single authorial individuality expressing itself directly in that language" (*Dialogic Imagination* 265). For a writer like Montaigne, meaning might be said to be constructed out of the dialogic interplay of different voices, an interplay in which the author is merely *maître de cérémonies*. The classical writer, on the other hand, sees himself as the unique maker ("poet") of meaning, and with this new notion of the author we already have the seed of the *Querelle des anciens et des modernes*. (In addition to, and reinforcing, the new semantic status of the writer as sole manufacturer of meaning, the writer also comes to acquire in this period a distinctly new social status.)[9] Foucault sums up the transformation of the author's role in this way:

> Dans l'ordre du discours littéraire, et à partir [du xviie siècle], la fonction de l'auteur n'a pas cessé de se renforcer: tous ces récits, tous ces poèmes, tous ces drames ou comédies qu'on laissait circuler au Moyen Age dans un anonymat au moins relatif, voilà que, maintenant, on leur demande (et on exige d'eux qu'ils disent) d'où ils viennent, qui les a écrits; on demande que l'auteur rende compte de l'unité du texte qu'on met sous son nom [...]. L'auteur est ce qui donne à l'inquiétant langage de la fiction, ses unités, ses noeuds de cohérence, son insertion dans le réel. (29-30)

The emergence of this radically new notion of the author's function and status coincides with the beginnings of Cartesianism. Bakhtin, as we have seen, links monologism with "Cartesian thought," though he refrains from any precise explanation of the nature of that link. The connection is to be found not in some vague appeal to "rational form" but rather in the Cartesian theory of mind and in its repercussions on contemporary thinking about language. The *cogito* argument is used by Descartes to establish the idea of the individual conscious subject. Thought is understood by Cartesians as the expression of this individual subject, indeed for Descartes it is a defining characteristic of the subject: "Je trouve ici," he writes in the Second Meditation, "que la pensée est un attribut qui m'appartient: elle seule ne peut être détachée de moi" (418).

It follows from this that language is the instrument which serves to communicate the thought of the individual subject. Such a view of language is first expressed in the seventeenth century before Descartes,[10] but it is reinforced by Cartesian thinking, and notably by the Port-Royal grammarians and philosophers; by the second half of the century it is assumed unquestioningly that the role of language is to give voice to pre-existent thought. It is this linguistic theory which underlies the classical principle of *clarté* and which makes possible La Bruyère's remark that there is one and only one "right" expression of a given idea. The Cartesian rhetorician Lamy makes the point explicitly:

> Il faut avant que de parler former en nous-mêmes une image reglée des choses que nous pensons, et que nous voulons peindre par nos paroles. Ceux qui nous écoutent ne peuvent pas appercevoir nettement ce que nous voulons leur dire, si nous ne l'appercevons pas nous-mêmes fort nettement: nôtre discours n'est qu'une copie de l'original qui est en nôtre tête. (*L'Art de parler* 4-5)[11]

Language is thus understood as the direct expression of an individual consciousness: behind any utterance there is a single speaking subject. This explains why, when he comes to define the qualities of "un bel esprit," Bouhours is so dismissive of those who "pillage continually the Romans and the Greeks," for to exhibit such subservience to the thoughts of others is to devalue, if not indeed to negate, the concept of the thinking self:

> Un bel esprit est riche de son fond: il trouve dans ses propres lumieres ce que les esprits communs ne touvent que dans les livres. Il s'étudie et s'instruit luy-mesme [...]. Sur tout il ne s'approprie point les pensées des autres. (*Entretiens* 119)

Pivotal to the classical theory of discourse is the assumption that a text has a single *sujet d'énonciation*.

The Renaissance model of discourse characterized by Terence Cave as the *cornucopian text* is eventually replaced in the seventeenth century by a classical model of discourse, that of the *singular voice*. A voice rather than a text, because for the classical generation the spoken word has come to have primacy over the written; and singular, because the dialogic model of the cornucopia has been supplanted by the monologic Cartesian ideal of a single enunciating subject. The classical voice is singular also in its need to remain discreet, for a highly self-conscious narrative voice would instantly create dialogic tensions; only if the voice is disembodied can the illusion be sustained that the literary utterance is the product of a single speaking subject. The singular voice is, in both senses of the term, *une voix discrète*.

Montaigne's treatment at the hands of his classicizers affords a revealing glimpse of the character of this new model of literary discourse. After being frequently reprinted during the earlier part of the century, not a single complete edition of the *Essais* was published between 1669 and 1724; in 1677 there did however appear a heavily abridged version, with the title *L'Esprit des Essais de Montaigne*.[12] The most striking feature of this gross bowdlerization is the omission of virtually all the Latin quotations, a fact which the anonymous editor explains in the "Préface" by saying that even those like himself who admire the charm of Montaigne's style cannot but baulk at "les trop frequentes citations Latines, qu'il devoit d'autant plus eviter, qu'elles sont inutiles; et que d'ailleurs elles interrompent la liaison de ses sujets, et la suite de son discours." The editor goes on to explain that he has retained "toutes les choses Historiques et divertissantes," while cutting out "leurs ornemens superflus"—in practice this amounts to the excision of all those passages in which Montaigne talks of himself, such as the beginning of "Du repentir" (III, 2); in the case of "Du démentir" (II, 18), the first two-thirds of the essay are simply lopped off; and, not surprisingly, the discussion of centos and of "notre incrustation empruntée" at the beginning of "De l'institution des enfants" (I, 26) disappears entirely. The voice of Montaigne is thus reduced to monologic singularity, first through the suppression of the Latin quotations, and then through the omission of all the most personal passages. This self-styled "agreable reduction" is a Procrustean attempt to refashion Montaigne's cornucopian text according to the classical model of the singular voice.

V

Disguising the Dialogic, or *l'art de se taire*

Barbier d'Aucour accused Bouhours of wholesale plagiarism in the *Entretiens*, remarking that entire sections had been lifted verbatim from Pasquier and Le Laboureur. The abbé de Villars countered with the ingenious argument that *vraisemblance* prevented Bouhours from naming his sources in a dialogue, but that he had quoted them verbatim precisely so as *not* to conceal the extent of his borrowing: "L'art du Dialogue l'a empesché de citer l'Autheur d'où cela estoit pris" (49-55).

The classical wish to expunge from the text all traces of alien voices amounts to an attempt to deny the essentially dialogic nature of all discourse. To the extent that dialogism is understood in opposition to monologism, we have been able to speak here of a shift during the classical period "against dialogism." But in another sense, all discourse must be seen as dialogic. "It might be said that any speech communication or speech interaction takes the form of an *exchange of utterances*, i.e. that of a *dialogue*," writes Bakhtin. "Dialogue, an exchange of words, is the most natural form of language" ("Construction of the utterance" 117).[13] Dialogism thus has a double sense: it describes both the essential nature of (all) human language, and also, more particularly, certain types of discourse. "In fact," writes Ken Hirschkop, "it is the status of monologism which is the most problematic: if dialogism is the nature of all language, then what gives rise to monologism? [...] Monologism must itself be recognized as a strategy of response toward another discourse, albeit a strategy which aims to 'ignore' or 'marginalize' the opposite discourse" (75). Whereas a "saussurean" literary critic might want to regard the burlesque as an aberration from the norm, a Bakhtinian will be inclined to consider classicism and its self-proclaimed monologism as the more aberrant, or at least as the more needful of explanation. A modern historian of seventeenth-century France writes that "the image of the absolute monarch did not correspond to the reality" (Parker 136)—the same could be said of the image of monologic classical discourse. How then does the dialogical reality manifest itself in classical discourse?

In a letter to a friend (1651), Pellisson considers "quatre manières d'alléguer un passage," according to the degree of assimilation of the quoted passage into the larger text (Marcou 465-67). When quoting a text as an authority, says Pellisson, it would be quite wrong to change it in any way. A second case is when one quotes "pour l'élégance et pour la gentillesse," and in this case, the author may wish to twist ("détourner") the sense of the original passage,

> parce que c'est une nouveauté qui surprend l'esprit et qui lui plaît, surtout quand elle est ingénieusement pratiquée. Cette variété même de sens dans les mêmes paroles a quelque chose de divertissant, et c'est ainsi qu'en usent votre Montaigne et votre Pline [...].

Thirdly, when quoting a passage in order to make a joke, it is positively recommended to distort the sense of the words, "parce que cela fait une plus grande surprise." In the final case of the device, distortion of meaning is obligatory, in order to create the mystery which is prescribed for this genre. In his discussion of the dialogue form, written for publication, Pellisson seemed blithely unaware of the dialogic potential of that genre; when however he comes to discuss the possibilities of quotation, in a letter not intended for publication, he is interested precisely in the literary effect ("surprise") to be derived from the appropriation and distortion of alien voices. Behind his meticulous categorizaton, Pellisson seems to be trying to come to terms with the dialogic nature of literary discourse.

Fundamental to classicism is the principle of imitation, and this very concept seems to assume the necessity of dialogue with other authors, even if the most obtrusive forms of intertextual dialogue, like the cento or the *florilège*, are frowned upon. Other more discreetly dialogic genres flourish, especially in the salons—the *maxime*, for example, or the *énigme*, a genre designed specifically to confound monologic expectations (Cronk "Enigma"). Pascal's *Pensées*—which speak of an "ordre par dialogues" (L. 2)—provide perhaps the most spectacular example of *une forme brève*, the fragment, being used to create a dialogic text.

It is however in the longer form of the novel that dialogism is best exemplified for Bakhtin, and he notes that the first French theoretician of the novel, Huet, appears just at the moment of classicism (*Dialogic Imagination* 22, 41, 372). The sudden appearance of *style indirect libre* in French writing of the second half of the seventeenth century has been remarked upon both by Bakhtin, who discusses the examples of La Bruyère and La Fontaine, and also by a number of other critics, who have independently identified instances of this style in, for example, *La Princesse de Clèves*.[14] Bakhtin offers no explanation for this development, beyond the rather tame suggestions that increasing grammatical regularity made *style indirect libre* more feasible, and that rationalism tended to curb "the individualization of reported speech" (*Marxism* 120, 151). *Style indirect libre* is of course an essentially dialogic device, but it is discreetly dialogic, and the most evident reason for the dramatically sudden appearance of *style indirect libre* in classical discourse is surely that it afforded the best means of producing a dialogic text without seeming to affront monologic appearances. The overtly dialogic devices of the *Roman comique* were not available to Madame de La Fayette as they had been to Scarron, and so she is obliged to resort to other techniques in order to achieve comparable narrative sophistication. The monologic constraints of classical discourse cannot suppress dialogism, but they do force it to find an outlet in other, more covert, forms, among them *style indirect libre*.

Classical poetics, if it cannot eliminate the dialogic, must at least strive to minimize it. One detail which is revealing of a broader shift is the change in meaning of the word *allusion*: it had originally signified a jokey play on words (as in Du Bellay's *Allusiones*), but in the classical period the term acquires its modern and radically different meaning of an indirect or covert reference (Goyet 314).[15] *Allusion* in Du Bellay's sense is overtly dialogic; with classicism, it becomes discreetly dialogic.

The classical *art poétique* thus becomes the art of disguising the dialogic, "la manière de déguiser facilement toute sorte de discours" —this last phrase being the subtitle of a work, *Le Masque des orateurs*, published in 1667. The author, aptly named Richesource, elaborates an "Art plagiaire" (6) in which he considers the various ways of appropriating other works so that they become unrecognizable:

> Le Plagianisme (*sic*) des Orateurs est l'Art ou la maniere ingenieuse et facile, dont les Orateurs Plagianistes se servent adroitement et heureusement, pour changer ou déguiser toutes sortes de Discours, ou de leur composition ou de celle de quelques Autheurs; ou pour leur plaisir ou pour leur utilité [...], de telle sorte qu'il soit tout à fait impossible à l'Autheur mesme de se reconnoistre dans son propre ouvrage, ni son air, ni son genie ni son style, ni son caractere, et par consequent qui que ce puisse estre, tant il sera bien deguisé. (8-9)

With great thoroughness Richesource details a whole series of available ploys for disguising borrowed voices (seven of the seventeen chapters have the word "déguisement" in their titles): phraseology may be changed, the order of topics altered, the material amplified or reduced, figures of speech removed, added, or changed. Richsource is insistent that his dissembling techniques can sometimes enhance the literary value of the text and even lead to the creation of new masterpieces (52). Above all, though, the semblance of monologism must be maintained; thus Richesource recommends comparison as an excellent means of amplifying a borrowed text, but adds the cautionary note that this should not be at the expense of the integrity of the whole:

> Mais il faut remarquer que c'est en cét endroit où se doit trouver le dernier effort du jugement, afin que dans ce mélange nous n'avancions aucune proposition qui détruise ce que nous avons dessein d'établir. (29)

The classical author is a *dialogiste malgré lui*, condemned to having to write dialogically while pretending not to. On being presented with a copy of Lamy's *L'Art de parler*, Cardinal Le Camus is supposed to have replied: "Voilà, sans doute, un excellent art; mais qui nous donnera l'art de se taire?" Bouhours has a similar thought: "C'est un grand art que celuy de se bien taire, il a ses principes et ses regles, comme l'art de bien parler" (*Entretiens* 106). *L'Art de se taire*: they had hit on the perfect title for a work on classical poetics. (The title was too good to waste, and the book was duly written, in 1696 by the abbé de Bellegarde.)

VI

The Ambivalent Voice

The tension between monologism and dialogism which is so fundamental to Bakhtin's theory of discourse is explicable only in a political context, and the fact that his ideas were first shaped in Stalinist Russia gives a particular resonance to his references to absolutism. (The possible literary-political parallel between Louis XIV's régime and Stalin's occurred also to a contemporary of Bakhtin's, Mikhail Bulgakov, who explores the idea in two plays and a novel about the life of Molière, all written during the 1930s.) Engels had remarked that absolute monarchy "*had* to be absolute just because of the centrifugal character of all elements" (quoted by Parker 146), and using a complementary image Bakhtin describes the poetics of classicism and the unitary language as the theoretical expression of "centripetal forces in socio-linguistic and ideological life" (*Dialogic Imagination* 271). The Académie française stands as the most potent symbol of central government's desire to control the literary establishment; the preamble to its Statutes, written in 1634 by Nicolas Faret, has recently come to light and it confirms that the political importance of linguistic "perfection" was understood by the Académie's architects from the very beginning (24). The establishment of the Académie is however only the best-remembered aspect of the progressive institutionalization of literature which occurred during Louis XIV's reign, a process which culminated in 1699 with the appointment of the abbé Bignon to head the newly-created Bureau de la librairie (Martin 760-62). This is a period which has acquired new insight into the historical and political dimensions of linguistic debate. When, in his "Discours sur la rhétorique françoise," Le Grand speaks of "cette habitude imperieuse qui regne absolument dans les coeurs, qui exerce une puissance legitime sur les volontez, et qui n'est pas moins le fonde-ment des empires, que la source des triomphes," one might think he was referring to the political régime; in fact, he is speaking of "cette éloquence souveraine" (sig. ã v v) The image is not a random one: another writer of the period, Macé, speaks of "la Puissance, la Sçiance, et l'Eloquence" as the three foundations of authority whose destinies are inevitably and inextricably linked (sig. * 3 r).

This idea of the interdependence of language and power is made the basis of the abbé de Lionnière's *Le Sort de la langue françoise* (1703), which may be considered the first history of the French language.[16] Written, so the author tells us in the "Préface," at the bchest of the King, he describes the triumphant rise of the French language from "un jargon grossier" (2), through adolescence, to arrive at "sa plus grande perfection" (97) in the reign of Louis XIV. He dwells at length on the politics of Richelieu—"Ici se presente un nouvel ordre, tout l'Etat change de face" (68)—and on its linguistic consequences, including the founding of the Académie française: "La *Langue* sur tout dans ce changement heureux, trouve les plus solides fondemens de sa perfection" (70). The fate of the language is inseparable from that of the monarchy: "Pour bien juger des derniers progrez de la *Langue*, il la faut mettre dans le même point de vûë de la *Monarchie*; car leurs avantages sont mutuels, et reciproques, ils rejallissent (*sic*) les uns sur les autres" (94-95). It thus follows naturally that the language should have become most noble and most expressive under the most noble and most forceful monarch (146). When Bouhours in the *Entretiens* conflates praise of the King and praise of the French language, as we saw at the beginning, he is not merely indulging in lavish eulogy of the King; he is also giving expression to a new awareness of the political underpinning of linguistic debate.

As there is a political dimension to monologism, so there is a philosophical dimension too, and the "abstract objectivism" which Bakhtin describes as the foundation of monologism and which he attributes to Saussure is in fact much better exemplified by Descartes. The Cartesian theory of mind and the emergence of the idea of the individual conscious subject are clearly crucial for the way in which monologism develops in the seventeenth century. Cardin Le Bret's *De la souveraineté du Roy* (1632), setting out the theory of absolutism, and the *Discours de la méthode* (1637), both appeared at the moment when Richelieu was planning the Académie française: the political theory of "une foi, une loi, un roi" combines powerfully with Descartes's theory of mind to produce a monologic model of literary discourse, the model of the singular voice.

But, of course, dialogism will out. We need look no further than Pascal's description of "le moi haïssable" to find an appreciation of the tensions underlying monologism: "En un mot le moi a deux qualités. Il est injuste en soi en ce qu'il se fait centre de tout. Il est incommode aux autres en ce qu'il les veut asservir, car chaque moi est l'ennemi et voudrait être le tyran de tous les autres" (L. 597). Bouhours's condemnation, quoted above, of those who "pillage the Romans and Greeks" occurs in a work, the *Entretiens*, in which he himself pillages both classical and contemporary authors extensively, as Barbier d'Aucour was quick to point out. La Bruyère's fulsome exposition of monologic discourse quoted above ("Il y a dans l'art un point de perfection...") comes from a text, *Les Caractères*, whose fragmented structure and lack of "unité" were explicitly criticized by contemporaries (Brody "Contextes" 56-58). That La Bruyère and Bouhours should have sought to expound monologism through dialogism is a pleasing (if unsurprising) paradox which only underlines monologism's essentially problematic status. The classical model of the singular voice is never more than an ideal, even if it is a highly potent and influential ideal. Bakhtin's theory of discourse insists on the essential oddity of monologic discourse, and reminds us that dialogism is always to be found, behind even the most assiduously constructed monologic facade. The classical voice is odd, singular in the other sense, because its—inevitable—dialogism has been, if not supressed, then at least rendered unobtrusive. Classical discourse is the product of monologic thinking yet manages also to subvert it. The singular voice is ambivalent in being simultaneously both an effect and a *mise en cause* of monologism.

We began with Bouhours's literary ideal of "une eau pure et nette qui n'a point de goust." The image was not of course new, and some poetic theorists of the pre-classical period fretted that the monologic diet of pure water prescribed by the grammarians would lead to poetic malnutrition. "Que ne sert-on en la faim de ces messieurs [...];" writes Marie de Gournay, "une belle nape blanche, lissée, polie, semée simplement de fleurettes, couverte de beaux vases clairs et luisants; mais pleins au partir de là d'une eau pure et fine à l'envy de l'argent de coupelle, et rien plus?" (71). The image recurs in a letter of 1647 in which La Mothe Le Vayer criticizes Vaugelas's newly published *Remarques* and argues the need for philosophy to be allied to eloquence: "La plus grande pureté de langage est insipide, et ressemble, si elle n'est accompagnée du bon sens, à un boüillon d'eau claire qui ne nourrit point" (*Petits Traitez*, 689). Filère, on the other hand, anticipates Vaugelas when in his *Discours contre les citations* he pleads the case for a unitary language:

> Il ne faut pas, que la peur de paroistre ignorans nous degouste de ce dessien [composer des Discours et des Oraisons d'une seule langue], on peut sans citer ny Grec ny Latin, monstrer avoir leu les Autheurs de ces deux langues. Certaines fontaines de Paphlagonie, selon Virtruve, n'estant qu'eau, avoient toutesfois le goust du vin: ainsi nos discours encor qu'ils soyent tous François, peuvent tenir des autheurs Grecs et Latin, en avoir la fleur, et la substance. Ce seroit de ceste façon, que je souhaiterois les discours des François, tirez avec peine de la moüelle des sciences, et formez avec industrie par le pinceau d'un langage rond, et uny; si bien qu'il les fallust loüer de l'elegance de leurs paroles, sans les pouvoir toutesfois reprendre d'une nonchalante et vicieuse ignorance. (37-38)

Filère's model of literary discourse is one of disguised dialogism, one in which language with the appearance of water has acquired the taste and substance of (foreign) wine. The abbé de Lionnière compares the slow formation of the language to the process by which diamonds take centuries to acquire the requisite mix of *clarté* and colour (140): the image of the clear-yet-colourful diamond here serves a like function to that of the pure-yet-appetizing water; with such metaphors, the monologic monarch's absolute voice is dialogized. The water spouting from the lips of the King in Bouhours's model may appear tasteless, but appearances deceive. The singular voice of the classical author has turned water into wine—not a new miracle, but a miracle nonetheless.

Notes

[1]Pierre Le Moyne similarly praises the royal powers of expression: "Vous parlez peu, Sire; et ce peu, au jugement de ceux qui sçavent entendre, ne laisse rien à dire aux grands parleurs. Toutes vos paroles sont choisies et ingenieuses: vos demy-mots mesme ont du fonds, et sont pleins de sens [....]" (*De l'art de régner*, sig. ã iv r).

[2] In the case of works formerly attributed to Voloshinov, I refer to the author(s) as Bakhtin in the text above.

[3]Compare Bakhtin, *Rabelais and His World*, 101

[4]In discussing "la varietà," Rizza quotes a text by Saint-Amant using the dialogic term *diversité* (176): the term was an important one, and more widespread than this single quotation suggests—I quote below other instances of its use, by Camus, Rambaud and La Mothe Le Vayer. Camus has a chapter "De la diversité" (*Les Diversitez*, Tome second, Livre X, chap. 17). On the dialogism of the burlesque, see my article "La défense du dialogisme." See also Floeck, *Literarästhetik*, on *diversité* and *variété* as key-terms of the baroque aesthetic (17-36), and on the shift from *diversité* to *unité* (242-47); and "*Diversité* und *simplicité*."

[5] See Beugnot, "L'Entretien"; Bray, "Le dialogue"; and Le Guern, "Sur le genre du dialogue." Christoph Strosetzki, *Rhétorique de la conversation* (100-03), considers the dialogue in the context of seventeenth-century discussion of "la conversation."

[6] The opposite view is argued by Beugnot: "La vogue de l'entretien correspond précisément à un moment de discrédit du dogmatisme, puis d'affranchissement" ("Dialogue, entretien et citation"). The (pre-classical) dialogues of La Mothe Le Vayer seem more truly dialogic; see Beugnot, "La fonction du dialogue chez La Mothe Le Vayer."

[7]He returns to the subject several times in later works: see *Petits Traitez*, "Lettre I" 6-8 and "Discours pour montrer que les doutes de la philosophie sceptique" (64).

[8]Compagnon cites Arnauld, Nicole and François Lamy as all having contributed to the debate in the latter years of the century (313)—Jesuits and Jansenists were evidently united in their distrust of *la rhétorique des citations*. See also the letter to d'Olivet (?), 1705, *Lettres de Maucroix*, 183-84; and Boucher d'Argis, "Citations de droit," *Encyclopédie*.

[9]See Viala, *Naissance de l'écrivain*.

[10]For example, by Jean-Pierre Camus, in 1610: "La parole est le truchement de nos conceptions, et l'instrument pour les produire et manifester à autruy," *Les Diversitez* (6: 503).

[11]The third edition, quoted here, asserts this point more forcefully than the first; compare *De l'art de parler* (1675), 4.

[12] The work was not republished, but an even more savage abridgement followed: *Pensées de Montaigne propres à former l'esprit et les moeurs*.

[13]Compare Emile Benveniste's analysis of *énonciation*: "[Le monologue] doit étre posé, malgré l'apparence, comme une variété du dialogue, structure fondamentale. Le 'monologue' est un dialogue intériorisé, formulé en 'langage intérieur', entre un moi locuteur et un moi écouteur. Parfois le moi locuteur est seul à parler; le moi écouteur reste néanmoins présent; sa présence est nécessaire et suffisante pour rendre signifiante l'énonciation du moi locuteur" (85-86).

[14]See *Marxism*, 142, 151; Lips, *Le Style indirect libre*, 130-48; Verschoor, *Etude de grammaire historique*, 124-30; and Delhez-Sarlet, "Style indirect libre et 'point de vue' dans *La Princesse de Clèves*."

[15]*Allusion* is first attested in 1574 with the sense "jeu sur la forme d'un mot," and in 1671 with the sense "évocation non explicite" (*Trésor de la Langue Française*, 2: 597).

[16] Bouhours had already sketched the history of the French language in the *Entretiens*, 67-76.

Works Cited

Aisy, Jean d'. *Le Génie de la langue françoise*. 2 vols. Paris: d'Houry, 1685.

Argis, Boucher d'. "Citations de droit." *Encyclopédie*. Vol. 3, 1753.

Bakhtin, M. M. [V. N. Voloshinov]. "The construction of the utterance." *Bakhtin School Papers*. Ed. Ann Shukman. Russian Poetics in Translation. Vol 10. Oxford: RPT, 1983. 114-38.

—. *The Dialogic Imagination*. Trans. C. Emerson and M. Holquist. Austin: U of Texas P, 1981.

—. *Marxism and the Philosophy of Language*. [V. N. Voloshinov] Trans. L. Matejka and I.R. Titunik. Cambridge: Harvard UP, 1973).

—. *Problems of Dostoevsky's Poetics*. Trans. C. Emerson Manchester: Manchester UP, 1984.

—. *Rabelais and His World*. Trans. H. Iswolsky. Cambridge: MIT, 1968.

—. *Speech Genres and Other Late Essays*. Trans. V.W. McGee. Austin: U of Texas P, 1986.

Barbier d'Aucour, Jean. *Sentimens de Cléante sur les Entretiens d'Ariste et d'Eugène*. Paris: Le Monnier, 1671.

Barthes, Roland. *Le Degré zéro de l'écriture*. Paris: Seuil, 1953.

Bayley, Peter. *French Pulpit Oratory 1598-1650*. Cambridge: Cambridge UP, 1980.

Bellegarde, abbé Jean-Baptiste Morvan de. *Conduite pour se taire et pour parler, principalement en matière de religion*. Paris: Bénard, 1696.

Benveniste, Emile."L' appareil formel de l'énonciation" *Problèmes de linguistique générale*. Vol. 2. Paris: Gallimard, 1974. 79-88.

Bercé, Yves-Marie. *Fête et révolte: des mentalités populaires du 16e au 18e siècle* . Paris: Hachette, 1976.

Beugnot, Bernard. "Un aspect textuel de la réception critique: la citation." *Œuvres et critiques* 1/2 (1976): 5-19.

—. "Dialogue, entretien et citation à l'époque classique." *Canadian Review of Comparative Literature* 3 (1976): 39-50.

—. *L'Entretien au XVIIe siècle*. Montréal: Presses de l'Université, 1971.

—. "Florilèges et polyantheae: diffusion et statut du lieu commun à l'époque classique." *Études françaises* 13 (1977): 119-41.

—. "La fonction du dialogue chez La Mothe Le Vayer." *CAIEF* 24 (1972): 31-41.

—. "Forme et histoire: le statut des *ana*." *Mélanges offerts à Georges Couton*. Lyon: Presses Universitaires, 1981. 85-101.

Bouhours, Dominique. *Les Entretiens d'Artiste et d'Eugène*. Paris: Armand Colin, 1962.

Bray, Bernard. "Le dialogue comme forme littéraire au 17e siècle." *CAIEF* 24 (1972): 9-29.

Brody, Jules. "Contextes." *Du Style à la pensée: trois études sur les* Caractères *de La Bruyère*. Lexington: French Forum, 1980. 55-67.

—. "La première réception des *Essais* de Montaigne: les fortunes d'une forme." *Lectures de Montaigne*. Lexington: French Forum, 1982. 13-27.

Caillières. *Des mots à la mode*. 2nd ed. Paris: Barbin, 1692.

Camus, Jean-Pierre. *Les Diversitez*. Vol. 2. Paris: Chappellet, 1609; Vol 6. Lyon: Pillehotte, 1610.

Caussin, Nicolas. *Eloquentiae sacrae et humanae parallela libri XVI*. Paris: Chappelet, 1619.

Cave, Terence. *The Cornucopian Text: problems of writing in the French Renaissance*. Oxford: Clarendon Press, 1979.

Compagnon, Antoine. *La Seconde Main ou le travail de la citation*. Paris: Seuil, 1979.

Cronk, Nicholas. "La défense du dialogisme: vers une poétique du burlesque." *Burlesque et formes parodiques: Actes du Colloque du Mans (1986)*. Ed. I. Landy-Houillon and M. Ménard. Biblio 17, 33. Tübingen: PFSCL, 1987. 321-38.

—. "The enigma of French classicism: a platonic current in seventeenth-century poetic theory." *French Studies* 40 (1986): 269-86.

DeJean, Joan. "Bakhtin and/in History." *Language and Literary Theory*. Ed. B.A. Stolz, I.R. Titunik, L. Dolezel. Ann Arbor: U of Michigan P, 1984. 225-40.

Delhez-Sarlet, Claudette. "Style indirect libre et 'point de vue' dans *La Princesse de Clèves*." *Cahiers d'analyse textuelle* 6 (1964): 70-80.

Descartes, René. *Œuvres philosophiques*. Ed. F. Alquié. Vol. 2. Paris: Garnier, 1967.

Dinouart, Abbé. *L'Art de se taire, principalement en matière de religion*. 1771. Preface by J.-J. Courtine and C. Haroche. Paris: Millon, 1987.

Du Pré. *Le Pourtraict de l'éloquence françoise*. Paris: L'Evesque, 1621.

Du Vair, Guillaume. *De l'éloquence françoise*. Ed. R. Radouant. 1907. Genève: Slatkine, 1970.

L'Esprit des Essais de Michel, seigneur de Montaigne. Paris: Sercy, 1677.

Faret, Nicolas. *Projet de l'Académie, pour servir de Préface à ses Statuts*. Ed. J. Rousselet. Saint-Etienne: Université de Saint-Etienne, 1983.

Filère, Alexandre Paul de. *Discours contre les citations du grec et latin es plaidoyés de ce temps*. Paris: Huby, 1610.

Fleury, Claude. *Dialogues sur l'éloquence judiciaire: si on doit citer dans les plaidoyers*. Ed. Fr. Gaquère. Paris: Gigord, 1925.

Floeck, Wilfried. "*Diversité* und *simplicité*: zur dramatischen Handlung im französischen Theater des 17.Jahrhunderts." *Romanistisches Jahrbuch* 22 (1971): 101-22.

—. *Die Literarästhetik des französischen Barock: Entstehung—Entwicklung—Auflösung*. Berlin: Erich Schmidt, 1979.

Foucault, Michel. *L'Ordre du discours*. Paris: Gallimard, 1971.

Fumaroli, Marc. *L'Age de l'eloquence: rhétorique et "res literaria" de la Renaissance au seuil de l'époque classique*. Genève: Droz, 1980.

Gillet. "Discours sur le génie de la Langue Françoise." *Plaidoyers et autres œuvres*. Paris: Boudot, 1696. 223-50.

Gournay, Marie de. *Les Idées littéraires de Mlle de Gournay*. Ed. A. Uildriks. Groningen: Kleine, 1962.

Goyet, Francis. "Imitatio ou intertextualité." *Poétique* 71 (1987): 313-20.

Guéret, Gabriel. "Si les citations sont necessaires dans les plaidoyez." *Entretiens sur l'éloquence de la chaire et du barreau*. Paris: Guignard, 1666. 129-82.

Hepp, Noémi. "Humanisme et cartésianisme: la guerre ou la paix?" *Travaux de linguistique et de littérature* 13.2 (1975) [Mélanges de littérature française offerts à M. René Pintard]: 451-61.

Hirschkop, Ken. "A response to the forum on Mikhail Bakhtin." *Bakhtin: Essays and Dialogues on His Work*. Ed. G. S. Morson. Chicago: U of Chicago P, 1986. 73-79.

Holmès, Catherine E. *L'Eloquence judiciare de 1620 à 1660*. Paris : Nizet, 1967.

Kapp, Volker. "Intertextualité et rhétorique des citations." *Recherches sur l'histoire de la poétique*. Ed. M. -M. Münch. Berne: Lang, 1984. 237-54.

La Bruyère, Jean de. *Les Caractères*. Ed. R. Garapon. Paris: Garnier, 1962.

Lafond, Jean. "Le centon et son usage dans la littérature morale et politique."
    L'Automne de la Renaissance 1580-1630. Ed. J. Lafond and A. Stegmann.
    Paris: Vrin, 1981. 117-128.
La Mothe Le Vayer, François de. *Considérations sur l'éloquence françoise*.
    Paris: Cramoisy, 1638. 138-55.
—. "De la lecture de Platon, et de son éloquence." *Opuscules ou petits traictez*.
    Paris: Sommaville, 1643. 1-41.
—. "Discours pour montrer que les doutes de la philosophie sceptique sont de
    grand usage dans les sciences."*Œuvres*. Nouvelle édition. Vol. 15.
    Paris: Billiane, 1669.
—. *Petits Traitez en forme de lettres*. Paris: Courbé, 1648.
Lamy, Bernard. *De l'art de parler*. Paris : Pralard, 1675.
—. *L'Art de parler*. 3rd edition. Paris: Pralard, 1678.
Le Grand. "Discours sur la rhetorique françoise." In R. Bary. *La Rhetorique
    françoise*. Nouvelle édition. Paris: Le Petit, 1659.
Le Guern, Michel. "Sur le genre du dialogue." *L'Automne de la Renaissance
    1580-1630*. Ed. J. Lafond and A. Stegmann. Paris: Vrin, 1981. 141-148.
Le Moyne, Pierre. *De l'art de régner*. Paris: Cramoisy, 1665.
—. *Les Peintures morales*. Paris; Cramoisy, 1640.
Lionnière, abbé l'Hérault de. *Le Sort de la langue françoise*. Paris: Barbin,
    1703.
Lips, Marguerite. *Le Style indirect libre* . Paris: Payot, 1926.
Loisel, Antoine. *Pasquier, ou Dialogue des advocats du parlement de Paris*. Ed.
    M. Dupin. Paris: Videcoq, 1844.
Macé, Jean ["Noël François"]. *La Politesse de la langue françoise pour parler
    puremant et ecrire nettemant*. 3rd edition. Bruxelles: Vivien, 1663.
Malebranche. *Œuvres*. Vol. 1. Ed. G. Rodis-Lewis and G. Malbreil.
    Bibliothèque de la Pléiade. Paris: Gallimard, 1979.
Marcou, F. L. *Etude sur la vie et les œuvres de Pellisson*. Paris: Didier and
    Durand, 1859.
Martin, Henri-Jean. *Livre, pouvoirs et société à Paris au XVIIe siècle (1598-
    1701)*. Vol. 2. Genève: Droz, 1969.
Maucroix, François de. *Lettres de Maucroix*. Ed. R. Kohn. Paris: PUF, 1962.
Parker, David. *The Making of French Absolutism*. London: Edward Arnold,
    1983.
Pascal, Blaise. *Œuvres complètes*. Ed. L. Lafuma. Paris: Seuil, 1963.
Pasquier, Etienne. *Lettres familières*. Ed. D. Thickett. Genève; Droz, 1974.
—. *Les Recherches de la France*. Paris: Sonnius, 1607.
Pellisson, Paul. "Discours sur les œuvres de M. Sarasin." *Les Œuvres de
    Monsieur Sarasin*. Paris: Courbé, 1656.
Pensées de Montaigne propres à former l'esprit et les moeurs. Paris: Anisson,
    1700.
Rambaud, Antoine de. *Discours parénétique aux advocats pour l'usage des
    citations du grec et du latin en leurs plaidoyez, contre le Discours du Sieur
    de Filaire*. Paris: Huby, 1611. [Bib. municipale de Grenoble].
Richesource. *Le Masque des orateurs, c'est à dire la maniere de déguiser
    facilement toute sorte de discours*. Paris: Académie des Orateurs, 1667.
Rizza, Cecilia. "Avviamento allo studio delle poetiche del barocco letterario in
    Francia." *Barocco francese e cultura italiana* . Cuneo: SASTE, 1973. 149-
    92.
Saint-Réal, César Vichard de. *De la critique*. Lyon: Anisson and Posuel, 1691.
Siguret, Françoise. *L'Oeil surpris: perception et représentation dans la première
    moitié du XVIIe siècle*. Tübingen: PFSCL, 1985.
Sorel, Charles. "Des dialogues, des harangues, et des panegyriques." *La
    Bibliothèque françoise*. Paris: Compagnie des Libraires du Palais, 1664.
    84-91.

Stanton, Domna. "On *la contestation* and *le carnaval*: a paradoxical preface." *Actes de Banff—1986*. Ed. Michel Bareau and others. Tübingen: PFSCL, 1987. 123-41.

Strosetzki, Christoph. *Rhétorique de la conversation* . Tübingen: PFSCL, 1984.

Temple, Nora. "The Decline of Urban Festivities in Seventeenth-Century France." *Newsletter of the Society for Seventeenth-Century French Studies* 3 (1981): 79-86.

Verschoor, Jan Adriaan. *Etude de grammaire historique et de style sur le style direct et les styles indirects en français*. Groningen: Kleine, 1959.

Viala, Alain. *Naissance de l'écrivain*. Paris: Minuit, 1985.

Vialart, Charles ["de Saint-Paul"]. *Tableau de l'éloquence françoise*. Paris, 1632.

Villars, abbé de. *De la délicatesse*. Paris: Barbin, 1671.

Fiction, Morality, and the Reader: Reflections on the Classical Formula *Plaire et instruire*

G. J. Mallinson
Pembroke College, Cambridge

Plaire et instruire, one of the most widely repeated aesthetic formulas in the 17th century seems to capture well two qualities often associated with classical writers: awareness of an audience and pride in the moral seriousness of their texts, and many novelists in the course of this period evoke it as an indication of the way their different fictions work. In his preface to *Francion*, Sorel likens his role to that of the apothecary who can make more palatable an unpleasant medicine (62), while Camus in the *Dilude* to *Petronille* , highlights the way his novels increase the persuasive force of moral precepts (469-70); later in the century, Mlle de Scudéry will stress the appealing yet enlightening nature of her art in *Clélie* (4:1141-2), and in the *Avant-Propos* to her *Annales galantes*, Mme de Villedieu refers to this same dual quality in her texts which she sees as the essence of their value. Similar characteristics will be uncovered too by literary theorists, and the praise of novelists, *heureux flatteurs* (64), in the second part of Langlois's early *Le Tombeau des romans*, is taken up by Huet among others in his *Lettre... sur l'origine des romans* as he underlines this same skill, *tromper par l'appât du plaisir* (47).[1]

Insistence on the moral worth of fiction often informs the novelist's defence of a genre against the charge that it is at best time-wasting fantasy, and at worst both corrupt and corrupting. In the first part of *Le Tombeau des romans*, for instance. Langlois voices the criticism that fictional invention is largely absurd and improbable:

> ...vous diriez qu'ils se sont estudiez à dire les accidens plus
> esloignez de l'ordinaire & de la croyance humaine...,(6)

a position from which attack on moral grounds readily follows:

> On laisse ce qui est veritablement arrivé pour ce qu'on faint
> d'estre arrivé; comme si la verité avoit moins d'appas que le
> mensonge...(31)

Against this background defenders of the novel are eager to assert both the veracity of their subjects and the value of their texts. The importance of the novelist is seen to lie in his transformation of historical data into an ordered and pleasurable vision. The difference between fiction and reality is not disguised, but used as an argument for the superiority of the former. In his preface to *Rosane*, for instance, Desmarets de Saint-Sorlin clearly relegates untreated facts to a lower order of significance, seeing them in need of embellishment and improvement:

> ...plus ils sont pleins de feintes parmy la verité, plus ils sont
> beaux & profitables, pource que la feinte vray-semblable est
> fondée sur la bienséance et sur la raison, et la verité toute simple
> n'embrasse qu'un récit d'accidens humains, qui le plus souvent
> ne sont pleins que d'extravagance.

Arguments used to attack novels are here used to attack history. Truth, in the form of historical event, is seen as composed of arbitrary and disordered *accidens*, and fiction, paradoxically, becomes the means to a more general and hence more valuable truth. Moral and aesthetic considerations are inextricably linked in this preference of *vray-semblance* and *raison* over *verité* and *extravagance*, both within the text and in its effect on the reader. The novelist brings coherence and consistency both to his presentation of actions and to their moral structure, as he ensures an appropriate outcome to good and evil characters; this double order itself then underlies a correspondingly double satisfaction for the reader. The apparent anarchy which characterizes reality as it is represented in history is seen to be an essential cause of the inferior pleasure provided by this genre; by implication, the structure of fiction is the basis of its greater value and effect:

> ...L'une est assujettie à suivre le fil des revolutions
> extravagantes que cause la fortune dans les Estats, sans oser
> employer que fort peu d'ornemens, qui ne sont pas capables de

> faire perdre aux Lecteurs le desplaisir de voir si souvent la Vertu
> opprimée & le Vice triomphant: L'autre se promene dans les
> libres campagnes d'une invention agreable, ayant tousjours la
> Raison & les Graces à ses costez.[3]

What Desmarets suggests here is pithily expressed in Boisrobert's
preface to his *Histoire indienne*, where he adopts the familiarly
moral reading of Aristotle's distinction between historical and poetic
truth:

> ...ceux qui composent des Poemes Epiques & des
> Romans...descrivent les actions non pas telles qu'elles sont,
> mais bien telles qu'elles doivent estre.

This conception of the novel echoes more general aesthetic
principles frequently expressed in the century. Desmarets'
arguments recall Chapelain's preface to Marino's *Adone* in which
he distinguishes between the moral chaos of history, subject to
chance and fortune, and the more pleasing order and significance of
poetry, and similar views are found much later in the *Reflexions* of
Rapin :

> Car la verité ne fait les choses que comme elles sont; et la vray-
> semblance les fait comme elles doivent estre...(41)

Once again text and reader are seen to meet on the ground of *vray-
semblance*, whose twin aesthetic and moral implications are seen to
be harmonised in the coherence it provides. It is on this basis that
the two aims of *plaire* and *instruire* theoretically coalesce. And in
his preface to *Adone*, Chapelain will suggest a close conformity
between the structure of a text and what he sees as man's natural
preference for order in all its manifestations:

> ...cette vraisemblance étant une représentation des choses
> comme elles doivent avenir, selon que le jugement humain, né et
> élevé au bien, les prévoit et les détermine...il n'y a point de
> doute que la poésie l'ayant pour partage... ne soit plutôt crue,
> ayant pour soi ce qui se fait croire simplement de soi-même, que
> l'histoire qui...n'a pour soi que la verité nue, laquelle ne se peut
> faire croire sans l'aide et le soulagement d'autrui. (87-8)

Significantly, this particular formula is not simply appropriated
and invoked by defenders of heroic fiction. Comic novelists, for
instance, may mock the idealised, exalted world of certain writers
throughout the century, and claim for their own texts a vision more
closely allied to experience; however, the same implicit assumption
of moral value and aesthetic appeal underlies these claims. In his

preface to *Chrysolite*, Mareschal argues that greater pleasure and profit will derive from his more imitable characters:

> ...icy, je n'ay rien mis qu'un homme ne pust faire; je me suis tenu dedans les termes d'une vie privée, afin que chacun se pust mouler sur les actions que je decry,[4]

and later in the century Pancrace voices in Furetière's *Roman bourgeois* a criticism of idealising fiction for failing to provide this same double stimulus:

> ...il n'y a que des amours de princes et de palladins, qui, n'ayant rien de proportionné avec les personnes du commun, ne les touchent point, et ne font point naistre d'envie de les imiter. (1006)

Comparable arguments will be advanced in defence of the *nouvelle*. In *Les Nouvelles françoises*, for instance, Aplanice stresses the gap between text and reader in many *romans*, a weakness which Segrais clearly seeks to avoid in his own work:

> ...Un particulier qui les lira, conformera-t-il ses entreprises sur les gens qui ont des Armees? (35)

and it is this attitude which underlies the praise of the Spanish novella expressed by La Garouffiere in Scarron's *Roman comique* :

> ...les exemples imitables estoient pour le moins d'aussy grande utilité que ceux que l'on avoit presque peine à concevoir. (645)[5]

Whatever the means employed, novelists frequently claim to offer a coherent moral vision on which the reader can base his behaviour or judgements; at different stages in the century, and in different registers they are seen to attribute the same value and effect to their work. In Gomberville's *Carithée*, for instance, the intended impact of the novel is made explicit when hero and heroine escape the villainous plotting of three schemers :

> Nostre salut, mon cher frere, & le chastiment de ces trois esprits enragez, seront deux exemples que la posterité regardera avec des admirations si grandes & si differentes qu'elle en pourra bannir les crimes du monde & y faire reflorir la vertu & la bonté que les hommes en ont chassées (452);

in Furetière's preface to his *Roman bourgeois*, the comic weapon of mockery is seen to be capable of inspiring an equivalent change in the reader:

> ...quand nous voyons le vice tourné en ridicule, nous nous en corrigeons, de peur d'estre les objets de la risée publique...;(900)

and in the preface to her *nouvelle, Eléonor d'Yvrée*, Catherine Bernard assumes a direct link between the structure of her tale and its effect:

> L'on y voit toujours le bien & le mal dans un certain jour qui donne de l'éclat à l'un & qui fait éviter l'autre.

Such comments imply a close relationship between novel and reader, textual coherence and moral control. Fiction assumes something of the status of a map both in the clarity of the guidance it offers and in the act of reading it inspires; its own authoritative order brings inevitably and unproblematically both knowledge and improvement. At the beginning of the century Corbin implicitly argues that his *Amours de Philocaste* provides valuable information from which all may benefit:

> ...il est autant necessaire de sçavoir le vice pour le fuir que la vertu pour la suivre: De mesme qu'un pelerin cheminant en des estranges contrées a autant & plus de besoin d'estre instruit des passages dangereux & mauvais qu'il doit soigneusement eviter que des bons qui le peuvent rendre en toute seureté où tendent ses desirs, (72-3)

and at the end of her *Portrait des foiblesses humaines* Mme de Villedieu outlines a sequel to this work which will together form a complete and indispensable guide to moral life:

> J'espere faire une suitte de cet ouvrage, qui traitera du retour des hommes à la vertu, afin que ces deux divers Traitez faisant envisager l'homme troublé par ses passions & vainqueur de ces mesmes passions, je tâche à donner de l'horreur pour la foiblesse humaine aux gens qui ne sont pas encore tombez, & à tracer un chemin vers le retour à ceux qui sont déjà dans l'égarement. (249-50)[6]

The frequent conjunction of these two aims implies an unexamined authority for what is often regarded as the essential classical literary doctrine. Such coherence, though, is deceptive. The easy relationship of text, moral and reader which lies at the heart of the theory becomes in different ways an important theme within many novels, and subtends a widespread scrutiny of the nature of fiction and its value. It is some aspects of this inquiry which I propose to explore in the rest of this article.

Frequently drawn into question is the very conception of the novel as the embodiment of a coded moral which the reader is invited to decypher. This notion is implicit in the images of sweetened medicines or veiled precepts often found in prefaces,[7] and extends to Le Bossu's definition of the fable, broadly conceived, in his *Traité du poème épique* :

> ...la Fable est un discours inventé pour former les moeurs par des instructions déguisées sous les allégories d'une action; (31)

however, the clearly delineated portrayal of good and evil on which the value and meaning of such texts ostensibly rests is itself the subject of examination.

Rosset's *Histoires tragiques* at times cast into doubt the moral attitudes they appear to illustrate. The narrator's portrayal of the incestuous lovers Doralice and Lyzaran, for instance, purports to carry total condemnation:

> Mon dessein est de dépeindre & de faire paroistre la saleté du vice & non de défendre, (182)

and yet in spite of this he sees a certain logic in the growth of their love:

> A la verité s'ils n'eussent esté si proches de sang, ils seroient plus excusables en leur folle passion: car elle estoit une des beautez les plus parfaictes que j'aye jamais veue, & luy l'un des plus beaux gentilhommes qu'on puisse voir. (185)

Moral considerations are enmeshed with other equally compelling principles of physical beauty and human attraction with which all readers—and the narrator—can identify. However culpable incest may be in principle, unequivocal censure cannot issue from this portrayal. The language of reproof may be retained, but beneath it is the suggestion of a different attitude, different values which see the characters as victims of circumstance, helpless and pitiful. When Doralice pleas to God on her execution, the eloquence of her own words combines with the narrator's implicit sympathy to suspend any simple moral evaluation:

> Pardonnez nostre iniquité, non pas comme aymant le vice, mais comme aymant les humains, en qui les vices sont attachez dès le ventre de leur mère. (196)[8]

Similar tensions are suggested in Lannel's comic novel, *Le Romant satyrique*. The novelist follows a traditional path, punishing vice and rewarding virtue, as he distinguishes, for instance, between the angelic radiance of the virtuous duchesse de Gonzanvert after her death and the infernal torments suffered by the lecherous reyne de Regnautchanfort. Nevertheless, this orthodox moral structure cannot conceal a more ambivalent attitude to characters and their feelings in the course of the narrative. The duchesse, however virtuous her resistance to an ardent attraction for the hero, Ennemidor, sees something cruel and even indiscriminate in the way praise and blame variously attach themselves to passions which have a common source in the divine creator:

> O grand Dieu, qui m'avez formée telle qu'il vous a pleu, & qui avez infus en mon âme les passions dont elle est agitée...Je brusle d'amour, & neantmoins, je ne puis sans perdre vostre grace...chercher la jouyssance de ce que j'ayme, dont mesme le desir m'est deffendu... (373)

As for the queen, responsibility for sin is seen to be attributable in part to the gods, who leave man powerless in the face of their own nature. Moral logic may require that vice be punished, and yet the justice of such an outcome is implicitly questioned by this alternative interpretation of events, itself carried in the equally authoritative form of a general statement which invites wide application:

> Ils nous prescrivent assez ce qu'il faut fuyr, mais ils ne nous en donnent point le moyen; nous voyons le mal, & nous ne le pouvons éviter. (58)

Such ambivalence also characterizes Sorel's *Francion* . As was seen earlier, the preface claims to identify and condemn vice and the hero is offered as the focus of much satirical comment, his experiences highlighting many different moral and social ills. He prides himself on his fierce exposure and punishment of these evils wherever he finds them:

> Mon coustumier exercice estoit de chastier les sottises, de rabbaisser les vanités et de me mocquer de l'ignorance des hommes. Les gens de Justice, de Finances et de Traficq passoient journellement par mes mains... (252)

and he constantly stresses the value of sincerity and naturalness; such qualities are seen as the marks of true virtue and nobility:

> Je leur apprenois qu'estre Noble, ce n'est pas sçavoir bien picquer un Cheval..., c'est avoir une ame qui résiste à tous les assauts que luy peut livrer la fortune, et qui ne mesle rien de bas parmy ses actions. (252)

However, this apparently stable perspective is deceptive and the force of the satire coloured by the very nature of the character through which it is expressed. Francion leads a life which in different ways reflects the qualities he condemns in others, and just a few pages after this assumption of a critical attitude, he is seen to justify with pride his deception of a friend as he pursues an amorous adventure:

> quelle sotise eussé je faite, si j'eusse laissé eschapper une si rare occasion? J'eusse merité d'estre mocqué de tout le monde; mon plaisir ne me devoit-il pas toucher de plus près que celuy d'un autre? (266)

Once again he dissociates himself from the *sottise* which he was keen to attack earlier, but the implications of the term and of the hero's condemnation of it are now significantly different; instead of vanity or hypocrisy, it now suggests self-restraint and fidelity, a shift in meaning which calls into question the basis on which Francion's judgements are made. Linguistic consistency can no longer be seen to reflect unchanging, absolute standards, but is exposed as an illusion beneath which the fluidity of moral values is clear. Indeed, even as Francion pursues Nays, established as the ideal object of his aspirations, he is quite prepared to compromise the frankness on which he bases his evaluation of others:

> ...de peur de se mettre en mauvaise odeur auprès de Nays, il desguisa les choses le plus qu'il luy fut possible. (408)

The authority of his seemingly superior insight is corrupted from within, and beneath its confident condemnation of vice, the novel suggests the instability of this moral stance.

This implicit questioning of the values a text claims to propose is also apparent in certain pastoral and heroic fiction. In *L'Astrée*, for instance, doubts, jealousies and deceptions frequently cut through the comforting order of a world where justice and virtue seem to reign, and many interpolated tales explore the inadequacies of moral judgements. Laonice, in the first part of the novel, is the unwitting pawn in the love affair of Cleon and Tirsis, courted by the latter at Cleon's suggestion in order to keep their relationship secret. When Cleon dies, the deception comes to light and Laonice, who loves Tirsis, lays claim to his affection; this he steadfastly refuses. The tale poses complex problems of guilt and innocence, fidelity and sincerity, but the resolution offered by the novel is self-consciously partial and problematic. Laonice is defended by Hylas, whose ironic mockery of Tirsis's love for his dead mistress blunts the force

of her appeal as the innocent victim of deceit. Phillis supports
Tirsis, but her defence of his right to remain faithful to Cleon is
superseded by another, more ambiguous argument to establish the
weakness of Laonice's position:

> ...ce n'a point esté tromperie, mais juste chastiment d'Amour,
> qui a fait retomber les coups sur elle-mesme, puis que son
> intention n'estoit pas de servir, mais de decevoir la prudente
> Cleon; que si elle a à se plaindre de quelque chose, c'est que de
> deux trompeuses elle a esté la moins fine. (1: 265-6)

A distinction between sincerity and deceit is voiced but implicitly
recognised as untenable—after all, the original *feinte* was Cleon's
idea—and Phillis is forced to shift to a consideration of outcome
rather than intention; Laonice, it is argued, can claim no redress, not
because she sought to deceive, but because she was less skilful at
deception than her rival. The problem is stifled rather than solved
with reference not to moral values but to guile, and this arbitrary
justice is then clad in the language of divine will as Silvandre
pronounces judgement:

> Et par ainsi, il soit d'ores en là deffendu aux recherches de
> Laonice de tourmenter d'avantage le repos de Cleon: car telle est
> la volonté du dieu qui parle en moy...(1: 267-8)

Such ambiguity is sensed also in the novel's portrayal of love.
Silvandre may claim that it is an ennobling force, and yet tales like
that of Laonice suggest the scheming and deceit which may spring
quite naturally from it. Indeed, self-interest is built into the very
fabric of the passion, and none who love—even Astrée herself—are
seen to be exempt from it. When the heroine agrees not to abuse the
confidence of Silvandre who has confessed to her his love of Diane,
the narrator first attributes this attitude to a nobility of spirit and her
dispassionate appreciation of moral worth:

> Astrée luy eust volontiers donné toute sorte d'aide,
> recognoissant la pure et sincere amitié qu'il portoit à Diane. (2:
> 204)

Beneath this, though, another instinct is suggested, and from these
particular, positive values the narrator moves on to invoke a more
general principle behind the behavior of lovers which, while
strengthening Astrée's outlook in this case, simultaneously
underlines the frailty of such virtue. Selflessness in love, it is
implied, is only possible when personal interests are not threatened:

> Aussi le naturel d'une personne qui ayme bien est de ne nuire jamais aux amours d'autruy, si elles ne sont prejudiciables aux siennes. (2: 204)

In *Clélie*, the figure of Plotine frequently calls into question the authenticity of the glittering world she inhabits. Virtues may be lavished on heroes, but the image of unalterable moral perfection created by individual actions and sustained by the stability of linguistic attributes is seen by her to be no more than a pleasing illusion; change, not stasis characterizes human nature, and all are prone to weakness:

> Ne me dites donc jamais...c'est un homme sage & genereux, incapable de faillir, car à parler sincerement, tous les hommes sont capables de manquer...tout le monde est envieux, tout le monde est médisant, tout le monde est menteur, tout le monde est foible, & il n'y a presque point de Héros qui en quelque moment de sa vie ne puisse trouver dans son coeur quelque petit sentiment bas & populaire, tant il est vray que les hommes sont imparfaits. (5: 485-6)

Later in the novel, this same character comments on the happiness which so often befalls lovers as a reward for their virtue; what may be conceivable in theory is rarely seen in practice, and Plotine dissociates herself from it:

> ...où trouvera-t-on deux personnes qui ayent assez d'esprit, assez de constance, assez d'amitié l'une pour l'autre, assez d'égalité d'humeur pour vivre tousjours bien ensemble. Il peut y en avoir, mais il y en a peu, & je ne croy pas estre assez heureuse pour trouver une si grande félicité. (5: 1065)

The order which is a commonplace in fiction—including this one—acquires the dubious status of fiction, whose links with reality are tenuous. The paradox implicit in the notion of a universal truth which embellishes and disguises the particularities of experience is translated here into tensions between the apparent moral harmony of the novel and an alternative vision which questions it from within.

Boissat's *Histoire nègre-pontique* embodies these tensions in its very structure. Its preface stresses the moral potency of the novel:

> ... la matière de ceste Histoire est si pleine de Vertu qu'elle peut à mon advis n'estre pas infructueuse au public, ny mesme à l'affermissement de nostre Religion...,

and yet the text itself undercuts the reader's expectations. The chaste Olympe is separated from Alexandre, her ideal lover and tricked into marrying Euryale; Alexandre, in despair, marries

Lindarache and ultimately finds happiness with her. A final reversal of fortune which brings merited relief to worthy protagonists is traditional in fiction, but here it is challengingly withheld. Instead, the tale ends on a tone of bleak helplessness as the heroine, soon widowed, is left to lament her innocent suffering which has no promise of an end:

> Elle en aymoit plus fort Alexandre de ce qu'elle estoit jalouze de Lindarache: elle en trouvoit Lindarache plus belle de ce qu'Alexandre l'avoit auprès de luy. C'est ainsi que passoit ses jours la belle Nègre-pontine, avec peu ou point d'espoir ou de posseder Alexandre ou de le mettre en oubly, qui estoient les seuls remedes de sa passion. (560)

This departure from literary tradition is seen explicitly by the author as proof that his tale is true: irregularity is the mark of a more complex reality which cannot be contained in conventional aesthetic structures:

> ...si ceste œuvre estoit purement de l'invention humaine, on y auroit observé plus religieusement les preceptes des vrays Romans, & se seroit-on bien empesché d'y introduire une Olympe pour espouse d'Euryale avant que l'estre d'Alexandre, le vray Heros de ceste Histoire.

The implications of a text in which virtue is not ultimately rewarded are left to stand in suggestive contrast with the claims of the preface: aesthetic and moral notions of truth—*vrays Romans, vray Heros*—are held alongside the novel itself which, in its own authenticity, subverts them.

A similar tension characterizes Mareschal's comic novel, *Chrysolite* . Once again its preface lays claim to a clear moral stance:

> ...peindre par figure les bonnes moeurs & les mauvaises; donner horreur du mal par la representation des peines & des mal-heurs qui suivent le vice, & nous encourager au bien par celle des recompenses que la vertu treuve & ne cherche pas...

but the text itself offers a probing commentary on these very aims. The author puts at its centre a heroine of quite unusual complexity, faithless and yet curiously innocent, scheming and yet pathetic, whose inconsistency and unpredictability are the only constants in her nature. The narrator is clearly fascinated by the moral problems raised by such a character who undercuts the possibility of stable and unequivocal judgement:

> Ne voilà pas d'estranges contradictions: & qui pourroit asseoir
> un jugement sur l'inegalité de cet esprit? (436)

This heroine may not conform to conventional notions of either aesthetic consistency or moral clarity, and yet the narrator justifies his enterprise by what he sees as the truth of his story, a truth which cannot be fitted artificially into an easy moral framework:

> Je la traiteray neantmoins avecque toute la modestie qui me sera
> possible, & suis marry que je ne puis donner quelque plus belle
> couleur à son action: mais où il ne faut point mentir, il faut dire
> le vray, bien que cette belle lumière soit quelquefois odieuse.
> (407)

The implications of *le vray* here are not limited to historical veracity, but are seen to embrace a wider truth. Chrysolite is neither simply a figment of the author's imagination, nor is she a mere oddity, an excentric part of the extravagance of history. All men bear something of the same character traits, and the reader, like the narrator, is invited to see himself caught up in this portrayal:

> ...il n'y a rien de si nouveau que je ne connoisse en un autre les
> mesmes qualitez, les mesmes habitudes & les mesmes
> inclinations que je remarque en moy-mesme. (318)

Novels such as these are seen to offer within their structures or characters judgements which balance or undermine the clear vision which they may elsewhere appropriate for themselves. If truth is claimed for such works, it is not simply to distinguish them from imaginative fantasy, but, more significantly, from the kind of moral order which distorts experience and oversimplifies problems. Against this background, certain *nouvelles* from the later part of the century suggest in their own thematic complexity the continuation of this already widespread inquiry, and not simply a new departure in reaction to the excessive idealism of heroic fiction.

In Mme de Lafayette's *Zaïde*, for instance, tensions are suggested between the main narrative and the interpolated tales which in different ways cut across its implicit values. The story of Alphonse is of a love destroyed by unsuspected and unconquerable human frailty. The hero recalls his supreme delight at the start of his relationship with Bélasire, its intensity seen as the ultimate mark of its authenticity and value:

> Je goûtai des délices dans ces commencements, que je n'avais
> pas imaginées; et qui n'a point senti le plaisir de donner une
> violente passion à une personne qui n'en a jamais eu, même

médiocre, peut dire qu'il ignore les véritables plaisirs de l'amour (109-10),

but whatever the virtues of the characters—Bélasire is beautiful and chaste, Alphonse is noble and generous—happiness is mercilessly elusive. When Alphonse's jealousy is aroused by the thought of a former suitor of his mistress, now dead, the two lovers find themselves powerless to eradicate or control the fears it inspires; mutual trust disintegrates into uncertainty and suspicion. Similarly, in another tale, Alamir, conscious of the dangerous appeal of his princely status, seeks through disguise to inspire a love devoid of ambition in which he can have total confidence. Such a love is awakened in Elsibery, but the hero is unable to appreciate it fully, compelled as he is by doubt and self-doubt to play the role of his own rival in ever more elaborate tests. However assured he may seem about this love, uncertainty cannot be suppressed; unease follows peace of mind as naturally and inevitably as these two in appearance self-contradictory sentences:

> ...il ne pouvait plus douter qu'elle ne fût à l'épreuve des sentiments d'ambition qu'il avait appréhendés. Le lendemain il essaya encore de lui faire donner une lettre de la part du prince....(195)

The hero's disguise destabilises the love even as it seems to guarantee its purity, and Alamir is led to acknowledge the frailty of its perfection which can only be sustained through deception:

> ...je ne saurais me résoudre à apprendre ma naissance à Elsibery; je perdrai, en la lui apprenant, ce qui fait le charme de mon amour. Je hasarderai le seul véritable plaisir que j'aie jamais eu, et je ne sais si je ne perdrai point la passion que j'ai pour elle. (197)

Such tales reveal and explore problems of trust, judgement and sincerity beneath the most apparently perfect relationships; characters are subjected not simply to external forces but to pressures from within which draw into question the stability of their love and the certainty of its rewards. Against this background, the turbulent fate of Zaïde and her lover, crossed by misunderstanding, coincidence and chance, but culminating in union, suggests in all its quite self-conscious fictionality a universe whose easy final harmony is a mere illusion. Like Alphonse and Alamir, Consalve is seen to stand on the threshold of happiness, but in the context of these tales expressions of incomparable joy and confidence in love are reduced to empty linguistic formulae, robbed of their authority and conviction; they do not imply now the superior worth of this particular hero but the potential fragility of his world:

> Apprendre qu'il était aimé de Zaïde, trouver des marques de tendresse dans tout ce qu'il avoit jugé des marques d'indifférence, c'était un excès de bonheur qui l'emportait hors de lui-même et qui lui faisait goûter dans un moment tous les plaisirs que les autres amants ne goûtent qu'interrompus et separés. (219)

The stable moral framework which Huet, in his preface to the novel, attributes to so much fiction is here ironically called into question:

> L'on y rencontre ces deux avantages en quoi Photius fait consister le fruit principal de la lecture des romans: d'y voir toujours le dérèglement & le vice suivi de la honte & d'un succès malheureux, après avoir longtemps vainement triomphé; l'honnêteté au contraire & la vertu glorieusement relevée, après de longues persécutions. (141)

Similar tensions characterize *La Princesse de Clèves*, which constantly juxtaposes the language of moral absolutes and its objects, intentions and effects, actions and interpretations. Clèves's much vaunted *prudence* dissolves under pressure into helpless suspicion and jealousy, and his praise of *sincérité* is transformed into a bitter regret of his lost ignorance. The heroine may attribute to herself and be credited by others with a superior moral strength, but the *aveu* on which this judgement is based is made at a moment of weakness and impulse, and is itself partial and misleading. She may interpret her reaction to Nemours's theft of her portrait in a morally advantageous way:

> ...il est vrai que je le vis prendre; mais je ne voulus pas faire paraître que je le voyais, de peur de m'exposer à me faire dire des choses que l'on ne m'a encore osé dire...(336)

and yet this contrasts with the narrator's earlier account of the same event which implies a more ambivalent collusion:

> ...elle fut bien aise de lui accorder une faveur qu'elle lui pouvait faire sans qu'il sût même qu'elle la lui faisait. (302)

No overall judgement is offered to resolve these evident discrepancies. Instead, divergent interpretations are left unqualified, each with its own authority, and together suggesting the irreducible complexity of actions which cannot be adequately summarized or evaluated in terms of honesty or self-deception, virtue or cowardice.

Similarly, when Nemours is seen to conceal his feelings for the heroine from the Vidame de Chartres, the narrator comments on the action in a characteristically challenging sentence:

> Il n'en parla pas même au vidame de Chartres, qui était son ami intime, et pour qui il n'avoit rien de caché. (370)

The paradoxical juxtaposition of concealment and confidence does not merely indicate here the hero's capacity for hypocrisy, but suggests the relative value of all moral labels. Intimacy of friendship can only extend so far, and however absolute may be its definition, it remains constrained by the limits of human nature; the language of moral evaluation is exposed as an unsophisticated and inadequate tool, both for the prediction of future action and for the understanding of what is past.

Such paradoxes are apparent also in Catherine Bernard's *Le Comte d'Amboise*. The preface stresses something of a crusading purpose with a clear-cut moral stance:

> ...mon dessein étoit de ne faire voir que des Amans malheureux pour combattre autant qu'il m'est possible le penchant qu'on a pour l'Amour..., (10)

and yet the attitude to love is particularly ambivalent in the course of the narrative. The novel's treatment of the count exemplifies this ambiguity. His willingness on several occasions to forsake his claim to Mlle de Roye in favour of Sansac, whom she loves, seems to embody the values of heroic self-control which the author promotes, and yet these very qualities find no reward in the text. Instead d'Amboise, who does finally marry the heroine, has his happiness immediately destroyed by an ill-timed letter from Sansac's sister which re-kindles jealousy of his rival and leads to his death. The author sees this outcome as a punishment of his love:

> Peut-être se plaindra-t-on de ce que je ne récompense pas la vertu du Comte d'Amboise, mais je veux punir sa passion...(9-10)

but the moral basis for this outcome is clearly fragile. D'Amboise suffers in the novel not because he loves, but because the heroine cannot love him; and this situation neither can alter. The same problems underlie the presentation of Sansac and the heroine. Both are seen to be the victims of circumstance rather than of moral failing, kept apart by the scheming of family and rivals and led to believe that each loves somebody else; nevertheless, the narrator's commentaries hover suggestively between compassion and severity.

When the two lovers meet after d'Amboise's death, purity and value are briefly sensed in their affection as they recognise each other's fidelity:

> La verité se montroit à eux à mesure qu'ils se parloient; ils se retrouvoient innocens, une douce joye que de longtemps ils n'avoient sentie, rentroit dans leurs coeurs. (197)

However, when Sansac himself dies soon afterwards, the countess, who has resolved to love only the memory of her dead husband, is shocked and surprised by the extent of her grief:

> ...elle retourna à la campagne, où elle passa le reste de ses jours remplie de ses diverses afflictions, & sans oser les démêler, de peur de reconnoître la plus forte. (202)

The contrast of these two attitudes to the same love, the one which stresses truth and innocence, the other which suggests concealment and shame, underlines all that is arbitrary in the evaluation of passion. Judgements vary not accordng to the nature of the love itself, but according to the circumstances in which it exists, circumstances over which the individual has no control. No character is "guilty" in this novel, each is the victim of a deeper inability to love to order. Absolute criteria are applied to actions born of the unalterable and unpredictable nature of human affection, and the tale explores the limits of their authority.

The slippage between text and gloss suggested in these examples constantly casts doubt on the stability of the novel's moral significance and the values on which it is based, and questions its assumed status of the vehicle for clear and coherent principles. Instead, such texts make play of a more elusively plural meaning, which in different ways proclaims its resistance to simple reduction. This exposure of the inherent ambivalence of fiction is complemented by a questioning of the relationship between text and reader, a relationship which is equally crucial to the very enterprise of *plaire et instruire* .

The apparently straightforward correlation of moral order and aesthetic appeal is recognized as problematic by certain apparently idealising novels. In Desmarets' *Rosane*, for instance, some of the assumptions of the author's confident theoretical preface are questioned within the text itself. In an incident which mirrors the novel's own strategies, Zabas tries to inspire with virtue the difficult and unruly Hormidas, and the heroine suggests to him a technique which echoes the classic arguments of *plaire et instruire* found in the preface:

> Je croy qu'il seroit plus à propos sous pretexte de le divertir, de luy dire quelques histoires pleines d'actions & de sentimens vertueux, & parmy la douceur du récit que vous luy feriez, il recevroit des instructions sans y penser, & sans que la rudesse de son naturel fust en garde pour les rejetter. (425-6)

Zabas proposes to recount the life of Uranie, whose spiritual purity has brought her control over all physical passion and weakness; nevertheless, he is quite aware that Hormidas may think that he is merely fantasizing, because such a character seemingly exceeds all human experience. These fears prove to be well founded, and when the tale is met with a *ris de moquerie* (518) the reason for this reaction is made quite clear:

> ...il ne pouvoit s'imaginer qu'une Vertu eminente qu'il ne cognoissoit pas fust au rang des choses possibles....(518)

Zabas defends his art by arguing that his vision is nevertheless true, and that the criticism levelled against him reflects the limited knowledge of the listener rather than the veracity or even verisimilitude of the tale itself:

> ...ceux qui sont sans vertu & sans estude, & qui ont de l'orgueil, ne veulent jamais rien croire de ce qui n'est point encore tombé sous leurs sens; & prennent pour des fables & des chimères tout ce qui passe leur imagination & leur cognoissance. (518)

The defence has its logic, but it cannot disguise the gap between the experience of the reader and the values of the text which inevitably weakens its claims to educate and enlighten. The incident ends with a compromise: Hormidas will put this seemingly ideal figure to the test, and try to win her love. What on one level may suggest a positive move forward is, on another, an indication of the tale's only limited powers of persuasion. To succeed, it needs to be verified in experience, and the outlet available to Hormidas is clearly not available to the reader. Partial success within the context of fiction remains to this extent a fiction which cannot be reproduced outside its confines.

This problem is sensed particularly acutely in the work of Camus, a writer whose aim it was to create a morally effective *histoire dévote* . His argument in the *Dilude* to *Petronille* that precepts can be both pleasurably and convincingly conveyed through examples suggests a smooth harmonisation of *plaire* and *instruire* and yet he clearly realises some of the difficulties of putting this into practice. In *Aristandre,* for instance, he is quite alive to the fact that his hero—who successfully resists the corrupt temptations of queen Argée and remains faithful to the virtuous Nicette—may not appeal. He may have a crucial place in the thematic structure of his novel, and yet the narrator realises that his radiantly moral attributes make of him too remote a character:

> C'est parlé en homme cela, & en homme de bien, mais las! Si Apollon estoit consulté encore une fois, qu'il treuveroit en ce temps peu de gens de bien de cette trempe, & qui ayent pour leur devise: Plustost mourir que de pecher. (321)

The general applicability of the term *homme de bien* is tested and immediately cast into doubt; everyday conceptions of the expression do not coincide with its meaning in this context. Aware that he may lose contact with his reader on the level of experience, the novelist is led to address himself instead to an assumed moral sense:

> Cependant je prie le Lecteur de peser bien serieusement en ces Lettres & en ces Responces, la foiblesse du Vice & la force de la Vertu, la folie de l'un & la sagesse de l'autre. (321-2)

The classic appeal to imitate which underlies the moral value and purpose of the text is displaced here by a more muted aim: to elicit acknowledgement that virtue is morally superior to vice.

Furthermore, Camus clearly senses that the overall moral structure of his novels may not necessarily counter the potentially corrupting influence of the portrayal of vice. In his preface to *Aristandre,* he foresees that Argée's letters to the hero which seek to justify her passion may lead a reader astray, even though the queen herself is ultimately punished, and he is even more reticent in *Petronille.* He tries to be as sketchy as possible about the worldly values of Tristan as he courts the heroine who has already promised herself to God (33), and when Tristan tries to coax Petronille from her calling, the narrator will report nothing:

> il luy enseigna une industrie dont je ne veux pas charger cet escrit de peur de faire comme ces Chirurgiens mal habiles qui blessent en voulant panser, & au lieu de faire une cure rendent la playe irremediable. (394)

Examples of good, it is implied, can have only limited influence; examples of vice, even when punished, are seen to appeal more. In Camus' tale "Le Despit inconsideré," the narrator wearily remarks on this bleak fact of human nature:

> ...l'experience nous fait tous les jours connoistre que les
> suggestions des mauvais ont beaucoup plus de pouvoir sur les
> ames que les inspirations des bons Anges (418),

a point which Rapin will echo later in the century:

> ...on est plus sensible au plaisir qu'à la raison. (22)

To this extent, a gap is sensed between the moral structure of a
text and the reader, which further undermines its ostensible
intention. In the *Remarques* appended to his *Berger extravagant* ,
Sorel lucidly recognizes that satire, for instance, which may be
defended as morally enlightening, may also easily corrupt:

> ...l'on me pourroit dire qu'il n'en faudroit donc pas deffendre la
> lecture puis qu'elle fait haïr le vice: mais cecy n'est entendu que
> pour les bons esprits, & l'on ne doit pas donner des penitences
> qui puissent faire entrer en tentation. Il n'y a que trop de
> personnes qui se plaisent à vivre dans l'ordure (543),

and later in the century, Huet will implicitly underline the extent of
this rift when he relieves the novelist of all responsibility for any
"misreadings" of his fiction:

> Une âme toute préparée au mal s'autorise des exemples mal
> entendus et mal appliqués; elle envisage les agréables
> engagements du crime sans en vouloir considerer la fin....La
> cause de ce désordre n'est pas dans l'ouvrage, mais dans la
> mauvaise disposition du Lecteur. (141)[9]

This dissociation of text and reader is only bridged in appearance.
Indeed, when writers do express confidence in the impact or moral
utility of fiction, it is with reference to the kind of reader who,
paradoxically, has no need of moral enlightenment. Desmarets'
supremely idealistic view of his *Rosane* is based precisely on the
notion of such a reader, one possessed, significantly, of a *naturel
facile:*

> ...Sur ces modelles un naturel facile qui n'a besoin que de bons
> exemples s'instruit pour acquerir les perfections qui luy
> manquent & pour fuir les vices auxquels il pourroit tomber,

and the same implication is to be found later in d'Aubignac's
Conjectures academiques, where he speaks of the *chef d'œuvre*
whose aim it is:

> de mieux faire que la nature, en nous traçant des modelles
> capables d'exciter les plus genereux à passer toujours au-delà de
> ce qu'ils sont. (226)

The enlightening power of fiction is recognized as partial at best, a self-authenticating illusion potently captured in Camus' *Petronille* where the reader seen to benefit from pious texts is the heroine herself, a character already proposed as a model of virtue:

> ...si elle jettoit les yeux sur des Histoires veritables & pieuses
> qui sont autant de vrais miroirs de Vertu, elle taschoit de former
> ses actions sur le modelle des personnes sainctes, & ainsi les
> perfections de son ame alloient croissant à veue d'oeil par cet
> arrousement spirituel à meme que celles de son corps
> s'espanouissoient. (21-2)

The impact of a novel is seen to depend ultimately on the disposition of the reader; it cannot itself influence that disposition. And in his preface to the second part of *Le Berger extravagant*, Sorel's characteristically enigmatic remark underlines the very selectivity of effect which novelists implicitly acknowledge for their work:

> En attendant, voyez cette Histoire qui ne sçauroit manquer de
> vous apporter de la delectation & de l'utilité, si vous la prenez du
> biais qu'il la faut prendre.

Such doubts about the moral effectiveness of fiction are built into many texts themselves. Rosset's tale of Vaumorin, for instance, offers the paradigm of a fault exposed and punished; the central character is arrested for theft and spends twenty years as a galley slave. The text offers the promise of enlightenment and correction when his son finally discovers him and secures his release, but this promise is illusory: punishment has not led to reform, and the old man soon falls back into his criminal ways. The narrator's wry conclusion about the ineradicability of this flaw suggestively casts into doubt the very moral enterprise on which he is embarked in these tales:

> il est bien mal-aisé de corriger les defauts de la nature. (283)[10]

In Mareschal's *Chrysolite*, the narrator similarly remarks on the uselessness of trying to reason with or enlighten a man in love. The preface to this novel may claim for the text the power to lead man to virtue, yet the force of this aim is significantly blunted by the narrator's own commentary on his characters:

> ...qui voudroit donner de la raison à l'amour ou de la mesure
> aux desirs d'un amoureux ne travailleroit pas plus inutilement
> que qui presenteroit de la lumiere à un aveugle; laissons-le donc
> aller jusques au bout. (457)

And in Sorel's *Francion* , it is significant that the hero, whose own
morally inconsistent nature cannot be convincingly stabilised by the
influence of Nays, is himself unable to dissuade friends from their
libertin ways:

> ...quelque remonstrance qu'il leur pust faire, ils employerent
> encore le reste du temps qu'ils vouloient passer dans Rome, à se
> saouler des plaisirs du monde. (527)

These doubts are equally apparent later in the century. Mme de
Villedieu, for example, proposes her *Portrait des foiblesses
humaines* as something of a guide to human nature, but the
characters in it are singularly incapable of the clear-sighted self-
examination which the reader would need to profit from it. Paul-
Emile, wracked by domestic strife is seen, for instance, to be quite
impervious to the advice of his sister:

> ...elle fit ce qui luy fut possible pour luy inspirer ces sentimens;
> mais comme on dit en commun proverbe, il n'est pas aisé aux
> malades de pratiquer les conseils des gens sains... (271)

and this particular tale is prefaced by remarks which stress its
general applicability:

> ...la foiblesse humaine s'introduit chez nous par diverses portes;
> & les desordres domestiques de Paul Emile viennent à propos à
> ma memoire, pour montrer que sans amour, & sans aucun des
> effets qu'il produit, la fermeté des plus grandes ames peut estre
> ébranlée & la tranquillité la mieux établie, sujette aux revolutions
> des troubles intérieurs. (252-3)

Similarly, Catherine Bernard's *Eléonore d'Yvrée* explores the
fundamental helplessness of its characters. Its preface, as has been
seen, suggests a salutory moral effect for the tale:

> Je mets donc mes Heros dans une situation si triste, qu'on ne
> leur porte point d'envie,

and yet the text offers a far more complex perspective. When
Eléonor finds herself betrothed to the ageing Retelois, although she
loves and is loved by the duc de Misnie, she may speak the language
of dutiful obedience, but she cannot overcome or even modify her

attitude to her love. For a long time she uses the excuse of illness to avoid marriage but although she realizes the full extent of her prevarication, she is powerless to do anything about it:

> ...elle se reprochoit neantmoins qu'elle abusoit de ce respect & de cette honnesteté; elle voyoit sa propre foiblesse dans toute son étendue, mais elle ne pouvoit la reparer, & quoy qu'elle fust plus d'une fois preste à parler, elle ne parloit cependant jamais. (194-5)

Mathilde, who also loves Misnie, realises the hopelessness of her own position, but she is equally conscious of her impotence; feelings of friendship for Eléonor cannot survive a deeply instinctive need to cling to the object of her desires, whatever the potentially harmful consequences both for herself and others:

> La plus grande marque d'amitié que je vous puisse donner à présent, c'est de me plaindre avec vous; je ne suis plus en état de vous servir. (119)

The reader may not be inspired with a wish to imitate these characters, but there is no suggestion that their predicament could have been avoided. The *malheur* of their position arises precisely from the fact that it is out of their control, and that they can neither overcome their respective loves nor find comfort in their duty. At the end of the novel, even the heroine's exercise of virtue is revealed to be an illusory triumph: she may offer the image of self-possession, but its significance as a moral example is undermined by the ineradicable presence of her love and the unhappiness it brings:

> ...elle vécut avec le Comte comme une personne dont la vertu estoit parfaite, quoy qu'elle fust toujours malheureuse par la passion qu'elle avoit dans le coeur. (236-7)

This problem is implicitly set at the centre, too, of Guilleragues' *Lettres portugaises*, which trace the heroine's attempt to come to terms with her lover's betrayal of her. Neither disillusionment with love nor moral scruple can lead to any permanent control, and even when she claims self-mastery in the final letter, such protestations cannot conceal her persistent confusion and self-deception:

> En vous renvoyant vos lettres, je garderai soigneusement les deux dernières que vous m'avez écrites, et je les relirai encore plus souvent que je n'ai lu les premières, afin de ne retomber plus dans mes faiblesses. (176-7)

The heroine may present herself here as the ideal "reader" of her own moral tale, instructed and strengthened by her experience; but what she adduces as proof and guarantee of her enlightenment reflects equally the continuance of her attachment to love. And indeed, her very act of communicating such feelings to a letter addressed to her lover suggests the deep-seated desire to communicate with him which colours any claims of a new-found independence.

At the end of the century, there is an important discussion of this problematic relationship of text and reader in the abbé de Villiers' *Entretiens sur les contes de fees*. The *provincial* echoes Huet as he argues that a reader's reaction does not undermine the moral worth of a novel:

> C'est la faute du Lecteur de prendre plûtot du goût pour le mal que pour le bien...(175)

but the *Parisien* draws attention back to the text itself, and in so doing suggests the paradox explored by many writers throughout the century: if a novelist is to lay claim to any moral value for his work, he has to be sensitive to the limits and complexities of human nature, both in his presentation of character and in his expectations of the reader, and yet novels so conceived are those precisely which imply the very impossibility of enlightenment or improvement:

> Mais croyez-vous que ce soit en effet la faute des seuls Lecteurs? N'est-ce pas une chose chimerique qu'une vertu qui se conserve toujours pure avec une violente passion? pourquoi flatter par de telles chimères la présomption du coeur de l'homme & l'accoutumer à ne pas faire scrupule de la plus déreglée des Passions en lui donnant l'esperance temeraire d'une vertu qui dans le fond ne sçauroit se conserver que par la haine ou la fuite de tout ce qui produit cette passion dangereuse? (175-6)

An imposed moral order is seen to be a dangerous illusion. Ultimately, it is implied, the organization of a text neither reflects nor can it adequately inspire a corresponding control in the reader over himself; he is no more able to emulate a virtuous hero than he is to avoid the downfall of a weak one, however these may be presented. Indeed, novels which themselves suggest a tension between their events or characters and the moral structures applied to them embody this very tension between claims to improve and conviction in their effectiveness. In his preface to *Francion*, Sorel challengingly and suggestively draws attention to this possible lack of communication:

> Mais il se peut bien faire que nous nous soyons flattez, & que
> nous ayons eu trop bonne opinion de mon ouvrage et du naturel
> des hommes. Ils n'ont pas tous deux assez de force, l'un pour se
> faire croire, l'autre pour suivre ses remonstrances... (1261)

and in his *Lettres sur La Princesse de Cleves*, Valincour highlights with particular clarity the fundamental rift between text and reader of which so many novelists are implicitly aware:

> L'auteur d'un roman arrête la passion où il veut dans ses
> personnages par un trait de plume; mais il ne l'arrête pas de
> même en ceux en qui il l'excite. On n'est pas maître de son
> coeur comme celui qui fait un livre est maître de son imagination.
> (227-8)

The aim to enlighten through pleasure is not simply a theory, blandly voiced by novelists in their prefaces and then displaced by works conceived as mere *divertissement*; it becomes an implicit part of their thematic fabric. Writers do not so much debate whether their texts should have a moral significance; they reflect rather on the nature of such a meaning and on its underlying values and effect. This speculation cuts across traditional literary historical divisions into the pre-Classical and the Classical, the age of the *roman* and the age of the *nouvelle*, and suggests a widespread preoccupation among novelists throughout the Seventeenth Century. Nor is it confined to this one particular genre, but may be seen as a significant concern in the work of many writers of the period, from Corneille whose plays examine the ambiguous nature of idealism and expose the tragic compromises involved in moral choice, to Molière whose comic insight leads not to unequivocal judgements about vice and virtue but to a more probing exploration of obsession; from La Fontaine, whose work frequently juxtaposes the simplicity of an authoritative *sentence* and the more complex implications of the illustrative fable, to La Rochefoucauld whose maxims uncover the elusive, and at times arbitrary nature of truth and knowledge, both in himself and the reader. Texts such as these expose tensions between the apparent authority of moral precepts and characters or events which question what they appear to exemplify, and suggest cracks in their own structural organization which cast doubt on their power of influence over the reader. The formula of *plaire et instruire*, so widely repeated in the course of the century, may be seen to this extent not as the summary of a confidently accepted approach to literature, but as the focus rather for a re-thinking of the moral and aesthetic assumptions which underlie this principle of Classicism.

Notes

[1]Cf. also Le Bossu, *Traité du poème épique* (31); Rapin, *Réflexions sur la poétique de ce temps...* (22).

[2]Cf. also the criticism of fiction as falsehood in Sorel, *La Maison des jeux* (406); Camus's mockery of the naive readers of sentimental and chivalric novels in the *Dilude* to *Petronille* (460); or later, P. Nicole, *Les Visionnaires* (253); P. de Villiers, *Entretiens sur les contes de fées* (174).

[3]For similar arguments later in the century, see Mlle de Scudéry, *Clélie* (4: 1143-44).

[4]Cf. also Sorel's preface to *Polyandre*.

[5]Cf. also du Plaisir's praise of the *nouvelle* in his *Sentimens sur les lettres et sur l' histoire* (50).

[6]Cf. similar implications in the theoretical remarks of Chapelain, *Adone* (87); Huet, *Lettre* (141-2).

[7]Cf. for instance, Sorel, Preface to *Francion* (62); Camus, *Dilude* to *Petronille* (469-70); Desmarets, Preface to *Rosane* .

[8]Cf. also, for instance, the ambiguous portrayal of Argée in Camus' *Aristandre*, where the passionate queen is both condemned and yet seen as subject to natural laws of frailty (27-32), or his tale "L'Infidèle Chastié" in *L'Amphithéâtre sanglant*, where the naivety of Mandalis who falls victim to the charms of a deceiver is seen as both blameworthy and inevitable (17-20).

[9]Cf. also Langlois, *Le Tombeau des romans*, (89-90); or Camus, *Dilude* to *Pétronille* (454-5).

[10]Cf also the revealing opening to Camus' tale "Le Puant Concubinaire" in his *Amphithéâtre sanglant*:

> Blanchir un More & oster les moucheteures à un Leopart sont deux choses plus aisées à faire que de porter au bien ceux qui sont accoustumez au mal...(148)

Works Cited

Aubignac, F. d'. *Conjectures academiques, ouvrage posthume*. Paris: F. Fournier, 1715.

Bernard, C. *Le Comte d'Amboise*. La Haye: A. de Hondt & J. van Ellinckhuysen, 1689.

— *Les Malheurs de l'amour: première nouvelle, Eléonor d'Yvrée*. Paris: J. Guerout, 1687.

Boisrobert, François Le Métel de. *Histoire indienne d'Anaxandre & d'Orazie*. Paris: F. Pomeray, 1629.

Boissat, P. de. *L'Histoire nègre-pontique*. 2nd edition. Paris: Musier, 1731.

Camus, Jean-Pierre. *Aristandre*. Lyon: J. Gaudion, 1624.

—. "L'Infidèle Chastié." *Amphithéâtre sanglant*. Paris: J. Cottereau, 1630.

—. *Petronille*. 2nd edition. Paris: F. Dehors, 1632.

—. "Le Puant Concubinaire." *Amphithéâtre sanglant*. Paris: J. Cottereau. 1630.

Chapelain, J. "Lettre....sur le poème d'Adonis du Chevalier Marino." *Opuscules critiques*. Ed. A.C. Hunter. S.T.F.M. Paris: Droz, 1936.

Corbin, J. *Les Amours de Philocaste*. Paris: J. Gesselin, 1601.

Du Plaisir. *Sentimens sur les lettres et sur l'histoire*. Ed. P. Hourcade. T.L.F. Genève: Droz, 1975.

Furetière, A. *Le Roman bourgeois. Romanciers du XVIIe siècle.* Ed. A. Adam. Bibliothèque de la Pléiade. Paris: Gallimard, 1958.

Gomberville, Marin Le Roy. *La Carithée.* Paris: J. Quesnel, 1621.

Guilleragues, G.-J. *Lettres portugaises.* Ed. F. Deloffre and J. Rougeot. T.L.F. Paris: Droz, 1972.

Huet, P.D. "Lettre à M de Segrais sur l'origine des romans." Ed. F. Gégou. Paris: Nizet, 1971.

La Fayette, Mme de. *La Princesse de Clèves. Romans et nouvelles.* Ed. E. Magne. Paris: Garnier, 1970.

—. *Zaïde. Romans et nouvelles.* Ed. E. Magne. Paris: Garnier, 1970.

Langlois, Fr. *Le Tombeau des romans, où il est discouru I. Contre les Romans; II. Pour les Romans.* Paris: C. Morlot , 1626.

Lannel, J. de *Le Romant satyrique.* Paris: T. du Bray, 1624.

Le Bossu, R. *Traité du poème épique.* Paris: M. Le Petit, 1675.

Mareschal, A. *La Chrysolite, ou le secret des romans.* Paris: N. & J. de la Coste, 1634.

Nicole, P. *Les Visionnaires.* Cologne: P. Marteau, 1683.

Rapin, René. *Réflexions sur la poétique de ce temps....* Ed. E.T. Dubois. T. L. F. Geneve: Droz, 1970.

Rosset, F. de. *Les Histoires tragiques de nostre temps.* 2nd edition. Paris: A. Brunet, 1615.

Saint-Sorlin, Desmarets de. *Rosane.* Paris: H. Le Gras, 1639.

Scarron, P. *Le Roman comique. Romanciers du XVIIe siècle.* Ed. A. Adam. Bibliothèque de la Pléiade. Paris: Gallimard, 1958.

Scudéry, Mlle de. *Clelie, histoire romaine.* Paris: A. Courbé, 1654-61.

Segrais, J.R. de. *Les Nouvelles françoises.* Paris: A. de Sommaville, 1657.

Sorel, Charles. *Le Berger extravagant.* Paris: T. du Bray, 1628.

—. *Histoire comique de Francion. Romanciers du XVIIe siècle.* Ed. A. Adam. Bibliothèque de la Pléiade. Paris: Gallimard, 1958.

—. *La Maison des jeux.* Paris: N. de Sercy, 1643.

—. *Polyandre.* Paris: A. Courbé, 1648.

—. *Remarques sur les XIIII Livres du Berger extravagant.* Paris: T. du Bray, 1628.

Urfé, Honoré d'. *L'Astrée.* Ed. H. Vaganay. Lyon: Masson, 1925-8.

Valincour, J.-B. *Lettres à Madame la Marquise*** sur le sujet de La Princesse de Clèves.* Ed. A. Cazes. Paris: Bossard, 1925.

Villedieu, Mme de. *Annales galantes.* Paris: C. Barbin, 1670.

—. *Portrait des foiblesses humaines.* Paris: Barbin, 1685.

Villiers, P. de. *Entretiens sur les contes de fées.* Paris: J. Collombat, 1699.

Comment on Recent Books

A Funhouse of a Book

Marcel Gutwirth
Graduate Center, City University of New York

The Labyrinth of the Comic—Theory and Practice from Fielding to Freud. BY RICHARD KELLER SIMON. Tallahassee: Florida State UP, 1985

The mirror and the maze—a maze more often than not literally constituted by a play of mirrors—offer themselves as the governing metaphors of this relentlessly overdetermined account of the nuptials of comic theory and comic practice, from Fielding to Freud. Comic theory, we learn early on, "has been self-consciously comic since Erasmus" (4). Bergson's *Le Rire* is offered as a case in point: does not the author introduce laughter as that little problem that has so far eluded all the great philosophers, and does he not admit himself that, like the child on the seashore who grasps at a wave, he ended up with no more than a handful of froth?

> The failure of all the great thinkers is repeated in the failure of Bergson. The confident Bergson is inverted by the defeated Bergson. Repetition and inversion, Bergson argues in the essay, are techniques of comedy, provocations to laughter. If that is so, then the essay titled "Laughter" is framed by a provocation to laughter and is itself a comic work.... If we have made our way carefully enough in the labyrinth we should also be laughing. (9)

True to its labyrinthine vocation the essay on the comic is a trap. Should we not laugh, should we fail to see the joke Simon discovers in Bergson, the laugh is on us—and the joke, though undetected, is preserved.

Fair warning: we read on at our peril, as a hall of mirrors forms around us, setting up a closed network of repetition and inversion that dazzles the understanding.

Three distinct pathways open up in this contribution to a "history of laughter" (15), later revised as, more modestly, "a first step" in "a major reinterpretation" of "the intellectual history of the comic" (244): the English comic novel from Fielding to Meredith, by way of Thackeray; Kierkegaard and German idealism; the modern scientific discourse on laughter eventuating in Freud. Tristram Shandy throws a bridge to Kierkegaard, in the writings of Schlegel; Freud binds together the scientific and the German philosophic tradition, so the three strands do flow into one another, but they nevertheless take us on a fairly discontinuous mental itinerary.

The claims made for the three major novels analyzed in these pages—*Tom Jones*, *Vanity Fair*, *The Ordeal of Richard Feverel*—are large, and in some way unverifiable (though forcefully argued). In keeping with the governing trope of specularity they mirror one another as they amplify almost comically from chapter to chapter. "The chaotic comic journey of Tom's present," we are told, "is ordered and controlled by the history of comic literature, Fielding's past" (58). An impressively Joycean progression is made to verify that claim, to wit:

> The journey is told in a chronology of styles beginning with Shakespeare (the bawdy tavern scenes with the soldiers, then Tom's speech on honor that parodies Falstaff's); and continuing with Cervantes (the reintroduction of Partridge as the barber from *Don Quixote*); the Puritan interregnum (the Man of the Hill's high seriousness and the Christian discipline); Restoration comedy (the sexual farce at Upton); sentimental comedy in the manner of Steele or Cibber (Mrs. Fitzpatrick's story); the attack on sentimental comedy (the relapse of the merry Andrew after the humorless puppet show); and finally concluding with Fielding (the adventure with the Gypsies and the fight with the highwayman, which both affirm and parody the techniques of *Joseph Andrews*). (57)

What *Tom Jones* is seen as doing for the history of comic literature *Vanity Fair* is viewed as doing for comic theory. We take a huge stride forward in the amalgamation of the book's twin concerns—the history of laughter, the intellectual history of the comic—when it is asserted that "laughter is the cipher key for character and plot; laughter theory is the cipher key for the novel as a whole" (133). Building on the opposing genealogies of true and false humor, adduced by Addison in his *Spectator* papers, Thackeray constructed *Vanity Fair* as "the genealogy of the female false humor, born of laughter and frenzy [Becky Sharp], as told by the genial male true humor, born of wit and mirth" [the 'harlequin' narrator] (127).

Inclusiveness and recapitulation of critical and literary forebears, either taken straight or, through mirroring, stood on their heads, reaches in Meredith's novel, hyperbolic multiplication. In a first breath, on page 141,

> Combining symmetries from Aristotle and Baudelaire, Meredith imposes an anatomy of laughter onto Fielding's symmetrical text and from that produces what is in neither the fiction nor the theory, a direct connection between the styles of laughter and the styles of comic literature from Aristophanes to the mid-nineteenth century.

A second breath, at an interval of thirteen pages, improves on this remarkable accumulation:

> Layering one symmetry, the combination of Aristotle and Baudelaire, onto the other, the architectonic of Fielding, Meredith multiplies the complexities of the labyrinth and in the reflections of the mirrors within mirrors produces *at least* two other layers of text, a history of comic literature from Aristophanes to the nineteenth century and a survey of the major prose style of the nineteenth century [*emphasis mine*].(155)

On page 167 a grid is offered "made up of four extremes and one absence at the center," which "is in turn a grid of four layers." To that debauch of symmetries two further importations are tacked on: "Celebrating his abandonment by the Peacock family, Meredith rewrites a Peacock novel—it is now not nearly so much fun. It is also, by a trick of mirrors, a rewrite of...*Tristram Shandy*" (173).

The rueful note, "it is now not nearly so much fun," fleetingly mirrors the reader's sense that the comic evaporates in that mirroring obsession. Not all mirrorings amuse. When Molière's *The Miser* is taken as half model for Fielding's symmetries (the other half Congreve's *Way of the World*) on account of the way Harpagon's family meshes with Anselme's, the daughter of the one (Elise) in love with the son of the other (Valère), and reciprocally, Mariane with Cléante, the symmetry no more pertains to what in that play is subject to laughter than does the duplication of blocking fathers, symmetrical and inverted, Allworthy and Western, move us to more than amused reflection, *après coup*. All the fun lies in Western's cantankerousness, little or none in Allworthy's deceived benevolence.

It is a relief to step out of the tangle of fearful symmetries evoked by the purely literary chapters to the transcendental buffoonery self-ascribed by Kierkegaard, in what is perhaps the most successful chapter in the book. Described as one who determinedly set out to "laugh against the laughter of others" (115) the Danish imp of Socratic irony appears to have played out consciously, and in the cause of the highest religious seriousness, the role prescribed by Folly in Erasmus' *Laus Stultitiae*, that of Fool wholly given over to the folly of the Cross. The complicated game of mutually parodistic pseudonymous writings, the journal entries outlining a strategy aimed at keeping Copenhagen off-balance, the ascending rungs in a theoretical scale that take us from the ironic through the comic to the religious, all add up to a pattern that lends to the-life-and-the-works of Kierkegaard, taken as a unitary enterprise, the cohesiveness in comedy which that baffling sage receives nowhere else.

Mirrored inversions gain plausibility in the chapter devoted to the beginnings of an encounter between the comic and Anglo-American science, in the form of speculations concerning the physiology of laughter, the psychology of the risible. That Herbert Spencer's trail-blazing account of the psycho-physiological mechanism of laughter—still, with added refinements, our sole explanatory model in that mode—owes its inception to the wish to "get back" at Meredith's caricature of Spencer in his novel, by inverting the terms of his explanation, adds, if verified, a note of piquancy to intellectual history. The veritable ballet of positions, borrowed without acknowledgement and inverted without ceremony, among the august founders of the infant disciplines involved, Charles Darwin, Alexander Bain, Stanley Hall, James Sully, and John Dewey, exhibits, all unawares, the comic spirit at its insouciant best. "What begins with Bain and then with Spencer and his mirror inversion of Meredith ends with Hall and Sully and their mirror repetitions of Meredith, and Dewey and McDougall and their mirror repetitions of Bain." (208) The upshot of it all is to organize along lines of comic force a set of formulations familiar to us from any standard bibliography of the field, which now fall into a pattern of thrust and counter-thrust that authentically mirrors their subject matter.

Enfin Sigmund Freud *vint* ... From German idealism he borrowed the notion of play as defining the aesthetic domain (Kant's *Zwecklos Zweckmäszigkeit*), melding it with the scientific requirement that the play make utilitarian sense in fitting the organism to survive. He posited "the unconscious as the location of the play within the self" (220). Evading the censor, the joke returns the adult to the heedless freedom of a long-forgotten childish past. In Freud's inversion of Spencer's wasteful scheme—an excess of unused accumulated energy dissipates in an outburst of wasted motion—into an economy of psychic energy saved by the lifting of inhibitions Simon sees, as a last instantiation of form mirroring matter,

> his own hidden Jewish joke, a joke at his own expense. The gentiles believe that laughter is the joy at waste, but the Jew knows better, for what would a Jew celebrate, waste or economy? What would the gentile stereotype of the Jew love more, spending or saving? For Freud the special value of the Jewish joke is that the maker demeans himself in a loving way and so diffuses criticisms and attacks from gentiles (227).

No more than Bergson's having the laugh on us in *Le Rire* is Freud's hidden joke fully persuasive. Some of the finest witticisms in his arsenal are of impeccably upper-class gentile provenance (N. on the ex-minister of agriculture, who like Cincinnatus is going back *before* the plough...), and his Jewish jokes invariably aim at the despised Ostjuden, the East European Jewry he scarcely identified with. The trick is neat, but the reader, while she cannot fail to be impressed with the sum of ingenious *rapprochement* that bombards us on all sides in this "fun-house" of a book, quails *à la longue*, eyes pleadingly in search of the exit.

"That Moving Voice..."

Michael S. Koppisch
Michigan State University

The French Essay. BY THEODORE P. FRASER. Boston: Twayne Publishers, 1986.

Montaigne created the essay, but for whatever reasons—and many have been put forward—it did not flourish on its native French soil. Although much of seventeenth-century French literature is a dialogue with the *Essais*, writers of the period were reluctant to adopt the form that Montaigne had perfected. Across the channel in England, Francis Bacon took up Montaigne's title and launched a genre which now thrived far better in his country than it had in France. Gustave Lanson has suggested that eighteenth- and nineteenth-century French writers who used the word *essais* in their titles did so, more often than not, under the pressure of an English influence: "L'*Essai*, parti de France, s'est acclimaté en Angleterre, y a évolué, et enfin nous a été renvoyé" (327). It is a critical commonplace that the history of the literary genre follows a similar course. No one denies that Montaigne is at the origin of the essay form, but most agree, as well, that the English imported it and have made it their own.

If Professor Fraser does not explicitly contradict this view, his project nonetheless implies that the essay has a rich tradition in France. For *The French Essay* proposes nothing less than a survey, chronologically organized, of the essay in France from Montaigne to the middle of the twentieth century. Preceded by a preface in which the author sets his course, successive chapters in the book treat Montaigne and each of the centuries after him. The sixth chapter is a very brief conclusion. In the chapters on the eighteenth, nineteenth, and twentieth centuries, the authors discussed are clustered under sub-headings which sometimes refer to a kind of essay ("The Periodical Essay," "The Dialogue Essay"), sometimes to the writers' place in the chronology ("The Second Generation of Major Nineteenth-Century Essayists: Baudelaire, Renan, and Taine") and sometimes to a characterization of the essayists or the essays they wrote ("Essayists Who Continue the Moralist Modes of Writing," "The Essay as World Mirror"). These divisions are more a convenient way to separate one author or group of authors from another than a gesture toward constituting a genuine taxonomy of the essay. Indeed this book's preface makes clear that systematically classifying various kinds of essays will be avoided.

Underpinning Professor Fraser's study is his conviction that, whatever its shortcomings by comparison with its English cousin, the French essay—"that brilliant, serious, and moving voice of an extremely intelligent, morally sensitive, and perceptive people" (166)—has played a major role in the history of French letters and, therefore, deserves consideration on its own merits. About this he is surely right. I am not convinced, however, that Professor Fraser is always best served by his decision to let chronology be his guide as he discusses the essay. Here and there, especially at moments when essays do not abound, some straining is necessary to show that the form is still alive and well. A chronological orientation holds yet another danger that is hard to avoid: the *vie et œuvres* syndrome. It is all too tempting to say a little bit about an essayist's life, discuss the subject of his essays briefly, and pass on to the next author in the given order. Study of the essay form and its history tends to take second place when this happens.

To his credit, Professor Fraser wastes no time in raising the most vexing question of all, how to define the essay. In the very first line of his book, he faces the dilemma squarely: "Any study of the essay must initially come to grips with the thorny problem of defining both the structure and the limits of this most diverse of all literary genres" (Preface). Emphasizing the last seven words of this sentence, the critic calls for a definition that is open-ended and flexible. He rejects the notion that the only form an essay worthy of the name may take is the one Montaigne invented. The *Essais* may be the finest French example of the genre, but they are not the only model. What Professor Fraser ultimately settles on is a description of the esssay like that offered by David Daiches in the introduction to his anthology *A Century of the Essay British and American*. In order to claim the status of an essay, a piece of prose writing must, as Professor Fraser sees it, satisfy three requirements: "first, the work must bear the stamp of the author's particular temperament;

second, it should clearly reflect his fundamental thought patterns; and third, it should reveal his most personal feelings or convictions on any topic with which it deals" (ibid.). The critical method of the present book is to apply these criteria to a series of writers, studied in roughly chronological succession. The author's goal is "to capture the spirit and psychology of the genre"(ibid.).

Although it would seem to be sanctioned by a standard, if dated concept of literary history, this approach has some serious limitations. In the first place, its critical language often lacks precision. I am not sure precisely what is meant, for example, by "the spirit and psychology" of a genre. What does come across in certain pages of this book is the flavor of a number of individual essays, but so strong is Professor Fraser's emphasis on diversity within the genre that a single "psychology" of the genre—whatever that might be—does not emerge. Despite the sensible insistence on elasticity of definition, "to apply the concept of the essay to a number of French authors and works" (ibid.) runs the risk of not allowing them to speak in their own authentic voices. The flexibility of the definition of an essay becomes a lasso used to herd into the corral of the genre a surprisingly mixed breed of writers.

The criteria of Daiches for determining what is and what is not an essay are all related to the author's mode of thought. Little attention is paid to the formal aspects of the writer's expression. Professor Fraser is well aware of this and seems untroubled by it: "What ultimately characterizes the essay for Daiches is not its specific form or content, but rather the state of mind and the intention of its writer"(ibid.). It is disconcerting that in so recent a study as this one, devoted as it is to a genre much in need of careful definition, the crucial question of form is virtually passed over. Is one to conclude that it is of no consequence for the essay genre? I do not believe that Professor Fraser is prepared to go this far, because he more than once makes reference to the essay form. However, deemphasizing form in favor of authorial intent and temperament permits him to include in the essay genre works that have not usually been thought of as essays. The suppleness of his definition leads Professor Fraser to conclude that "forms traditionally attributed to it [the genre]—the character sketch, the dialogue, and the aphoristic piece—though initially seeming to differ markedly from one another—can, upon analysis, be regarded as sharing to varying degrees the essential characteristics of the genre, hence as different yet authentic manifestations of the essay form" (ibid.). I take this to mean that a dialogue may well be considered an essay, as along as it passes the three tests articulated by David

Daiches and Theodore Fraser. If no constraint of form is imposed, the essay genre becomes significantly more encompassing. What strikes me as especially problematic in all this is that, considerations of form aside, the case could reasonably be made that works taken from a variety of genres meet these conditions.

Relying heavily on Pierre Villey and Hugo Friedrich, Professor Fraser writes about Montaigne in general terms. Students of the *Essais* will recognize the material discussed here: the influence of the letter and the dialogue on the form of Montaigne's work, the difference between Montaigne and Rabelais on education, the phases through which the author supposedly passed under the successive stars of Seneca, Plutarch, and Sextus Empiricus. The conclusion reached is that as Montaigne "perfected the essay form, he also evolved, through a marvelous process of intellectual alchemy, a philosophy of nature that could accept without regret or recrimination the sum total of all that makes up the human person" (26). What remains unclear is just what this form is. Can it be described? Could it be duplicated? Does the essay have some formal characteristics against which other similar literary texts might be measured to determine whether they too are essays? These kinds of questions go unanswered, and the last word is given to a citation from Henri Peyre to the effect that thanks to Montaigne, the essay form becomes a literary means of self-discovery equalled only by the epistolary. Professor Peyre's comparison is on the mark, as is his understanding that similar content is possible in very different literary genres. The key to the distinction between the essay and the epistolary genres lies substantially in their formal constitution.

It would be reasonable to expect the seventeenth century not to figure prominently in a book on the essay. Professor Fraser begins his chapter on that period like this: "After Montaigne's death, the essay form as he created it virtually vanished from the French literary scene" (28). Yet this chapter of *The French Essay* is marginally longer than the one on Montaigne. Having said what he does about the essay form, Professor Fraser asks whether the essay tradition disappears as well. Predictably, "the response to this question hinges to a great extent upon the latitude allowed in defining the essay as a genre" (35). H.V. Routh's contention that the classical period saw no successors to Montaigne is treated as "too rigid" and "too myopic" (36). Since the moralists are preoccupied with the study of man, they can be folded into the essay tradition, even though they neither use the personal "I" nor go in for self-analysis. To include them, all we need do is to cast off "unwarranted rigidity and an obsession with the Montaigne model bordering on the belief that literay forms can be likened to Platonic essences" (37). If we accede to this call for flexibility, we shall perhaps agree also that the essay tradition includes two groups of writers: three who use the authorial "I"—Guez de Balzac, Madame de Sévigné, and Saint-Evremond, and three who do not—La Rochefocauld, Pascal, and La Bruyère. Whatever the divergence in form among these writers, "they still had the temperament of the essayist" (58). Professor Fraser's working hypothesis is that the seventeenth century is a period of transition during which the French essay grows away from the model of Montaigne to become "an amalgam of forms, levels, and styles of expression"(ibid.).

While it may be true that the seventeenth-century French moralists, along with other writers of the period, contributed to the development of the essay in France, they ought not be referred to as "seventeenth-century French essayists" (ibid.). La Bruyère, for example, has much in common with Montaigne. In a recent book on the author of the *Caractères*, Floyd Gray knowingly compares the two writers: "Quand La Bruyère juge la dose de l'esprit chez les gens, il peut être rapproché de Montaigne par sa tendance à peser; mais tandis que la pesée de Montaigne est un moyen d'amplifier le sujet, celle de La Bruyère aboutit très souvent à son annihilation" (17). This is not a minor distinction. The paths of the writer of character portraits and the essayist often converge, but their literary projects and destinies remain fundamentally different. The broadly divergent forms that the *Essais* and the *Caractères* take signal essential differences of substance. That character sketches appear in essays is obviously true, but this does not justify treating the work of La Bruyère as if it were part of the essay tradition.

Questionable use of the generic terms "essayist" and "essay" occurs in other parts of Professor Fraser's book as well. He simply casts his net too widely. On the other hand, one cannot but be impressed by the amount of material that he has mastered in order to study the essay. His enthusiasm for this genre has led him to bestow too easily the title of essayist on some writers, but it also encourages the reader to think again about a literary form often neglected in studies of French letters.

Works Cited

Gray, Floyd. *La Bruyère, Amateur de caractères.* Paris: Nizet, 1986.
Lanson, Gustave. *Les Essais de Montaigne.* Paris: Mellottée, n.d.

The Day of the Locus

Doranne Fenoaltea
University of Florida

Poems in Their Place: The Intertextuality and Order of Poetic Collections. EDITED BY NEIL FRAISTAT. Chapel Hill and London: U of North Carolina P, 1986.

The interest of this collection of essays, devoted primarily to Anglo-American texts, lies, for readers of this journal, in the issue addressed, that of poetic collections as meaningfully organized works.

The essays which compose the volume attempt to show, from different perspectives and for a broad body of works, how attention to questions of composition or disposition affects interpretation of the work and, to a greater or lesser degree, its individual components. As a result, a number of the essays elucidate aspects of meaning not otherwise readily apparent, and they provide suggestive models for exploration of French works along similar lines.

Several of the more interesting discussions are in fact devoted to English works from the late sixteenth to early eighteenth centuries, and Joseph Wittreich's "'Strange Text!': *Paradise Regain'd....*To Which is Added *Samson Agonistes*" furnishes an excellent model. It explores the expression of Milton's views, on crucial issues in a period of censorship, achieved by textual strategies and intertextual reference: "It is as if Milton were using explicit intertextuality between *Paradise Regained* and the Gospels, between *Samson Agonistes* and the book of Judges, to signal a hidden intertextuality between the poems themselves, with *Samson* relating to *Paradise Regained* as each poem relates to its biblical context, and thus as text relates to pre-text. An intertextuality achieved through allusion masks an elusive intertextuality, with the presuppositions governing the former now transferred to and providing the controls for the latter. Surface intertextuality, at least in *Paradise Regained* and *Samson Agonistes*, holds the reader within the confines of inferential meaning whereas, in these same poems, a covert intertextuality leads the reader into the realm of specified but subversive meanings" (p. 165). The demonstration of this thesis is developed through close analysis of the texts, informed by the historical context, the essential intertexts, modern scholarship and interpretation, and Wittreich arrives at an overall reading of the volume which differs in some important respects from interpretations of the two works considered independently.

Similarly, Annabel Pattersons's discussion of Jonson's *Under-Wood* and Marvell's *Miscellaneous Poems* seeks to demonstrate that poems written independently can be collected in ways that affect the individual poems and suggest to the reader attentive to order a meaning which transcends that of the individual elements. Like Wittreich, Patterson undertakes an historically sensitive, probing but never didactic reading to explore how grouping and juxtaposition, through effects readily discernible to an alert contemporary reader, are means of affecting and expanding the implications of the works. Here, too, Patterson argues, there is an element of subversion, the voice of political opposition. Thus, for both Wittreich and Patterson, the ordering of works may draw attention to positions which cannot be overtly expressed.

Vincent Carretta's study of Pope suggests that the composition of the *Collected Works* of 1717 is to some extent a polemical response to criticism of his work. His argument is based less on order, grouping and juxtaposition of the texts, than on the illustrations, initials and head and tailpieces, which, he argues, play an intertextual role by drawing attention to specific episodes and contexts, thus highlighting certain aspects of the texts and permitting the creation of visual as well as thematic links between sections and a significance which, once again, goes beyond that apparent in individual poems. The concept of "work" here includes issues of layout and illustration, thereby broadening, in valuable ways, the concept of the ordered work.

John Shawcross's focus in his essay on Donne is rather different from that of the preceding discussions, which dwell on implications of presumably authorial arrangement, since his principal concern is editorial practice. This is a detailed study of editorial problems, particularly in respect to placement of individual lyrics in the appropriate generic category and in the light of an extremely rich manuscript tradition. Of particular interest is

Shawcross's demonstration of the effect of generic categorization on meaning: a verse letter in sonnet form will be read differently if classed among epistles or among sonnets, due to readers' expectations concerning genre. Where the essays discussed above are in principle more closely tied to elucidaton of authorial intention (without, of course, being restricted to it), Shawcross's discussion of "poems in their place" uses a reader-response model to show that placement will affect in various ways the interpretation of a poem.

Finally, for the period of particular interest here, S. K. Heninger has traced changes in the relation between lover and lady in sonnet sequences, as a structuring principle. While there is less detail here on the specific arrangement of individual works than in the essays previously discussed, Heninger draws attention to the importance of the intertextual tradition from which a work derives and to its transformation of that tradition, seen here as a function of a changing philosophical view of the world which profoundly affects the poet's definition of experience. Heninger rightly calls attention to those philosophical and literary intertexts which, in addition to those supplied by religion and politics, variously affect the microcosm which is the work and can usefully be explored in the search for fundamental structuring elements of a collection.

All these essays raise questions about order and arrangement in poetic collections which, *mutatis mutandis*, may suggest fruitful avenues of exploration for the French lyric of the same general period. It is worth remarking, perhaps, that these analyses are based for the most part on thematic evidence of order and arrangement rather than on more strictly formal patterning. (Shawcross's discussion of Donne is, naturally, a partial exception.)

It is only for works of the nineteenth century, in Stuart Curran's essay on Wordsworth's 1807 *Poems, in Two Volumes* and George Bornstein's analysis of Browning's *Dramatic Lyrics* of 1842 that strong arguments are made for strictly formal patterns: the symmetrical disposition of Wordsworth's lyrics within sections which allows for "a continual readjustment of perspective" within elaborate formal symmetries and Browning's disposition of paired and freestanding poems (the latter devoted to political events) which draws attention to the underlying overall theme of the contrast between virtuous and vicious characters.

Bornstein's essay, like Wittreich's, furnishes a clear model of procedure: the reading of the poems is carefully maintained at the level of the collection, focusing on the aspects of the works which the pairing and the arrangement bring out, a "reduction" of detailed analysis useful for clarifying the overall program of the work. A specific aspect of the collection of interest here is the addition, at the last minute, of a final poem to the (finished and coherent) collection, which the printer found too short. Thus, the originally circular and closed work focused on moral issues becomes, by the addition of "The Pied Piper of Hamelin"—which affects the entire collection retrospectively—a more open-ended work, drawing attention to the role of the poet. (This practical fact of book production usefully reminds us that artistic endeavors are often subject to constraints, which artists often find means of turning to formal or thematic advantage.) Bornstein points out that a contemporary reviewer was fully aware of the pairing pattern in the 1842 version of the work and that he thus anticipated modern criticism by over one hundred years. (An alternate formulation—that modern readers may be recognizing something perfectly evident to a contemporary and since lost sight of—may draw attention both to the importance of contemporary comment and to differences of reading practice at different times.)

That choices of inclusion and exclusion, as well as arrangement, profoundly affect the sense of a collection is the telling point made by Marjorie Perloff in her discussion of Plath's *Ariel* as the poet planned it and as it was in fact published. The discussion makes abundantly clear that works change as (even relatively small) changes are made in their contents, a point which can also be of value to students of successive editions of poetic works. Emphasizing the impact of poems on other poems in a collection, Perloff's discussion most usefully calls attention to effects of order and juxtaposition as they affect interpretation.

Finally, Earl Miner's analysis of the composition of Japanese collections shows that types of order and arrangement can in some contexts be highly codified yet not readily available as system to a reader lacking the key. In arguing that minimal narrative, a combination of sequence and continuity, can be used to form integrated collections (in this case, works ordered not by authors, but by by compilers), Miner reminds us of the variety of forms that arrangement can take. This is salutary, especially in light of another essay in collection, William Anderson's diatribe against arguments for concentrical patterning in Augustan poetry, a position which, whether ultimately right or wrong, seems to set an unfortunate example in a collection in principle devoted to exploring the variety of ways in which collections may be integrated. One fails to see why only one kind of pattern should obtain in a collection, when it is obvious that different kinds of patterning operate in a single element of that collection.

In his suggestive introduction, Neil Fraistat calls attention to a variety of issues for the "contextual poetics" he advocates. The elaboration of a theory would, however, require the making of careful distinctions among types of collections and kinds of issues to be addressed. Thus, collections ordered by authors, or with their approval, are likely to require discussion, at least initially, along different lines than anthologies, both here contained within the same general framework. Different critical issues are raised when dealing with authorial intent and/or decision or a reader-response based approach. Intertextual and ideological questions will probably have varying impact for works from different historical periods. In addition, the entire issue is of necessity complicated by the fact that different organizing principles may be at work in a given collection, and that just as poems constitute a unique formulation of experience, so too will the collections, that is to say, that while the types of pattern that are seen to be present may belong to recognizable types, they will also most probably be work-specific as well.

In sum, this collection sets the scene for a kind of exploration of poetic texts which might well prove fruitful for studies of the French lyric tradition. It is provocative and suggests a number of ways to approach the issue. In particular, several of the discussions show how context—the effects of juxtaposition, of arrangement, of inclusion and exclusion—can be a considerable factor both for expression and interpretation; it is an issue which may too often be only indirectly acknowledged or implicitly ignored, although to focus closely on its effects can, as several of the essays demonstrate, bring out facets of works which may not be apparent in isolated readings. The reasons for retrospective ordering can be infinitely varied, ranging from playfulness and appreciation of the simple pleasure which order can give to a desire to express indirectly forbidden or unpopular views. Where the author's control is strong, study of the collection as a formally structured whole can reveal different aspects of a poet's conception of his work and its meaning. Readers may of course discover patterns which go beyond authorial intent in collections, as they do in individual poems. What is eminently clear is that much can be gained from close attention to "poems in their place," and to the structure of poetic collections.

The Semiotics of the Dance:
A State of the Art in the Renaissance

Margaret M. McGowan
University of Sussex

The Dancing Body in Renaissance Choreography. BY MARK FRANCO. Birmingham, Alabama: Summa Publications, 1986.

By the end of the sixteenth century, a large body of texts on the practice and theory of the dance had been assembled. Relevant Greek and Latin texts (notably Plato's, Plutarch's, and Lucian's) had been translated; dance manuals such as those of Arbeau, Arena, Cornazano, Caroso, Negri or Tuccaro (some of which had been circulating freely in manuscript form), were increasingly available in print; and contemporary comments either in courtesy books on the art of dancing in general or, in the works of poets or in the records of court festivals or individual performance, had become *de rigueur*. More than enough matter, one might think, for theatre historians, dance reconstructors and linguists to exercise their analytical talents.

Yet, despite the mass of material, we are still at the beginning of the "science" of dance analysis. Methods of investigating the dances of the past, and even their social and cultural contexts, have remained imperfect. Abundance of texts does not make up for imprecise description, for inadequacies of technical language and for the complex inter-connections which any study of the dance involves. Pamela Jones has built on the evidence of musical scores only, while Yves Guilcher, in a series of penetrating articles, has questioned (rightly in my view) whether reconstruction is possible at all, given our prejudices, put alongside the technical uncertainties and the particular character of the "texts"—tablature, dance manuals, drawings—on which any reconstruction might be based.

Consider for a moment the different classes of so-called "dance texts." Some commemorate particular events, but there are no set ways of doing this. Thus, at different points in time, Francesco Colonna and Balthazar de Beaujoyeulx offer very precise accounts of what they intended to happen, the latter in the *Balet Comique* (1581), the former in the "beau bal" (1499), based on a game of chess;[1] while others resolutely offered perplexing and highly generalized views of the dancing. One might cite the anonymous witness of the ball given after the wedding of Mary Queen of Scots; he names all the royal dancers and depicts the bride, performing with her new sister Elizabeth de France, and yet "avoit l'Espouse une queue longue de bien de six toises, que portoit apres elle un gentilhomme"! With equal unhelpfulness, Simon Goulart summarily ends his account of the festivities for the wedding of Marguerite de Valois and Henri de Navarre with "elles se mirent à danser un bal fort diversifié, et qui dura plus d'une grosse heure."[2] Other "dance texts" were written in the guise of retrospective *apologiae:* for example, Arena's *Rules of Dancing* (1529) or Archange Tuccaro's *L'Art de sauter* (1599). Then there are the "texts" (those of Thoinot, Arbeau or Cesare Negri, for instance), which offer practical advice concerning the steps which ideally should be made for any particular dance, but which lack the technical tools which would have given an indisputable view of what actually was performed. Finally, some "texts" were socially prescriptive (*The Courtier* of Castiglione and some *Essais* of Montaigne), implicitly or explicitly assuming that gesture and class are mutually reinforcing.

From this conspectus, it can be seen that dancing had many functions in the Renaissance. Although its status was often argued about, no one denied its importance, especially as the high authority of Plato had established a significant role for the dance in his plans for political and moral harmony in the state. The frequency of reference to the dance in Plato's dialogues would be astonishing if it were not for his conviction that

> the Gods who, as we say, have been appointed to be our companions in the dance, have given the pleasurable sense of harmony and rhythm and so they stir us into life, and we follow them, joining hands together in dance and songs...

He also maintained "he who is well educated will be able to sing and dance well" (5: 31).

Basing his argument on these twin persuasions, the Greek philosopher in the *Laws* set out the links between dancing and goodness (2: 654); excluded vicious dances (2: 656); chose with care directors of music and gymnastic (6:765-773); described the dances which were appropriate to generous souls (7: 797-817) and had defined gymnastics as having two branches:

> dancing and wrestling; and one sort of dancing imitates musical recitation, and aims at preserving dignity and freedom, the other aims at producing health, agility and beauty in the limbs and parts of the body, giving the proper flexion and extension to each of them, a harmonious motion being diffused everywhere, and forcing a suitable accompaniment to the dance. (7: 795).

Such wide benefits for health, education, moral being, and general harmony were eagerly accepted by Renaissance writers whose thoughts on dancing were often mere reworkings of Platonic ideas. Sir Thomas Elyot had thoroughly grasped the educational values of dancing and his moral instructions in *The Governour* were specifically based on the various movements of the dance:

> the first meuyng in every daunse is called honour, whiche is a reverent inclination or curtaisie...by the seconde motion...may be signified celeritie and slowness (241-42),

and so on, until all the steps had been assigned their moral counterparts, at which point, Elyot could conclude, that dancing "shall appiere to be as well a necessary studie as a noble and vertuous pastime" (269). Medieval moralizing habits were still preeminent in this work; on the other hand, Tuccaro's influential *L'art de sauter* (1599), written in dialogue form, was more closely modelled on Plato's works. Tuccaro himself underlined the affinities when, in his preface, he recalled the role given to the dance by Plato in his *Republic* and when he had one of the interlocutors—seigneur Cosme—refer explicitly to "ceste lice Platonique" (f. 20; see also f. 59).[3] For other writers—Béranger de la Tour d'Albenas (1556), or Sir John Davies (1596)—the dance was an infinitely expandable metaphor capable of describing all visible activity even to the motions of the Universe. Everything danced on every plane— physical, philosophical, moral, social and political.[4] It is clear that many sixteenth-century 'dance texts' had less to do with the actual contemporary dance scene than might be imagined.

Tasks of analysis are further complicated by the fact that, in theoretical discussion in the Renaissance, one art was easily substitutable for another; and aesthetic criteria were common to all the arts.[5] Thus, Plutarch was quoted on the expressive power and transferability of poetry and dancing:

> Bref, il faudroit transferer le dire de Simonides de la peinture au bal pource que le bal est une poesie muette, et la poesie un bal parlant...entre le bal et la poesie toutes choses sont communes, et participent en tout l'une de l'autre, toutes deux representants une mesme chose, mesmement es chansons à danser ou la representation se fait plus eficacement de l'une par les gestes et mines, et de l'autre par les paroles (2: 250).

This kind of definition was manipulated by sixteenth-century writers when they tried to explain what dancing was. Tuccaro, for instance, cites "les doctes [qui] tiennent que la danse est une espece de Rhetorique muette." This was, apparently, an important observation, for it was later repeated and expanded by François de Lauze in his *Apologie de la Danse* (1623) where dancing is described as follows: "C'est une eloquence muete... bien plus forte et plus persuasive que celle de Ciceron." Assessments of performance, whether ideal or real, were couched in the same language as that employed in the appreciation of a painting or the judgement of a poem. Grace, the natural, comeliness and decorum were the ever-recurring terms, used by Vasari to praise a work of art, by Du Bellay to command an ode, by Castiglione to characterize behavior of which he would approve, or by Brantôme to describe the dancing prowess of Marguerite de Valois who delighted the French court with "sa belle grace, apparence et grave majesté" (5: 73).

Into this turmoil of transferable criteria and variable status of "texts" Mark Franko has attempted to inject some order by using Riffaterre's model of intertextuality which subjects a number of "texts"—variants of the same structure (whether referential or utopistic)—to the same, minute analysis.The results of his enquiry are enlightening. Franko freely acknowledges the difficulties encountered by dance reconstructors; indeed, the inadequacies of their methods serve his own purposes well, for in his search for the specificity of movement in Renaissance "dance texts," he is quickly obliged to admit that movement was unrepresentable at this time. It was unrepresentable, partly because most texts were, as we have seen, ideal or apologetic in intent, and partly because of the limitations (verbal and representational) cogently stated on page 9; in Renaissance "dance texts," whatever their nature, "the body is conspicuous by its absence"—a challenging paradox.

In order to reconstitute a presence from this absence, to give substance and then to attempt to fix movement which cannot be analysed directly, texts relevant to the dancing body are studied and made to interpenetrate each other: passages from Quintilian which show the orator's posture is the same as that of the dancer; citations from courtesy books where the term "measure" defines virtue in both civility and dance; pedagogical precepts intended to control gesture; and political exchange which reveals how silence and speech, like pose and movement, are interdependent. The process of analysis is skilful and cumulative. What emerges for the dance is the discovery that theatricality, in its broadest sense, is central for human conduct and judgement in the Renaissance, and that in our understanding of its operations, dance plays a key role. The discovery should not be underestimated: although the world defined as a theater or a stage were commonplaces at the time, and although it is well known that Montaigne (for instance), on innumerable occasions, revealed civility as strategy and gesture as covering rather than exposing intent, nonetheless the intricacies, complexities and riches of the gestural code are made manifest in Franko's analysis.

Self-consciousness, the awareness of being watched and assessed are inherent in the act of dancing, which exposes to a peculiar extent conditions present in all social intercourse at the time. The dancer was both performer—acutely sensitive to the gaze of his/her onlooker—and orator, in so far as his/her movements were persuasive and effective. Ideally, the nature and purpose of the dance were to display the person and his/her skills, and to do it so with such adroitness that, paradoxically, display seemed denied. "Showing-off, as though one were some professional *baladin*, was to be avoided at all costs."[6] On the contrary, the nonchalance or *sprezzatura* desired in the courtier were also requirements for the dancer so that (in the words of Thoinot Arbeau) the slow and solemn *pavane* could show to advantage a magnificent dress and rich jewels, and the dignified nobility of the person, while the *galliard* (more quick and gay) offered a spectacle of individual dancing skill.

In practice, since analysis of movement could only begin once the dancer is momentarily at rest (Franko 64-5) how did one assess the quality of a dance, particularly when it was (as so often in the Renaissance) a question of awarding prizes.[7] Two texts, infrequently quoted, are instructive since they lead us back once again to the real difficulties of notating performance. The first comes from Montaigne's *Journal de Voyage* where the traveller reports the criteria he proposed to use in awarding the prizes at the ball he offered to the noble citizens of Lucca in 1581.

> En effet j'allois choisissant des yeux, tantot l'une, tantot l'autre, et j'avois toujours egard à la beauté, à la gentilesse: d'ou je leur faisois observer que l'agrément d'un bal ne dépendoit pas seulement du mouvement des pieds, mais encore de la contenance, de l'air, de la bonne façon et de la grace de toute la personne (174).

In Montaigne's assessment, the steps of the dance were not preeminent; although they played a focal role within a larger aspect. It is also obvious that Montaigne's opinion was based on very general, all embracing and indefinable qualities—the bearing, the beauty and grace of the whole person. In short, judgement here came from a shared instinct of quality rather than any precisely defined factors.

On the surface, our second "text"—Brantôme's account of the dancing abilities of Marguerite de Valois and her brother Charles IX —seems to offer the analyst more.

> J'ay veu assez souvent la mener dancer la pavanne d'Espagne, dance où la belle grace et majesté font une belle representation; mais les yeux de toute la salle ne se pouvoient soullcr, ni assez se ravir par une si agreable veue; car les passages estoient si bien dansez, les pas si sagement conduicts, et les arrests faicts de si belle sorte, qu'on ne sçavoit que plus admirer, ou la belle façon de danser, ou la majesté de s'arester, representant maintenant une gayeté, et maintenant un beau et grave desdain; car il n'y a nul qui les aye veus en ceste dance, qui ne die ne l'avoir veue danser jamais si bien (5: 183).

A rare spectacle is conjured up with royal performers and ready-to-praise audience; expectation of skill and pleasure is shared; the movement of the dance, described in a set of superlatives, is regulated: steps, sequences, pauses and poses—now appropriately majestic, now gay or haughty. Brantôme picks out the essential elements of the dance and places them in an admiring social context, yet he can only transmit, in most general terms, the sense of a dance superbly done.

Perhaps, in the end, only art can serve, and it is vain to strive for a sophisticated "scientific" model which will reinvest with substance the Renaissance dancing body. Its gestures can after all—even in Franko's account —only be glimpsed.

There are, moreover, further difficulties for those who wish to reconstruct, even approximately, the nature of dancing in the

Renaissance. So far, in this discussion, we have concentrated on the social dance and on individual performances. What of dance ensembles? or of imitative or representational dances which were more frequent than Franko allows and which create different conditions for analysis. The circular dance forms of which we have depictions from the earliest times change the relationship between dancers and onlookers, and the links between the dancers themselves are modified (Ferrand). Then there are the imitative masquarades or ballets where the account is not centered on a person but on the story, not on the individual's choreographic prowess but on his/her ability to convey feelings; in other words, to fulfill Plutarch's contention that 'le bal est une poesie muette.' In such dances the audience and dancers assumed different roles, as may be demonstrated from a brief look at the *Masquarade du Triomphe de Diane sur Cupidon,* performed at Carnival time 1575 in honor of Montaigne's friend, Diane de Foix.

   Pierre de Brach, in his account of this spectacle, emphasized the symbolic content of the characters' costumes; spelt out the signifying gestures—for instance, Phoebus "portant sa teste basse en signe d'humilité...encore tout poureux et craintif, Cupidon faisoit le superbe et le brave"; or the amorous looks exchanged between dancers, and between performers and ladies in the audience; and he differentiated between the dancers playing the same part—four pelerins d'Amour or the four nymphs of Diana. The spectators' interest was variously elicited. Sometimes it was concentrated on a single performance as when each dancer made his/her entrance and performed variations on known social dances—*pavanes, branles,* or *voltes*; or attention could be much more fragmented as when the tiny drama required dancers to perform together in specially prepared ensembles or simulated combats, or to dance simultaneously in different parts of the hall. In order to capture and analyze the larger patterns of this choreography and to include the dimensions of emotional appeals which are involved, other strategies are needed, other intertexts perhaps. The *masquarade*, in so far as it blends social dances into a larger choreographed ensemble, is halfway between the restricted interpretation of social dancing as used by Franko, and the fully-fledged geometric designs of *ballet de cour*. As such a hybrid, it provides matter for further reflection on how Franko's approach might be modified or extended to accommodate danced transmission of emotion and performance as demonstration. "New insights into the origins of the Ballet-Spectacle" (blurb for Franko's book) is an extravagant claim; however, if one takes into account the formidable problems that confront any analyst and reconstructors of Renaissance dance, then the vision of gesture as "a descanting on the book"—the verbal swagger that closes Franko's discourse—is justified.

Notes

[1]See my introduction to the facsimile edition of *Le Balet Comique*, and Jean Martin's translation of Colonna's *Le Songe de Poliphile*.

[2]The text for Mary, Queen of Scots' wedding was printed in D. Godefroy's *Le Cérémonial françois*; Goulart's comments occur in his *Memoires de l'Estat de France* 1: f. 269.

[3]His comment on Plato in the Preface, sig. aijv, runs as follows: "le divin Platon, pour asseurer et affermir sa Republique tant renommee, sagement et prudemment voulut introduire en icelle toutes les parties [including the dance] qui luy sembloient utiles, profitables et necessaires en son entretien et bon gouvernement." François de Lauze, *Apologie de la danse* copies Tuccaro in this influence.

[4]Béranger de la Tour d'Albenas, *Choréide, Autrement Louenge du bal* and Sir John Davies, *Orchestra*.

[5]For a detailed discussion of this common aesthetic, see chapter 2 of my book, *Ideal Forms in the Age of Ronsard*, 51-88.

[6]For strong antagonism towards such professionalism, see Montaigne, *Essais*, "Des Livres" and de Lauze, 35-6.

[7]The use of prizes is clear from texts such as Mellin de Saint Gelais, *Œuvres*, 1: 235-6: and Montaigne, *Journal de Voyage*, 173-5.

Works Cited

Arbeau, Thoinot. *Orchésographie*. Trans. by Mary S. Evans. New York: Kamin Dance Publications, 1948.

Arena, Antonius. *Rules of Dancing*. Trans. John Guthrie and Marino Zorzi. *Dance Research* 4 (1986): pp. 3-53.

Béranger de la Tour d'Albenas. *Choréide, Autrement Louenge du bal*. Lyons: Jan de Tournes, 1556.

Brach, Pierre de. *Poésies*. Bordeaux: Simon de Millanges, 1576.

Brantôme, P. de. *Œuvres Complètes*. Paris: Foucault, 1822.

Colonna, Francesco. *Le Songe de Poliphile*. Paris: Les Libraries Associés, 1963.

Elyot, Sir Thomas. *The Boke named the Governour*. Ed. H.H.S. Croft. London: Kegan Paul, Trench & Co., 1883.

Ferrand, Françoise. "Esprit et fonctions de la danse au XIIIe siècle." *La Recherche en Danse* 1 (1982): 29-39.

Godefroy, D. *Le Cérémonial françois*. Paris: S. & G. Cramoisy, 1649.

Goulart, Simon. *Memoires de l'Estat de France*. Meidelbourg: H. Wolf, 1578.

Guilcher, Yves. "Les différentes lectures de l'*Orchésographie* de Thoinot Arbeau." *La Recherche en Danse* 1 (1982): 39-50.

—."L'Interprétation de l'Orchésographie par des danseurs et des musiciens d'aujourd'hui." *La Recherche en Danse* 2 (1983): 21-32.

—. "*Orchésographie* de T. Arbeau en tant qu'essai pour transmettre la danse par l'écriture." *La Recherche en Danse* 3 (1984): 25-8.

Jones, Pamela. "Spectacle in Milan: Cesare Negri's torch dances." *Early Music* May, 1986: 182-97.

McGowan, Margaret M., ed. *Le Balet Comique*. Binghamton: MRTS, 1982.

—. *Ideal Forms in the Age of Ronsard*. U of California P, 1985.

Montaigne, Michel de. *Essais*. Ed. Pierre Villey. Paris: PUF, 1965.
—. *Journal de Voyage*. Ed. Maurice Rat. Paris: Garnier, 1955.
Negri, Cesare. *Nuove inventioni di Balli*. Milan: Bordoni, 1902.
Plato. *The Dialogues*. Ed. and trans. B. Jowett . Oxford: Oxford UP, 1892.
Plutarch. *Les œuvres meslées*. Paris & Genève: J. Stoer, 1621.
Riffaterre, Michael. "Syllepsis." *Critical Inquiry* 6 (1980): 625-38.
Saint Gelais, Mellin de. *Œuvres*. Ed. Prosper Blanchemain. Paris: Paul Daffis, 1873.
Tuccaro, Archange. *Trois Dialogues de l'Exercice de sauter et voltiger en l'air*. Paris: C. de Monstr'oeil, 1599.

Topoi: Origin and Ordering

Floyd Gray
University of Michigan

A travers le seizième siècle. BY HENRI WEBER. Tome I: Dix études sur la poésie. Paris: Nizet, 1985.

Reading, or better, rereading Weber today, is to realize how much literary studies have changed in recent years. A good deal of academic writing, originating at the point at which criticism merges into scholarship and, conversely, scholarship into criticism, has traditionally been concerned with the exploration and explanation of themes and sources. When, therefore, Weber wrote his monumental thesis on *La Création poétique au XVIe siècle en France*, he focussed quite naturally on the problem of imitation and originality. Using themes and their transformations to ascertain the precise qualities of creativeness discernable in the poetry of the age, he opened an interesting and seminal line of inquiry. Not only was he able to put order and continuity into a highly complex and diffuse subject, he helped as well to renew our perception of the way in which themes, with their variants and variations, contribute to the overall poetic phenomenon.

The present volume, in many ways a continuation of the former, brings together ten articles published separately in a number of various periodicals between 1958 (and not 1961, as the back cover erroneously states) and 1983. It begins with three studies of a general nature: the question of the existence of hermetic poetry in the sixteenth century, Platonism and sensuality in Pléiade poetry, Prometheus and the torments of love. These are followed by four articles on Ronsard, dealing successively with the structure of the *Odes*, self-correction in the *Amours* of 1552, cosmic order and human activity in the *Hymnes*, old age and death in the last sonnet. The final three articles are on or around d'Aubigné: the satirical and polemical tradition prior to and in the *Tragiques*, the presentation and discussion of a manuscript fragment of *La Chambre Dorée*, the structure of four poems from the *Printemps*. All of these topics are of some importance, and Weber treats them pertinently, with the thoroughness we have come to expect from his work. Reading them once again, however, especially in the light of everything we have learned about poetics in recent years from linguistics and, more particularly, about sixteenth-century poetics from, among others, Glauser, Rigolot, and Cave, one cannot help but be struck by a certain methodological and even bibliographical anachronism. It is true that the articles have been reproduced as originally printed, but this only makes it all the more apparent that Weber has not always availed himself even of what was being written around him. A substantial introduction (or even a brief preface) would have provided a platform for a much needed corrective or, at least, a commentary on past material from a present standpoint.

The articles dealing with hermeticism and the baroque hold probably the greatest appeal for anyone interested in the antecedents of pre-classical French literature. Weber demonstrates that those sixteenth-century poets who were most strongly influenced by the *Corpus Hermeticum* tended paradoxically to avoid the hermetic style in their writings, and that obscurity in "scientific" poetry as in Ronsard, informed by readings in astronomy, astrology, mythology, is not at all incompatible with stylistic and thematic clarity: the *poeta doctus* addressed and expected a *lector doctus*. This tendency towards relative transparency is confirmed by a detailed study of Ronsard's corrections in the *Amours* of 1552 (in which Weber takes a stance midway between Desonay and Terreaux), followed by a comparison with d'Aubigné's corrections in the aforementioned fragment. Whereas Ronsard seeks to modify instances of *furor poeticus* in favor of a more sustained and disciplined discourse, d'Aubigné would seem to be more concerned with maximum lexical and dynamic expressivity. Ronsard, consequently, anticipates certain "classical" preoccupations, while d'Aubigné's aesthetic remains fundamentally baroque. In his "Poésie polémique et satirique de la Réforme sous les règnes de Henri II, François II et Charles IX," Weber provides a useful survey of various contemporary collections of sonnets, chansons, epigrams, etc., in which this literature has survived, and discovers reoccurrences of these same themes and techniques in the *Tragiques*. This analogy leads him to conclude that d'Aubigné's vision of the world may have been shaped as much by traditional reform literature as by the emergence of a baroque temperament or style.

In his final study, "Structures de quelques poèmes d'Agrippa d'Aubigné," Weber examines four texts from the *Printemps* (*Stances* I, XX, and *Odes* XIV, XXIII) in an effort to determine if it is possible to formulate a more precise definition of the baroque. He acknowledges Marcel Raymond's contribution in the matter, especially his transposition of Wölfflin's architectural categories to the literary domain, and credits structuralism for opening the way to a more independent analysis of the plastic arts. He himself, however, preferring to avoid premature generalizations (these remarks date from 1968) adheres to a more traditional approach. Although Weber's conception of structure and structuralism remains disconcertingly impressionistic, his analysis of what he calls the "structure de cet ensemble de structures," i.e. thematic, rhythmic, metaphoric, permits him to identify a succession of violent contrasts caught up in a movement towards a prefigured and increasingly evident conclusion. Other poets, moreover, namely Saint-Amant and Malherbe, display similar patterns of extreme antitheses coupled with orderly progression. This similarity leads him to consider, over and above the play of structures, the individual or collective attitude towards life which may influence or regulate them. It would seem obvious that the intense and tormented movement of a poem by d'Aubigné, whatever its subject, is an expression of personal as well as poetic tension. Contrast here is combat, a virtual struggle between content and form. And even when treating a subject to which he may be indifferent, he cannot help but bring it to its moment of paroxysm. Stylistic and structural erethism translates the ambition, audacity and tenaciousness of the man, just as potential equilibrium tends to dominate in Malherbe and Saint-Amant: "Cependant, à travers la diversité des caractères, la différence des époques et des milieux, un même souci d'exploiter dans la direction qu'ils ont choisie toutes les resssources du langage, tous les artifices de la rhétorique se retrouvent également chez Malherbe, chez d'Aubigné et chez Saint-Amant. Rien ne serait plus faux que d'opposer les calculs et les artifices de l'un à la spontanéité des deux autres; c'est le point d'application, la direction choisie qui diffèrent" (230).

Some mention of the structural significance of the poetic landscape in these four poems would not have been inappropriate. While the Petrarchan and Pléiade depictions are conventionalized or stylized in such a manner that the mood they are intended to accompany or heighten is immediately perceived, d'Aubigné's is more intimately involved in the total conception and ultimate resolution of the poem. Weber's emphasis, however, is on structure viewed as composition, which, in d'Aubigné, subordinates details to the whole, anticipating thereby the logical arrangement of Malherbe's argumentation in his *Ode pour le Roy allant chastier la rebellion des Rochelois*, or the spatial and chronological unity of Saint-Amant's *La Solitude*.

Weber's preoccupation with themes and sources inevitably results in a profusion of examples, and this occasions a marked disproportion between quotations and critical commentary. Finally, the explanation of poetry by the examination of topoi, their origin and ordering, seems to respond at times to a desire to discuss literature in terms of something else. Content and context are indispensable adjuncts to literary analysis, but they should not be made so predominant as to obscure the very reasons for considering them at all. Although there are numerous passages in which Weber shows his understanding of poetry *qua* poetry, his usual tendency is to view sources and themes explicitly, and not as integral parts of a complex process of intertextual reappropriation.

Work cited

Weber, Henri. *La Création poétique au XVIe siècle en France*. Paris: Nizet, 1956.

The Authority of the Baroque

Alison Weber
University of Virginia

Culture of the Baroque: Analysis of a Historical Structure. BY JOSÉ
ANTONIO MARAVALL. TRANSLATED BY TERRY COCHRAN. FOREWORD BY
WLAD GODZICH AND NICHOLAS SPADACCINI. Theory and History of
Literature 25. Minneapolis: U of Minnesota P, 1986.

Current literary scholars seem to have lost enthusiasm for debate
over the concept of the baroque, in spite of the fact that there is still
wide divergence in opinion over its chronological and geographical
extension as well as its constellation of formal and thematic features.
The publication of the English translation of José Antonio
Maravall's 1975 *Cultura del Barroco* is therefore a welcome
challenge to keep the baroque alive as a "working hypothesis."

Maravall, who died last year, was an important liberal presence
in Franco's Spain, and exerted an enormous influence on the post-
Franco generation of scholars. A "historian of mentalities," he
defines the baroque as a culture—a complex of values, beliefs, and
myths—rather than a style, which predominates roughly from 1600
to 1670-80. Although his focus is on Spain as the nation which felt
the crisis of the seventeenth century most intensely, frequent
parallels are drawn with other European countries, especially
France. In brief, Maravall conceives of the baroque as an urban,
conservative, mass culture "guided" to preserve the authority of the
monarchical-seignorial *status quo*.

Maravall's description of seventeenth-century crisis, with its
rampant inflation, plague, vagabondage, endemic banditry, and rural
depopulation will be familiar to readers of Braudel. But Maravall
argues that it was the profound awareness of instability at all levels
of society that created the distinctive baroque mentality. Geographic
mobility and urban growth allowed for some social mobility, but an

increase in anonymity, crime, and unemployment were much more pervasive results of the breakdown of stable rural communities. There was a consciousness that human welfare was precariously dependent to a greater extent than before on impersonal institutions of power. Maravall creates a fascinating composite picture of the period, drawing from little-studied contemporary sources— sermons, the letters of Jesuits, proto-journalistic handbills, and the treatises of *arbitristas*—would-be political and economic reformers. The existence of a large body of literature dedicated to reform supports Maravall's claim that the possibility for change through human intervention was accepted, although change was quite pessimistically associated with instability and risk. In a sense, the century was marked by a revolution of rising expectations— expectations which were nonetheless immediately frustrated. Society, in short, was perceived as a zero sum game. If Méré remarked "Le bonheur de l'un serait souvent le malheur de l'autre," Spanish pamphleteer Barrionuevo complained more bitterly, "Some get rich making others poor" (166-67). Prudence, discretion, psychological perceptiveness, wariness—all were baroque virtues precisely because of the conviction that *homo homini lupus est*. Maravall obviously does not create his concept of the baroque *ex nihilo*, but *leitmotifs* made familiar by Hatzfeld, Spitzer and especially Rousset acquire more density when related to these non-literary works and a wealth of other unusual facts. The mentality of the baroque begins to take shape from these cultural nexes, which juxtapose, for example, the baroque obsession with time and innovations in clockmaking or the spread of the interest loan. Maravall places the topos of mutability in the context of the passion for gambling and rise in stock speculations, explains ostentation in dress in terms of urban anonymity, and connects the aesthetic of difficulty to the fascination with optical illusions and anamorphosis.

In one of his most original chapters, Maravall convincingly moves Ortega's concept of mass society back by two centuries. The concentration of uprooted rural populations in baroque cities created the conditions under which the lower classes were anonymous, but visible and audible to an unprecedented degree. They eagerly bought booklets and news pamphlets, attended plays and festivals, formed "public opinion" and asserted their claim to have "taste." For this reason, Maravall places the first manifestations of kitsch— art as a mass commodity—in the baroque, and adds more startlingly, "there is scarcely a baroque work of high quality—from Bernini's *Santa Teresa* to Poussin's *Pastoral*, to Calderón's *La vida es sueño*—that escapes being touched by kitsch elements.

Everything that belongs to the baroque emerges from the necessities of manipulating opinions and feelings on a broad public scale" (90).

For Maravall, stylistic features are subordinate to this pragmatic aim. Thus the baroque can embrace both excessive ornamentation and severe laconism, in the sense that both are seen as expressions of the baroque extreme. Extremeness is in turn motivated not by aesthetics, but by ideology—the desire to evoke from the public a heightened admiration for the power of the state: "The baroque ceased imitating, lost restraint, took pleasure in the terrible, and sought to cultivate the extreme, all to impress a public more forcefully and with greater freedom" (212). Rousset's concept of a baroque art which "seduces and transports" is thus tied much more explicitly to the power of the state which seeks to entice the public and direct its potentially disruptive energies into non-threatening channels. The expansion of public architecture (triumphal arches, retables, tombs and fountains) and mass spectacles (fireworks, festivals, processions, and above all, the national theater) are adduced as examples of a culture directed by the ruling classes.

Maravall gives few examples of direct secular or religious censorship, because he appears to be more interested in the propagandistic than the repressive mechanisms of control. Consequently, he slights an area which merits much more research, and tends to assert rather than demonstrate the success of the state's cultural manipulation. One of the salient characteristics of Ortega's mass man is his unwillingness to be led by a minority. It is likely that the seventeenth-century *vulgus* was equally intractable. As Donald Cruickshank has argued, the economics of the book trade (in which individual buyers cast their own monetary votes) probably was more significant in determining what the public read or didn't read than church or state restrictions. Maravall asserts that the privileged groups used baroque techniques of suspense and ostentation to manipulate the masses, but we know that authors frequently complained of the *vulgus*—of its demand for sensationalism and for novelty, its taste for the artificial. The limited success of Cervantes's "classical" theater is generally attributed to his unwillingness to conform to the more extravagant taste of the *vulgus*, which Lope de Vega was able to exploit so well. In other words, there is evidence to suggest that the masses directed as much as they were directed in matters of taste.

Also questionable is Maravall's assumption that the middle strata of society, which would have included most playwrights, unqualifiedly cast their lot with the ruling elite and used their plays as political and social propaganda in its behalf. However, the national theater simply does not reflect a monolithic code of values. An extensive bibliography on the subject attests to the fact that Lope, Calderón, and others were capable of treating even the quintessential baroque value of socio-sexual honor problematically. Recent scholarship on Calderón's *Life is a Dream* has suggested that, rather than an apologia for absolutism, it is, in fact, a *problem* play about kingship. Granted, plays depicting weak or corrupt kings too easily identifiable with present or recent Hapsburgs did not last long on the stage, but monarchical fallibility was not a censored concept in principle. Charlotte Stern has written a thorough and well-reasoned response to the sociological approach of *comedia* criticism, in which she proposes that Northrop Frye's "myth of concern" is a more appropriate term than propaganda for the baroque literature of social cohesiveness. It is essential, she adds, to consider that different genres refract reality in diverse ways and demand different kinds of identification from the audience or reader; pastoral, romance and historical drama are the most "propagandistic" genres, and require emotional participation whereas comedy and tragedy demand a critical and detached attitude. There are many plays which are patriotic, communal and celebratory, others which are problematic, norm-breaking and non-conformist and still more which lie between these extremes.

Maravall's experience in post-Civil War Spain undoubtedly sensitized him to the psychologically coercive potential of state-sponsored culture (one has only to think of the intimidating enormity of Franco's Valley of the Fallen), but this perspective may also have led him to overstate his thesis and perceive absolutism as totalitarianism. Although the seventeenth-century state was demonstrably repressive, it seems to have lacked both the technology and the organizational efficiency necessary to function successfully as a totalitarian society. There is simply too much evidence of variety in opinion, subverted censorship, open dissent and freedom of artistic expression to support Maravall's claim that the baroque was effectively controlled from above. An increase in literacy, the proliferation of inexpensive reading material, the construction of permanent theaters accessible to men and women of all classes, urban populations who were eager consumers of public spectacle—all were factors which undoubtedly changed the face of Renaissance culture, and we owe it to Maravall that these connections are much clearer now than before. But if some writers and artists reacted to these phenomena with nostalgia for a traditional, authoritarian society, others responded to the new audiences, means of production, and tastes with works which were innovative in technique and non-conformist in content.

Scholars who feel that the baroque is an important but secondary current or style in seventeenth-century France will undoubtedly reject Maravall as a baroque "imperialist." But *Culture of the Baroque*—ambitiously and courageously synchronic—has made more than a few points of the classicism/ baroque antithesis moot. Pascal and Gracián are revealed as kindred spirits no matter what their period appellation. For French scholars, his thesis above all might stimulate a reexamination of Tapié's idea of baroque absolutism—this time with the Spanish situation in the formula. Was it rural or urban? Did the urban middle classes identify with monarchical-seignorial values? How pervasively did absolutist ideology influence the new mass culture? To what extent was the Counter Reformation Church an instrument of state power? These questions should help keep the baroque alive as a working hypothesis, and a supra-national one at that.

By placing high culture within the context of mass culture and by relating both to the instability of a pre-modern society, Maravall has suggested intriguing interrelationships between style and thought in the seventeenth century. Evangelina Rodríguez, a distinguished student of Maravall's, has called *Culture of the Baroque* a great historical novel, precisely because of the author's ability to create an image of the period as a tightly woven web of attitudes and material existence. Unfortunately, the writing in the original suffers from Maravall's unwillingness to consider anything extraneous, and the translator, Terry Cochran, was clearly not up to the challenge of reining in this intractable prose. Most disturbing are the endless parenthetical remarks and lack of parallelism; it takes considerable ingenuity to reconcile a subject with its predicate. Supposedly untranslatable terms are pretentiously retained in brackets, and other key words are left unglossed. Five pages in which Maravall specifically addresses the relationship of classicism to the baroque inexplicably have been omitted from the Introduction. The best approach for those not able to consult the Spanish is to push on and even skim when the syntax seems especially exasperating. The image of a European baroque, seen from the Spanish perspective, will emerge nonetheless from the surprising juxtaposition, the vivid journalistic quotation, and the illuminating detail.

Works Cited

Cruickshank, Donald. "'Literature' and the book trade in Golden-Age Spain."
    MLR 73 (1978): 799-824.
Stern, Charlotte. "Lope de Vega, Propagandist?" *Bulletin of the Comediantes* 34
    (1982): 1-36.

Sous le signe des échanges culturels

Marie-Odile Sweetser
University of Illinois (Chicago)

Corneille, Tasso and Modern Poetics. BY A. DONALD SELLSTROM. Columbus: Ohio State UP, 1986.

Le mérite essentiel de cet important ouvrage, élégamment présenté par les soins des presses universitaires d'Ohio State, consiste à nos yeux à placer Corneille et sa poétique dans le contexte des échanges culturels entre la France et l'Italie et à établir des correspondances idéologiques et esthétiques entre deux grands écrivains incarnant l'un et l'autre l'esprit de la renaissance culturelle et spirituelle post-tridentine. Les historiens de la littérature les plus autorisés avaient bien vu en Corneille le dramaturge qui avait traduit avec le plus de force, grace à des dons remarquables d'intelligence et d'imagination, le génie de la Contre-Réforme en France. A. Donald Sellstrom s'appuie d'ailleurs sur les travaux essentiels d'André Stegmann, de Marc Fumaroli et de Germain Poirier, les deux premiers s'étant surtout attachés à l'influence des théoriciens et du théatre italien sur Corneille, le dernier à la tradition philosophique, psychologique et morale venue de l'antiquité gréco-romaine, reprise et modifiée par les pères de l'Eglise et par les penseurs italiens et français dans les temps modernes. L'auteur de *Corneille, Tasso and Modern Poetics* s'adresse de façon précise à des textes et n'hésite pas, avec audace et modestie à la fois, à passer par dessus les frontières linguistiques, chronologiques et génériques pour établir des ponts, proposer des rapprochements et dégager une vision commune à deux grands écrivains appartenant à des langues et à des générations différentes, suffisamment proches toutefois l'un de l'autre par la culture et l'esprit pour justifier de tels rapprochements. A. Donald Sellstrom, en bon comparatiste, reprend les choses d'assez haut et d'assez loin pour montrer, de façon pertinente, l'existence, chez les deux poètes, d'une conception similaire de l'essence et du but de leur art.

Un témoignage artistique tout à fait révélateur l'a confirmé dans son intuition initiale. Dans l'inventaire de 1653 des meubles et d'objets d'art appartenant au cardinal Mazarin, se trouve la description d'un "cabinet" décoré de dix miniatures représentant Apollon et les neuf muses avec aux quatre coins des portraits, ceux de deux poètes anciens et de deux poètes modernes: Homère et Virgile d'une part, le Tasse et Corneille de l'autre. Voici donc chez un fin connaisseur et collectionneur averti, chez un homme d'état doublé d'un mécène, un signe certain de la position éminente et conjointe du Tasse et de Corneille, placés au même rang que les deux plus célèbres poètes de l'antiquité classique. Le fait que trois de ces grands hommes étaient surtout connus pour leurs créations dans le domaine épique, Corneille dans celui du théâtre ne devait pas constituer une différence notable aux yeux du mécène ou du public lettré du 17ième siècle: ils étaient tous quatre poètes, placés au premier rang et avaient chacun, illustré leur langue, leur pays et leur siècle.

D'ailleurs, l'œuvre du Tasse ne se limitait pas au genre épique. Il avait écrit pour le théâtre un *Torrismondo* qui avait dû connaître un succès assez marqué, car la pièce fut traduite en français par Charles Vion d'Alibray en 1636. Dans un très intéressant article, Daniela Dalla Valle souligne judicieusement la signification d'un tel choix et cite une phrase de *l'Avis*, rédigé par d'Alibray, à la louange du Tasse "autheur universel" qui "sans parler de tant de discours et de dialogues qu'il nous a laissés en prose, a travaillé et réussy parfaitement en toutes sortes de Poésie, mais particulièrment en la Dramatique et aux pièces de Théâtre" (106). D. Dalla Valle met également en valeur l'attitude "moderniste" du traducteur qui a choisi un poète moderne et "moderniste" lui aussi, ayant su montrer son indépendance à l'égard des règles dans le choix du sujet du *Torrismondo*.

C'est bien un modernisme partagé par le Tasse et Corneille qui est au coeur de l'argument développé par A. D. Sellstrom. Si Corneille n'a pas mentionné le Tasse à côté d'autres théoriciens italiens, ceci ne veut pas dire qu'il n'ait pas connu l'œuvre théorique, dramatique et poétique d'un écrivain dont la réputation était répandue à travers l'Europe. Il est avéré que le *Torrismon* avait été joué au Marais l'année du *Cid*, avec le même acteur Mondory, que Corneille et d'Alibray étaient tous deux Normands et avaient un ami commun, Saint-Amant. Des rapports personnels entre le traducteur du Tasse et Corneille étaient donc probables. De plus, une traduction française par Beaudoin des *Discorsi del Poema Eroico* (1594) avait paru en 1638. Avant ces *Discours* consacrés au poème héroïque, le Tasse avait écrit un premier groupe de *Discorsi dell' Arte Poetica*, publiés en 1587, mais rédigés plus tôt et incorporés par la suite dans les *Discorsi* de 1594. C'est dire que les questions générales de poétique avaient occupé le poète italien tout au long de sa carrière. Comme Corneille, il n'avait publié ses vues qu'assez tardivement.

Selon A. D. Sellstrom, ce fut la querelle du *Cid* qui amena Corneille à prendre clairement conscience des tendances fondamentales de sa poétique, et à lui communiquer l'ambition de faire pour la littérature française ce que le Tasse avait fait pour la littérature italienne. Le nom du poète italien apparaît en effet à propos du *Cid*. Fortin de la Hoguette compare la réussite de Corneille à celles d'Homère, de Virgile et du Tasse; Chapelain, dans les *Sentiments de l'Académie* évoque les conséquences bénéfiques des querelles littéraires suscitées par la *Jérusalem Délivrée* et le *Pastor Fido*. Pour le critique, le poète doit modifier ses sources pour rendre son œuvre conforme aux mœurs et aux valeurs morales de son temps, théorie soutenue par le Tasse pour l'épopée: c'est de ce point de vue que le dénouement du *Cid* est condamné. Dans sa lettre à l'Académie, Scudéry citait également le Tasse qui avait répondu à l'Accademia della Crusca par une *Apologia della Gerusalemme liberata* avec modestie, tandis que Corneille avait montré beaucoup de hauteur dans sa *Lettre apologétique*. L'auteur du *Cid* allait toutefois adopter une autre attitude dans *l'Epître* de la *Suivante* en 1637 et reconnaître que l'écrivain devait s'efforcer d'approcher le plus possible de la perfection afin d'obtenir un "applaudissement universel". S'il ne mentionne pas le Tasse, c'est sans doute pour ne pas paraître céder aux arguments avancés par Scudéry, suggère l'auteur qui entend montrer que d'*Horace* à *Héraclius*, Corneille allait entreprendre de faire pour la tragédie ce que le Tasse avait accompli pour l'épopée.

C'est dans ce sens qu'il interprète *Polyeucte*, à la lumière du célèbre livre IV de l'*Enéide*, centré sur les amours tragiques de Didon et d'Enée: celles de Polyeucte et de Pauline en seraient une reprise christianisée. Nous avions, de notre côté, soutenu qu'il s'agissait bien dans les deux cas d'une femme abandonnée par un héros chargé d'une mission d'origine divine, mais que Pauline, contrairement aux héroïnes antiques, Didon et Médée, ne se livrait ni au désespoir ni à la vengeance. Les héroïnes cornéliennes, Pauline, Cléopâtre (dans *La Mort de Pompée*), sont représentées comme chastes, contrairement à leurs modèles; les princes héritiers,

Antiochus en particulier, dans *Rodogune*, comme vertueux, contrairement aux sources historiques. L'auteur décèle dans ce perfectionnement moral opéré par le dramaturge l'influence de la querelle et du Tasse.

Si *Polyeucte* peut être considéré comme une version moderne et christianisée du livre IV de l'*Enéide*, Marc Fumaroli a montré que dans *Rodogune*, Corneille reprenait en la modifiant la tragédie d'*Electre*. De plus, la mère coupable qui se préparait à empoisonner son fils, comme Médée, est punie: un dénouement moral s'attache donc aux actions criminelles de cette "nouvelle Médée".

Dans ces transformations, l'auteur voit l'influence indéniable des principes exposés dans les *Discorsi del poema eroico* sur le caractère élevé des héros et de l'amour devenu une passion noble. Polyeucte par sa vertu correspond plutôt au héros épique qu'au héros tragique, selon le Tasse, qui suit Aristote dans sa définition d'un personnage ni tout à fait bon ni tout à fait méchant. Corneille affirme donc ainsi son indépendance à l'égard même du Tasse.

L'auteur estime qu'en voulant égaler Virgile et le Tasse, Corneille, opérant dans le cadre plus restreint de la tragédie, devait avoir recours à une suite de pièces pour réaliser un effet à l'échelle de l'œuvre épique: *Horace*, *Cinna* et *Polyeucte* doivent donc être considérées comme formant un tout, une trilogie retraçant l'histoire de Rome de ses origines à son apogée et à sa transformation en capitale du monde chrétien. Corneille réussit à créer dans sa trilogie un effet semblable à celui créé par Virgile dans l'*Enéide*: la naissance de l'empire romain annoncée dans *Horace*, réalisée dans *Cinna*, christianisée dans *Polyeucte*.

L'auteur suggère également la possibilité d'une interprétation allégorique de la trilogie, comme dans la *Divine Comédie* avec l'enfer, *Horace*; le purgatoire, *Cinna*; le paradis, *Polyeucte*.

Le chapitre sur *La Mort de Pompée* reprend un brillant article paru dans *PMLA* en 1982. Pour cette pièce, Corneille se tourne vers une source épique, la *Pharsale* de Lucain, mais inverse la signification de sa source. Lucain avait montré les horreurs de la guerre civile, Corneille insiste sur la grandeur romaine face à la corruption de l'Egypte. Cette grandeur morale apparaît dans la conduite de César à l'égard de Cornélie, dans celle de Cornélie à l'égard de César bien qu'ils appartiennent à des camps opposés; Cléopâtre montre, elle aussi, une générosité toute romaine. Pourtant, contrairement aux pièces précédentes, le dénouement n'aboutit pas à une réconciliation. En face de ces généreux, le roi d'Egypte et ses conseillers représentent la décadence politique et morale dans le machiavélisme et l'assassinat. L'action inspirée par l'histoire ne correspond pas à la vision épique choisie par le dramaturge, montrant l'opposition entre la vertu et le crime, d'où l'impression d'ambiguité, César est bien un héros épique, inspiré par la colère et l'amour. Mais l'intrigue amoureuse n'aboutira pas, à cause de la loi romaine: un dénouement heureux, avec une intervention providentielle, n'est donc pas possible.

Dans les pièces centrées sur des personnages monstrueux, *Rodogune, Théodore, Héraclius*, Corneille a dû tenter de réduire le champ où s'exercent les forces du mal pour ne pas lui conférer des proportions épiques. Les sinistres menées de Cléopâtre, de Marcelle et de Phocas ont lieu à l'intérieur d'une famille.

Il y a sans doute des différences entre l'amour pastoral évoqué dans l'*Aminta* du Tasse et l'amour spiritualisé de Théodore, mais le schéma fondamental des deux pièces est très proche. L'amour généreux se voit récompensé dans l'*Aminta* par le mariage, par une union spirituelle dans le martyre, dans *Théodore*. Il nous semble que Corneille a voulu compenser les aspects atroces de cette tragédie par des éléments pastoraux: amour idyllique de Théodore et de Didyme, rêves de bonheur dans l'évasion de l'amoureux repoussé, Placide. On consultera à ce sujet l'article récent d'Alain Couprie.

Dans le *Torrismondo*, le Tasse avait utilisé un héros de type aristotélicien, et la pièce se terminait par un double suicide. Héraclius, au contraire, est un généreux, et la pièce comporte un dénouement providentiel avec le rétablissement de l'héritier légitime sur le trône. Corneille applique une fois de plus à la tragédie ce que le Tasse avait recommandé pour l'épopée, et réaffirme sa préférence pour un héros supérieur sinon parfait, de Rodrigue à Héraclius.

La conscience aiguë que le poète a de son art se trouve confirmée par une lecture allégorique des pièces, selon l'auteur. Horace serait une allégorie du combat singulier que Corneille avait dû livrer contre lui-même après la querelle du *Cid* pour se soumettre aux critiques de l'Académie et prendre sa revanche par une nouvelle pièce. L'iconoclasme de *Polyeucte* traduirait dramatiquement celui que Corneille pratiquait dans le domaine de la création littéraire en transformant ses modèles. En mettant en valeur le thème de la persécution dans *Théodore*, Corneille devait songer à la "persécution" subie par le *Cid*. L'héroïne représenterait la muse cornélienne, chaste et pure. Une *Teodora* de Rospigliosi avait connu un grand succès à la cour d'Urbain VIII Barberini, protecteur de Mazarin: une Théodore française pouvait paraître la meilleure forme d'hommage au mécénat de Mazarin et à la cour de Rome.

Le principe fondamental de la poétique cornélienne reste, à la fin des années 40, celui de la liberté de l'artiste, son droit de modifier à son gré, pour le plus grand plaisir du spectateur le matériau utilisé. Dans l'*Avertissement* du *Cid* de 1648, après avoir loué Aristote et les principes fondamentaux de sa *Poétique*, il déclare que "pour le reste" des modifications sont toujours possibles lorsque les conditions changent. La même position de relativisme selon une évolution culturelle et morale se retrouve dans le *Discours* de la tragédie où il invoque la différence de mentalité et de goût entre la Grèce du Ve siècle et la France de 1660. Il se voyait comme un moderne et son art comme un art de son temps, implicitement accordé aux valeurs d'une culture contemporaine.

Les spécialistes des théories dramatiques, du théâtre et de l'histoire des mentalités et du goût au 17e siècle trouveront donc dans cet ouvrage élégant et concis, mais riche de substance, des vues extrêmement neuves et stimulantes, et une véritable ouverture sur la culture et l'art suscités par la Contre-Réforme, en Italie et en France. On y perçoit une évolution caractéristique par rapport à la première Renaissance, marquée surtout par le retour à l'antiquité gréco-latine et par la création d'une littérature vernaculaire inspirée par les Anciens. La génération du Tasse à la fin du 16e siècle, celle de Corneille au début du 17e vont plus loin, sans toutefois rejeter les œuvres canoniques appartenant à la tradition antique—Homère et Virgile restent des maîtres, même si l'on se permet de les améliorer—mais en y ajoutant d'autres œuvres choisies parmi les plus grandes des Modernes, en modifiant les anciennes et en y infusant les croyances et l'idéal moral et spirituel légués par une autre tradition, judéo-chrétienne celle-là.

Une conséquence curieuse et inattendue de la thèse brillamment soutenue par l'auteur: Corneille émule du Tasse et créateur d'un héros tragique moderne et d'une véritable vision providentielle, consiste à privilégier les chefs-d'œuvre *Horace*, *Cinna* et *Polyeucte*, ce qui semblerait un retour aux vues traditionnelles, alors que depuis la grande thèse de Georges Couton, *La Vieillesse de Corneille*, le mouvement de la critique a été vers la redécouverte de l'œuvre dans son ensemble, dans sa variété et dans sa richesse. Il est certain qu'avec *Polyeucte*, Corneille était parvenu à l'achèvement d'un cycle, et qu'il a dû chercher ailleurs d'autres sources d'intérêt dramatique. Le mythe de Rome offre sans doute une fascination particulière pour des spectateurs et lecteurs formés dans la tradition "classique" et pour des esprits du 20ième siècle qui se penchent sur les causes de la grandeur et de la décadence des empires. Toutefois, l'auteur de cet excellent ouvrage ne s'offusquera pas de nous voir réaffirmer notre admiration et notre goût pour les chefs-d'œuvre "barbares" que sont *Rodogune*, *Théodore*, *Nicomède*, *Pertharite*,

Attila, Suréna, pour ceux de la décadence romaine, *Sertorius* et *Othon*, et pour la byzantine, *Pulchérie*.

Ouvrages cités

Couprie, Alain. "Corneille et le mythe pastoral." *Dix-septième siècle* avril-juin 1986: 159-166.

Dalla Valle, Daniela. "*Le Torrismon du Tasse* par Charles Vion d'Alibray. Entre tragédie et tragi-comédie." *Cahiers de littérature du 17e siècle* 6 (1984): 105-114.

Fumaroli, Marc. "Tragique païen et tragique chrétien dans *Rodogune*." *Revue des Sciences humaines* oct.-déc. 1973: 599-631).

Sellstrom, A. Donald. "*La Mort de Pompée*: Roman History and Tasso's Theory of the Epic." *PMLA* (Oct., 1982): 830-43.

An Unusually Informed Teacher

Philip A. Wadsworth
University of South Carolina (retired)

La Fontaine. BY MARIE-ODILE SWEETSER. Twayne World Author Series 788. Boston: Twayne Publishers, 1987.

It is good news that the Twayne World Author Series has finally added La Fontaine to its French list, entrusting the assignment to a dedicated scholar in the field of seventeenth-century French literature. Professor Marie-Odile Sweetser is widely known for her books on Corneille and for various articles on other classical writers. Her volume on La Fontaine follows a familiar Twayne pattern. Its purpose is to provide a compact "life and works" written in English, presented so that it can be read easily or consulted by most members of the academic community, and based on up-to-date scholarship and the best critical editions.

This last goal gives the book much of its originality. It contains not only the standard information on La Fontaine but also a well-digested survey of pertinent recent research. The author does not propose any new theories or adhere to any particular school of analysis. Her approach to texts is that of an unusually well-informed teacher. Her comments are derived from a wide range of critical materials, including the methodologies developed in the last thirty or forty years. On almost every page she cites her authorities and indicates her indebtedness to them. They are far too numerous to list here but some of the names that recur frequently are: Bernard Beugnot, J.-P. Collinet, Patrick Dandrey, Richard Danner, Madeleine Defrenne, Nathan Gross, Marcel Gutwirth, John Lapp, Beverly Ridgely, David Lee Rubin, Jacqueline Van Baelen, Michael Vincent, and Philip Wadsworth.

After some preliminary materials—preface, acknowledgements, chronology—the book's main text unfolds swiftly, filling only 133 pages. It consists of seven dense chapters and a brief Conclusion and is followed by a substantial scholarly apparatus: notes and references, an extensive bibliography, and a rather limited index (it covers the central text but not the notes). The first chapter deals with La Fontaine's family and social background and the little that is known about his first thirty years. Then the emphasis shifts from biography to the study of his literary productions. Professor. Sweetser groups his works in roughly chronological order, with chapters on the Vaux period, on his *contes* and *Clymène*, on the fable collection of 1668, on *Psyché*, on the fables published in 1678-79, and finally on the late poems and the fables of Book 12. Along the way she introduces many passages by La Fontaine, given in both French and English. Quotations from the fables are accompanied by Marianne Moore's rhymed but very inaccurate English version; other texts are translated, more literally, by Professor Sweetser herself.

This kind of book tends to focus on old favorites and selected masterpieces. Some of La Fontaine's minor poems are left unmentioned or brushed aside. The author devotes only a few sentences to his early comedy based on Terence, *L'Eunuque*, and scarcely alludes to his various failures as a dramatic poet and opera librettist. These omissions are doubtless unavoidable.

The first work to be treated at length is the mythological idyll, *Adonis* (13-26). Professor Sweetser recounts the history of the poet's two versions, the early manuscript in honor of his wealthy patron, Nicolas Fouquet, and the printed edition many years later. As she summarizes the poem she pauses to discuss its many facets, such as its reflections of ancient literature and mythology, its themes that foreshadow *Psyché* and the fables, its many ironic and humorous touches, and its rather flowery "heroic" style. In this same chapter on the poet's works inspired by Fouquet and the artistic ambience at Vaux one finds an excellent treatment of *Le Songe de Vaux* (26-31) and a brief account of the *Relation d'un voyage de Paris en Limousin* (33-35).

At least half of Professor Sweetser's book is devoted, naturally, to the fables. She provides useful background information—on the history of the genre, on the poet's chief sources, on his announced intentions. Then, in the course of three important chapters, she studies the fables book by book in the order that La Fontaine gathered them together and published them, i.e., in the collections of 1668, 1678-79, and 1693. This approach, although monotonous at times, has the merit of being roughly chronological; one can watch the maturing of the poet's thought and art. Also, each of the twelve books has a partially visible structure of its own: often an introductory passage (in a dedication or in the initial fable), a striking finale, and in the midsection some clusters of fables with subtle thematic relationsips that scholars have tried to decipher, with some degree of success.

Professor Sweetser's Chapter 4 covers Books 1-6 of the fables. Her method is to salute many of these poems in passing and to linger over a few of them that are perennial favorites or that have features demanding special attention. In Book 1 she examines "La Cigale et la Fourmi," "Le Loup et le Chien," "Le Loup et L'Agneau," and "Le Chêne et le Roseau," discussing their ideas and style, along with diverse critical interpretations. This groundwork enables her to quicken the pace and, regrettably, give fewer details in dealing with Books 2 through 6.

La Fontaine's later fables, i.e. those in Books 7 through 12, are generally considered to be his greatest achievement. Professor Sweetser allows herself to comment carefully on at least fifteen of these fables, selecting two or three from each book. She refers to other investigators nearly all questions of literary form, preferring to concentrate on the explanatory material—in areas of hitory, science, philosophy, and religion—that any reader needs to bear in mind in order to grasp the intellectual content of these fables. I recommend this section of her book, together with the fables themselves, to any student seeking to understand seventeenth-century culture (see 92-115 and 123-31). As for textual nuances, ironies, and ambivalences, many of the fables are being studied again and again, with new insights and research methods being employed. Problems of interpretation abound in La Fontaine and are likely to be debated indefinitely.

Professor Sweetser's valuable commentary on the fables is matched by her treatment of La Fontaine's "novel" in prose and verse, *Les Amours de Psyché et de Cupidon* (75-88). She examines not only the story and its themes but also its mysterious framework (the conversations among four literary friends as they visit the gardens at Versailles) and several related topics: the memories of Vaux, the heroine's spiritual itinerary, the use of comic and tragic effects etc. She also deals sympathetically with a number of La Fontaine's occasional poems on diverse themes, whether amorous (the group of four elegies), religious (*Saint Malc*), scientific (*Le Quinquina*), literary (the *Epître à Huet*) or introspective and self-critical (the second *Discours à Mme de La Sablière*). The pages devoted to these brief works and several others provide a good illustration of the poet's versatility.

I have a small complaint to make concerning the brevity of Chapter 3, entitled "*Les Contes, Clymène.*" Professor Sweetser gives an adequate description of only one story, *Joconde*, among the 70 or so that La Fontaine composed. Some readers dislike these tales in verse because of their frequent use of a popular, singsong style or their persistent satire of the clergy and of women. But they are not really vulgar, shocking, or irreligious, and many are masterpieces of humorous fiction. They deserve to be better known. Similarly, the two pages on *Clymène* seem quite insufficient. This comic fantasy, in which the nine Muses act out dramatic scenes and recite various types of love poems, is full of ideas about poetry. It shows La Fontaine experimenting with many styles and genres and almost amounts to an *art poétique*. It is one of the keys to his apirations as a poet.

But these reservations arise from questions of emphasis or differences in personal tastes; they do not detract from my very high opinion of Professor Sweetser's book. It provides a reliable guide to the life and writings of La Fontaine and to most of the works written about him. It will be valued for many years to come by students and teachers of French literature.

L'être sous le paraître

Roger Duchêne
Université d'Aix-Marseille

"Appelle-moi Pierrot," Wit and Irony in the Lettres *of Mme de Sévigné.* PAR JO ANN RECKER. Purdue University Monographs in Romance Languages. Philadelphia: Benjamins, 1986.

A condition de comprendre le français, les lecteurs de *"Appelle-moi Pierrot," Wit and Irony in the* Lettres *of Mme de Sévigné* ne s'ennuieront pas. Le livre de Jo Ann Marie Recker est une excellente anthologie des passages les plus amusants de la "spirituelle marquise," comme on dit volontiers depuis Voltaire. A tort, souligne l'auteur, dans la mesure où l'expression privilégie le talent de l'épistolière pour raconter des bagatelles avec vivacité au détriment de son acuité intellectuelle et de la profondeur de sa vision des êtres et des choses. Les exemples donnés par Jo Ann Marie Recker et ses brillants commentaires ont vite fait de convaincre le lecteur que Mme de Sévigné n'est pas une femme superficielle et qui gaspillerait son esprit. Elle l'emploie à séduire ses correspondants, mais aussi à démasquer les hypocrisies et à dénoncer les incongruités, bref à saisir l'être sous le paraître.

La justesse du projet, sur un sujet moins frivole qu'il n'en a l'air, et la finesse que Jo Ann Marie Recker manifeste dans maintes analyses de détail font d'autant plus regretter qu'elle ait choisi une méthode qui la conduisait nécessairement dans un impasse. "L'étude que voici," annonce-t-elle, "utilise la critique moderne sur Molière comme moyen de comprendre Mme de Sévigné." Son plan même reproduit les points de vue (*areas*) de W.G. Moore (*Mask, Scene, Speech*), précédés d'un chapitre "Transitions." Il faudrait un miracle pour que des catégories définies à propos d'un comédien auteur de pièces de théâtre conviennent sans modification à une grande dame qui écrit des lettres privées à sa fille et à ses amis. Jo

Ann Marie Recker, qui a bien senti l'importance du témoin-destinataire (et non du spectateur) dans l'art épistolaire aurait mieux fait de suivre cette piste pour analyser précisément et systématiquement quand et comment l'esprit et l'ironie conviennent ou non à la lettre. Le plaisir de "rabutiner" avec Bussy crée un climat quasi constant. Le souci de retenir l'attention de Mme de Grignan par des morceaux de bravoure ou des rapides signes de complicité dans des lettres régulières brillent comme des éclairs dans une correspondance où il y a beaucoup d'autres modes d'expression et quelquefois des "landes."

Mme de Sévigné aimait Molière. Elle l'a souvent cité. Ce n'est pas suffisant pour conclure à l'étroite parenté de leur esprit et de leur technique. La différence des genres, des sexes, des milieux sociaux change presque tout. Jo Ann Marie Recker s'abrite derrière un commentaire de Mme Gérard pour citer un passage où la marquise regrette que Molière soit mort, qui aurait fait une "scène merveilleuse" de Daquin "enragé de n'avoir pas le bon remède." Mais voilà, justement, Mme de Sévigné a "étranglé" le sujet, ne consacrant que quelques lignes à ce qui aurait pu être une scène, et son esprit se marque au changement d'échelle. Jo Ann Marie Recker compare un passage plein de sous-entendus racontant la dernière soirée de l'épistolière avec Guitaut à la fameuse scène du le de *L'Ecole des Femmes*. C'est oublier que dans la lettre, les doubles sens tirent leur sel et leur force de ce qu'ils ont eu lieu entre personnes averties et qu'ils sont racontés à une tierce personne également avertie, alors que chez Molière le comique vient du décalage entre la peur d'Arnolphe et l'innocence d'Agnès.

Appliquer aux lettres de Mme de Sévigné la théorie du ridicule de la *Lettre sur l'Imposteur* est sans doute de meilleure méthode. Mais il aurait fallu d'abord se demander d'où venait cette théorie et si elle était originale. On ne devrait pas écrire sur l'esprit et l'ironie au XVIIème siècle sans rappeler que rien n'est alors plus répandu et plus vague que la première notion alors que la seconde y est inconnue. Jo Ann Marie Recker aurait, selon nous, mieux fait de partir des mots sévignéens (*folie* ou *plaisant* par exemple) et de suivre grâce à eux la méthode cartésienne des dénombrements complets. Au lieu de brillantes intuitions, on aurait eu quelques conclusions sûres.

Racine, texte et prétexte

Jean Dubu

Re-lectures raciniennes: nouvelles approches du discours tragique.
EDITÉ PAR RICHARD L. BARNETT. Biblio 17. Tübingen: PFSCL, 1986.
Racine: le jansénisme et la modernité. PAR M.-F. BRUNEAU. Paris:
José Corti, 1986. *Dramatic Narrative: Racine's Récits.* PAR NINA C.
ECKSTEIN. New York: Peter Lang, 1986.

Trois volumes en provenance directe ou indirecte des Etats-Unis
ont marqué au cours de l'année 1986 la contribution d'outre-
Atlantique principalement à cet outre-tombe de Racine, l'une des
formes de la survie devant et par la postérité, cette survie constituant
elle-même un aspect du classicisme.

Les titres, on le voit, balancent du projet ambitieux au simple
énoncé, voire à la résignation au fragmentaire. Sous un certain
angle, c'est résumer assez correctement le statut actuel des
publications consacrées à Racine. De prime abord, certes, on peut
s'interroger sur l'usage, et l'abus éventuel, du terme *lectures* (ou *re-*
lectures). Faut-il redire, une fois encore, et en dépit du trop fameux:
"Si l'on s'était contenté de la mettre sur le papier, j'en serais encore
plus content..." de Quesnel, que les pièces de Racine n'ont jamais
été conçues comme "spectacle dans un fauteuil"? Elles sont
destinées à être jouées, interprétées sur scène, donc vues et
entendues. Même si les erreurs des comédiens nous choquent
parfois, elles ne laissent pas de nous instruire, sinon sur la pièce
elle-même, du moins sur le goût de nos contemporains, dont les
acteurs cherchent *munerum causà* à se concilier l'approbation. Il est
au demeurant plus aisé d'admettre une divergence de goût (Horace a
même fourni une excellente formule qui l'autorise) que de voir les
délicatesses du poète, les finesses d'une langue souveraine, bref
l'art, soumis au lit de Procruste des doctrines, livré à l'arbitraire des
"grilles," meurtri par l'inéluctable et fallacieuse cohérence des

systèmes. Un créateur, un poète, n'est pas un philosophe. Platon
que Racine a si bien su entendre et traduire, l'aurait banni de la
République!

Toute déliée que soit son intelligence dans l'exercice délicat du
maniement des concepts, si bien rompue à saisir l'enchaînement des
doctrines (ses premier et troisième chapitres, avec l'exposé des
thèses de Blumenberg en apporte la preuve), M.-F. Bruneau
n'échappe pas à cet écueil. Au simple aspect du volume et à la
lecture du titre, on a pu, à bon droit, ressentir quelque effroi devant
l'énoncé du jansénisme et à la perspective qu'il soit réduit à ne
former que l'une des trois composantes de l'ouvrage. On l'est
encore davantage—et peut-être par contraste—à la lecture du texte:
assez fréquemment utilisé, le terme n'est jamais défini avec clarté, à
supposer d'ailleurs que cela soit possible. Il semble pris comme une
évidence. La caution invoquée (63, n.10) du livre d'Alexander
Sedgwick, est certes rassurante, pour l'auteur; mais l'esprit critique
nous semble, en l'occurrence, requérir une définition, une tentative
de réflexion personnelle. De fort bons esprits (le chanoine
Martimort, par exemple) ont parfois soutenu que le jansénisme n'a
jamais existé; moins catégoriques, d'autres inclinent à penser avec
Sainte-Beuve et pour s'en tenir à Port-Royal que divers jansénismes
ont co existé et se sont succédé. Un coup d'oeil aux sept ou huit
plus récentes livraisons annuelles des *Chroniques de Port-Royal*
permet de mesurer les nuances importantes qui séparent sans les
opposer fondamentalement solitaires ou moniales pris chacun dans
leur autonomie de personnes adultes et responsables. Pour
demeurer dans les entours de Racine, à quelques semaines
d'intervalle, on peut distinguer le modeste: "Je ne pense ceci que
pour moi, car je n'aime à juger ni condamner personne" de Duguet,
à propos d'*Esther* qu'il a "trouvée parfaitement belle" mais à laquelle
il ne voudrait "pas néanmoins avoir assisté," de la phrase plus
abrupte de Quesnel que nous avons rappelée plus haut. Le fond de
l'opinion n'est pas essentiellement différent, mais que de nuances de
l'un à l'autre! Comme il paraît hasardeux alors de nommer *le*
jansénisme et de l'invoquer comme une idée claire, un concept
immanent. Des coupes plus fines, une approche moins simple
auraient sans doute réclamé un propos plus étendu, ou bien une
ambition plus restreinte. Quant à la *modernité*!... Troquant au
besoin Blumenberg pour Goldmann, Barthes, Foucault, voire Mme
Kristeva (M.-F.Bruneau s'avance rarement seule dans l'aventure
intellectuelle, et elle en est si consciente lorsque cela se produit,
qu'elle ne néglige pas de nous en instruire (v. notamment p. 136, n.
11), l'auteur voit en *Athalie* un exemple d'affirmation de soi, de

"libération féminine," pour ne pas dire féministe. Sans doute, Racine a placé ironiquement sur les lèvres de Mathan, l'apostat, le terrible:

> Elle flotte, elle hésite, en un mot elle est femme.

(On conviendra bien volontiers qu'on n'est guère surpris de ne pas voir ce vers cité dans ce savant ouvrage). Plutôt que de chercher, après L. Marin, à opposer assez simplement l'écrivain chargé d'écrire l'histoire du roi et l'écrivain de théâtre, on peut, à cette occasion, souligner chez Racine une remarquable cohérence (apologie de la légitimité incarnée en Joas, condamnation du régicide en la personne d'Athalie, respect de la loi salique, trois données conformes à la pratique judicieuse de Louis XIV après les trois régences féminines que ce pays avait connues en un siècle). Une autre héroïne de la pièce est injustement négligée: Josabet, l'inquiète, la discrète et touchante Josabet. A ce sujet, deux données historiques ne sauraient être négligées. L'une concerne Racine: lorsque Mme de Maintenon décide qu'il n'y aura pas de représentations publiques d'*Athalie* à Saint-Cyr, le jour même Louis XIV attribue au poète pour une somme infime—ce qui revient à un présent de sa part—une charge anoblissante. Les chansonniers du temps n'ont pas manqué d'établir un lien entre les deux événements:

> Ta famille en est anoblie,
> Mais ton nom ne le sera pas.

L'autre donnée concerne la pièce elle-même, qui sera reprise et représentée en 1702 à Versailles; les pensionnaires de Saint-Cyr ne feront que chanter les chœurs; les rôles seront tenus par des princes de la famille royale: la duchesse de Bourgogne sera justement Josabet et l'on demandera à la femme d'un parlementaire, Mme de Chailly de jouer Athalie. N'est-ce pas la preuve qu'il n'était pas concevable qu'un personnage aussi affreux puisse fournir, fût-ce par jeu, un rôle à une princesse, le cas échéant future régente? C'est pourquoi nous ne pouvons souscrire à l'une des conclusions de M.-F.Bruneau:

> En somme le portrait que Racine nous fait d'Athalie est celui du monarque idéal qui aurait bien pu servir de modèle à Louis XIV. (131)

Mais l'auteur a hâte d'en venir à la conclusion brillante que voici, qui ne surprend pas après l'énoncé des thèses de Mme Kristeva:

Le texte de Racine expose que l'absolutisme quel qu'il soit est
toujours un signe de fragilité. Si la fragilité du moi, dans son
désir d'absolutisme, peut le mener au carrefour de la phobie, de
l'obsession et de la perversion, la fragilité de l'absolutisme social
et politique mène au carrefour du sacré et de la mystification.
Racine en créant une héroïne moderne, libre de la représentation
du féminin fabriquée par le patriarcat monothéiste nous permet
de nous poser la question d'une telle métaphore dans ce système.
Effet du patriarcat, la métaphorisation de l'abject par les femmes
est en même temps un instrument qui permet de justifier et de
perpétuer au niveau de l'inconscient politique l'oppression et la
répression des femmes. (137-38)

Lorsqu'en 1702, Racine mort et Guillaume d'Orange agonisant,
Louis XIV faisait représenter *Athalie* à Versailles tandis qu'Anne
Stuart montait sur le trône d'Angleterre, quelle était la part de la
conscience politique, du hasard ou de la conjoncture? La question
n'est pas posée dans l'ouvrage, et nous n'entendons pas y apporter
de réponse. Mais le vers de Mathan cité plus haut ("Elle flotte, elle
hésite..."), remarquable par l'économie des moyens, dévalorise
simultanément Athalie par le jugement qu'un homme en qui elle a
mis sa confiance, un de ses "courtisans," porte sur la reine, et
Mathan lui-même, par la médisance si bien dénoncée par B.
Castiglione (129).

Il y a contre-sens évident à voir en Athalie un possible modèle de
Louis XIV: dans l'optique monarchique, le prince qui a causé
sciemment la mort d'un chef d'Etat se trouve disqualifié *ipso facto*:
c'est l'erreur de Créon dans *La Thébaïde*, c'est la raison qui autorise
Titus à retourner contre Bérénice l'arme du chantage au suicide. La
Reine montre qu'elle a parfaitement compris l'Empereur lorsqu'elle
déclare:

...je vivrai, je suivrai vos ordres absolus.

Mais M.-F. Bruneau n'a cure de tels détails. En appelant à Barthes
(133), ne déclare-t-elle pas: "Racine ne s'embarrasse pas d'un
maladroit grand-mère dans les imprécations d'Athalie:

Voici ce qu'en mourant lui souhaite une mère (v. 1783),

sans que ni l'un ni l'autre apparemment ne songe que, d'une part,
les bienséances de la scène tragique concourent admirablement à
l'ironie du texte et que, d'autre part, Racine lui-même, trente ans
auparavant, employait le terme de mère en parlant de Marie Des
Moulins, sa grand'mère (lettre du 3 janvier 1662 notamment). Les
bienséances!... Même en faisant la part d'une certaine "épate au
bourgeois" (*nil novi..*!) qui colore le nouveau discours critique, M.-

F. Bruneau réussit à renchérir sur la paronomase de Mme Kristeva objet/abject, grâce à une amphibologie:

> "A chaque moi son objet, à chaque sur-moi son abject" (Kristeva, 10). Bérénice, en qui sont confondus l'objet et l'abjec, ne peut être combattue par Titus que par une adéquation totale de son moi à la Loi. (109)

Moi de Titus, ou moi de Bérénice, on peut hésiter; mais ce qui est sûr, c'est que, *o tempora! o verba!*, Bérénice est *l'abject* de Titus. Mais l'auteur est moins heureuse encore lorsqu'elle en vient aux données proprement historiques. On peut ainsi lire: "Le Vatican reproche à Quesnel..." (76), l'innocent raccourci abolit deux siècles d'histoire. Plus loin la comtesse d'Armagnac devient princesse (79); quant à déclarer à la page suivante à propos d'*Alexandre*:

> Lue de cette façon, la pièce cesse d'être un irritant problème pour devenir une illustration de cette fable qui, à partir du droit romain et de la théologie catholique et de la croyance populaire, a forgé la notion de monarchie de droit divin...

—pour ne rien dire de l'anglicisme sous-jacent *forgé* (*élaboré* ou *créé de toutes pièces* conviendraient beaucoup mieux ici)—il convient de ne pas oublier que l'un des premiers théoriciens du droit divin des rois n'est autre que Jacques Stuart: du temps qu'il était Jacques VI d'Ecosse, il publiait anonymement *The True Law of a Free Monarchy* (1598), et l'année suivante, sous son nom, *Basilikon Doron*, lui, l'élève de George Buchanan. Quant à l'engoûment du public pour *Alexandre* en 1666, il s'explique par un processus d'identification et d'héroïsation. Après Louis XIII, prince mélancolique et parfois malchanceux, après deux cardinaux-ministres, dont un italien, après deux régentes, princesses étrangères, la France cultivée admire un prince jeune, séduisant, vigoureux, victorieux, jusqu'alors pacifique, et elle s'admire en lui; voir dans cet événement simple l'illustration de théories socio-politiques récentes, ne serait-ce pas, selon les propres paroles de Bossuet "prendre les choses pour ce qu'on voudrait qu'elles fussent," à quoi correspond bien le mot anglais *self-delusion*. Une toute récente mise en scène de la pièce (Cartoucherie de Vincennes, avril 1987) a montré qu'*Alexandre* n'est pas une pièce aussi insipide que l'ont répété ceux qui ne l'avaient que lue et que Racine, celui des chefs-d'œuvre, y est déjà présent en plus d'un endroit.

A la page 25, n.1, l'auteur reconnaît avoir emprunté le titre de son second chapitre: "Phèdre, Christ noir" à M. Gutwirth. L'image n'est pas dénuée de grandeur, mais l'introduction (26) d'une donnée non explicitée: "le Dieu de la scolastique," ne facilite en rien l'intelligence du reste, même s'il nous est précisé:

> Le divin dans cette pièce a toutes les caractéristiques paradoxales, contradictoires et mutuellement exclusives du dieu de la scolastique. Ces contradictions ne relèvent pas d'un héritage double affectant l'éducation de Racine, l'un antique, l'autre chrétien. Elles proviennent de plus loin, de l'origine même de la théologie chrétienne élaborée par les Pères de l'Eglise à partir du Dieu biblique, de la métaphysique antique et du Dieu Chrétien. Il s'agit de cet héritage même que la scolastique, désireuse de n'en abandonner aucun élément, essaya en vain d'amalgamer. (28)

Avouons notre déception: aucun nom à quoi rattacher tous ces vocables. Racine déclare lui-même lire Saint Thomas à Uzès; il a laissé de nombreuses notes de lecture de l'*Ecriture sainte* et des Pères de l'Eglise; mais on a ici l'impression que le vocable "scolastique" a valeur incantatoire, tout comme "jansénisme" ailleurs. Quant à la "modernité," il semble surtout qu'elle s'inscrive, *in fine*, dans le plaidoyer *pro femina* de Mme Kristeva relayé en ce chapitre 2 par Mme E. Berg, éventuellement par Mme E. Zimmermann.

Mais ne serait-ce pas jouer la difficulté pour la difficulté que de ne pas se souvenir de la remarque de Jean Giraudoux? Dans son petit essai sur *Racine* (Paris 1930), ne déclare-t-il pas avec un mélange inimitable de finesse et d'élégance qui n'exclut en rien la pénétration: "Si Racine s'est tû après *Phèdre* ce n'est pas que *Phèdre* fût par nature la dernière de ses pièces. Elle était au contraire la première d'une série terrible..." (57-58). Cette série n'a jamais été écrite, mais cette remarque ne devrait-elle pas décourager toute tentative d'intégration et d'interprétation structuraliste de *Phèdre*?

N'est-il pas assez curieux de voir cette situation comme reflétée dans les propos de M. Delcroix ("Racine et la fonction fabulatrice: le cas de *Phèdre*," in: *Re-lectures raciniennes*, 37): "En fait le cas de *Phèdre* est particulièrement complexe et clôture la série par une exception à bien des égards, si même la pièce intègre nombre d'éléments présents et dispersés dans les œuvres antérieures"?

E. Gans utilise un langage beaucoup moins simple pour, nous semble-t-il, dire à peu près la même chose, notamment dans la conclusion de "Racine et la fin de la tragédie" (*Re-lectures raciniennes*, 49-67) Loin de s'en tenir au seul Racine, il lui faut cependant reconnaître (50, n.5) qu'il néglige délibérément Schiller, Goethe et Alfieri, pour arriver à ses fins. Mais c'est toujours *Phèdre*—ou bien ne serait-ce que le personnage de Phèdre?—qui fait problème.

Réserve faite de nos remarques antérieures sur le titre de ce recueil, il faut avouer que le début accumule quelques étrangetés: 1) en épigraphe, une citation de V. Hugo qui paraîtra incongrue à plus d'un; un portrait reconnu comme inauthentique et un avant-propos "Sous Racine," titre sur lequel on se gardera bien d'ironiser, car il annonce une adhésion, une allégeance, pour ne pas dire plus à R. Barthes, qui, comme tout ce qui relève du sentiment personnel est éminemment respectable: *De gustibus coloribusque non disputandum est...*

Peut-être est-ce E.Gans qui, dans les premiers paragraphes de l'article déjà cité, fait le plus rapidement le point et aide le mieux à comprendre certains des travaux ici présentés, comme aussi bien, pour partie, celui de Mme Bruneau: recherches nourries essentiellement des divers discours critiques tenus à propos de Racine depuis Goldmann jusqu'à Foucault auxquels on joint des vivants, surtout d'Outre-Atlantique: Gutwirth, Apostolidès, L. Marin, Reiss et quelques autres. Il s'agit bien souvent d'un discours au second degré qui sera très utile lorsqu'on en viendra à établir la Fortune critique de Racine au XXième siècle. On comprendra qu'au moment où le *Sur Racine* de Barthes vient d'être le sujet d'une sérieuse remise en question dans une thèse de doctorat d'Etat à Paris (R. Pommier), où vient de paraître "Un âge critique: Les trente ans du *Dieu Caché*" sous la plume de G. Ferreyrolles et de Thomas Pavel on fasse toute réserve sur la valeur que l'on peut encore accorder à des textes *prétextes* de préférence à Racine lui-même et à ses œuvres; tel, certes, n'est pas le travers dans lequel tombent M. Delcroix, qui tente une délicate conciliation de thèses divergentes dues à R.C. Knight et Ch. Delmas, ni celui de M. Gutwirth lequel avec la pénétration à laquelle nous sommes accoutumés de sa part voit en Jéhu, ou plutôt en son évocation la prise de conscience du tragique de l'existence chez Athalie. (Dommage qu'à l'avant-dernière ligne le mot *loi* reste énigmatique: faut-il lire *lieu*, ou *loisir*? (Serait-ce l'avènement d'une critique au ...3e degré, celle qui requiert la collaboration active du lecteur ?) A la lumière de ce que nous avons dit *ab initio*, on comprendra que nous saluions comme elle le mérite "La lecture métadramatique et théâtrale" que nous propose Judd Hubert, lecture qui "privilégie tous les signes se rapportant au côté performatique en évitant dans la mesure du possible de retomber dans une simple thématique de la théâtralité." Ces "Ecarts de Trézène" (81-97) sont donc une étude minutieuse du texte de *Phèdre*, lecture qui s'assigne un but précis, limité, et qui sait s'y tenir, démontrant à la fois puissance d'analyse et originalité de la méthode. On avouera avoir été moins séduit par le propos de L. Marin qui aurait gagné, peut-être à se voir éclairé d'une anecdote: Louis XIV écoutant Racine lui lire des fragments déjà rédigés de son *Histoire*, et murmurant "Gazettes! gazettes!" De même, il y a beau temps que G. Delassault a montré que, dès 1669, Racine était virtuellement réconcilié ave Port-Royal. Le "pardon" d'Arnauld après *Phèdre* (103) pourrait bien ne signaler que le caractère exceptionnel de la pièce, ou bien ne s'appliquer qu'au ridicule jeté sur l'une des mères Arnauld par l'anecdote des capucins. On est surpris qu'il faille une dizaine de pages à M.-J. Muratore ("Racinian Stasis") pour, Goldmann et Barthes *juvantibus*, montrer le caractère statique de la tragédie; n'est-ce pas une des lois du genre? Quatre pages de G. Poulet ("Racine et la pensée indéterminée") lui permettent de cerner, disons de poser un sujet, plus que de le traiter réellement, mais ce peut-être, exposé clairement comme il l'est, l'esquisse d'une piste de recherche fructueuse. T. Reiss a bien vu, pour sa part (133-160), l'importance de l'assentiment populaire aux actes du prince tant pour Louis XIV que pour Titus, c'est-à-dire la mesure dans laquelle le souverain (celui de Rome perçu comme une projection de celui de la France) peut exercer son pouvoir, d'ailleurs moins absolu que ce que l'on a dit (voir plus haut, M.-F. Bruneau). Sous un titre qui pourra paraître spécieux: "Authority and authorship: Néron's Racine," Mme H.-B. Stone est amenée, après un parallèle des deux figures féminines, Agrippine et Junie, à se poser une question qui paraîtra assez abstruse à d'aucuns: "Is Racine the subject (creator) or the object (created) of his work?" pour d'ailleurs conclure que Racine "refuse d'assumer l'autorité dont il a dépouillé ses personnages" (Notre traduction, sous toute réserve). C'est aussi vers *Britannicus* que s'est tourné R. Tobin, pour y étudier un sujet à la mode: "Néron et Junie: fantasme et tragédie." Toujours à l'affût des nouvelles recherches, le fantasme lui procure l'occasion de situer Néron, grâce à des épisodes parallèles, entre Junie qui serait sa rédemption et qui lui échappe, et Agrippine qui, jusque dans sa mort, sera la voie de sa damnation.

Esther a retenu l'attention de Mme Woshinsky; mais on regrettera que, pour son étude des sources bibliques, elle ne se soit pas tournée de préférence vers l'édition procurée par Le Maistre de Sacy dont, dans divers articles, nous avons eu l'occasion de démontrer l'influence. Pour Racine, il est clair que cette édition, avec son commentaire littéral et spirituel, représente le dernier mot de la critique scripturaire. C'est la porte à laquelle il faut frapper si l'on veut ne pas risquer de s'égarer.

On le voit, ces seize études sur Racine, ou bien acceptent de se tourner vers le texte, et font progresser notre connaissance, ou bien préfèrent le discours au second degré dont j'ai parlé plus haut. On regrettera que, parfois, les éditions les plus récentes de R. Picard ne soient pas citées, malgré les améliorations constantes que l'auteur leur a apportées.

C'est sans doute avec les meilleures de ces études qu'il faut placer celle de Mme Ekstein sur le *récit* chez Racine, recherche exhaustive de tous les récits dramatiques (*Plaideurs* compris) de l'œuvre de Racine, conduite selon les principes reconnus de la narratologie (le vilain hybride que voilà!). Etude minutieuse, méticuleuse, avec dénombrements et classifications. Aurait-il été possible d'aménager les catégories existantes, pour placer correctement le plus long de tous, le "récit" d'Agrippine à Néron dont Mme Eckstein, avec une exquise sincérité reconnaît: "...it does not fit neatly into the recognized categories" (94)? A cette réserve près, ce volume rendra service en permettant une vue d'ensemble rapide d'un aspect important de l'œuvre de Racine.

Trois volumes bien différents donc dans leurs ambitions, leurs buts et leur ton. Les uns se réjouiront à la pensée que la Nouvelle Critique est toujours lue et inspire de nouvelles publications. D'autres parmi lesquels nous nous plaçons, se féliciteront de voir se poursuivre un approfondissement méthodique de l'œuvre et de la vie de Racine, loin des phraséologies absconses et des néologismes prétentieux. Tous constateront avec plaisir la vitalité des études raciniennes d'un rivage à l'autre du Nouveau Continent.

Ouvrages cités

Castiglione, B. *Le Livre du Courtisan.* Paris: Editions Gérard Lebovici, 1987.

Ferreyrolles, G. "Un âge critique: Les trente ans du *Dieu Caché.*" *Commentaire* 34 (1986).

Pavel, Thomas. *Le mirage linguistique, essai sur la modernisation intellectuelle.* Paris: Minuit, 1988.

(Dis)continuité(s) de La Bruyère

Edward Knox
Middlebury College

La Bruyère. Amateur de caractères. BY FLOYD GRAY. Paris: Nizet, 1986.

Les *Caractères* de La Bruyère sont entrés voilà vingt-cinq ans dans une nouvelle ère critique avec la parution de la préface de Roland Barthes à une édition en 10/18, reprise dans ses *Essais critiques* en 1964. Jusqu'alors on nous avait conviés à considérer La Bruyère—quand bien même on parlait de lui—sous les angles classiques de l'histoire littéraire (et surtout sous l'angle des clefs) et de l'organisation de l'ensemble, tâche rendue ardue en l'occurrence par son aspect discontinu, fragmenté. En attirant l'attention sur ce "premier écrivain moderne," Barthes a inspiré une sorte de nouvelle continuité critique, alimentée d'une dizaine de monographies (et plusieurs bibliographies) en moins de vingt ans, portant sur la place des *Caractères* dans l'histoire des idées, et surtout sur l'écriture comme mariage forme/sens qui engendre sa propre réalité.

Contre cette toile de fond F. Gray nous propose un La Bruyère "poète...[qui] se manifeste surtout dans les portraits, les 'caractères'" (13) et auteur d'une "œuvre qui vise à instruire, condamner les vices, à dire ses vérités au monde, mais qui, par son exercice même, ne signifie qu'elle-même, prouve son autonomie dans le détachement d'une intention morale ou sociale" (14).

Ce propos prometteur sinon bien original se développe cependant selon une organisation quelque peu déroutante par son aspect tout aussi classique, avec 45 pages sur 150 qui traitent des "Ouvrages de l'esprit" et des "Maximes," avant d'aborder successivement "Caractères, Jeux intertextuels, et le Moraliste-poète." De plus—était-ce inévitable à propos d'un ouvrage aussi fragmenté que les *Caractères*?—la thèse de F. Gray n'est nulle part nettement perçue et nous assistons plutôt à une série de motifs qui n'ont jamais la force d'un argument développé de front et appuyé sur des exemples introduits en temps voulu: ainsi, il est question au fil du livre du portrait-pensée, de l'amour de la pointe finale, de la recherche de la clarté, de la litote (!), du jeu entre le statique et le mouvement ou la surface et la profondeur, de la (fausse) théâtralité des caractères. On est plutôt déconcerté de ne découvrir qu'à la page 50 une définition de *caractère* (cf. p. 13 son équivalence, après Furetière, avec *portrait*), ou de voir opposer (151) "portrait hyperbolique" et "'caractère possible," mais surtout le discontinu de l'œuvre n'exigeait-il pas un plus grand suivi dans son étude? Même le chapitre qui propose de traiter des caractères à proprement parler, et des "constantes qui fonctionnent comme le point neutre auquel il revient toujours à la suite de ses errances du côté de l'exceptionnel" (67) décevra les amateurs de cohérence ou tout au moins de convergence.

Les remarques les plus intéressantes de F. Gray concernent, nous semble-t-il, le rapport éventuel entre la maxime et le portrait (57 et suiv.); l'intertexte, notamment (ce n'est pas surprenant sous sa plume) vis-à-vis de Montaigne (92-102); et la tentation du sur-réel chez La Bruyère (passim). Mais c'est peu, et on trouve ailleurs de vrais problèmes.

Nous éviterons de relever, malgré leur nombre, les remarques peu claires et les affirmations lancées un peu dans le vide sans appui immédiat et souvent sans définition, pour signaler plutôt deux aspects plus troublants et sans doute plus fondamentaux, à savoir sa tendance à afficher l'intention de l'auteur à tel ou tel tournant du texte, et—ce n'est pas complètement étranger à cette première tendance—une certaine circularité dans sa perception du rapport moyens/fins, pour ne pas dire un quasi-malaise devant l'autonomie de l'écriture comme moment originel dans l'existence d'un caractère. Ceci n'exclut pas de pouvoir citer des remarques de F. Gray qui semble croire, dans le passage de la page 14 plus haut par exemple, au détachement esthétique de cette écriture; mais sa pratique critique ne justifie pas de ces quelques déclarations de principe. Ainsi, la troisième phrase de la conclusion: "La Bruyère tient à exprimer sans ambiguïté apparente ce qu'il est destiné à dire" (149).

Dans son chapitre sur les Ouvrages de l'esprit nous trouvons, par exemple, "La Bruyère introduit nécessairement beaucoup de lui-même dans ces remarques sur l'écriture et la lecture et c'est encore à sa manière habituelle qu'il pense, puisque c'est dans le particulier des 'caractères' qu'il excelle" (49). Un paragraphe plus tôt F. Gray nous faisait remarquer qu'il "condamne les figures qu'il emploie constamment, dont il use malgré son idée du mot juste." Mais ce chapitre-ci n'était-il pas justement l'endroit qui s'imposait pour une réflexion sur (le degré de) la participation de l'auteur à une certaine continuité d'idées...classiques sur le style? Ou encore: "[la maxime] doit refléter une grande diversité, car La Bruyère tient à présenter une œuvre qui plaise par ses surprises, ses chocs, et ses errances. Il est curieux de voir que La Bruyère, qui semble croire à la vérité, n'ait pas, dans les sujets divers qu'il traite, dégagé une vérité..." (65). Mais n'y aurait-il pas d'autres explications possibles et surtout un peu plus complexes, en ce qui concerne le rapport entre l'opinion personnelle, les idées de l'époque et l'écriture?

Plus loin dans ce même paragraphe, qui clôt le chapitre sur les maximes: "une des conditions de son jeu scriptural: détailler pour que le sujet qu'il traite soit véritable matériau littéraire. Le fragment chez La Bruyère témoigne de la crainte du mouvement, du développement...." Il ne s'agit bien entendu pas de nier ici même la trajectoire probable observation-écriture, mais de mettre en question la pertinence d'en faire un principe qui opère à chaque fois et pour chaque instance "scripturale." Est-ce en fin de compte autre chose qu'une version un peu plus acceptable de l'approche par les clefs? —je vois, je désapprouve/ressens, j'écris (et me venge). F. Gray peut écrire "voyons dans Hermippe l'exemple du personnage impossible, si ce n'est dans les réseaux de l'écriture" (119), il a trop de formules ambiguës du genre "Etonnante mimésis: le texte est le sot" (114) pour nous rassurer sur la primauté de l'écriture. Qu'est-ce à dire enfin que "Les personnages de La Bruyère perdent leur identité, d'êtres humains, dans la mesure où ils s'accommodent du milieu irréel dans lequel les plonge le texte" (153)? Ceci n'est pas un problème chez F. Gray seul en ce qui concerne les *Caractères*, mais le point de vue se rachète malheureusement moins ici que chez d'autres qui nous ont déjà permis de regarder plus en détail ce "réel" dont est fait un caractère, sans parler de sa place dans l'écriture et de son évolution—encore une continuité—à travers les éditions. Il est d'ailleurs frappant de voir à quel point F. Gray semble préférer Thibaudet et autres Sainte-Beuve à ses prédécesseurs plus immédiats.

C'est dire en fin de compte que même si F. Gray nous laissait moins sur notre faim en ce qui concerne tel aspect des *Caractères*, tout porte aussi à croire qu'il n'en dirait pas vraiment autre chose que ceux qui l'ont précédé sur le même terrain. Or il n'est pas le premier à se heurter à ce problème: il y a bien assez de redites sur La Bruyère depuis vingt ans pour parler. . . d'une surcontinuité. Mais quand on le fait simplement sien, n'a-t-on pas l'impression de venir un peu trop tard? Le moment n'est-il venu d'un nouveau départ dans la continuité La Bruyère, dans une optique plus résolument anthropologique (sémiologique historique), psychanalytique (homme/œuvre, l'autre comme aberration), esthétique (du côte du réalisme magique) ou même foucaldienne (discours du fragment, fragment du discours)?

Index

Adam, A., 20
Aristotle, 53, 63, 80, 83, 84, 85, 205
Aubignac, F. H. d', 221

Bakhtin, M., 23, 176, 177, 178, 192, 194, 196
Balzac, G. de, 16, 67
Barthes, R., 2, 3, 9, 19, 21, 22, 23, 25, 26, 176,
Bayle, P., 52
Bayley, P., 182
Beaudoin, 271
Benedetto, L., 18, 19, 20
Borgerhoff, E., 19, 54, 111
Bernard, C., 207, 217, 223
Beugnot , B., 54, 179, 188
Bloom, H., 83, 86, 87, 88, 89, 92, 93
Boileau, N., 4, 9, 10, 11, 12, 14, 16, 31, 53, 61, 62, 65, 66, 81, 86, 87, 111
Boissat, P. de, 212
Borgerhoff, E., 19, 20, 53, 97, 111
Bossuet, J.-B., 4, 6, 8, 9, 10, 11, 13, 16, 18, 31, 32, 52, 81
Bouhours, D., 54, 58, 63, 175, 176, 180, 189, 191, 194, 195, 196

Bourdaloue, L., 4, 16
Brams, S., 119, 120, 121,122, 123, 124, 126, 127, 128
Bray, R.,14, 15, 52, 90, 117
Brody, J., 1, 2, 18, 20, 21, 111, 182, 196
Brunetière, F., 22, 43
Brunot, F., 15, 180

Camus, J.-P., 178, 179, 185, 203, 219, 220
Cave, T., 189
Chapelain, J., 16, 67, 205
Clarac, P., 41, 44
Corneille, P., 4, 9, 10, 12, 14, 16, 37, 62, 65, 66, 72, 79, 80, 81, 83, 84, 85, 86, 87, 88, 89, 90, 91, 92, 93, 97, 100, 112, 142, 144, 145, 146, 147
Cousin, V., 9, 10, 11, 13
Cuénin, M., 52
Cyrano de Bergerac, S., 178

Dassoucy, C. C., 177
Davidson. H., 54
De Ley, H., 138
De Man, P., 81, 94, 95
DeJean, J., 177
Derrida, J., 136

Descartes, R., 11, 16, 66, 67, 69, 81, 133, 151, 152, 153, 154, 155, 156, 157, 158, 159, 160, 163, 165, 167, 169, 170, 171, 188,
Desmarets de Saint-Sorlin, J., 204, 205, 218, 221
Du Vair, G., 183, 185, 186

Edelman, N., 20
Elizabeth of Bohemia, 151, 152, 153, 154, 155, 156, 157, 158, 159, 160, 164, 169

Faguet, E., 22, 43
Fénelon, F., 6, 8, 9, 10, 11, 16
Filère, A. P. de, 183, 184, 185, 187, 197
Fleury, C., 186
Fléchier, E., 8, 9, 10
Fontenelle, B. L. B. de, 67, 69, 71, 152, 153, 159, 160, 161, 162, 163, 164, 165, 166, 168, 169, 170
Foucault, M., 2, 23, 24, 25, 26, 66, 136, 137, 139, 140, 178, 188,
Freud, S., 231, 234
Fumaroli, M., 54, 61, 65, 66,
Furetière, A., 206, 207

Goldmann, L., 23
Gomberville, M. R. de, 206
Gournay, M. de, 180
Guéret, G., 186
Guilleragues, G., 224

Hegel, G., 109, 110, 113
Homer, 271
Horace, 62, 84
Huet, P. D., 203, 221

Kuhn, T., 138, 141

La Bruyère, J. de, 9, 16, 62, 65, 66, 81, 112, 113, 116, 117, 187, 189, 192, 196
Lafayette, Mme de, 52, 81, 112, 115, 116, 193, 214
La Fontaine, J. de, 9, 10, 11, 12, 16, 18, 31, 52, 53, 81, 111, 112, 192
La Rochefoucauld, F., duc de, 16, 22, 81, 114, 111, 115, 116, 164,
LaCapra, D., 134, 135, 141, 148
Lafond, J., 179
La Mothe Le Vayer, F. de, 180, 181, 185
Lamy, B., 187, 189, 194
Lanson, G., 12, 13, 15, 16, 19, 22, 25
Le Moyne, P., 182, 186
Lemaître, J., 43
Lukacs, G., 23
Lulli, J.-B., 4

Malherbe, F. de, 16, 64, 65, 66, 180, 183
Mareschal, A., 206, 213, 222
Massillon, J.-B., 8, 9, 10, 32
Ménage, G., 180
Molière, J.-B. P., 4, 9, 10, 11, 12, 18, 19, 31, 32, 33, 34, 35, 36, 37, 38, 39, 40, 42, 52, 53, 62, 81, 83, 90, 91, 92, 94, 95, 96, 99, 112
Montaigne M. de, 9, 63, 64, 65, 86, 87, 182, 188, 190
Montchrestien, A. de, 120, 123, 124

Moore, W., 20
Mornet , D., 16, 17, 19, 20, 53

Nisard, D., 9, 10, 11, 12, 22, 43

Pascal, B., 6, 9, 11, 16, 21, 52, 81, 83, 88, 91, 99, 100, 101, 165, 192, 196
Pasquier, E., 182, 186, 190
Perrault , C., 59, 71
Peyre, H., 2, 17, 20, 90, 112, 117
Picard, R., 21, 22
Poullain de La Barre, F., 168, 170, 171

Quinault , P., 4

Rabelais, F., 177
Racine, J., 4, 9, 10, 11, 12, 14, 18, 19, 21, 22, 37, 53, 62, 63, 66, 69, 79, 80, 81, 83, 84, 85, 86, 87, 88, 89, 90, 91, 92, 97, 98, 100, 101, 102, 111, 112, 114, 120, 125, 126, 129, 187
Rambaud, A.,184, 185, 186
Rapin, R., 205, 220
Recker, M., 281,
Reiss, T.,139, 148, 151, 153, 156,
Retz, J. F. P. Gondi, cardinal de, 14
Rémond de Saint-Mard, 69, 70, 71
Rizza, C., 178
Romanowski, S., 136
Rorty, R., 139, 140, 146
Rosset, F. de., 222

Saint-Amant , M.-A. de, 177
Sainte-Beuve, C. A., 2, 10, 11, 12, 15, 16, 23, 25, 43
Saussure, F. de., 176
Scarron, P., 178, 193, 206
Scudéry, M. de, 203
Sévigné, Mme de, 16, 21, 52, 81, 112
Sorel, C., 181, 203, 209, 221, 222, 223, 225
Staël, Mme de, 7, 10, 23
Stanton, D., 177
Stendhal, 6, 7, 10

Taine, H., 12, 13, 14, 15, 16, 23, 25

Valincour, J.-B., 226
Vaugelas, C., 180, 197
Verville, B. de, 178
Vialart, C., 185
Viau, T. de, 177
Villedieu, Mme de, 203, 207, 222
Voltaire, 3, 4, 5, 9, 11, 25, 52, 69, 79, 86

Wölfflin, H., 109, 110, 113,

Zuber, R., 52, 54